T0178713

Models and Analysis in Distributed Systems

Models and Analysis in Distributed Systems

Edited by

Serge Haddad
Fabrice Kordon
Laurent Pautet
Laure Petrucci

First published 2011 in Great Britain and the United States by ISTE Ltd and John Wiley & Sons, Inc.

ISTE Ltd
27-37 St George's Road
London SW19 4EU
UK

www.iste.co.uk

John Wiley & Sons, Inc.
111 River Street
Hoboken, NJ 07030
USA

www.wiley.com

© ISTE Ltd 2011

Library of Congress Cataloging-in-Publication Data

Models and analysis in distributed systems / edited by Serge Haddad ... [et al.].
    p. cm.
  Includes bibliographical references and index.
  ISBN 978-1-84821-314-2
  1. Distributed parameter systems--Simulation methods. 2. System analysis. I. Haddad, Serge.
  T57.62.M63 2011
  003.78--dc23
                                                                                    2011012244

British Library Cataloguing-in-Publication Data
A CIP record for this book is available from the British Library
ISBN 978-1-84821-314-2

Printed and bound in Great Britain by CPI Antony Rowe, Chippenham and Eastbourne.

Contents

Foreword

Verification and hence modeling are a mandatory but intricate problem for engineers developing embedded distributed real-time systems that are entrusted with critical safety applications like medical care, transportation, energy production, industrial processes, military operations. Therefore, while emerging 40 years ago, first for circuit design, avionics and finally for all domains, verification environments are now widely exploited by industry and fully integrated into the development processes.

Volume 1 presented design and algorithms for developing these large-scale distributed systems, real-time embedded ones, security concepts for peer-to-peer and ubiquitous computing. However the crucial problem of their correctness is made hard by their complexity, the difficulty of managing fault tolerance, the real-time constraints that they must satisfy, asynchronism of worldly spread units as well as the heterogeneity of devices, networks and applications.

This second volume presents different approaches for mastering these verification problems, beginning with the main concepts and formal methods used for modeling and well structuring distributed systems and for expressing their logical and timed properties. Then it explores the theoretical approaches, mainly logic and automata theory, for behavioral verification of these models. It goes thoroughly into the decidability issues and algorithmic complexity that are the inherent obstacles to overcome particularly for dealing with infinite state spaces and timed models. Collecting the experience of researchers from several laboratories, this volume covers advanced topics of distributed system modeling and verification. It aims at giving a deep knowledge of theory, methods and algorithms to Masters and PhD students as well as to engineers who are already good experts in verification.

Semi-formal specifications and models are a first step for a precise system description. The Unified Modeling Language (UML), widely used in industry, provides diagrams for describing the relations between classes, objects, operations, activities, and allows for examining the system action sequences, reachable states and desired properties. Such specifications provide a good understanding of the system and allow early detection of some errors. Furthermore, formal models, such as algebraic specification, automata, Petri nets (PN), process algebras, bring abstraction, precision and rigor by precisely describing all the possible behaviors of a system. They allow for performing exhaustive simulation and therefore checking some safety and liveness properties. Moreover temporal logics like Linear Time Logic (LTL) and Computation Tree Logic (CTL) are introduced to express properties of sequences of states generated by these formal models. However the size of the generated sets of states may be so huge that it raises the problems of complexity of the space and time needed to build and explore them. These sets may even be infinite and their manipulation requires sophisticated methods.

Whatever the chosen formalism, system modeling has to keep verification in mind. The abstraction level needs to identify the system elements that must be taken into account, while neglecting those which are out of the verification purposes. Once identified, the system relevant elements are progressively taken into account, and refined. Incremental construction allows us to validate successive refinements. Model oriented engineering approaches may be based on problem frames, architectural or component architectures. Property oriented approaches may use languages like the Common Algebraic Specification Language (CASL) extended with a Labelled Transition Logic to express conditions satisfied by states, requirements on the transitions and incompatible elementary actions.

As modern distributed systems and consequently their models become very large and complex it is important to express their structure. Architecture and Analysis Description Languages (AADL) help to manage and improve it by component composition via interfaces and packages, providing a convenient analysis support in case of future reconfigurations or evolutions.

System verification depends heavily upon the interrelated choices concerning the expressiveness of the formal model, the system requirements and expected properties, the adequate verification methods and moreover the quality of the available tools. Axiomatic proof of properties is highly desirable, but even if computer-aided it needs intensive work for system formalization (much more difficult than modeling) and rigorous checking by highly trained engineers. Moreover, repetitions for each design correction increase cost and delay. Therefore engineers mainly use automatic verification based on numerous model checking methods. Researches combine the advantages and drawbacks of methods, extend the models and develop new strategies. Many subtle variants of models and classes of properties may drastically change complexity in time or in space, or require ingenious extensions of methods and algorithms at the decidability borders. Often expressiveness is costly for analysis. Inhibitor or reset arcs of PN make reachability undecidable. Decidability of counter automata may be obtained by restricting their counters and avoiding zero tests. Association of time with tokens instead of transitions requires more complex constructions for reachability proofs. Fortunately some powerful extensions have been defined without theoretical loss. Colored PN still allow positive linear flows and easily understandable invariants, symmetries and parameterization. Recursivity is smartly introduced for PN keeping their most useful properties. Colored semantics of PN by unfolding although rather cumbersome, allows for efficient verification and reductions. PN box calculus allows CCS-like process algebra but nevertheless decidability of verification.

Expression of properties is the most sensitive choice. Generic ones like boundedness, liveness, even home states are useful but not sufficient for verifying the complex behavior of distributed systems. Therefore temporal logics expressing the intricate succession of events are so essential that for the past 40 years much research has focussed on them, thus leading to effective automatic verification of complex systems. For this reason, the pioneer fundamental work of E. Clarke, A. Emerson and J. Sifakis has been recognized by the 2007 ACM Turing Award.

The state graph is the key object for verification. Even when finite, it may be exponentially huge w.r.t. the model size so that its reduction is a major goal. Some model simplifications, like agglomerations of actions, allow us to suppress many intermediate states and meaningless interleaving effects, provided suitable conditions preserve behavioral properties. For Petri nets, intricate behavioral conditions on firing sequences provide powerful agglomerations but the help of structural properties simplifies their checking. Avoiding the state graph, structural verifications of PN use flows, invariants, systems of integer linear inequalities and distinguished place subsets. For better behavioral verification, a system is abstracted as an automaton accepting transition sequences of infinite length. To be checked, a Linear-time Temporal Logic formula Φ is automatically translated into a second automaton, called a Büchi automaton, whose language is the sets of words that contradict Φ. Their "synchronized product" is built to check if they have no common word (emptiness test) and Φ holds, otherwise a counter example is found.

The memory space for these automata may be reduced by representing only the index states in a hash table, or by neglecting parts of the state space irrelevant for checking a particular formula. Better still, the widely used Binary Decision Diagrams (BDD) provide an extremely compact representation of a state space as a Directed Acyclic Graph of Boolean functions sharing most of their common subexpressions. BDD may grow linearly even when state graphs grow exponentially. They are also extended to represent whole graphs and automata allowing us to check paths and to achieve model checking for CTL as well as for LTL. Variants again provide more compactness (Zero suppressed BDD) or larger scopes (Algebraic DD, Multi-valued DD and Data DD). Interleaving partial executions of actions is a major cause of space explosion; therefore important gains are obtained by using equivalence classes of independent action subsequences. Covering Step Graphs, partial order methods and trace unfoldings lead to many improvements like persistent sets, sleep sets, stubborn sets. Distributed systems often have identical components, modeled by Colored Petri

Nets (CPN) so their behavioral symmetries allow us to use quotient state graphs and compact symbolic representations. All these improvements now help model checking of large distributed systems, mainly hardware and embedded ones.

Verification of infinite state systems is a challenging problem because all systems use integer and real variables, dynamic data structures, recursive calls, list processing, process creation, parameterization that lead to infinity or unknown bounds. Infinity raises specific difficulties for verification because it requires finite representations with special decision techniques. Only subproblems with strong restrictions become decidable.

Counter systems are finite-state automata with counters, that are non-negative integer variables. Their transition relation is expressed by Presburger formulae which control guards and counter modifications. The Presburger arithmetic allows addition but not multiplication of variables with relational and Boolean connectors and quantifiers. It is one of the most expressive fragments of arithmetic that is decidable. Vector Addition Systems are restricted, hence called "succinct" counter automata without zero test, shown equivalent to Petri nets, and allowing us to decide boundedness and reachability of a target marking. Conversely satisfiability for Presburger arithmetic may be solved by the non-emptiness test for finite state automata. Many tools have been implemented for Presburger decision procedures and for verification of infinite state systems with counters.

Petri nets may be extended by recursion while still allowing for decidability and model checking. Recursive PN (RPN) introduce abstract transitions for creating and resuming processes. The simpler model of Sequential RPN (SRPN) allows us to run only the child process by stacking its father. Each abstract transition is provided with the initial marking of the child process and a Presburger condition for its termination. An "extended marking" is the stack of saved occurrences of abstract transitions having created a child process (modeling the saved interrupt points) with their corresponding marking at the creation (modeling the saved contexts). A termination pops up the stack and fires the abstract transition with the saved marking. SRPN are a fundamental model of great practical and theoretical interest because they are a strict extension of PN able to naturally describe key system features like interruptions, exceptions, management and even fault tolerance while reachability and verification of LTL formulae remain decidable and extended structural linear invariants may be computed.

Real-time systems deal with time, dates and delays which must be carefully taken into account for sound verification and for performance evaluation. The underlying problems are difficult because concurrency and distribution involve subtleties and moreover because continuous time variables require managing dense sets. Markings are extended to also represent clocks or time variables. Different semantics are used for time modeling: event dates and action delays with either clock ticks for discrete time or real variables for continuous time. Timed automata are the basic model equipped with a finite set of real synchronous clocks. These clocks are synchronously increased by special delay transitions, they may be compared with constants for guards and also be reset by firings. Although they can generate an infinite state space, most decision problems remain decidable. Among Time Transition Systems (TTS) variants, Time PN (TPN) associate time with transitions and model urgency or time out, but they cannot disable transitions that become obsolete. Conversely, Timed PN (TdPN) more subtly associate age to tokens. Their input arcs specify an age interval during which tokens may be consumed, and their output arcs give initial ages to created tokens. Their lazy semantics do not model urgency but allow for disabling transitions when time elapses. The state descriptions and firings become far more complex for all TTS with elapsing of time, durations of transitions, minimum and maximum delays for firing. The often assumed instantaneity of some actions or guard evaluations may be not always compatible with real hardware speed. Temporal logic CTL must be extended for timing, giving in particular CTLT. Strong or weak equivalences between time automata may also be defined. Despite the difficulties, these new logics with their rather efficient and scalable model checking algorithms, provide time modeling and verification for industrial systems.

Real-time systems involve time represented by clocks that are continuous variables forcing us to deal with infinity by means of new "finite-state abstractions". For the classical timed automata, "configurations" are defined as the product of a state and the set of clock values. These clocks are increased by the delay transitions. Subspaces of configurations are delimited by guards which combine comparisons of clocks with constants (that may be all chosen as integers). An equivalence between configurations allows us to divide this space into regions delimited by the constraints and also by the steps of integer values crossed by the clocks, up to the maximum constant to which the clocks are compared. Some infinite region gathers all the values above this maximum. This partition distinguishes regions from all their boundaries of decreasing dimension, down to elementary points. Thus, the continuous transition system is reduced to a region automaton with a finite number of regions for which reachability and language emptiness are decidable. Finite-state abstraction has been extended to more expressive time automata and to Time Petri nets (TPN). The Büchi automata approach and the emptiness test may be applied to these nets for temporal logic verification of LTL and TCTL formulae.

Problems are far more complex for models with an infinite number of regions. This is the case for Timed Petri Nets (TdPN) because tokens have ages. A more complicated construction makes the coverability problem still decidable by using a finite recurrence to compute the predecessors of the configuration to be covered. The problem of token liveness which arises because some tokens may become useless (i.e. dead) when time elapses, is also shown decidable. A Zeno execution is one where an infinite number of actions or message transmissions must be performed within a finite delay that is unrealistic for real systems. Existence or non-existence of such a sequence is also decidable. Verification of real-time systems being theoretically well founded, tools have been developed for them. However they raise several axiomatic issues about clock precision, time progress and Zenoness. Therefore a new semantics "Almost As Soon As Possible" (AASAP) has been introduced as an emerging research domain.

Controlling a system G consists in designing an interacting controller C so that the controlled system (C/G) satisfies its requirements whatever the actions of the environment of S. However some system actions may be uncontrollable. Also the controller may only have a partial observation of the state of G. The formal control problems are very representative of the ones appearing in real peer-to-peer systems and take into account the complete underlying architecture. Verifying that the controller effectively keeps the systems within the requirements is simpler than its synthesis which aims at automatically producing a correctly controlled system.

The completed tasks are represented by the action sequences whose end states are in the set of terminal states of G, called markers. The controller is modeled by an automaton S over the same actions and a control function Ψ that indicates whether each action s of G is enabled by C. By convention it must enable all uncontrolled actions. L(C/G) is the language of sequences generated by G whose actions are enabled by C. A subset K of L(G) specifies all the "legal" sequences. K is controllable if any prefix followed by an uncontrollable action remains legal. If K is not controllable, a fixed-point algorithm builds a supremal sublanguage of K that is controllable. Local and modular specifications and solutions have been proposed for decentralized control. Each controller C_i makes local observations of the system and can disable only a subset of controllable actions. It takes local decisions. An arbiter mechanism is required for a final decision when there is no consensus between the controllers. Moreover deadlocks must be avoided. Intricate conditions define tolerance and co-observability of controllers and distinguish disjunctive or conjunctive arbiters. A general controller may be obtained by a shuffle of local controllers of the two types. Cooperative control allows local controllers to exchange information when their local views are not sufficient.

The synthesis problem for distributed systems is, in some sense, very general. The system architecture defines a set of processes and their possible communications, A variable belongs to the partition corresponding to a process if it can be modified by this process. Indeed at most one process can have a writing access to a given variable. This very general architecture may be refined. The control is very difficult to achieve: the problem is in general undecidable in particular for LTL or CTL specifications. For the decidable sub-cases, the theoretical complexity is very high. For decidability with LTL specifications, the processes must be organized in a pipeline with restricted access to variables. For asynchronous communications via shared variables and controllers with causal memories, the synthesis needs extremely restrictive conditions.

The control problem may be viewed as a game where the controller plays against the environment. A distributed controller is a team of players able to play actions simultaneously but each one does not know the other's choices. At each state, each player can concurrently choose one move among available ones. Each state is evaluated w.r.t. a set of desired properties. A player strategy is a function determining his moves after a state sequence. The logic ATL (Alternating-time Temporal Logic) is suited to open systems with multiple agents. It can express that some agent can enforce a property. It appears as an extension of CTL offering besides the connectors X, G and U, a selective quantification over paths. For any subset P of players, possibly empty, called a coalition, this new quantifier "P" selects the paths enforced by the strategies of the P players: "P" Φ means that P can enforce Φ and the dual [[P]] Φ means that P cannot avoid Φ. The implemented model checking algorithm extends those of CTL. Like CTL with CTL*, ATL may be extended to ATL*, allowing both state and path formulae. However it cannot express that an infinite number of requests implies an infinite number of grants. Extensions of ATL have been proposed for more expressiveness as well as for games where the players have incomplete information.

This volume provides strong bases for new research extending verification methods in open fields such as composition and refinement, aspect orientation, new algorithms and heuristics, distributed verification, synergies with theorem provers, scheduling, performance evaluation, and more.

Claude Girault, Emeritus Professor
Pierre & Marie Curie University

Chapter 1

Introduction

Problematics

The complexity of dynamic systems grows much faster than our ability to manage them [LEV 97]. In particular, the parallel execution of the threads of a distributed system requires the elaboration of sophisticated models and methods.

The oldest technique, simulation, is a straightforward way to increase confidence about the correctness of an implementation. Such a simulation is based on a model of the system with operational semantics in order to perform the elementary steps of the system. Unfortunately due to the non-determinism of distributed systems, replaying a simulation is a difficult task.

More precisely this problem is a consequence of two factors: the variable transit time of any message and the relative speed of the machine processors. Thus with the help of (vectorial) logical clocks associated with every station, additional information can be managed during the simulation so that it can be replayed [BON 96]. Such mechanisms can easily be integrated within a framework for distributed execution (called middleware).

Even if simulation techniques point out some bugs, they can never fully reassure to the designer of the system. Thus tests must be combined with other techniques in order to obtain a more complete validation of the system.

Introduction written by Serge HADDAD, Fabrice KORDON, Laurent PAUTET and Laure PETRUCCI.

Among these alternative approaches, the more efficient ones are associated with the early stage of the design. The most appropriate method consists of equipping the design step with a formal model such as UML [1] [CHA 05]. Unfortunately UML is not intended to have an operational semantic and this feature is required for the analysis of distributed systems. In particular, a formal semantic for the component behavior and for their composition is essential in view of checking the properties of the system.

Once a model with a formal semantics is obtained, the properties can be expressed either in a specific way (absence of deadlocks, mutual exclusion, etc.) or in a generic way via some logic (such as temporal logics) that can express fairness, liveness, etc. Furthermore, in order to combine performance evaluation, and verification, quantitative logics have also been introduced.

There are also difficulties with verification methods [LUQ 97]: the competency of the designer, the adaption to industrial case studies, the ability to tackle large-scale applications. Thus pragmatism is a key factor in the success of formal methods: without tools and methodology formal methods would never be adopted by engineers [KOR 03].

Objective of this book

The objective of this book is to describe the state of the art in formal methods for distributed and cooperative systems. These systems are characterized by:

– several components with one or more threads, possibly running on different processors;

– asynchronous communications with possible additional assumptions (reliability, order preserving, etc.);

– or local view for every component and no shared data between components.

These are the most common features in modern distributed systems. Numerous issues remain open and are the topic of European research projects. One current research trend consists of intricately mixing the design, modeling, verification, and implementation stages. This prototyping-based approach [KOR 03] is centered around the concept of refinement of models.

This book is more specifically intended for readers who wish to get an overview of the application of formal methods in the design of distributed systems. Master's and PhD students, and engineers will obtain a thorough understanding of the techniques as well as references for the most up-to-date work in this area.

---

1. UML stands for Unified Modeling Language.

Organization of the book

This book follows the two stages of a formal method: modeling, and verification.

Part 1 is concerned with the initial step of system design: modeling.

– Chapter 3 discusses a modeling approach to design a consistent specification. After identifying the key elements of the system to be modeled, they are step by step taken into account, and refined until the model is obtained.

– Chapter 4 is devoted to efficient handling of time. Timed models address mechanisms to manipulate time within distributed systems. They make use of discrete clocks and variables, while hybrid systems consider continuous evolution of time.

– Chapter 5 is concerned with the description of software architectures using dedicated languages that are ADLs (architecture description languages).

Part 2 is concerned with the next step of system design: verification.

– Chapter 7 covers the finite-state verification. Historically it is the oldest line of research that has been developed. The main objective of finite-state verification is the reduction of complexity due to the combinatory explosion of the system. Possible approaches are structural methods, which try to avoid developing the behavior of the system, and data representation which reduces the explosion by sharing substructures or exploiting the properties satisfied by the formalism.

– Chapter 8 addresses the problem of verifying infinite-state systems. Most of the research is devoted to the design of formalisms, which are slightly less expressive than Turing machines (or equivalent computational models), and to study which properties are decidable. In this chapter, the main focus is put on extensions of Petri nets and on different variants of counter machines. It emphasizes the fact that small variations lead to drastically different theories.

– Chapter 9 studies timed systems. Time is a particular source of infinity. However, its specificity leads to efficient verification procedures such as those developed for timed automata. Moreover, time can be combined with other sources of infinity such as in time(d) Petri nets. In addition, this chapter tackles the problem of implementing timed systems when the abstractions achieved at the theoretical level (such as the perfect synchronization of the clocks) are no longer satisfied.

– Chapter 10 studies control and synthesis of distributed systems. After recalling the centralized case, it develops, with the aid of specific examples, the specifics of the distributed case and the different possible approaches.

The *MeFoSyLoMa* community

MeFoSyLoMa (Méthodes Formelles pour les Systèmes Logiciels et Matériels [2]) is an association gathering several world-renowned research teams from various laboratories in the Paris area [MEF 11]. It is composed of people from LIP6 [3] (P. & M. Curie University), LIPN [4] (University of Paris 13), LSV [5] (École Normale Supérieure de Cachan), LTCI [6] (Telecom ParisTech), CÉDRIC [7], (CNAM), IBISC [8] (University of Évry-Val-d'Esssone), and LACL [9] (University of Paris 12). Its members, approximately 80 researchers and PhD students, all have common interest in the construction of distributed systems and promote a software development cycle based on modeling, analysis (formal), and model-based implementation. This community was founded in 2005 and is federated by regular seminars from well-known researchers (inside and outside the community) as well as by common research activities and the organization of events in their domains such as conferences, workshops, or book writing.

The editors of this book, as well as most authors, are from this community.

Bibliographie

[BON 96] BONNAIRE X., BAGGIO A., PRUN D., "Intrusion Free Monitoring: An Observation Engine for Message Server Based Applications", *9th International Conference on Parallel And Distributed Computing Systems (ISCA)*, p. 88-93, 1996.

[CHA 05] CHARROUX B., OSMANI A., THIERRY-MIEG Y., Eds., *UML2*, Pearson Education, 2005.

[KOR 03] KORDON F., HENKEL J., "An overview of Rapid System Prototyping today", *Design Automation for Embedded Systems*, vol. 8, num. 4, p. 275–282, Kluwer, december 2003.

[LEV 97] LEVESON N., "Software Engineering: Stretching the Limits of Complexity", *Communications of the ACM*, vol. 40(2), p. 129–131, 1997.

[LUQ 97] LUQI, GOGUEN J., "Formal Methods: Promises and Problems", *IEEE Software*, vol. 14(1), p. 73–85, January / February 1997.

[MEF 11] MEFOSYLOMA, "MeFoSyLoMa, home-page", www.mefosyloma.fr 2011.

---

2. This acronym stands for Formal Methods for Software and Hardware Systems (in French).
3. Laboratoire d'Informatique de Paris 6.
4. Laboratoire d'Informatique de Paris Nord.
5. Laboratoire de Spécification et de Vérification.
6. Laboratoire Traitement et Communication de l'Information.
7. Centre d'Études et de Recherche en Informatique du CNAM.
8. Informatique, Biologie Intégrative et Systèmes Complexes.
9. Laboratoire d'Algorithmique, Complexité et Logique.

FIRST PART

Formal Models for Distributed Systems

Chapter 2

Introduction to Formal Models

2.1. Motivation

Systems that are developed nowadays are of increasing complexity, and their functioning may have dramatic consequences on their environment, even irreversible ones, be it economical or human, e.g. avionics mission systems [PET 03], healthcare management [JØR 04], etc. [Dep 09].

It is thus of the utmost importance to design secure and safe systems, and their behavior must be checked before they become operational.

Verification of such critical systems is usually carried out using methods and techniques that largely depend on the problem at hand. For example, for hardware systems, such as avionics mission systems, physical test-beds are used. In such a case, a plane model, reproducing the exact system, is used on the ground. Simulation traces are logged and analyzed. Such an approach obviously necessitates a hardware infrastructure, as well as qualified staff, to conduct tests. Setting up this kind of test-bed is also usually very time-consuming. Moreover, the simulation traces obtained present the functioning in so much detail that their interpretation is a difficult task. It is thus clear that for verification to be efficient, an adequate *abstraction level* corresponding to the problem at hand is necessary.

To achieve these safety goals, one should abstract away from the physical system, using a *model*. Such an approach has many advantages:

– as no hardware is involved, its cost is relatively small;

Chapter written by Laure PETRUCCI.

– it can be analyzed using computer tools, and modified without a significant additional cost;

– the designer of the system model has a better and more rigorous understanding of the characteristics that need to be put into operation;

– once the verification of the expected properties of the model is satisfactory, an experimental prototype can be developed, with sufficient confidence, as many of the design errors have already been eliminated;

– moreover, such a formal specification helps with future maintenance, especially by a person not involved in the initial project.

Several types of specification models and languages can be considered, with complementary goals. They are detailed in the following sections.

2.2. Semi-formal models

System specification can be more or less formal, according to the techniques employed. The use of *semi-formal models*, such as UML (*unified modeling language*, [PIL 05]) may achieve part of the intended goals:

– while writing the specification, the designer improves his understanding of the expected behavior of the system, as well as the interactions between its various components. Writing the model enables reconsideration of some conceptual choices, and provides a more accurate understanding of the system itself;

– a model written in a simple notation facilitates communication with clients;

– during a maintenance phase, the model constitutes precise documentation of the system.

A UML specification is composed via various development steps, each of them represented by diagrams, which have the advantage of being relatively easy to understand. Here, we present some of the main aspects of UML.

Firstly, a *use case diagram* depicts the context: it describes the relationship between use cases and the actors within the system under study. *Use cases* summarize action sequences carried out by the system. The *actors* are the external parts (either people or other systems) that interact with the system that is being modeled. Use cases may correspond to several execution scenarios.

EXAMPLE.– Let us consider a car insurance problem. Two actors are involved: the *client* and the *insurance agent*. The client may *declare an accident* to the insurance agent. This operation is composed of several elementary actions, such as filling in a declaration, sending it by electronic or surface mail, etc. The insurance agent may decide, according to the case, to *refund* the client or not. There are thus several possible scenarios. A corresponding use case diagram is presented in Figure 2.1.

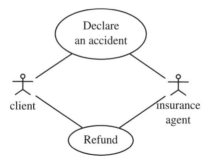

Figure 2.1. *Use case diagram*

These diagrams clarify the system that will be modeled and enables a better under-standing of what should or should not happen without getting lost in technical details. They also help to provide, at a later stage, *test sets* for the validation of the system's behavior.

The model of a system can be structured into classes, represented by a *class dia-gram*. The different classes contain their own *attributes* and *operations*, and are linked to one another via *relations* of different kinds.

EXAMPLE.– Let us consider the class diagram of our accident declaration example, shown in Figure 2.2. A vehicle has several associated attributes, such as its license plate number, its type, and its brand. Similarly, a client has a name, a surname, and an insurance number. The client can execute a `declare()` operation, in order to declare an accident. A declaration concerns exactly one vehicle and one client.

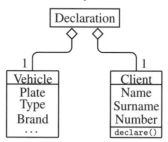

Figure 2.2. *Class diagram*

Each object in the system implements part of the intended functionalities. The global behavior is obtained through the cooperation between the different objects. These communications between objects are realized by exchanges of messages, which can be described in a *communication diagram*.

EXAMPLE.– The communication diagram in Figure 2.3 shows that the client should declare an accident by sending a message declare. He can then send the declaration to the insurance agent who makes a decision in order to reply to the client.

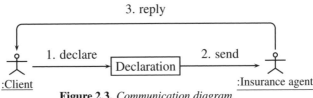

Figure 2.3. *Communication diagram*

This information can also be represented by *sequence diagrams*, which, in addition, show how objects are created.

EXAMPLE.– The sequence diagram in Figure 2.4 indicates message exchanges between the different objects. Note that the operation initiated by the client to declare an accident also generates a declaration object.

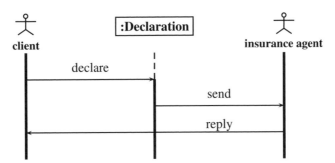

Figure 2.4. *Sequence diagram*

The flow of information in the system is represented by an *activity diagram*, which gives additional information complementary to those of the communication and sequence diagrams. It depicts the system evolution as seen by one of its actors.

EXAMPLE.– From the insurance agent point of view, the activities take place as pictured in Figure 2.5: he receives a declaration, handles it, and then sends his reply to the client.

A behavioral description of classes, use cases, actors, etc. is described through a *state diagram*. During the system evolution, the involved entities change state. This may be the result of external events triggering a particular activity.

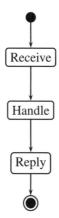

Figure 2.5. *Activity diagram – the insurance agent viewpoint*

EXAMPLE.– The state diagram for our accident declaration example is shown in Figure 2.6. The insurance agent initially waits. When he receives a declaration, he moves to a new state in which he is ready to handle it. After checking the declaration, two cases may occur: either there is no problem (OK) and the reimbursement can take place (a positive response is sent to the client), or there is a problem (NOK) and the insurance agent sends a negative response to the client.

Software tools enable a complex specification to be built. They check the consistency among the different diagrams. Moreover, they propose automatic generation of code and test scenarios.

Some diagrams, other than those mentioned in this section, exist, but their presentation is outside the scope of this book. For further information, see e.g. [PIL 05].

To conclude, semi-formal techniques such as UML enable the characteristics of the system to be studied in depth during modeling, with a high level of abstraction, and the implementation detail can be addressed. The diagrams thus obtained provide a good view of the different aspects of the system. However, even though these diagrams are easy to understand for a non-specialist, grasping the full picture can be a challenge. Moreover, system validation cannot be exhaustive. Therefore, formal models aim to tackle these problems.

2.3. Formal models

Formal models enable the correct behavior of a system to be formally (i.e. mathematically) proven. Then, whatever the evolution of the system, it is guaranteed to behave as expected.

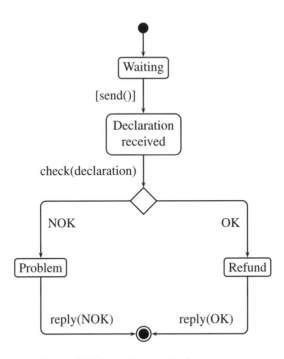

Figure 2.6. *State diagram for the insurance agent*

In addition to the advantages of the previous techniques, formal models offer analysis tools for the system under study:

– simulation provides evidence of the correct behavior or eventually errors to be discovered, especially severe ones. Correction at this stage is relatively cheap, compared to the correction of an already existing system, either implemented as software or hardware;

– exhaustive verification of system behavior can be performed. First, simulation is applied, leading to a coarse-grained debugging, and then the model is refined by verification of its expected properties.

A wide range of specification models and languages exists. In this book, we shall focus on *algebraic specifications*, *automata* [BÉR 01a], *Petri nets* [GIR 03, DIA 09], and *process algebras* [BER 01b]. This is justified by the existence of a specification methodology, the possibility of using structural methods, and introducing temporal constraints in the models considered. Finally, *architecture description languages* (ADLs) [MED 00] enable model composition.

2.3.1. *Algebraic specifications*

Algebraic specifications historically originate from data abstraction ("abstract data types"), and are the origin of object-oriented programming languages (see the class concept). They were further developed and enhanced to become formal specifications of the functional requirements for software modular design. Following the design of numerous algebraic specification languages, CASL (*common algebraic specification language*) was developed in the context of the CoFI international project (*Common Framework Initiative for algebraic specification and development*). This language is based on a careful selection of already explored constructs, such as sub-sorts, partial functions, first-order logics, structured and architectural specifications [AST 02]. The CoFI project website [COF11] contains the documents produced within the project, the language is described in a user manual [BID 04], and the reference manual [CoF 04] provides the complete formal semantics.

A CASL specification may include declaration for types, operations, and predicates (together with their arity), as well as axioms, which are first-order formulae. Some operations are considered as generators (or constructors) and are part of the type declaration ("*datatype declaration*"). A simple specification is described as follows:

spec NOMSPEC=
    type $type\_name ::= gen\_name(args) \mid \ldots$
    op $op\_name : op\_args \rightarrow op\_res$
    $\ldots$
    pred $pred\_name : pred\_arg$
    $\ldots$
    axioms   % %first-order formulae
    end

The language includes constructs for modular design of specifications: union **and** and **then** extensions can be used for specification structuring.

spec NOMSPEC= SP_1 **and** $\ldots$ **and** SP_j **then**
    type $type\_name ::= gen\_name(args) \mid \ldots$

EXAMPLE.– Let us consider the example from section 2.2. An accident declaration specification imports the modules specifying vehicles and clients.

spec DECLARATION = VEHICLE **and** CLIENT **then**
    type $Declaration ::= \ldots$
    end

In practice [BID 04], a realistic system specification involves both partial and total operations. Hence, the ? symbol distinguishes partial operations and generators, and their definition domains are provided by axioms.

spec NOMSPEC=
    type   *type_name* ::= *gen_name(args)* | ...
    op   *op_name* : *op_args* →? *op_res* %%partial operation
    ...
    axioms
          def op_name(args) ⇔ ...

The **free** construct forces the use of the initial semantics, avoiding explicit negation. Indeed, in the **free** specification models, term values are distinct unless their equality follows from the specification axioms [BID 04].

spec NOMSPEC= SP_1 **and** ... **and** SP_j **then**
    free { **type**   *type_name* ::= *gen_name(args)* | ...
    op   *op_name* : *op_args* →? *op_res* ...
    axioms ...}

EXAMPLE.– A counter modulo 3, using increments by 1 and by 2 as operations (see example in section 2.3.2) can be specified as follows:

spec COUNTER =
    free { **type**   *Counter* ::= *0* | *suc(Counter)*;
    %%   suc adds one
    axioms *suc(suc(suc(0)))* = *0*;
    op   *add2* : *Counter* → *Counter*
    axioms   *add2(0)* = *suc(suc(0))*;
          add2(suc(0)) = *0*;
          add2(suc(suc(0))) = *suc(0)*; }
    end

Generic specifications are most useful for reuse purposes. Specifying their parameters is simple, and an instance of the generic specification is obtained by providing a specification argument for each parameter. The specification below is an extension of the generic specification SET[ELEM] instance by INT (these specifications are part of the basic library [ROG 04]):
spec NOMSPEC = SET [INT] ... **then** ...

Note that algebraic specifications include the properties as axioms. Hence, theorems having some impact on these properties can be proven.

The extensions of algebraic specification languages have been proposed so as to take into account dynamic systems and temporal logic properties. For example, CASL-LTL [REG 03] uses *labelled transition logic* [AST 01], thus the states of a system and transitions between states triggered by events can be described.

2.3.2. *Automata*

Automata explicitly describe the possible states of the system. Different kinds of automata exist (communicating automata, timed automata, with variables, etc.), each with specific characteristics.

An automaton can be illustrated using a graph where states of the system are nodes. The evolution from one state to another is performed by *firing a transition*, represented on the graph by an arc linking the two states. The choice of which transition to fire is non-deterministic as several transitions may be fired from a single state. This enables different evolutions of the system to be represented.

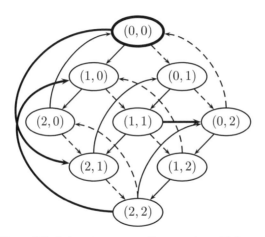

Figure 2.7. *Automaton representing a system with 2 counters*

EXAMPLE.– Let us consider a system with two counters modulo 3, i.e. taking the following values successively: 0, 1, 2, 0, etc. The two counters can either evolve independently, by incrementing their value, or together when they have the same value. In this latter case (and this example), the first counter is incremented by 2 while the second is only incremented by 1. This example is modeled by the automaton in Figure 2.7.

In this description, the name of states contains the value of both counters, i.e. $(0, 2)$ represents the state where the first counter has value 0, and the second value 2. The arcs with a plain line correspond to the increment of the first counter only, and those dashed to the increment of the second counter only. Finally, the arcs depicted with a bold line increment the first counter by 2 and the second by 1. The initial state of the system is also bold-faced (both counters have value 0).

2.3.3. *Petri Nets*

Petri nets [GIR 03, DIA 09] are another formalism giving a view of both states and transitions of the system. The corresponding graph contains two types of nodes: *places* (represented by circles or ellipses) and *transitions* (rectangles). Places represent part of the system state. They contain *tokens*, which indicate the number of occurrences of this particular sub-state. As for automata, transitions represent events that can occur. The arcs entering a transition indicate the *pre-conditions* required to enable transition firing, i.e. the conditions that must be satisfied for the action to occur. Similarly, the output arcs of the transition indicate its *post-condition*, i.e. the result of the firing. The *firing* semantics for a transition t thus consists of deleting the input tokens of t, as specified by the pre-conditions, and adding the tokens in the output places of transition t, as specified by the post-conditions.

EXAMPLE.– The Petri net in Figure 2.8 models our counters system example.

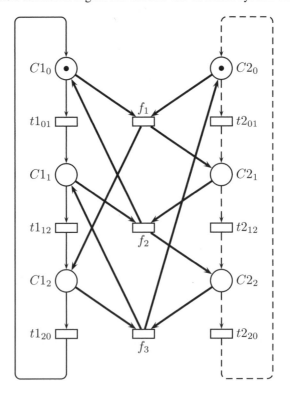

Figure 2.8. *Petri net representing a system with 2 counters*

The conventions used to indicate the meanings of the arc lines is the same as in the automaton of Figure 2.7. Places on the left-hand side of the figure ($C1_0$, $C1_1$, and $C1_2$) indicate the different values the first counter can take, while those on the right hand-side ($C2_0$, $C2_1$, and $C2_2$) correspond to the values of the second counter. Similarly, transitions on the left-hand side ($t1_{01}$, $t1_{12}$, and $t1_{20}$) correspond to the increment of the first counter, and transitions on the right-hand side ($t2_{01}$, $t2_{12}$, and $t2_{20}$) correspond to the increment of the second counter. Transitions in the center of the figure (f_1, f_2, and f_3) represent actions that increment the first counter by 2 and the second by 1. Note that these transitions can only be fired when all their preconditions are satisfied, i.e. when both counters have the same value. The initial state of the system is represented by the distribution of tokens among places: both counters have value 0.

The behavior of Petri nets is often analyzed through its *reachability graph* or *state space*. This graph shows an exhaustive representation of all states the system can reach. Starting from the initial state, all possible transition firings are examined, the resulting markings are added as nodes of the reachability graph, and transitions label the arcs between states, thus explicitly showing how one state is obtained from another. The state space of the Petri net in Figure 2.8 is similar to the automaton in Figure 2.7 (up to the arc labels not present in the automaton), where a marking $(C1_x, C2_y)$ is represented by the pair (x, y).

As systems are becoming larger and larger, Petri net models have evolved towards *high-level nets* [JEN 91], in which the flow is captured by a Petri net structure, and data are explicitly represented using a data specification language. This language can either be dedicated to the kind of model [AMI11], a programming language [CPN11], or an abstract data type specification [REI 91]. High-level nets are easily understood by those with a good programming experience.

In high-level nets, tokens carry data that may be tested or changed while firing a transition. To express data manipulation, the net arcs are labeled with terms specifying the required preconditions and values associated with the created tokens.

EXAMPLE.– Figure 2.9 presents a high-level net model of the counters system.

The net has a single place that always contains a unique token. The token value is (x, y) where x is the value of the first counter and y the value of the second counter. Place *counters* initially contains a token with value $(0, 0)$. The 0..2 inscription next to the place indicates that tokens take their value in the interval from 0 to 2. Transition $t1$ increments the first counter, whatever its value. It thus corresponds to a folding of transitions $t1_{01}$, $t1_{12}$, and $t1_{20}$ from Figure 2.8. Similarly, transition $t2$ increments the second counter (folding of $t2_{01}$, $t2_{12}$, and $t2_{20}$). Finally, transition f increments the first counter by 2 and the second by 1 (folding of f_1, f_2, and f_3). A guard $[x = y]$, associated with transition f, indicates that both counters must have the same value for f to be firable. Such a constraint could also have been captured within the arc expressions of transition f, replacing variable y by x.

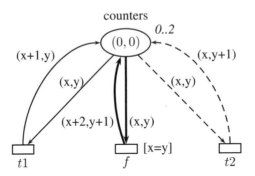

Figure 2.9. *High-level net representing a system with two counters*

2.3.4. *Process algebras*

Process algebras are a family of mathematical formalisms with the aim of describing concurrent systems. Numerous algebras have been defined, the two main families being those derived from CSP (*communicating sequential processes* [HOA 78]) and CCS (*calculus of communicating systems* [MIL 80]).

The most expressive process algebras often include *parameterized definitions*, *process expressions*, and *actions prefixes*. The data manipulated can be simple values (CCS), structured events (CSP), or even *names* (as in e.g. π-calculus [MIL 92]).

A process expression is generally built using the following operators [1]:

– 0 is the *inactive process*;

– $\alpha.P$ is the *sequential composition* of action prefix α followed by the expression of process P;

– $P\|Q$ represents the *parallel composition* of processes P and Q expressions. The semantics considered is often an *interleaving semantics* possibly with a synchronization of processes P and Q. Processes P and Q coexist;

– $P + Q$ is a *non-deterministic choice* between processes P and Q. Only one of them is executed;

– finally, $A(v_1, \ldots, v_n)$ represents a call to a *parameterized definition*.

The elementary *actions* of processes are often limited to the following:

– τ represents an *internal action* that cannot be observed outside the process itself;

---

1. Here, a mixed CCS/CSP syntax is used, but equivalent expressions exist in most process algebras.

– *c!v* represents the *emission* of a value *v* on name *c*, used as a communication channel. The *c!* prefix corresponds to an emission without value passing (as for a signal);

– *c?(x)* represents the *reception* of a name on a channel *c*. Variable *x* is then instantiated with the value received, for the sequel of the process. Reception without value *c?* corresponds to an emission without value *c!*;

– $[a = b]$ tests the *equality* of values or names *a* and *b*;

– $[a \neq b]$ tests the *inequality* of values or names *a* and *b*;

– (νx) corresponds to the *construction of private name x*. This name is visible only for the process that created it. This construct is also called *restriction*.

EXAMPLE.– Let us consider a simplified machine delivering drinks. The communication channels explicitly describe the interface between the machine and its user: channel *coin* is used for inserting coins, and channels *coffee*, *tea*, and *water* for selecting a drink. A possible specification is the following:

$$
\left[
\begin{array}{l}
Machine = coin?(p).\, ([p = 1e]\, Coffee\, Tea + [p = 50cts]\, Water) \\
Coffee\, Tea = tea?.Machine + coffee?.Machine \\
Water = water?.Machine
\end{array}
\right.
$$

The machine operates as follows. If the inserted coin is a 1 euro coin, the machine offers a choice (external choice, performed by the environment) between coffee and tea. If it is a 50 cent coin, only fresh water is proposed.

It is also possible to compose this machine with e.g. a client, so as to obtain a complete system *Sys*:

$$
\left[
\begin{array}{l}
Client = coin!(1e).tea!.coin!(50cts).water!.0 \\
Sys = Client \parallel Machine
\end{array}
\right.
$$

Here, a parallel composition of the client and the machine is used. The behavior of the client consists of first paying and then choosing tea, followed by paying and choosing water.

Process algebras admit many variants: timed, probabilistic, distributed, asynchronous algebras, etc.

2.4. After specification, verification

Once the system has been modeled, simulations can be carried out to gain increased confidence that its behavior is correct. To do so, we start from an *initial state* of the system and execute the model step by step. For automata or Petri nets, transitions are fired one after the other. Simulation can follow two main modes:

– *automatic simulation* is entirely performed using a computer tool. When a choice between transitions occurs, it is done in a non-deterministic fashion;

– *guided or manual simulations* provide the user with a choice either at each step or when several firings can occur. This allows the tool to be guided towards possible errors.

In any case, execution traces will be studied for coarse-grained checking of the behavior of the system for these particular executions. This also enables correction of major errors.

One of the main criteria to consider for simulation is the stop condition. It can be expressed according to:

– the *number of firing steps* to execute during each simulation. The fixed limit should be large enough for the simulation result to be significant;

– a *property that should not be satisfied*. The goal is then to find an execution trace that violates a desired property. As soon as a state violating the property is found, the simulation terminates, and an inspection of its trace enables the source of the error to be determined.

This latter technique is close to verification issues. Verification techniques are applied as a second step, after simulation, in order to perform a more detailed analysis of the system. Then, intended properties must be expressed using a formalism compatible with both the model and the chosen tool.

In order to check specific system properties, they must be written according to an appropriate formalism. Petri nets propose a set of "standard" properties, generic for any Petri net (boundedness, liveness, deadlocks, etc.). However, the properties of interest are often more complex and depend on the system under study (e.g. mutual exclusion between two processes). Such properties are then formalized using an appropriate language, such as *temporal logics* [BÉR 01a, CLA 00]. Temporal logics aim at expressing the sequentialisation of events. It is basically divided into two kinds of logics:

– LTL (*linear time logic*) expresses properties on execution paths;

– CTL (*computation tree logic*) expresses properties on the states encountered during the system evolution.

Verification of properties can be performed in different ways, as will be explained in part II:

– *structural analysis* is concerned with validation of intrinsic properties of the system, valid whatever the initial state;

– *behavioral analysis* is based on a total or partial representation of the system's behavior.

Each of these techniques has its pros and cons. Making the appropriate choices from the start of the modeling phase is thus a key issue.

2.5. Outline of Part I

Formal models are key to the design and validation of secure and safe systems. For such an approach to be efficient, the system under study must first be *specified*. This first step is of utmost importance since it has consequences on later stages of the process. The designer should consider many aspects of his system and answer questions that are not always obvious initially, so as to choose the most appropriate model or specification language. The expected properties that will be checked at a later stage must already be considered as well. Hence, the chosen abstraction level will allow these properties to be expressed without the burden of useless details. Once all these aspects have been considered, writing a specification using knowledge of the system is key to a successful *modeling approach*. This is detailed in Chapter 3.

For some systems, temporal or dynamic constraints should explicitly be considered. Then, the use of *temporal* or *hybrid models* will be privileged. They make it possible to verify not only the usual properties of untimed systems, but also real-time constraints. Thus, the duration of some events, the occurrence of a particular event before a time delay elapses, etc., can be checked. Time can be modeled using a global clock, i.e. shared by all components of the system, a local clock for each component, chronometers, etc. Adapted verification techniques are applied to these kinds of models. These models and their associated verification techniques constitute the subject of Chapter 4.

When dealing with real systems, models are usually too large to be dealt with and to guarantee complete understanding, follow-up, and analysis. Moreover, parts of such systems can be reused within other similar systems, or during maintenance, e.g. when replacing one subsystem with another. Some models, such as hierarchical high-level nets [JEN 92, JEN 09] or modular nets [CHR 00, KIN 09], include a modular structure from the start. But, these concepts are extended further so as to harness heterogenity issues, hence allowing for the development by components, which may be heterogenous. Then, not only should the component be modeled – and its individual behavior checked, but its interface with other system components must also be detailed (input/output, connectors, etc.). ADLs follow such an approach. Chapter 5 presents formal ADLs, which aim to verify properties, and implementation ADLs, which enable real tools to be obtained from their specification.

2.6. Bibliography

[AMI11] CPN-AMI website,   http://move.lip6.fr/software/CPNAMI/index.html, February 2011.

[AST 01] ASTESIANO E., REGGIO G., "Labelled transition logic: an outline", *Acta Inf.*, vol. 37, 2001.

[AST 02] ASTESIANO E., BIDOIT M., KIRCHNER H., KRIEG-BRÜCKNER B., MOSSES P. D., SANNELLA D., TARLECKI A., "CASL: the common algebraic specification language", *Theoretical Comput. Sci.*, vol. 286, p. 153–196, 2002.

[BÉR 01a] BÉRARD B., BIDOIT M., FINKEL A., LAROUSSINIE F., PETIT A., PETRUCCI L., SCHNOEBELEN PH., *Systems and Software Verification. Model-checking Techniques and Tools*, Springer, 2001.

[BER 01b] BERGSTRA J. A., PONSE A., SMOLKA S. A., *Handbook of Process Algebra*, Elsevier Science, 2001.

[BID 04] BIDOIT M., MOSSES P. D., CASL *User manual*, LNCS 2900 (IFIP Series), Springer, 2004, with chapters by T. Mossakowski, D. Sannella, and A. Tarlecki.

[CHR 00] CHRISTENSEN S., PETRUCCI L., "Modular analysis of Petri nets", *The Computer Journal*, vol. 43, p. 224–242, 2000.

[CLA 00] CLARKE E. M., GRUMBERG O., PELED D. A., *Model Checking*, MIT Press, 2000.

[CoF 04] CoFI (THE COMMON FRAMEWORK INITIATIVE), CASL *reference manual*, LNCS 2960 (IFIP Series), Springer, 2004.

[COF11] CoFI, http://www.cofi.info, February 2011.

[CPN11] CPN TOOLS HOMEPAGE, http://cpntools.org/, February 2011.

[DEP09] DEPARTMENT OF COMPUTER SCIENCE, DAIMI, Examples of industrial use of CP-nets, http://www.daimi.au.dk/CPnets/intro/example_indu.html, May 2009.

[DIA 09] DIAZ M., Ed., *Petri Nets: Fundamental Models, Verification and Applications*, ISTE-Wiley, 2009.

[GIR 03] GIRAULT C., VALK R., *Petri Nets for Systems Engineering: a Guide to Modeling, Verification and Applications*, Springer, 2003.

[HOA 78] HOARE C. A. R., "Communicating sequential processes", *Communications of the ACM*, vol. 21, p. 666–677, 1978.

[JEN 91] JENSEN K., ROZENBERG G., *High-level Petri Nets*, Springer, 1991.

[JEN 92] JENSEN K., *Coloured Petri Nets: Basic Concepts, Analysis Methods and Practical Use. Volume 1: Basic Concepts*, Monographs in Theoretical Computer Science, Springer, 1992.

[JEN 09] JENSEN K., KRISTENSEN L., *Coloured Petri nets: modelling and validation of concurrent systems*, Monographs in Theoretical Computer Science, Springer, 2009.

[JØR 04] JØRGENSEN J., BOSSEN C., "Executable use cases: requirements for a pervasive health care system", *IEEE Software*, vol. 21, p. 34–41, 2004.

[KIN 09] KINDLER E., PETRUCCI L., "Towards a standard for modular Petri nets: a formalisation", *Proc. 30th Int. Conf. Application and Theory of Petri Nets and Other Models of Concurrency (PetriNets'2009)*, vol. 5606 of *LNCS* , Springer, p. 43–62, 2009.

[MED 00] MEDVIDOVIC N., TAYLOR R. N., "A classification and comparison framework for software architecture languages", *IEEE Transactions on Software Engineering*, vol. 147, p. 225–236, 2000.

[MIL 80] MILNER R., "A calculus of communicating systems", vol. 92 of *LNCS* , Springer, 1980.

[MIL 92] MILNER R., PARROW J., WALKER D., "A calculus for mobile processes", *Information and Computation*, vol. 100, p. 1–40, 1992.

[PET 03] PETRUCCI L., KRISTENSEN L. M., BILLINGTON J., QURESHI Z. H., "Developing a formal specification for the mission system of a maritime surveillance aircraft", *Proc. 3rd Int. Conf. on Application of Concurrency to System Design (ACSD'03), Guimarães, Portugal, June 2003*, IEEE Comp. Soc. Press, p. 92–101, 2003.

[PIL 05] PILONE D., PITMAN N., *UML 2.0 in a Nutshell*, O'Reilly, 2005.

[REG 03] REGGIO G., ASTESIANO E., CHOPPY C., CASL-LTL: A CASL extension for dynamic reactive systems, version 1.0 – Summary, Report num. DISI-TR-03-36, University of Genova, 2003.

[REI 91] REISIG W., "Petri nets and algebraic specifications", *Theoretical Computer Science*, vol. 80, p. 1–34, 1991.

[ROG 04] ROGGENBACH M., MOSSAKOWSKI T., SCHRÖDER L., "CASL Libraries", [CoF 04], part V.

Chapter 3

Specification and Design Approaches

3.1. Introduction

The aim of this chapter is to describe how to write a consistent system specification. The question under study here is the following: "how do you write and develop a specification?" It is obvious that before starting to write the specification of a complex problem, the problem should be studied, structured, and split into parts, using processes that will be detailed at a later stage. Moreover, appropriate choices should be made at an early stage so that the specification reflects the important characteristics of the system for which some properties must be guaranteed. The choice of an appropriate modeling language and associated verification techniques, within the large existing zoo, is thus a major issue.

Therefore, section 3.2 presents criteria that should be taken into account for the specification to fulfill its intended objectives. Thus, before even starting to write the specification, the important characteristics of the specification should be carefully considered, i.e. which modeling language should be chosen, which abstraction level should be selected, the expected properties that should ultimately be verified.

Then, section 3.3 introduces a modeling methodology. Such an approach helps the designer to choose the constituent features of the system to model, as well as the relevant actions. It helps him in formalizing the essence of the relations between these and constructing a formal model step by step, starting from an informal description.

Chapter written by Christine CHOPPY and Laure PETRUCCI.

3.2. Criteria for developing specifications

It is necessary, before starting the development of a specification, to consider the important characteristics of the system under study. Such an approach enables an appropriate formalism to be chosen with respect to the system, and also enables the model to be structured, so that it will be easier, at a later stage, to enrich the model by incorporating additional details. Finally, the formalism used must provide analysis techniques for the intended properties.

In this section, we describe the different aspects to be considered before starting to write the system specification. Then, a rather simple case study illustrates this approach.

3.2.1. *Relevant concepts*

The first step identifies the *relevant concepts* in the system under study. The key elements constituting the system are exhibited, thus guiding the choice for a formalism.

System data types   More or less complex *data* can appear in the system under study. Hence, it is important to determine whether details for these data are necessary or not. Indeed, in general, the higher the description level, the less efficient the associated verification techniques are.

EXAMPLE.– Let us consider a communication protocol, with a special focus on the adequate functioning of retransmissions with this protocol. The detail of the message content is not necessary, whereas the kind of messages exchanged may very well be. Then messages can be modeled using solely their type (request, indication, response, confirm) and their sequence number.

When handling complex data that should explicitly be modeled, the choice of formalism is preferably high-level models, such as abstract data types or colored Petri nets. Conversely, if the actual data are not that important, but only their availability is required for the system to operate, lower-level formalisms, such as automata or Petri nets will be preferred. In an intermediate case, where few simple types are used and can be mapped to integers or enumerations, counter automata or symmetric Petri nets [1] are more appropriate.

Time   Among critical systems are real-time systems, which include *temporal* constraints of different types such as:

---

1. Symmetric Petri nets were formerly named *well-formed nets*. The name changed during the standardization process for Petri nets (ISO/IEC 15909 standard).

– a *waiting time*, such as a timeout;

– an action *execution time*, such as the movement of a robot.

Several extensions of automata and Petri nets include time. They will be detailed in Chapter 4. Two main paradigms are used when considering time. Some formalisms assume a *global clock* exists, which is used by all operations with timing constraints. Others consider there is no such global clock and operations can occur within a time interval from the moment all their preconditions are satisfied; or each of the different system components have their own *local clock*.

Time can be modeled along two main trends:

– *discrete time* corresponds to the observation of the system at regular clock ticks, or to a sampling;

– *continuous time* reflects the evolution of the system without considering time slices. This is particularly relevant when studying *hybrid systems* where variables values may evolve according to time (for example, acceleration, change in temperature, etc.).

It is not always necessary to take time into account in the specification. Indeed, this is the case when the focus of interest is *qualitative properties*, in which time is not considered.

Determining whether time should be considered in the specification is hence an issue. Moreover, if it is the case, the nature of time, i.e. discrete or continuous, and which clocks (local, global, time intervals) are chosen is in accordance with the problem studied.

The choice between the *synchronous* or *asynchronous* model paradigm [LYN 96] will also have to be carefully considered. Subsystems of a synchronous model evolve at the same rate, whereas in an asynchronous model, one subsystem may progress while another waits for a particular event to happen.

Communication   Complex systems are generally composed of communicating subsystems. Communications may take different forms:

– *rendez-vous* enforces a *synchronization* between the different participating entities. A subsystem sends a message that is received simultaneously by one or more other subsystems. If one of these is not yet ready to synchronize, the other subsystems have to wait. This kind of communication is explicitly modeled in communicating automata and in Petri nets.

– a *communication channel* may be used according to different policies: the channel can be modeled by a *message queue* with a FIFO (*first in first out*) ordering, or another order (in which case desequencing of messages is possible); it can either eventually *lose messages* or be *reliable*. *Queuing automata* and high-level Petri nets provide such modeling mechanisms.

3.2.2. *Abstraction level*

Writing a specification is definitely not a one-shot process. A major notion in this process is the *abstraction level*. The modeling starts at a very abstract level, before applying *incremental construction* through several *refinement* steps. At each step, the model should be analyzed and proven correct before the next refinement. Refining consists of considering more elaborate data structures so as to consider additional details, but also to augment the automaton or Petri net structure, in order to elicit a complex action by breaking it down into several more elementary actions.

Thus, such a specification approach starts with a rather abstract model, where only the key aspects of the system are modeled, and sequentially adds more and more details.

EXAMPLE.– Let us consider again the example of the modulo-3 counters introduced in section 2.3.2. Even though this example is extremely simple, it could be seen as a system with two counters and two kinds of operations: incrementing a single counter by one unit and incrementing both counters, the first one by 2 and the second by 1. This leads to the model in Figure 3.1. This model can then be refined into the one in Figure 2.8.

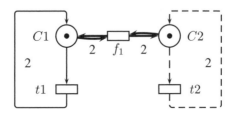

Figure 3.1. *Abstract Petri net for a system with 2 counters*

Choosing an adequate abstraction level is all the more important as taking into account unnecessary details complicates the analysis of the system.

Moreover, as for program development, a step-by-step construction enables parts of the model to be validated one by one. The designer then ensures that the subsystems studied have the correct behavior before proceeding with an additional subsystem.

3.2.3. *Specification structuring*

Since writing a complex system specification is a multistep process, structuring mechanisms are necessary. Such a system is usually composed of several interacting subsystems. An interesting approach is to specify each of these subsystems in isolation, and then specify their interactions. Such an approach has several advantages:

– the design of each subsystem focuses on its own behavior. Hence, the designer is not bothered with other subsystem specifics;

– a subsystem may allow for different variants. The whole system can then be analyzed with these different possibilities, only replacing one model of the subsystem by another within the complete model;

– similarly, a component (or subsystem) designed for a particular problem may be *reused* within another complex system. Therefore, it is not necessary to model this component again;

– several *instances* of a same component may be integrated in the model, using parameterized modeling features, so as to clearly identify each individual instance during the analysis phase. Hence the subsystem model is not duplicated;

– This approach enables generic components or subsystems to be used, which are available in libraries of frequently used components, with as little adaptation as possible.

EXAMPLE.– Consider the specification of a communication protocol. Such a system usually involves *sender* and *receiver* processes, as well as a *communication medium*. These three components can be specified independently of each other. It may be of particular interest to e.g. model two kinds of senders, and verify the characteristics of the protocol with each of these.

Some specification formalisms include structuring concepts, either intrinsic or integrated. This is the case for hierarchical colored Petri nets [JEN 92, JEN 09], in which the model architecture follows a tree-like structure. The highest level (tree root) corresponds to the most abstract description of the system, while the lowest levels (tree leaves) describe the different elements in great detail.

3.2.4. *Properties*

Expressing the system's intended properties is complementary to its specification. Indeed, not only should the formalism used for expressing properties be compatible with the language used for the system specification, but also the elements constituting the property should actually be represented within the model. For example, real-time constraints or schedulability can be expressed on a timed model.

3.2.5. *Future evolution of model and properties*

Both the system and properties specifications are deemed to evolve during the design and verification phases. This aspect must also be taken into account, in order to guarantee that the intended abstraction level is reached.

EXAMPLE.– The Petri nets in Figures 3.2, 3.3, 3.4 and 3.5 all model the problem of mutual exclusion between two processes, competing for access to a critical section.

These models comprise a loop to represent a process behavior: it is initially not in the critical section (place P), it can ask to enter the critical section (transition *Enter*), after which it is in the critical section (place CS), which it can leave (transition *End*) to return to its initial state. At any time, only a single process can be in the critical section. As a consequence, the right for a process to enter the critical section is pre-conditioned by the status of the other process, which should not be in the critical section itself. This is modeled by the double arcs (i.e. arcs with two arrow heads) in Figure 3.2. A standard way of handling the access to the critical section is to grant some "access right", modeled by a token in place *MutEx* in all other Petri nets presented for this problem. In Figure 3.3, the loop is explicitly shown for each process, whereas in Figure 3.4, both cycles are superposed and the two processes specified by two tokens in place P. Figure 3.5 is similar, using a colored Petri net that enables the two processes to be distinguished by naming them $p1$ and $p2$.

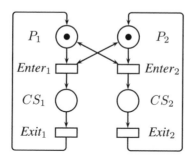

Figure 3.2. *Mutual exclusion between two processes (version 1)*

Let us now consider the first approach to this specification development: the designer wants to extend his model so as to cater for the mutual exclusion between three processes. The net in Figure 3.2 should then include a new cycle for the additional process. Transition $Enter_3$ must be connected by a double arc to places P_1 and P_2, and similarly, transitions $Enter_1$ and $Enter_2$ must be connected to place P_3. Hence the model becomes less readable. When adding the same extension to the Petri net in Figure 3.3 a new loop must be added for the third process and connected to place *MutEx*. This is also not very readable. Conversely, the extension of the other two models is simply made by adding a new token in place P to model the third process.

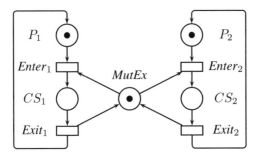

Figure 3.3. *Mutual exclusion between two processes (version 2)*

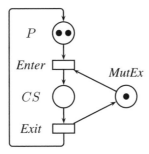

Figure 3.4. *Mutual exclusion between two processes (version 3)*

Now, assume that the internal behavior of the critical section for each process has to be detailed. Only the Petri net in Figure 3.5 enables the different processes involved to be distinguished while maintaining a relatively compact model (the net in Figure 3.3 also distinguishes the process identities).

Similarly, if verifying that a process can enter the critical section, whatever its identity, nets in Figures 3.3 and 3.5 are more appropriate. Hence, this shows that even for a very simple example, the design choices must definitely take into account future evolutions of the model as well as checking the properties.

3.2.6. *Using specification and verification tools*

Several tools (e.g. [AMI11, CPN11, HEN 95, LAR 97]) provide an environment for designing formal models as well as the associated analysis techniques. However, the kind of model considered and the analysis provided differ from one tool to another. The choice of a formal specification and verification tool should then consider both aspects. The recent standard for Petri nets [ISO 11] provides a unified language

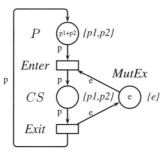

Figure 3.5. *Mutual exclusion between two processes (version 4)*

to describe these models in order to exchange them between different software tools, and thus take advantage of the particular analysis techniques they implement. A companion framework to the standard [HIL 10] is provided to ease the implementation of writing and reading such standardized Petri nets files.

3.2.7. *Case study: modeling a railway system*

In this section, we consider the more complex design example of a model railway. This example is taken from a students' project [BER 01] with the aim of formally designing and analyzing an electrical model railway before implementing it on the actual hardware. It is thus mandatory to ensure that no collision will occur before the final solution is tested on the real devices.

The physical layout of the railway track is presented in Figure 3.6. It is composed of approximately 15 m of track divided into 16 sections (blocks B1 to B16), plus two garage side tracks (ST1 and ST2). These are connected with four switches and one crossing. The hardware allows for several trains to circulate simultaneously. It is connected to a computer, which sends information on the tracks and transmits orders to trains (stop, advance, go backwards) and also to switches. Each track section is equipped at both ends with a sensor to detect that a train is entering or leaving the section.

When catering for several trains, the model can very quickly become extremely complex. Hence, the formalism chosen is a high-level specification language. Moreover, in a first approach, a very abstract model, close to the actual layout, can be designed. In a subsequent step, details to move from one track section to the next will be considered. Therefore, hierarchical colored Petri nets will be an adequate choice. Figure 3.7 illustrates an abstract model "fitting" the physical tracks layout, easily reflecting a mapping between net elements and physical ones.

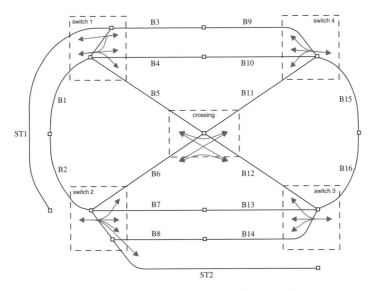

Figure 3.6. *Setup of the model railway track*

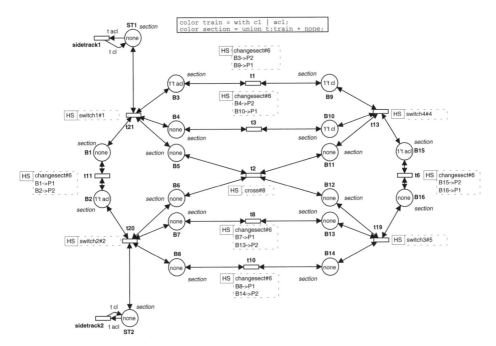

Figure 3.7. *Abstract Petri net for the model railway*

The policy to move from one track section to the next can then be detailed: each transition of the net in Figure 3.7 is thus a *substitution transition*, i.e. its behavior is described by a subnet. Figure 3.8 shows a simple policy to move from one section to the next, in the simple case where there is neither a switch nor a crossing. This subnet explicitly describes the behavior of transitions $t1$, $t3$, $t6$, $t8$, $t10$, and $t11$. The subnets for the switches and the crossing can be found in [BER 01].

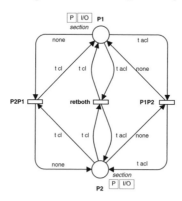

Figure 3.8. *Petri net model for the move from one track section to the next*

Let us now focus on the data manipulated in this model. The railway is represented by Petri net places. Each track section can contain either a single train or no train at all. The *type* associated with places thus reflects these two possibilities. It is also necessary to know which way each train is heading, thus a direction (*clockwise* or *anticlockwise*). The designer is tempted to assign an identity to each train, so that he knows at all times where each train is. However, this information is superfluous. Indeed, for the system to behave as expected, knowing if a train is present on a track and its direction suffices. Even though naming trains is possible, it entails problems: when verifying the absence of collisions, the state space explosion problem is encountered (unless symbolic techniques are used, see Chapter 7). An approach without train identities avoids this problem.

3.3. Specification development methodologies

A common characteristic of all development methods considered is thus that they can lead, one way or another, to a decomposition of the system under study. An initial decomposition can very often be obtained through unified modeling language (UML) use cases. This structuring step must then be pursued further, for example using *patterns* and guidelines so as to ultimately reach a precise formal specification.

Patterns represent families of structures that are frequently used, and that the user is invited to "try" on (and possibly to adapt to) the problem under study, so as to benefit from its "off-the-shelf" structuring concepts. *Patterns* can thus be viewed as an elaborated means to reuse knowledge acquired from experience. *Problem frames* [JAC 01] were proposed by M. Jackson to structure problems in a global way. Structures of a finer grain and often used for design are offered by *architectural styles* [GAR 93, BAS 98]. *Components architecture* [CHE 01] is interesting to describe precisely how the components (that structuring yields to develop independently) should be integrated. It may be worth combining these different approaches so as to benefit from their combined advantages [CHO 04c].

Once a convenient level of decomposition is reached, the precise specification of the system may be developed, and guidelines are useful to achieve this in a methodical way that should cover the different relevant points as much as possible. An approach presented in section 3.3.1 relies on a distinction between data structures, simple dynamic systems, and structured (with subsystems) dynamic systems, and for each case proposes the characteristic elements to consider and the kind of properties to look for. The methods developed further are based on problem frames, architectural styles, as well as the specification development based on components and the composition of the different parts for the solution.

3.3.1. *Guidelines for specification development*

Following the approach described in [CHO 06], a software item may be:

– a simple dynamic system (for instance a sequential system);

– a structured dynamic system (with interacting subsystems, that may themselves be either simple or structured);

– a data structure.

Software items are characterized by their *parts* and by their *constituent features*. For instance, the parts of a simple system are its data structures and its constituent features are its states and elementary interactions. A dynamic system (simple or structured) is considered as a *labeled transition system lts*, where lts is a triple $(State, Label, \rightarrow)$ that comprises the system $State$, the transition $Label$ (composed of elementary interactions), and the transition relation $\rightarrow$, with $\rightarrow \subseteq State \times Label \times State$.

Precise guidelines indicate which properties should be expressed and in which way.

It is also possible to choose a specification style, for instance a *property-oriented* style (also called axiomatic), or a *model-oriented* style (also called constructive). The property-oriented style is focused on the description of the system properties expressed at an abstract level (it may be possible to prove some consequences of these properties), while the model-oriented style deals with the possibility of achieving some computations (and also to perform *model checking*).

Whichever style is chosen, it is always recommended to adopt a graphical representation that facilitates the reading and understanding of the formal specification.

This method was initially developed for the languages CASL [BID 04] and CASL-LTL [REG 03] (see section 2.3.1), but it was also applied to other languages, such as Petri nets [CHO 04a, CHO 08] or UML [CHO 04b]. We describe below the method for simple dynamic systems.

Simple dynamic systems

We sketch out a description of the method for producing a property-oriented specification of simple dynamic systems, and we illustrate this using the train example described in section 3.2.7.

A simple dynamic system has no internal component, and it may be a sequential/non deterministic process or a distributed/parallel system. As mentioned above simple dynamic systems are formally considered as labeled transition systems lts. The states s of an lts represent the intermediate situations in the system life, each transition represents its capacity to evolve from state s to state s', and the label l contains information about the necessary conditions to enable this transition and on the transformations resulting form the transition execution.

The labels are a set of elementary interactions. Each elementary interaction corresponds to an elementary exchange with the external environment. Elementary interactions have different types, and one type is characterized by a name and arguments (that belong to data structures). Elementary interactions belong to the simple system constituent features.

The state is also a constituent feature of a simple system and, depending on the specification style adopted, it will be described by means of state observers (for a specification in the property-oriented style) or by state constructors (for a specification in the model-oriented style).

The data structures used in the state descriptors and by the elementary interactions are the parts of the system.

The properties of a simple system correspond to properties on lts that areproperties on the labels, states, and transitions. These properties may express what the admissible sets of elementary interactions are in order to form a transition label, and the links between the source state, the target state, and the label of a transition. These properties may also provide information on the values observed by the different state observers. More precisely:

1) label properties express that elementary interactions are incompatible under some conditions;

2) state properties describe the conditions that should be satisfied by the values returned by state observers for any state;

3) state properties may also include special atoms that express properties on the execution paths (sequences of transitions) leaving/arriving this state (thus properties of the future/past behavior of the system);

4) transition properties are conditions on the state observers that apply to the source and target states of the transition.

Properties should be described both informally using a comment expressed in natural language, and formally with a formula. A complete list of the properties is given in [CHO 06], and they will be illustrated in the train specification example. Some examples of properties are detailed below: an elementary interaction precondition and its incompatibilities with itself and other elementary interactions.

pre-cond1 (TransitionProp) If a transition label contains an instance of ei, then the transition source state should satisfy the condition:

if $cond(args)$ **then** $ei(args)$ **happens**

Some observers on the source state may appear in $cond(args)$ while observers on the target state may not appear.

incompat1 (LabelProp) Under some conditions on the arguments, an instance of ei is incompatible with another instance of itself (no transition label may contain both):

$ei(arg_1)$ **incompatible with** $ei(arg_2)$ **if** $cond(arg_1,arg_2)$

Under some conditions on the arguments, an instance of ei is incompatible with an instance of ei' (no transition label may contain both):

$ei(arg_1)$ **incompatible with** $ei'(arg_2)$ **if** $cond(arg_1, arg_2)$

In the next section these ideas are applied to guide the specification of part of the train example described in section 3.2.7.

The train example specification

In order illustrate the ideas above, we consider the train as a simple dynamic system.[2]

Hence, system characteristics should be identified and expressed as state observers and elementary interactions, as shown in Figure 3.10.

---

2. Of course, a more complete approach, taking into account a moving policy, can be described as a more elaborate structured system, as described in [CHO 08].

The description of a state of the system is first based on the physical system layout, i.e. the tracks on which the trains circulate, as well as the switches. The state observers must then tell which track sections are contiguous ("*connected*") or connected via a switch ("*switched*"), and if a train is present on a section ("*train_present*"), which direction it is heading (here "*clockwise*" or "*anticlockwise*").

The elementary interactions (associated with a train changing state) are thus the track section changes for the train, be they connected directly or via a switch. The properties of the state observers will of course show that the track positions and the switches connections are fixed.

The identified elementary interactions and state observers should be named in a consistent manner. Their parameter types must also be determined and specified.

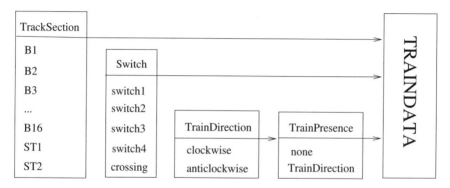

Figure 3.9. *Data structures*

Data structures that constitute part of the system are identified and designed while working on elementary interactions and state observers. The names of track sections and switches are those of the physical layout in Figure 3.6, and they are also the possible values for the associated data types. When the number of different values being rather small, the types are defined as enumerations (see Figure 3.9 and the CASL specification below). Similarly, the direction in which trains are heading has two possible values. The CASL specification for these data is given below. The **free** construct guarantees that no property relates these values with one another, and that they are therefore actually distinct. The **sort** construct is used here to express that each element of type *TrainDirection* is also an element of type *TrainPresence*.

spec TRAINDATA =
    free type
            TrackSection ::= *B1* | *B2* | *B3* ... | *B16* | *ST1* | *ST2*
    free type
            Switch ::= *switch1* | *switch2* | *switch3* | *switch4* | *crossing*

free type
　　　　TrainDirection ::= *clockwise* | *anticlockwise*
free type
　　　　TrainPresence ::= *none* | **sort** (*TrainDirection*)
end

Note that these data appear in the names of the Petri net places and transitions, or in the token colors (see Figure 3.6). The presence of a train on a track section evolves with the system behavior according both to the initial state and the changes that occurred since then. It is thus necessary to record the system "History" and "State".

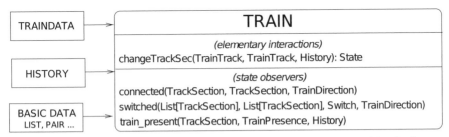

The auxiliary type TrainTrack is defined as Pair[TrainPresence, TrackSection]

Figure 3.10. *The train elementary interactions and state observers*

spec STATE =
　sort　*State*;
　op　　*initial* : *State*;
　end

spec HISTORY = STATE **then**
　type　*History* ::= *initial* | __.__(*History*; *State*);

　　　　. . .

　end

The **then** construct introduces the elements added after importing the STATE specification module.

Once the constituent characteristics are identified and the system parts specified, the system properties can be formulated. The properties of the elementary interaction *changeTrackSec* are altogether a pre-condition, a post-condition, and an incompatibility property.

pre-cond1 (transition property) The track section change is possible when two track sections are connected (either directly or via a switch), when a train is on the departure track for this connection, and there is no train on the destination track:

if $(connected(TS_i, TS_j, TP_i) \vee$

$\exists sw : Switch \; s.t. \; switched((\ldots, TS_i, \ldots), (\ldots, TS_j, \ldots), sw, TP_i)) \wedge (TP_j = none)$

then $changeTrackSec(< TP_i, TS_i >, < TP_j, TS_j >)$ **happens**

post-cond1 (transition property) After changing track section, the train is on the destination track:

if $changeTrackSec(< TP_i, TS_i >, < TP_j, TS_j >)$ **happens then** $(TP'_j = TP_i)$

incompat1 (label property) The idea here is to express that a train cannot simultaneously make several track changes at a given time in the system's history h. Since the direction the train is heading is known, the possibility that the train takes two different directions while using a switch should be avoided:

$changeTrackSec(< TP_i, TS_i >, < TP_j, TS_j, h >)$ **incompatible with**

$changeTrackSec(< TP_i, TS_i >, < TP_k, TS_k, h >)$

if $\exists sw : Switch \; s.t. \; switched((\ldots, TS_i, \ldots), (\ldots, TS_j, \ldots, TS_k, \ldots), sw, TP_i) \wedge (T_j \neq T_k)$

The properties for state observers *connected* and *switched* reproduce the track layout, which never changes:

value1 (state property)

$connected(B1, B2, anticlockwise)$

$connected(B2, B1, clockwise)$

$\ldots$

$switched((ST1, B1), B3), switch1, clockwise)$

$switched((B1), (B3, B4, B5), clockwise)$

$switched((B3), (B1, ST1), anticlockwise)$

$switched((B3, B4, B5), (B1), switch1, anticlockwise)$

$\ldots$

The properties for state observer *train_present* concern the initial state values (for example trains are or are not occupying some tracks) and the way these values evolve when elementary interactions occur (here *changeTrackSec*).

value1 (state property) $train\_present(B1, none, initial) \ldots$

how-change (transition property)

if $train\_present(TS_i, TP_i, h) \wedge train\_present(TS_j, none, h)$

$\wedge \; changeTrackSec(< TS_i, TP_i >, < TS_j, none >, h)$ **happened**

then $(TP_i \neq none) \wedge train\_present(TS'_i, none, h') \wedge train\_present(TS'_j, TP_i, h')$

where h and h' are the system history before and after the move, respectively.

A parallel can be drawn between this CASL-LTL specification and a Petri net model. This modeling step can be pursued by other steps introducing additional details (specification *refinement*).

Moreover, this specification can be used (e.g. be imported) as part of a structured system specification, or part of another system. In the following, we describe problem frames, and illustrate how the specification developed above is used at a larger scale by using the train example.

3.3.2. Problem frames

A *problem frame* [JAC 01] is a schema defining, in intuitive manner, a class of problems with their context, domain specific characteristics, interfaces, and requirements. The system to be developed is represented by the "machine".

A diagram is associated with each problem frame (such as that in Figure 3.11). Rectangles represent the already existing application domains, while those with a double bar represent the "machine" domains to be constructed, and the requirements are denoted by a dashed oval. The lines linking them represent interfaces, also called *shared phenomena*. Jackson distinguishes *causal* domains, which obey some rules, *lexical* domains, which are physical representation of data, and *"biddable"* domains, which correspond to people. Jackson also defines five basic frames (*required behavior, commanded behavior, information display, workpieces* and *transformation*). Figure 3.11 pictures the control-command (*commanded behavior*) problem frame, proposing a structure for problems where the domain is controlled according to an operator's commands.

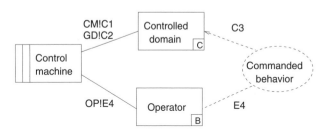

Figure 3.11. *Control-command problem frame*

The C indicates that the *controlled domain* is causal, and CM!C1 means that the C1 phenomenon is controlled by the machine (CM, *control machine*). The dashed line refers to requirements, and the arrow indicates that it is a constraining reference.

Using a problem frame consists of instantiating domains, interfaces, and requirements according to the problem under study. A problem frame corresponding to the problem studied will therefore be sought. The basic frames provided by Jackson being very simple, either a first decomposition (e.g. using UML use cases), an adaptation of existing frames, or the use of more elaborate ones (obtained by combination of several problem frames) will be necessary. The domain nature (causal, lexical, "biddable") is key to obtaining the appropriate frame.

With respect to the model railway example described in section 3.2.7, the control-command problem frame cannot be used as it does not refer to a train user. The train can be considered has having an autonomous behavior as soon as it is started. The problem frame "*required behavior*" (without a user, see Figure 3.12) is more adequate. It corresponds to applications where an automatic behavior prevails, and humans seldom intervene (only for the bootstrap and eventually a few settings).

Figure 3.12. *Problem frame "required behavior"*

The specification associated with this problem frame involves a specification of the controlled domain, that for the required behavior, and also for the design of the system that will operate. In our train example, the controlled domain is composed of trains that circulate according to the railway layout. The intended behavior must be described, e.g. by imposing circulation rules (a train advances as long as it does not result in a collision). In order to guarantee this behavior, the system must be aware of the controlled domain state (in practice, this is often achieved with sensors), and should be able to change this state (using actuators). In the train example, sensors can transmit the $train\_present$ information, and the system controls the $changeTrackSection$ event.

In the above, only the structure deduced by the nature and the elements of the problem is considered. When describing a global system structure, frames given by architectural styles are advocated, either immediately if the problem is well known, or after initial processing of the problem specification (then following a refinement approach).

3.3.3. *Architectural styles*

Architectural styles [GAR 93, BAS 98] are patterns of software architecture, so they are *a priori* structures less abstract than problem frames and that will therefore not be used as a first line, but to a level of development (and specification) close to the design. Architectural styles are characterized by:

– a set of component types (for instance a directory of data, processes, etc.) that perform certain functions upon execution;

– a topological distribution of these components indicating their relationships at run time;

– a set of semantic constraints;

– a set of connectors for communication, coordination, or cooperation among components.

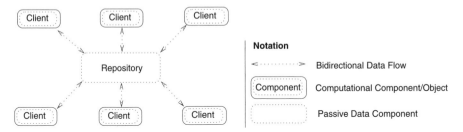

Figure 3.13. *A data-centered architectural style*

Among the major styles of architecture, the *"repository"* style (see Figure 3.13), data-centric, where different clients access shared data, is well-suited for information systems.

As for problem frames, it must provide an instance of an architectural style. This style will be chosen depending on the type of problem considered, but it often leaves several choices. Non-functional specifications can then come into play. It is also possible to guide the choice from the problem frame(s) used in the first step.

The associated formal specification shall take all elements of the chosen architecture into account.

3.3.4. *Component-based specifications*

The basic idea of component-based software engineering is to build software from parts of already existing software, which are well encapsulated and relatively independent [SZY 99]. These pieces of software are also named "components", but in this context, the *components* must satisfy the following conditions:

– all services provided and all services required by a component are accessible only via well-defined *interfaces*;

– a component adheres to a *component model*. This model specifies, among others, syntactic conventions for defining interfaces and how the components communicate. It serves to ensure the interoperability of several components that adhere to the same component model;

– components are integrated in binary form, and the source code is often not accessible to the "client" components. It is therefore important that the specification of a component contains all information needed for its use.

In the component-based software engineering approach, architectural principles also play an important role, since the composition of a system from components is performed using a chosen architecture. The two areas are quite tightly linked.

The idea here is to break down a problem into sub-problems. For each sub-problem, a software must be developed, and the whole system consists of an appropriate combination of the software that solves these sub-problems. Each sub-problem is constructed as a component that must comply with the constraints on the interfaces. The combination of different components can be achieved using a *component architecture*, such as that proposed by Cheesman and Daniels [CHE 01].

3.4. Conclusion

Developing a formal specification is a crucial step in the development of the system. However, achieving this specification raises many issues, but these are not insurmountable. Indeed, the various points discussed here are intended to help to quickly and accurately identify the nature of the problem studied and to enlighten the reader with the crucial aspects to consider (for example, choosing a level of abstraction, the choice of elements to take into account immediately or to leave open up to the implementation stage, and determine the responsibilities of the system).

We have also seen how a specification might evolve, for example in the case of mutual exclusion.

Finally we showed how schemas or patterns can also be used in the specification, and we have provided guidelines for writing specifications that indicate which elements to look for and which properties should be expressed.

3.5. Bibliography

[AMI11] CPN-AMI: home page, http://move.lip6.fr/software/CPNAMI/, 2011.

[BAS 98] BASS L., CLEMENTS P., KAZMAN R., *Software Architecture in Practice*, Addison-Wesley, 1998.

[BER 01] BERTHELOT G., PETRUCCI L., "Specification and validation of a concurrent system: an educational project", *Journal of Software Tools for Technology Transfer*, vol. 3, p. 372–381, 2001.

[BID 04] BIDOIT M., MOSSES P. D., CASL *User manual*, Lecture Notes in Computer Science 2900 (IFIP Series), Springer, 2004, with chapters by T. Mossakowski, D. Sannella, and A. Tarlecki.

[CHE 01] CHEESMAN J., DANIELS J., *UML Components – a Simple Process for Specifying Component-based Software*, Addison-Wesley, 2001.

[CHO 04a] CHOPPY C., PETRUCCI L., "Towards a methodology for modelling with Petri nets", *Proc. Workshop on Practical Use of Coloured Petri Nets*, p. 39–56, 2004, Proceedings published as report DAIMI-PB 570, Aarhus, Denmark.

[CHO 04b] CHOPPY C., REGGIO G., "Improving use case based requirements using formally grounded specifications", *Fundamental Approaches to Software Engineering (FASE)*, Lecture Notes in Computer Science 2984, Springer, p. 244-260, 2004.

[CHO 04c] CHOPPY C., HEISEL M., "Une approche à base de 'patrons' pour la spécification et le développement de systèmes d'information", *Proceedings of Approches Formelles dans l'Assistance au Développement de Logiciels - AFADL'2004*, p. 61–76, 2004.

[CHO 06] CHOPPY C., REGGIO G., "A formally grounded software specification method", *Journal of Logic and Algebraic Programming*, vol. 67, p. 52–86, Elsevier, 2006.

[CHO 08] CHOPPY C., PETRUCCI L., REGGIO G., "A modelling approach with coloured Petri nets", *Proc. 13th Int. Conf. on Reliable Software Technologies — Ada-Europe*, Lecture Notes in Computer Science 5026, Springer, p. 73–86, 2008.

[CPN11] CPN TOOLS HOMEPAGE, http://cpntools.org/, 2011.

[GAR 93] GARLAN D., SHAW M., "An introduction to software architecture", AMBRIOLA V., TORTORA G., Eds., *Advances in Software Engineering and Knowledge Engineering*, vol. 1, World Scientific Publishing Company, 1993.

[HEN 95] HENZINGER T. A., HO P., WONG-TOI H., "HYTECH: the next generation", *Proc. 16th IEEE Real-Time Systems Symposium (RTSS'95)*, IEEE Computer Society Press, p. 56–65, 1995.

[HIL 10] HILLAH L., KORDON F., PETRUCCI L., TRÈVES N., "PNML framework: an extendable reference implementation of the Petri net markup language", *Proc. 31st Int. Conf. Application and Theory of Petri Nets and Other Models of Concurrency (PetriNets'2010), Braga, Portugal, June 2010*, vol. 6128 of *Lecture Notes in Computer Science*, Springer, p. 318–327, June 2010.

[ISO 11] ISO, "ISO/IEC 15909-2: software and systems engineering – high-level Petri nets. Part 2: transfert format", 2011.

[JAC 01] JACKSON M., *Problem frames. Analyzing and structuring software development problems*, Addison-Wesley, 2001.

[JEN 92] JENSEN K., *Coloured Petri Nets: Basic Concepts, Analysis Methods and Practical Use. Volume 1: Basic Concepts*, Monographs in Theoretical Computer Science, Springer, 1992.

[JEN 09] JENSEN K., KRISTENSEN L. M., *Coloured Petri Nets: Modelling and Validation of Concurrent Systems*, Monographs in Theoretical Computer Science, Springer, 2009.

[LAR 97] LARSEN K. G., PETTERSSON P., YI W., "UPPAAL in a nutshell", *Journal of Software Tools for Technology Transfer*, vol. 1, p. 134-152, Springer, 1997.

[LYN 96] LYNCH N., *Distributed Algorithms*, Series in Data Management Systems, Morgan Kaufmann, 1996.

[REG 03] REGGIO G., ASTESIANO E., CHOPPY C., CASL-LTL: a CASL extension for dynamic reactive systems. Version 1.0 – summary, Report num. DISI-TR-03-36, University of Genova, 2003.

[SZY 99] SZYPERSKI C., *Component Software – Beyond Object Oriented Programming*, Addison Wesley, 1999.

Chapter 4

Modeling Time

This chapter is devoted to the modeling of applications involving quantitative time constraints. We briefly show how timed models can be useful (section 4.1), then we describe semantical aspects of such models in section 4.2. Sections 4.3 and 4.4 respectively present several timed models and logics that have been largely studied in the last 15 years for the specification of timed properties.

4.1. Introduction

We now explain in an informal way when time constraints should be integrated in the modeling of systems and we describe the problems involved by this process of adding explicit time.

4.1.1. *Introducing explicit time in models*

Reactive systems have to take into account actions from the environment and maintain adequate reactions throughout their executions. Timed systems are a subclass of these systems, where possibly critical requirements are enforced by using explicit time constraints.

A classical example is the response time property: "each time a dangerous event occurs, an alarm is triggered". In a model that does not handle explicit time, there is no way to specify a precise delay between the dangerous event and the triggering of

Chapter written by Béatrice BÉRARD.

an alarm. Thus, when the property is satisfied, we only know that "sometimes in the future", the alarm will be triggered, which is not enough in some critical systems. On the contrary, when time is explicitly represented, it is possible to require that at most 30 seconds elapses between these events. Another feature occurring frequently in reactive systems is the time-out requirement, for instance: "if no action takes place, return to initial state". Again in this case, a precise time duration is needed to implement the constraint.

Moreover, some systems involve more complicated *dynamic variables* evolving with time, such a the room temperature obtained with a heating device or the water level in a tank. In both cases, these variables satisfy differential equations and the system should satisfy some requirements stating that their values must stay between minimal and maximal thresholds.

Similar examples are described more formally in the following.

4.1.2. *Some issues related to explicit time*

There are various difficult aspects related to handling explicit time; we only show some of them below.

The first concerns the language used to express time requirements. Consider again the example of the response time property and assume that $p(\tau)$ and $a(\tau)$ denote, respectively, the occurrence of a problem and the triggering of an alarm at time τ. Writing the property in first-order logic would give the following formula:

$$\forall \tau \ (p(\tau) \Rightarrow \exists \tau' \ (\tau \leq \tau' \leq \tau + 30 \ \wedge \ a(\tau'))).$$

This would lead to large formulas for more complicated properties. Therefore, new logics better suited to the timed framework have been introduced and will be described in section 4.4.

The second problem concerns the more general issues of modularity and compositionnality. The design of large systems is easier if it is possible to separately describe subparts of a system, which are subsequently composed to obtain a global representation. The classical synchronization problems between modules are increased by the necessary additional time synchronization. In a simplified framework, a global clock can be introduced, thus leading to a strong synchronization between timed modules. However, this hypothesis is not realistic when dealing with distributed components executing on different machines, and introducing several asynchronous clocks often yields undecidability for most verification problems.

Finally, similar to the design of large models, the questions of hierarchical structure and model refinement arises. Until recently, few studies have been devoted to these questions at the model level [BÉR 08b, BER 09].

4.2. Semantics of timed models

Labeled transition systems are a natural framework well suited to the description of the behaviors of dynamic systems. This framework has been extended to timed models, by adding duration transitions to the classical action transitions. We first describe the structure of time domains, then the timed transition systems, and the corresponding languages, and we explain the problems resulting from the addition of timed transitions.

4.2.1. *Time domains*

Classically, the time domains are the sets $\mathbb{N}$ of natural numbers, $\mathbb{Q}_+$ of non-negative rational numbers and $\mathbb{R}_+$ of non-negative real numbers. The first domain is a particular case of *discrete* time domain, sometimes also modeled by sequences of special events called *ticks*, where the system state can be observed. The other two represent *dense* time domains. In [NIC 93], a unified model is proposed for the time domains, as a commutative monoid $(\mathbb{T}, +)$, with 0 as its identity, satisfying the following properties:

- $\forall \tau, \tau' \in \mathbb{T}$, $\tau + \tau' = \tau$ if and only if $\tau' = 0$

- the relation $\leq$ defined by $\tau \leq \tau'$ if $\exists \tau'' \in \mathbb{T}$ such that $\tau' = \tau + \tau''$, is a total order on $\mathbb{T}$.

This definition implies that 0 is the minimum of $\mathbb{T}$ for $\leq$ and if $\tau \leq \tau'$ then there exists a unique $\tau'' \in \mathbb{T}$, denoted by $\tau' - \tau$, such that $\tau' = \tau + \tau''$.

Thus, elements in $\mathbb{T}$ represent *dates* and the difference between two dates naturally corresponds to a *duration*, also in $\mathbb{T}$. Within this framework, discrete or dense time can be characterized.

A *date sequence* is a non-decreasing sequence in $\mathbb{T}$. When the domain is $\mathbb{Q}_+$ or $\mathbb{R}_+$, an infinite sequence can be convergent, in which case it is called *Zeno*, in reference to the famous greek philosopher and his paradox. Behaviours occurring along such sequences are often excluded from the semantics of timed models, since they are not considered realistic. They were nevertheless studied, for instance in [HAN 95, BÉR 00]. In the following, for the sake of simplicity, the time domain $\mathbb{T}$ is considered as a subset of $\mathbb{R}_+$.

4.2.2. *Timed transition systems*

Recall that a labeled transition system is usually defined by a quadruple $\mathcal{T} = (L, S, s_0, E)$, where L is the set of labels, S is the set of configurations, s_0 is the initial configuration and E is the transition relation, given as a subset of $S \times L \times S$. A transition (s, ℓ, s') in E is also written as $s \xrightarrow{\ell} s'$ and $\xrightarrow{\ell}$ is the set of transitions labeled by ℓ.

A timed transition system is obtained by introducing delay transitions, in addition to action transitions:

DEFINITION 4.1 *A timed transition system (TTS) is a transition system $\mathcal{T}$ labeled by $L = \Sigma \cup \mathbb{T}$, where Σ is a finite alphabet and $\mathbb{T}$ a time domain.*

Transitions $\xrightarrow{d}$, with $d \in \mathbb{T}$, correspond to time elapsing for a duration d and must satisfy specific conditions expressing consistency of the system with respect to time operations:

- null delay: $s \xrightarrow{0} s'$ *if and only if* $s' = s$,
- addition rule: *if* $s \xrightarrow{d} s'$ *and* $s' \xrightarrow{d'} s''$, *then* $s \xrightarrow{d+d'} s''$,

The timed transition system $\mathcal{T}$ is *time deterministic* if $s \xrightarrow{d} s_1$ and $s \xrightarrow{d} s_2$ implies $s_1 = s_2$. The system is *continuous* if $s \xrightarrow{d} s'$ implies for all d' and d'' such that $d = d' + d''$, there exists s'' such that $s \xrightarrow{d'} s''$ and $s'' \xrightarrow{d''} s'$.

Transitions $\xrightarrow{a}$, with a in Σ, correspond to usual actions and are considered instantaneous. Some variants include a non-observable action represented by the empty word ε, so that actions are labeled by $\Sigma_\varepsilon = \Sigma \cup \{\varepsilon\}$ instead of Σ. In other variants like durational Kripke structures (see definition 4.5), there are only delay transitions with a set of labels reduced to $\mathbb{T}$.

A variant of this semantics is obtained by combining a delay transition with an action transition into a single step of the system by defining:

$$s \xRightarrow{(a,d)} s' \text{ if there exists } s'' \in S \text{ such that } s \xrightarrow{d} s'' \text{ and } s'' \xrightarrow{a} s'$$

which leads to a single type of transitions with labels as pairs $(a, d) \in \Sigma \times \mathbb{T}$. The associated transition system $\mathcal{T}_m = (\Sigma \times \mathbb{T}, S, \Rightarrow)$ is called the *mixed transition system* associated with $\mathcal{T}$ in [LAB 98]. These semantics are used in [ALU 90, ALU 94], where they are directly defined from the machine model.

In all the above cases, executions (or runs) of $\mathcal{T}$ or $\mathcal{T}_m$ are defined as paths in the graph starting from the initial configuration, sometimes with additional conditions leading to so-called *admissible* runs. Observe that with the property of null delay and the additivity rule, all runs in $\mathcal{T}$ can be obtained by a strict alternation of action transitions and delay transitions.

4.2.3. *Timed languages*

A *timed word* is a pair $w = (\sigma, \theta)$, where σ is a word $a_1 a_2 \ldots$ over the alphabet Σ and $\theta = \tau_1 \tau_2 \ldots$ is a sequence of dates in $\mathbb{T}$ with same length as σ. The timed word w can also be written $w = (a_1, \tau_1)(a_2, \tau_2)\ldots$ and its untimed part is obtained by projection on the alphabet of actions: $untime(w) = a_1 a_2 \ldots$. In this framework, a pair (a_i, τ_i) is called a *timed action*, since it can represent an observation of a system at time τ_i, where action a_i takes place in an instantaneous way.

From the sequence of labels $(a_i, d_i)_{i \geq 1}$ on the run of a mixed transition system $\mathcal{T}_m$, a timed word $w = (a_i, \tau_i)_{i \geq 1}$ is obtained by accumulating the delays: $\tau_i = \sum_{j \leq i} d_j$, for $i \geq 1$. Conversely, from a timed word, a sequence $(a_i, d_i) \in \Sigma \times \mathbb{T}$ can be recovered by setting $d_i = \tau_i - \tau_{i-1}$ (with the convention $\tau_0 = 0$). Thus, d_i can also be viewed as the maximal duration of action a_i.

When the labels belong to $\Sigma \cup \mathbb{T}$, a timed word is obtained by considering paths with an alternation of actions and durations. Moreover, if action labels belong to $\Sigma \cup \{\varepsilon\}$, unobservable actions (a_i, τ_i) (i.e. such that $a_i = \varepsilon$) must be removed. Note that in this case, absolute dates must be computed before erasing non-observable actions, in order to take the corresponding delays into account.

A *timed language* is a set of timed words. Untiming is extended to languages: for a timed language L, the projection on the alphabet of actions yields a standard language $untime(L) = \{\sigma \mid \exists \theta \, (\sigma, \theta) \in L\}$. Timed languages have not been greatly studied independently of timed transition systems. However, some studies have investigated the notion of timed regular expression [ASA 97, HEN 98b, BOU 99, BOU 02, ASA 02, BRI 10] and algebraic approaches have been proposed in [GRO 95, DIM 00, BOU 01].

4.2.4. *Some issues related to timed semantics*

A typical question raised by the timed model concerns urgency [BOR 98b]. A transition labeled by some action $a \in \Sigma$ is *urgent* in a configuration s of a transition system if it cannot be delayed. This means that no delay transition can be fired in this configuration, that is, a transition $s \xrightarrow{a}$ must occur in a null delay. This notion is very useful for practical modeling purposes, for instance if several action transitions must be executed in an instantaneous way. This is the case in some models where this feature is used to simulate a synchronization of several components when only binary synchronization is allowed. However, there can be ambiguous interpretations of urgency in some models, for instance when two urgent actions are enabled simultaneously in two components, and urgency can lead to deadlocks in the composition of modules [BOR 98a]. These two points are illustrated in the next section.

4.3. Classical timed models

This section shows how an explicit notion of time was added in classical (untimed) models, such as finite automata or Petri nets, to obtain timed behaviors. In all models presented hereafter, a labeling of states by a set of atomic propositions is usually added for verification purposes. This labeling is omitted here for the sake of simplicity, we consider that this role is played by the names of states.

The mechanism for introducing explicit time in existing models consists of adding a time domain and time constraints associated with the firing of transitions, in order to produce a timed transition system. Essentially two variants have been proposed: either adding variables evolving with time or adding time intervals, which can be seen as a particular case of the first variant.

4.3.1. *Adding a discrete clock*

This first approach has been largely used since [EME 92], with $\mathbb{N}$ as the time domain, based on the idea that system observations always take place along discrete time sequences, produced, for instance, by sampling. With a fine enough granularity, a global clock can be represented by a sequence of *ticks* and synchronized with the system. This technique amounts to unfolding the original model by representing all time units.

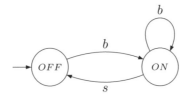

Figure 4.1. $\mathcal{A}_1$: *a time-switch*

EXAMPLE.– Consider a time-switch for light in a staircase. If the button is pressed, the light is switched on (action b). If the button is not pressed again, the light switches off after some time (action s). In this very simple case, the system is modeled by the finite automaton $\mathcal{A}_1$ in Figure 4.1 with two states ON and OFF (also called control modes). A timing requirement can be added, for instance: "If the button is not pressed again, the light switches off after three time units". Introducing the action $\mathbb{1}$, which represents a duration of one time unit, automaton $\mathcal{A}_1$ is synchronized with the (reduced) clock $\mathcal{H}$ from Figure 4.2, which corresponds to unfolding the previous automaton and yields the timed system $\mathcal{A}_2$ in Figure 4.3. Note that in this timed transition system, there are no explicit transitions of duration two or three time units, so they should be added for the addition rule to hold.

Figure 4.2. $\mathcal{H}$: *three consecutive ticks*

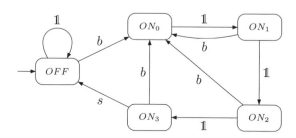

Figure 4.3. $\mathcal{A}_2$: *a time-switch with time-out of three time units*

A serious drawback of such models lies in the constants involved in the unfolding, which can produce a very large number of configurations. It then becomes difficult to use a symbolic representation for the constraints.

4.3.2. *Adding variables*

Another technique consists of explicitly adding variables to describe different features of a system [DIL 89, ALU 97]. These variables are functions over the time domain, which evolve with time in the control modes and can be updated when a discrete transition is fired. This mechanism yields the general class of hybrid automata, with real valued variables evolving according to differential equations. A detailed presentation can be found in [HEN 96] when the control modes belong to a finite set.

Timed automata Timed automata were introduced in [ALU 90, ALU 94] and form a basic subclass of hybrid automata, where most verification problems have been proved decidable. In this framework, the underlying structure is a finite automaton to which variables called *clocks* are added. In a given control mode, these variables evolve synchronously with time, at the same speed. When a discrete transition is fired, clock values can be compared to constants and some clocks can be reset.

EXAMPLE.– Consider again the specification of the time-switch with a three time units time-out. The time constraint can be modeled by adding a clock x, which is reset when b occurs and compared to 3 for switching off the light. This yields the timed automaton $\mathcal{A}_3$ in Figure 4.4, which is simply obtained from $\mathcal{A}_1$ (Figure 4.1) by decorating the transitions with operations on clocks.

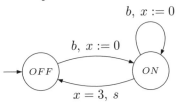

Figure 4.4. $\mathcal{A}_3$: *a time-switch with a time-out of three time units*

We now give a formal definition of timed automata. For a (finite) set X of clocks, $\mathcal{P}(X)$ denotes the power set of X and $\mathcal{C}(X)$ is the set of conjunctions of atomic constraints of the form $x \sim c$ where x is a clock, c is a constant (usually a natural number) and $\sim$ is in $\{<, \leq, =, \geq, >\}$. A constraint in $\mathcal{C}(X)$ is called a *guard*.

DEFINITION 4.2 *A* timed automaton *over alphabet* Σ *is a tuple* $\mathcal{A} = (\Sigma, X, Q, q_0, \Delta)$, *where*

- X *is a finite set of clocks,*
- Q *is a finite set of states (also called control modes or locations),*
- $q_0 \in Q$ *is the initial state and*
- $\Delta \subseteq Q \times \mathcal{C}(X) \times \Sigma \times \mathcal{P}(X) \times Q$ *is the set of transitions.*

A transition (q, g, a, r, q') in Δ, also written $q \xrightarrow{g,a,r} q'$, represents switching modes from q to q' with action a, when the guard g is satisfied. All clocks in $r \subseteq X$ are reset, which is often written $r := 0$, such as in Figure 4.4.

Timed automata semantics We now more precisely define the semantics of a timed automaton. Recall that the time domain is a (discrete or dense) subset of $\mathbb{R}_+$. The guards are interpreted over *clock valuations*, which are mappings from X to $\mathbb{R}_+$: valuation v satisfies a guard $g \in \mathcal{C}(X)$ if, replacing each clock by its value yields *true* for the constraint g. For instance, if $X = \{x, y\}$ and if g is the constraint $x < 5 \wedge y \geq 3$, the valuation v defined by $v(x) = 1.2$ and $v(y) = 3$ satisfies g. Operations on clock valuations are defined as follows:

- time elapsing of duration d from valuation v results in the valuation $v + d$ defined by: $(v + d)(x) = v(x) + d$ for each clock x. This describes synchronous evolution of duration d for all clock values,

- reset of the clocks in $r \subseteq X$ from valuation v results in the valuation $v[r \mapsto 0]$ defined by: $v[r \mapsto 0](x) = 0$ if $x \in r$ and $v(x)$ otherwise.

DEFINITION 4.3 *The semantics of* $\mathcal{A} = (\Sigma, X, Q, q_0, \Delta)$ *is the timed transition system* $\mathcal{T} = (\Sigma \cup \mathbb{T}, S, s_0, E)$, *where*

– *the set of configurations is* $S = Q \times \mathbb{R}_+^X$. *Hence, a configuration is a pair* (q, v) *where* $q \in Q$ *and* v *is a valuation;*

– *the initial configuration is* $(q_0, \mathbf{0})$, *where* $\mathbf{0}$ *is the valuation for which all clocks are assigned the value 0;*

– *the transitions in* E *are of two types:*

- *delay transition with duration d, defined by* $(q, v) \xrightarrow{d} (q, v + d)$,
- *action transition with label a, defined by* $(q, v) \xrightarrow{a} (q', v')$ *if there is a transition* $q \xrightarrow{g,a,r} q'$ *in* Δ *such that* v *satisfies the guard* g *and* $v' = v[r \mapsto 0]$.

EXAMPLE.– For automaton $\mathcal{A}_3$ in Figure 4.4, the beginning of a run can be:
$$(OFF, 0) \xrightarrow{1.5} (OFF, 1.5) \xrightarrow{b} (ON, 0) \xrightarrow{3} (ON, 3) \xrightarrow{s} (OFF, 3) \cdots$$

Such a transition system contains an infinite number of states, uncountable if the time domain is $\mathbb{R}_+$. Adding acceptance conditions to a timed automaton $\mathcal{A}$, for instance final states for finite runs or Büchi conditions for infinite runs [ALU 94], allows the language of timed words associated with $\mathcal{A}$, denoted by $\mathcal{L}(\mathcal{A})$, to be defined. This leads to the definition of the family of *recognizable* timed languages, which contains those timed languages accepted by a timed automaton.

The transition system $\mathcal{T}$ associated with $\mathcal{A}_3$ is represented in a compact way in Figure 4.5. For instance, all configurations of the form (OFF, d), $d \geq 0$ have been grouped together and all time transitions are dotted lines. These systems can be compared to the automaton $\mathcal{A}_2$ from Figure 4.3 obtained with a global discrete clock. The analysis of timed automata relies on an abstraction similar to these representations, which amounts to finding an equivalence relation and considering sets of states of the form (q, v) for a given state q together. Valuations are equivalent if they produce "similar" behaviors in the automaton. Using this technique, the emptiness test was proved decidable for the class of timed languages accepted by timed automata (or equivalently the reachability problem for timed automata) [ALU 90, ALU 94].

Urgency and liveness Note that the previous system has an incorrect behavior, where it stays longer than three time units in state ON and can later reset the time switch. This problem led to the addition of liveness conditions to the definition of timed automata. Various solutions have been proposed, among them Büchi conditions, as undertaken in the original model from [ALU 90], but also the addition of *invariants*, which are clock constraints associated with control modes [NIC 92], or *deadlines*, which are also clock constraints viewed as limiting conditions for the firing of transitions [SIF 96].

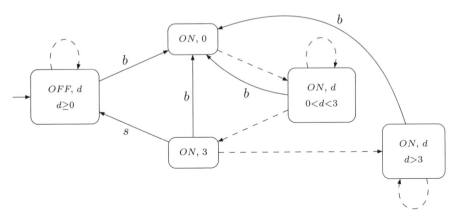

Figure 4.5. *A compact representation of* $\mathcal{T}$

For instance, the specification will be satisfied if automaton $\mathcal{A}_3$ is modified as follows: the constraint $x \leq 3$ is associated with state ON, with an additional restriction in the semantics: a configuration (ON, d) belongs to S if and only if $d \leq 3$. The relations between the different liveness conditions are investigated in detail in [BOR 97, LAB 98] and other mechanisms ensuring urgency of transitions have been implemented in analysis tools for timed models such as KRONOS [DAW 96] or UPPAAL [LAR 97a, BEH 10].

Hybrid automata   First consider the (simplified) example of a thermostat from [JAF 91] in Figure 4.6. This hybrid automaton describes the behavior of a thermostat, which starts or stops a heating device according to the temperature information from a sensor in a room (in winter). There are two control modes: ON and OFF, with a variable H representing the temperature in the room. In each mode, the temperature change is described by a (linear) differential equation. Assume that the system is initially in the mode ON with a temperature of $0°C$, the constant K is associated with a decrease in temperature and H_a depends on the heating device. In this mode, the device is heating the room and the temperature increases according to the equation, until it reaches a maximal value H_{max}. The system then switches to mode OFF, where the device is switched off and the temperature decreases. When it reaches H_{min}, the device is again switched on.

We now give a formal definition of linear hybrid automata. For a set X of real valued variables, a *linear expression* over X is an expression of the form $k_0 + k_1x_1 + \cdots + k_mx_m$, where the x_is are variables in X and the k_is are constants in (a subset of) $\mathbb{Q}$. If ℓ_1 and ℓ_2 are linear expressions, $\ell_1 \leq \ell_2$ is a *linear inequality*. A *linear constraint* is a conjunction of linear inequalities. The set of linear constraints over X is denoted by $\mathcal{C}_{lin}(X)$. Similar to timed automata, a valuation is a mapping $v : X \rightarrow \mathbb{R}$,

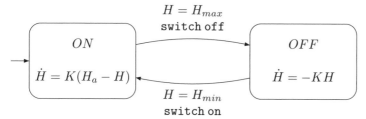

Figure 4.6. *Hybrid automaton for the modeling of a thermostat*

which can also be viewed as a tuple of real values $\mathbf{x} \in \mathbb{R}^n$ where $n = |X|$ is the number of variables in X. A valuation $\mathbf{x}$ satisfies a constraint $\varphi \in \mathcal{C}_{lin}(X)$, denoted by $\mathbf{x} \models \varphi$, if the closed predicate $\varphi[X := \mathbf{x}]$ is evaluated to $true$.

To describe a linear hybrid automaton, the following notations are used: $X' = \{x' \mid x \in X\}$ is a copy of X for the values of variables updated by a discrete transition, and $\dot{X} = \{\dot{x} \mid x \in X\}$ is another copy of X representing the slopes of the variables of X. These slopes describe the evolution of the variables in the control modes. With these notations, a reset of variable x is written $x' = 0$.

DEFINITION 4.4 *A linear hybrid automaton over alphabet Σ is a tuple $\mathcal{A} = (\Sigma, X, Q, q_0, V_0, \Delta, Inv, \Pi)$, where*

    – *X is a finite set of variables;*

    – *Q is a finite set of states (or control modes), with $q_0 \in Q$ the initial state;*

    – *V_0 is a set of intial valuations;*

    – *$\Delta \subseteq Q \times \mathcal{C}_{lin}(X \cup X') \times \Sigma \times Q$ is the set of transitions;*

    – *Inv : $Q \to \mathcal{C}_{lin}(X)$ associates an invariant with each state, which is a constraint that variable values must satisfy in the state;*

    – *$\Pi : Q \to \mathcal{C}_{lin}(\dot{X})$ associates a constraint over the variable slopes with each state.*

We do not formally define the semantics, which is similar to that of timed automata, and is obtained by adapting the variable evolutions and updates. An element in $\mathcal{C}_{lin}(X \cup X')$ is called a *jump* and describes a firing condition for a transition, combined with an update. A transition in Δ, denoted by $q \xrightarrow{j,a} q'$ describes a switch from q to q' with action a and jump j. For instance, a transition labeled by $x \leq 2 \wedge y = 3 \wedge x' = 0 \wedge y' > 2x + 1$ can be fired only if the current valuation satisfies $v(x) \leq 2$ and $v(y) = 3$, the variable x is then reset, and a new value for y chosen non-deterministically in the open interval $]2v(x) + 1, +\infty[$.

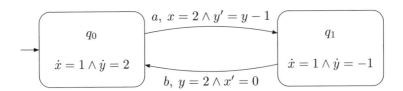

Figure 4.7. *An example of linear hybrid automaton*

Similarly, if $\Pi(q)$ is the constraint $2 \leq \dot{x} \leq 5 \wedge \dot{y} = 0$ for some state $q \in Q$, then in this state, the slope of x is chosen between two and five while y stays unchanged.

EXAMPLE.– Consider for instance the automaton in Figure 4.7. In this basic case, the sequence of transitions starting from q_0 with both variables x and y having value 0 is:

$$\left(q_0, \begin{bmatrix} 0 \\ 0 \end{bmatrix} \right) \xrightarrow{2} \left(q_0, \begin{bmatrix} 2 \\ 4 \end{bmatrix} \right) \xrightarrow{a} \left(q_1, \begin{bmatrix} 2 \\ 3 \end{bmatrix} \right) \xrightarrow{1} \left(q_1, \begin{bmatrix} 3 \\ 2 \end{bmatrix} \right) \xrightarrow{b} \left(q_0, \begin{bmatrix} 0 \\ 2 \end{bmatrix} \right)$$

$$\xrightarrow{2} \left(q_0, \begin{bmatrix} 2 \\ 6 \end{bmatrix} \right) \xrightarrow{a} \left(q_1, \begin{bmatrix} 2 \\ 5 \end{bmatrix} \right) \xrightarrow{3} \left(q_1, \begin{bmatrix} 5 \\ 2 \end{bmatrix} \right) \xrightarrow{b} \left(q_0, \begin{bmatrix} 0 \\ 2 \end{bmatrix} \right) \cdots$$

and from there, the system stays in a loop, producing the trajectory depicted in Figure 4.8.

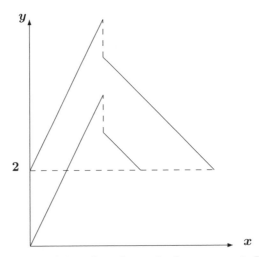

Figure 4.8. *Geometrical view of a trajectory for the automaton in Figure 4.7*

Note that for hybrid automata where the constraints on the derivatives are of the form $\alpha \leq \dot{x} \leq \beta$, the timed transition system is not time deterministic, in the sense defined in section 4.2.2.

Most verification problems are undecidable on such models, as soon as two variables with different slopes are used (see for instance [ALU 95, ASA 95, HEN 98a, LAF 01, ASA 07, BRI 10, LEG 10] for analysis results). However, several tools such as HYTECH [HEN 95], HCMC [CAS 00], TReX [ANN 01], or more recently, PHAVer [FRE 05] and SpaceEx [FRE 09] have been developed, often implementing semi-algorithms or approximations.

Composition Like in the untimed case, the composition of several models is obtained from the cartesian product of the states, with a synchronization function on the transition labels. When several transitions can synchronize, the corresponding components progress simultaneously. When some action is internal to a component, this component evolves separately. For timed or hybrid systems, the additional delay transitions correspond to time elapsing, which is the same for all components and hence plays a synchronization role. The main problem occurring in this case is the following, explained in [SIF 96]. Suppose that an untimed model $\mathcal{M}$ is obtained by composition of two models $\mathcal{M}_1$ and $\mathcal{M}_2$. If these models are then extended in $\mathcal{M}^t$, $\mathcal{M}_1^t$ and $\mathcal{M}_2^t$ by adding timing constraints, the timed composition must guarantee that the product of $\mathcal{M}_1^t$ and $\mathcal{M}_2^t$ corresponds exactly to $\mathcal{M}^t$.

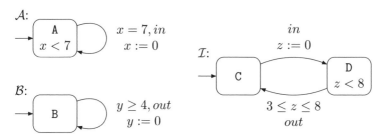

Figure 4.9. *Three processes communicating through in and out*

The example proposed in [SIF 96] illustrates this problem with the specification of three processes, described by timed automata with invariants (Figure 4.9): the first one ($\mathcal{A}$) produces in messages every seven time units, the second ($\mathcal{B}$) produces out messages separated by at least four time units and the third ($\mathcal{I}$) implements the communication by transmitting to $\mathcal{B}$ the messages received from $\mathcal{A}$ within a delay between three and eight time units. Figure 4.10 shows how the product $\mathcal{A} \mid \mathcal{B} \mid \mathcal{I}$ is performed with a synchronization on actions in and out. Now if the transmission interval $[3, 8]$ is replaced by $]7, 8]$, a *timed* deadlock is reached in configuration ABD, with clock values

$x = 7$ and $z = 7$, since action *out* cannot take place and time progress is restricted by invariant $x < 7$.

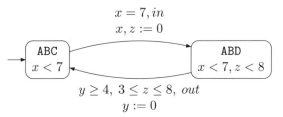

$$x = 7, in$$
$$x, z := 0$$

$$y \geq 4, \ 3 \leq z \leq 8, \ out$$
$$y := 0$$

Figure 4.10. *Synchronized product* $\mathcal{A} \mid \mathcal{B} \mid \mathcal{I}$

Thus, problems mainly result from the combination of action synchronization and time synchronization. Several solutions have been proposed to answer this question, for instance using priorities on actions [BOR 98a, BOR 00].

4.3.3. *Adding time intervals*

In this section, we show how a timed transition system can be obtained by equipping transitions with time intervals. When an interval (min_e, max_e) from the time domain is associated with a transition $e : q \xrightarrow{a} q'$, the limits of the interval represent respectively the minimal and maximal delay for firing the transition. In this case, an implicit clock can be associated with the transition and the transition can be fired only if the clock value belongs to the interval. This mechanism, first used for time Petri nets in [MER 74] was also applied to timed systems in [MAL 91, HEN 92, HEN 94a], and durational Kripke structures in [CAM 95, LAR 02]. The model of Petri nets is well suited to the modeling of concurrent processes and numerous timed extensions have been proposed for this model, which also associates timing parameters with arcs, places, etc. We present here DKS as well as two versions of Petri nets with dense time: time Petri nets and timed Petri nets [VAL 99, ABD 01], where intervals are used on arcs.

DKS   Note that until now, the timed models defined over the time domain $\mathbb{R}_+$ have a *continuous* semantics, in the sense defined in section 4.2.2: an infinite (non-countable) number of configurations appear between two configurations s and s' separated by a delay d, namely all intermediate configurations s_δ, with $s \xrightarrow{\delta} s_\delta$, for $0 \leq \delta \leq d$. DKS, as studied in [CAM 95, LAR 02] for instance, are a discrete time model with a so-called *jump semantics*, where these intermediate configurations do not exist.

We write $\mathcal{I}(\mathbb{N})$ for the set of intervals in $\mathbb{N}$ with lower bound in $\mathbb{N}$ and upper bound in $\mathbb{N} \cup \{\infty\}$.

DEFINITION 4.5 *A* DKS *is a triple* $\mathcal{K} = (Q, q_0, \Delta)$ *where* Q *is a finite set of states,* $q_0 \in Q$ *is the initial state and* $\Delta \subseteq Q \times \mathcal{I}(\mathbb{N}) \times Q$ *is the set of transitions.*

EXAMPLE.– Figure 4.11, borrowed from [LAR 02], describes (a simplified view of) the activity of a researcher. The transitions are equipped with an interval, possibly reduced to a single value. Intuitively, a value is chosen in this interval in order to switch to the next state.

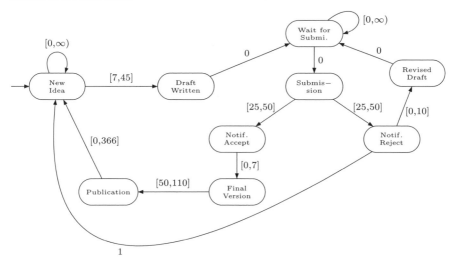

Figure 4.11. *Durational Kripke structure for a researcher's activity*

Observe that no action labels are used in these structures.

Jump semantics   Several semantics can be defined for this model, according to the interpretation given to the firing of a transition from q to q' with delay $d \in \mathbb{N}$. Similar to timed automata, it can be assumed that the system waits in state q for a duration of d time units and then switches in an instantaneous way to state q'.

The jump semantics rather consider that the system is in state q at time n and will be in state q' at time $n + d$, with no intermediate states for times $n + 1$, ..., $n + d - 1$. This is similar to viewing the durations as costs. The associated timed transition system is $\mathcal{T} = (\mathbb{N}, Q, q_0, E)$, with only one type of transitions in E, defined by: $q \xrightarrow{d} q'$ if there exists a transition (q, I, q') in Δ such that d belongs to interval I. This semantics can then be considered as a mixed transition system, where only one (unobservable) action is associated with the durations.

EXAMPLE.– For the system in Figure 4.11, the beginning of a run could be:
New Idea $\xrightarrow{15}$ New Idea $\xrightarrow{10}$ Draft Written $\xrightarrow{0}$ Wait for Submi. $\cdots$

Finally observe that this semantics is not robust with respect to the composition. In contrast, verification problems can be solved with a lower complexity than in timed automata (see for instance [LAR 02]).

Time Petri nets   In an analogous way, time Petri nets extend standard Petri nets by associating intervals with transitions. We denote here by $\mathcal{I}$ the set of closed intervals with a lower bound in $\mathbb{Q}_+$ and an upper bound in $\mathbb{Q}_+ \cup \{\infty\}$. For such an interval I, we define the backward closure by: $I^{\downarrow} = \{x \mid \exists y \in I, \; x \leq y\}$.

Similar to classical Petri nets, a marking is a mapping from the set P of places into $\mathbb{N}$.

DEFINITION 4.6 *A* time Petri net *over alphabet* Σ *is a tuple* $\mathcal{N} = (P, T, \Sigma_\varepsilon, Pre, Post, M_0, \lambda, I)$ *where:*

– *P is a finite set of* places;

– *T is a finite set of* transitions *with* $P \cap T = \emptyset$;

– *Pre and Post are mappings from* $T \times P$ *into* $\mathbb{N}$ *called, respectively, the* precondition *and* postcondition;

– $M_0 \in \mathbb{N}^P$ *is the* initial marking;

– $\lambda : T \to \Sigma_\varepsilon$ *is the* labeling function *of transitions;*

– $I : T \to \mathcal{I}$ *associates with each transition a* firing interval.

EXAMPLE.– Figure 4.12 illustrates the graphical representation of a time Petri net. Each transition is equipped with its label and its firing interval. For instance, transition t_1 has label a and interval $I(t_1) = [1, \infty[$. The initial marking has two tokens in place p_1 and one token in place p_2.

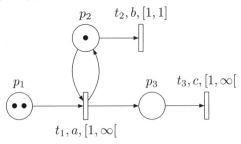

Figure 4.12. *A time Petri net*

Semantics of time Petri nets   For a marking M in $P^{\mathbb{N}}$, $M(p)$ represents the number of tokens in place p. For a transition t, we denote by $^\bullet t$ (respectively $t^\bullet$) the mapping from P to $\mathbb{N}$ such that $^\bullet t(p) = Pre(t, p)$ (respectively $t^\bullet(p) = Post(t, p)$). A transition t is enabled in marking M if $M \geq \,^\bullet t$ and we write $En(M)$ the set of enabled transitions. As in standard Petri nets, firing t leads to a new marking $M' = M - \,^\bullet t + t^\bullet$.

We now explain the timing conditions, with $\mathbb{R}_+$ as dense time domain. A transition can be fired if the time elapsed since the last update belongs to interval $I(t)$. Moreover, for all enabled transitions, time cannot progress when one of the upper bounds is reached, thus enforcing urgency.

A configuration of $\mathcal{N}$ is a pair (M, ν), for a marking M and a valuation $\nu \in (\mathbb{R}_+)^T$. Relevant values of ν are those for which t belongs to $En(M)$, and $\nu(t)$ contains the time elapsed since the last update in this case. We write $\nu(t) = \bot$ otherwise. A configuration is *admissible* if for all enabled transitions, $\nu(t) \in I(t)^{\downarrow}$. We denote by $ADM(\mathcal{N})$ the set of admissible configurations.

The important point that remains to be defined is the update of timing information upon transition firing. In other words, we should specify when the implicit clock associated with the transition is reset: transition t' is said to be *newly enabled* after firing t from marking M if the predicate $\uparrow enabled(t', M, t)$ defined by:

$$\uparrow enabled(t', M, t) = (t' \in En(M - {}^{\bullet}t + t^{\bullet})) \wedge (t' \notin En(M))$$

evaluates to *true*.

Thus, t' is newly enabled if it was not enabled before firing t but becomes enabled by this firing. This corresponds to the so-called *persistent atomic* semantics, which is not the most frequently used but is easier to explain and equivalent to the others for safe time Petri nets (see [BÉR 05a, REY 09] for discussions).

DEFINITION 4.7 *The semantics of a TPN $\mathcal{N}$ is the timed transition system $\mathcal{T} = (L, S, s_0, E)$ where:*

- $L = \Sigma_\epsilon \cup \mathbb{R}_+$;
- $S = ADM(\mathcal{N})$;
- $s_0 = (M_0, \mathbf{0})$, where $\mathbf{0}$ denotes the valuation with null values for all transitions enabled in M_0 and $\bot$ otherwise;
- $E \subseteq S \times (\Sigma_\epsilon \cup \mathbb{R}_+) \times S$ contains the two following types of transitions, from an admissible configuration (M, ν):

- for each transition t enabled in M such that $\nu(t) \in I(t)$, a discrete transition $(M, \nu) \xrightarrow{\lambda(t)} (M - {}^{\bullet}t + t^{\bullet}, \nu')$ with for all $t' \in En(M - {}^{\bullet}t + t^{\bullet})$,

$$\nu'(t') = \begin{cases} 0 & \text{if } \uparrow enabled(t', M, t), \\ \nu(t') & \text{otherwise}, \end{cases}$$

- for each $d \in \mathbb{R}_+$, such that for each t in $En(M)$, $\nu(t) + d \in I(t)^{\downarrow}$, a delay transition $(M, \nu) \xrightarrow{d} (M, \nu + d)$.

EXAMPLE.– A possible run of the TPN in Figure 4.12 is the following:

$$(M_0, [0, 0, \bot]) \xrightarrow{1} (M_0, [1, 1, \bot]) \xrightarrow{a} (M_1, [1, 1, 0]) \xrightarrow{a} (M_2, [\bot, 1, 0])$$

$$\xrightarrow{b} (M_3, [\bot, \bot, 0]) \xrightarrow{1.5} (M_3, [\bot, \bot, 1.5]) \xrightarrow{c} (M_4, [\bot, \bot, 1.5]) \cdots$$

with markings $M_0 = (2, 1, 0)$, $M_1 = (1, 1, 1)$, $M_2 = (0, 1, 2)$, $M_3 = (0, 0, 2)$ and $M_4 = (0, 0, 1)$.

This model has been extensively studied (see for instance [JON 77, BER 91]), and tools such as ROMÉO [GAR 05] and TINA [BER 06] have been developed for the analysis of (bounded) time Petri nets.

Timed Petri nets   We finally present a (simple) variant of timed Petri nets, where the timing information is related to the tokens by giving them an *age*. In this model, intervals are associated with arcs: when a transition is fired, the tokens removed from the input places of the transition and the tokens added to the output places should have ages lying in the intervals of the corresponding arcs. Thus, input arcs correspond to guards over the token ages while output arcs perform non-deterministic updates on these ages, resulting in the association of an implicit clock with each token. The definition is restricted here to the case where at most one token travels along an arc. Note that the token may become too old to be used in a transition, in which case it is said to be *dead*. This means that, unlike for the previous model, urgency constraints are relaxed here.

We again denote by $\mathcal{I}$ the set of closed intervals with a lower bound in $\mathbb{Q}_+$ and an upper bound in $\mathbb{Q}_+ \cup \{\infty\}$.

EXAMPLE.– Figure 4.13 depicts a timed Petri net modeling a producer/consumer problem, borrowed from [VAL 99], with a buffer of size three. In this particular case, all missing intervals on the output arcs are $[0, 0]$, which means that the token's age is reset by each transition. Moreover, the labeling of transitions has been omitted, so that it can be considered that Σ is the set T of transitions.

The notion of marking in a TdPN is slightly modified to integrate the ages of tokens. Let $Bag(Z)$ denote the set of finite multisets (also called bags) on a set Z, i.e. the set of mappings with finite domain from Z into $\mathbb{N}$, the image of an element being its multiplicity. Operations of union, set difference, and inclusion apply to multisets by taking multiplicities into account.
A marking M is an element of $Bag(P \times \mathbb{R}_+)$. For instance, the initial marking M_0 in the TdPN of Figure 4.13 contains one token in place p_1, one in place p_3 and three in place p_5, all with age 0. Using the standard notations for multisets, it can be written $M_0 = (p_1, 0) + (p_3, 0) + 3.(p_5, 0)$.

DEFINITION 4.8 *A timed Petri net (TdPN) over alphabet Σ is a tuple $\mathcal{N} = (P, T, \Sigma_\varepsilon, Pre, Post, M_0, \lambda)$ where:*

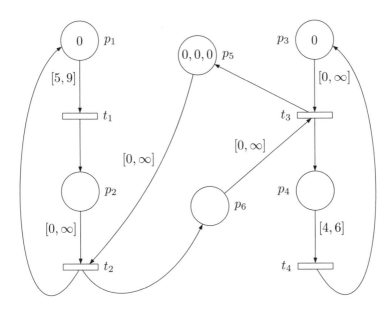

Figure 4.13. *A timed Petri net for the producer/consumer problem*

    – *P is a finite set of* places;

    – *T is a finite set of* transitions *with* $P \cap T = \emptyset$;

    – *Pre and Post are mappings from* $T \times P$ *into* $\mathcal{I}$ *again called, respectively, the* precondition *and* postcondition;

    – M_0 *is the* initial marking, *with all tokens aged* 0;

    – $\lambda : T \to \Sigma_\varepsilon$ *is the* labeling function *of transitions*;

Note that the case where place p is not an input place (respectively an output place) for transition t now corresponds to the empty interval for $Pre(t, p)$ (respectively $Post(t, p)$). We denote here by $^\bullet t$ (respectively $t^\bullet$) the subset of P of intput places (respectively output places) of t.

Semantics of timed Petri nets   As in previous models, time elapsing of d time units (where d is a nonnegative real number) results in increasing all clock values by d. For instance, from initial marking M_0 time elapsing of 2.1 produces the marking $M_1 = (p_1, 2.1) + (p_3, 2.1) + 3.(p_5, 2.1)$. More generally, for a marking M and a duration $d \in \mathbb{R}_+$, we denote by $M + d$ the marking obtained by increasing the age of each token by d. Firing a discrete transition t from a marking M is possible if a token with an age in the specified interval $Pre(t, p)$ exists in each input place of t. The new marking M' is obtained by extracting these tokens from M and adding a new token with an age chosen in the interval $Post(t, p)$, for each output place of t.

More formally:

DEFINITION 4.9 *The semantics of a TdPN $\mathcal{N}$ is the timed transition system $\mathcal{T} = (L, S, s_0, E)$ where:*

- *$L = \Sigma_\varepsilon \cup \mathbb{R}_+$;*
- *$S = Bag(P \times \mathbb{R}_+)$: a configuration is a marking;*
- *$s_0 = M_0$ is the initial marking where all tokens are aged 0;*
- *$E \subseteq S \times (\Sigma_\varepsilon \cup \mathbb{R}_+) \times S$ contains the two following types of transitions, from configuration M:*

   - for each $d \in \mathbb{R}_+$, there is a delay transition $M \xrightarrow{d} M + d$,

   - given a transition $t \in T$, there is a discrete transition $M \xrightarrow{\lambda(t)} M'$ if and only if for $\bullet t = \{p_1, \ldots, p_h\}$ and $t^\bullet = \{p'_1, \ldots, p'_k\}$, there exist two bags $B_{pre} = \{(p_1, \tau_1), \ldots, (p_h, \tau_h)\}$ and $B_{post} = \{(p'_1, \tau'_1), \ldots, (p'_k, \tau'_k)\}$ such that:

$$\left\{ \begin{array}{l} B_{pre} \subseteq M \text{ and } \tau_i \in Pre(t, p_i) \text{ for each } i, \\ \text{for each } j, \text{ token } (p'_j, \tau'_j) \text{ is such that } \tau'_j \in Post(t, p'_j), \\ M' = M - B_{pre} + B_{post}. \end{array} \right.$$

Note that due to the restrictive framework, the bags B_{pre} and B_{post} are in fact plain sets here.

EXAMPLE.– An execution for the TdPN in Figure 4.13 can be as follows:

$$
\begin{array}{ll}
(p_1, 0) + (p_3, 0) + 3.(p_5, 0) & \xrightarrow{5.7} (p_1, 5.7) + (p_3, 5.7) + 3.(p_5, 5.7) \\
& \xrightarrow{t_1} (p_2, 0) + (p_3, 5.7) + 3.(p_5, 5.7) \\
& \xrightarrow{t_2} (p_1, 0) + (p_3, 5.7) + 2.(p_5, 5.7) + (p_6, 0) \\
& \xrightarrow{t_3} (p_1, 0) + (p_4, 0) + 2.(p_5, 5.7) + (p_5, 0) \\
& \xrightarrow{4.9} (p_1, 4.9) + (p_4, 4.9) + 2.(p_5, 10.6) + (p_5, 4.9) \\
& \xrightarrow{t_4} (p_1, 4.9) + (p_3, 0) + 2.(p_5, 10.6) + (p_5, 4.9) \ldots
\end{array}
$$

The absence of urgency constraints led to verification methods for unbounded nets. Extensions of this model and analysis results can be found for instance in [SRB 05, BOU 08, ABD 07] and in [FRU 00] for discrete time semantics.

4.3.4. *Timed process algebras*

The mechanisms of parallel composition offered in process algebra can be a partial answer to some of the problems mentioned above. The first timed process algebra was timed CSP, proposed in [REE 86] as a real-time extension of CSP. It was quickly followed by a large amount of work (a retrospective can be found in [OUA 06]).

EXAMPLE.– We first present an example from [OUA 03] (a modification of the classical coffee machine), which defines a "chocolate-biscuit machine" by the following equation:

$$M \stackrel{def}{=} in.[(choc.M + bisc.M) \stackrel{60}{\triangleright} (out!.M)]$$

The machine accepts a coin (action in), then the client selects a chocolate or a biscuit. However, if he waits more than 60 seconds before choosing, he receives his money back (action $out!$) and the machine returns in its initial state. The timed automaton in Figure 4.14 can be associated with this process.

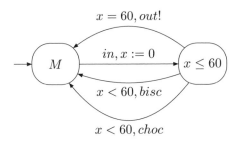

Figure 4.14. *A timed automaton for the vending machine*

This definition integrates a *time-out* operator, where process $P \stackrel{d}{\triangleright} Q$ behaves like P within d time units, and like Q after this delay. Moreover, *urgent* actions are added, like $out!$, which must be executed immediately.

We give here a simple definition, mainly based on binary synchronization, but many more elaborated variants appear in the literature. The set Σ contains a set of actions and their complementary actions denoted, respectively, by a and $\bar{a}$ and we consider again the augmented set Σ_ε. The set $\mathcal{E}$ of *expressions* (or terms) of a process algebra over Σ_ε contains constants, variables, and is defined by the grammar:

$$E ::= \mathbf{0} \mid a \cdot E \mid (d) \cdot E \mid E_1 + E_2 \mid E_1 \parallel E_2$$

where a is an action in Σ_ε, the delay d belongs to the (discrete or dense) time domain $\mathbb{T}$, and $\mathbf{0}$ is the null process, which executes nothing but may let time elapse. The basic delay mechanism is represented by $(d)E$, which lets d time units elapse and then behaves like E. A *process* is an expression without free variable and a constant (other than $\mathbf{0}$) is a process defined by an equation using operator *def* (as in the example above).

Of course, this *def* operator can be replaced by explicit recursion. Sometimes, a constant process, which cannot execute any action and can also not let time elapse, is introduced, as well as classical operators of restriction, renaming, or timed operators.

The timed transition system associated with a definition such as the one above is $\mathcal{T} = (\Sigma_\varepsilon \cup \mathbb{T}, \mathcal{E}, \Delta)$, where configurations are expressions in $\mathcal{E}$, and transitions in Δ are given by the following rules, with $\ell \in \Sigma_\varepsilon \cup \mathbb{T}$, $a \in \Sigma_\varepsilon$ and $d \in \mathbb{T}$:

– definition and action prefixing:

$$\text{Def}: \frac{E \xrightarrow{\ell} F}{P \xrightarrow{\ell} F} \text{ if } P \overset{def}{=} E$$

$$\text{D0}: \frac{}{\mathbf{0} \xrightarrow{d} \mathbf{0}} \qquad \text{Act1}: \frac{}{a \cdot P \xrightarrow{a} P}$$

– choice is usually a commutative and associative operation, the third rule is a time synchronization between processes:

$$\text{Ch1}: \frac{P \xrightarrow{a} P'}{P + Q \xrightarrow{a} P'} \qquad \text{Ch2}: \frac{Q \xrightarrow{a} Q'}{P + Q \xrightarrow{a} Q'}$$

$$\text{Ch3}: \frac{P \xrightarrow{d} P' \quad Q \xrightarrow{d} Q'}{P + Q \xrightarrow{d} P' + Q'}$$

– parallel composition:

$$\text{Comp1}: \frac{P \xrightarrow{a} P'}{P \parallel Q \xrightarrow{a} P' \parallel Q} \qquad \text{Comp2}: \frac{Q \xrightarrow{a} Q'}{P \parallel Q \xrightarrow{a} P \parallel Q'}$$

with action (for $a \neq \varepsilon$) and time synchronization:

$$\text{Comp3}: \frac{P \xrightarrow{a} P' \quad Q \xrightarrow{\bar{a}} Q'}{P \parallel Q \xrightarrow{\varepsilon} P' \parallel Q'} \qquad \text{Comp4}: \frac{P \xrightarrow{d} P' \quad Q \xrightarrow{d} Q'}{P \parallel Q \xrightarrow{d} P' \parallel Q'}$$

– delays:

$$\text{D1}: \frac{}{a \cdot P \xrightarrow{d} a \cdot P} \qquad \text{D2}: \frac{P \xrightarrow{a} P'}{(0) \cdot P \xrightarrow{a} P'}$$

$$\text{Ddec}: \frac{}{(d + d') \cdot P \xrightarrow{d} (d') \cdot P} \qquad \text{Dac}: \frac{P \xrightarrow{d} P'}{(d') \cdot P \xrightarrow{d + d'} P'}$$

Similar rules can be defined to distinguish lazy actions and urgent actions, and for the *time-out* operator. Following this line, several classical process algebras have been extended to the timed framework. A detailed presentation can be found in [NIC 91a, BAE 01], comparisons and various propositions are given in [YI 91, COR 99, COR 03, OUA 03].

Remarks This short presentation of timed models only describes a small part of the work done in the last 20 years with the aim of producing models for real-time systems and verifying them. Several of these models have been studied both in dense and discrete time. A question that arises then concerns the relation between all these models, both for their expressive power and their ability to support analysis. Some comparisons have been investigated, based either on language equivalence (do models $\mathcal{M}_1$ and $\mathcal{M}_2$ accept the same timed language?) or on various behavioral equivalences, such as strong or weak timed bisimulation (see next section). We only give a few references here for the interested reader. Comparisons can be found in [BOY 08] about the different timing mechanisms for Petri nets, while time Petri nets or timed Petri nets are compared to timed automata, for instance in [BÉR 05b, BOU 08, BÉR 08a]. The ability of Petri nets to model concurrency led to comparisons with networks of automata. This was done for timed Petri nets and networks of timed automata in [SRB 05] for instance. Relations between hybrid systems and process algebra are described in [NIC 91b, NIC 93, BOR 98a].

4.4. Specification of timing requirements

In this section, we specifically address the problem of formalizing properties involving explicit time constraints. The initial section is devoted to timed extensions of classical temporal logics, with the example of timed CTL (TCTL), then, considering the representation of properties by models, we present the behavioural equivalences, which form the basis of some verification techniques.

4.4.1. *Timed Logics*

The temporal logic CTL We briefly recall the syntax of the branching time temporal logic CTL introduced by Pnueli [PNU 77]. Formulas are defined by the following grammar:

$$\varphi, \psi ::= P_1 \mid P_2 \mid \ldots \mid \neg\varphi \mid \mathsf{EX}\varphi \mid \mathsf{AX}\varphi \mid \varphi \wedge \psi \mid \mathsf{E}\varphi\mathsf{U}\psi \mid \mathsf{A}\varphi\mathsf{U}\psi$$

where P_i are atomic propositions in a set AP.

These formula are interpreted over usual Kripke structures, hence without the intervals presented in definition 4.5, but with the addition of a labeling function, which associates a subset of atomic propositions in AP with each state. Let $\mathcal{K} = (Q, q_0, \Delta, \ell)$ be such a Kripke structure, where Δ is simply a subset of $Q \times Q$ and ℓ is the labeling function from Q into $\mathcal{P}(\text{AP})$. A formula is interpreted on a state $q \in Q$, and we denote by $Exec(q)$ the set of runs in $\mathcal{K}$ starting from q. Let $\sigma : q \to q_1 \to q_2 \cdots$ be a run in $\mathcal{K}$ and for $i \geq 0$, write $\sigma(i)$ for the state of index i in σ (*i.e.* q_i). The semantics is defined inductively by:

$q \models P$	if P belongs to the set $\ell(q)$ of labels of state q;
$q \models \neg\varphi$	if q does not satisfy φ;
$q \models \varphi \wedge \psi$	if q satisfies both φ and ψ;
$q \models \mathsf{EX}\varphi$	if there exists a run σ in $Exec(q)$ such that $\sigma(1) \models \varphi$;
$q \models \mathsf{AX}\varphi$	if each run σ in $Exec(q)$ is such that $\sigma(1) \models \varphi$;
$q \models \mathsf{E}\varphi\mathsf{U}\psi$	if there exists a run σ in $Exec(q)$ and an integer $j \geq 0$ such that $\sigma(j) \models \psi$ and for each k, $0 \leq k < j$, $\sigma(k) \models \varphi$;
$q \models \mathsf{A}\varphi\mathsf{U}\psi$	if, for each run σ in $Exec(q)$ there exists an integer $j \geq 0$ such that $\sigma(j) \models \psi$ and for each k, $0 \leq k < j$, $\sigma(k) \models \varphi$.

Modalities X and U are temporal modalities, interpreted along a run, while E and A are, respectively, the existential and universal quantifier on runs. Hence, if state q satisfies the formula $\mathsf{A}\varphi\mathsf{U}\psi$, this means that ψ will be true at some point in the future in all runs starting from q and φ remains true in the meanwhile. Modality X, also denoted sometimes by next, has a natural interpretation: $\mathsf{X}\varphi$ is true in a state if φ is true in the next state.

For this logic, all boolean operators can be defined and some abbreviations are frequently used, such as for instance:

– $\mathsf{EF}\varphi$, defined by $\mathsf{E}(\text{true})\mathsf{U}\varphi$, means that for a state q that property φ will be true at some point in the future in at least an execution starting from q (formula true is satisfied by any state);

– $\mathsf{AG}\varphi$ is defined by duality as $\neg\mathsf{EF}(\neg\varphi)$. It means that for a state q that property φ is always true along any execution starting from q;

– $\mathsf{AF}\varphi$, defined by $\mathsf{A}(\text{true})\mathsf{U}\varphi$, means that for a state q, for any execution starting from q, property φ will be true at some point in the future.

Timing CTL   Adding time constraints to these formulas can also be done in several ways, including adding variables or adding intervals. We present here the original definition of TCTL [ALU 91, ALU 93, HEN 94b], which is interpreted over timed transition systems, where configurations are equipped with sets of atomic propositions. We consider a dense time domain and continuous executions. In this case, the X modality is meaningless and is removed. For the subformula $\varphi\mathsf{U}\psi$, the idea consists of associating a time constraint of the form $\sim c$ with modality U for a comparison operator $\sim$ and a constant c (usually in $\mathbb{N}$), in order to enforce that property ψ will occur at a time t satisfying $t \sim c$.

The syntax of TCTL is defined by:

$$\varphi, \psi ::= P_1 \mid P_2 \mid \ldots \mid \neg\varphi \mid \varphi \wedge \psi \mid \mathsf{E}\varphi\mathsf{U}_{\sim c}\psi \mid \mathsf{A}\varphi\mathsf{U}_{\sim c}\psi$$

where P_i are atomic propositions in AP, operator $\sim$ belongs to $\{<, >, \leq, \geq, =\}$ and c is a constant in $\mathbb{N}$.

To define TCTL semantics, we consider a timed transition system $\mathcal{T} = (\Sigma \cup \mathbb{T}, S, s_0, E, \ell)$, where ℓ is the function labeling configurations in S by atomic propositions, and we still denote by $Exec(s)$ the set of paths starting from configuration s. For such an execution $\rho : s \xrightarrow{d_1} s_1' \xrightarrow{a_1} s_1 \xrightarrow{d_2} s_2' \xrightarrow{a_2} s_2 \cdots$, where durations alternate with actions, continuity allows all intermediate positions in time to be considered. These positions are totally ordered and the strict order along ρ is denoted by $p' <_\rho p$. For a position p on ρ, the corresponding configuration is denoted by s_p and $\rho^{\leq p}$ is the prefix of ρ before (or at) p. The duration of this prefix, written $\mathsf{Dur}(\rho^{\leq p})$, is the sum of all delays spent along $\rho^{\leq p}$.

The satisfaction relation for TCTL is defined on a configuration s of $\mathcal{T}$, in a way similar to CTL. We only give it for the $\mathsf{U}_{\sim c}$ modalities:

$s \models \mathsf{E}\varphi\mathsf{U}_{\sim c}\psi$ if there exists a run $\rho \in Exec(s)$ such that $\rho \models \varphi\mathsf{U}_{\sim c}\psi$;
$s \models \mathsf{A}\varphi\mathsf{U}_{\sim c}\psi$ if, for each run $\rho \in Exec(s)$, $\rho \models \varphi\mathsf{U}_{\sim c}\psi$;
with
$\rho \models \varphi\mathsf{U}_{\sim c}\psi$ if there exists a position p along ρ such that $\mathsf{Dur}(\rho^{\leq p}) \sim c$ and
$s_p \models \psi$, and for each position $p' <_\rho p$, $s_{p'} \models \varphi$
and if $\mathsf{Dur}(\rho^{\leq p'}) \sim c$, $s_{p'} \models \varphi \vee \psi$.

Observe that the standard U modality is now obtained by $\mathsf{U}_{\geq 0}$.

EXAMPLE.– If we consider again the property at the beginning of this chapter: "if a dangerous event occurs, an alarm will be triggered after at most three time units". With abbreviations similar to those of CTL, and atomic propositions danger and alarm, the property can be expressed by the following TCTL formula:

$$\Phi : \mathsf{AG}(\mathsf{danger} \Rightarrow \mathsf{AF}_{\leq 3}\,\mathsf{alarm})$$

To interpret TCTL formulas over timed automata or time(d) Petri nets, the models must be completed with a labeling of states by atomic propositions. This labeling is then extended to the associated timed transition system in a natural way: P belongs to the set of labels of state q if and only if it belongs to $\ell((q, v))$ for each configuration $s = (q, v)$. A timed automaton $\mathcal{A}$ is said to satisfy formula Ψ in TCTL, denoted by $\mathcal{A} \models \Psi$ if the initial configuration $s_0 = (q_0, 0)$ of $\mathcal{T}_\mathcal{A}$ satisfies Ψ.

As proved in [ALU 93], TCTL model checking is decidable for timed automata with a PSPACE-complete algorithm: given a timed automaton $\mathcal{A}$ and a TCTL formula Ψ, this algorithm decides whether $\mathcal{A} \models \Psi$ or not. The tool KRONOS [DAW 96] implements (an optimized version of) this algorithm, while UPPAAL [LAR 97a] allows on-the-fly verification of a TCTL fragment to be performed. A compositional method is applied in the tool HCMC [CAS 00].

Other timed logics   The same kind of method was used to produce timed versions of other temporal logics. For instance, the linear time temporal logic, LTL, was extended in [KOY 90] to the timed framework, yielding MTL (the metric temporal logic). Unfortunately, it turned out that model checking MTL is undecidable over timed automata. Thus, several expressive fragments were studied later [ALU 96, OUA 05], with positive results. In a similar way, operators with quantitative constraints have been added to a fragment of the μ-calculus, producing the logic L_ν [LAR 95, ACE 02]. Furthermore TCTL itself was extended, either with parameters [BRU 03], or with modalities extending the expressiveness to "almost everywhere" properties [BEL 05].

In a slightly different direction, to overcome undecidability in hybrid automata, other extensions of timed automata have been proposed, for instance by associating costs with states or transitions [BOU 04]. The logic WCTL [BRI 04] was then defined for these models, by adding cost constraints to CTL modalities. Since model checking WCTL is still undecidable, fragments were also proposed.

4.4.2. *Timed bisimilarity*

Note that in the previous section the response time property "if a dangerous event occurs, an alarm will be triggered after at most three time units" was easily expressed by the formula Φ in TCTL above. It could also be expressed by a timed automaton $\mathcal{B}$ similar to $\mathcal{A}_3$ (see section 4.3.2). Consider now a system, modeled by a timed automaton $\mathcal{S}$, where this property must be satisfied. Rather than solving the problem by model checking, the two models $\mathcal{S}$ and $\mathcal{B}$ can be compared, in order to decide whether all behaviors of $\mathcal{S}$ satisfy the specification expressed by $\mathcal{B}$. For this aim, model equivalences have been introduced and extended to the timed framework. However, it should be noted that it is not always possible to represent a TCTL formula by a timed automaton [ACE 03].

Strong simulation   Let $\mathcal{T}_1 = (L, S_1, s_0^1, E_1)$ and $\mathcal{T}_2 = (L, S_2, s_0^2, E_2)$ be two timed transition systems, over the same set of labels $L = \Sigma_\varepsilon \cup \mathbb{T}$.

DEFINITION 4.10 *A binary relation $\mathcal{R}$ on $S_1 \times S_2$ is a strong t-simulation of $\mathcal{T}_1$ by $\mathcal{T}_2$ if (s_0^1, s_0^2) belongs to $\mathcal{R}$ and*

1) if $s_1 \xrightarrow{d} s_1'$ is in E_1 for a delay d and $s_1 \mathcal{R} s_2$ then there exists s_2' in S_2 such that $s_2 \xrightarrow{d} s_2'$ is in E_2 and $s_1' \mathcal{R} s_2'$,

2) if $s_1 \xrightarrow{a} s_1'$ is in E_1 for an action a and $s_1 \mathcal{R} s_2$ then there exists s_2' in S_2 such that $s_2 \xrightarrow{a} s_2'$ is in E_2 and $s_1' \mathcal{R} s_2'$.

The timed transition system $\mathcal{T}_2$ strongly t-simulates $\mathcal{T}_1$ if there exists a strong t-simulation of $\mathcal{T}_1$ by $\mathcal{T}_2$. When a relation $\mathcal{R}$ is a strong t-simulation of $\mathcal{T}_1$ by $\mathcal{T}_2$ and the inverse relation $\mathcal{R}^{-1}$ (defined by $(s_2, s_1) \in \mathcal{R}^{-1}$ iff $(s_1, s_2) \in \mathcal{R}$) is also a strong t-simulation of $\mathcal{T}_2$ by $\mathcal{T}_1$, this relation is called a strong t-bisimulation. The two systems $\mathcal{T}_1$ and $\mathcal{T}_2$ are then said to be *strongly t-bisimilar*.

Similar to simulation in the untimed framework, this relation means that $\mathcal{T}_2$ can "imitate" $\mathcal{T}_1$, the delay transitions are considered as ordinary transitions.

Weak simulation   The relation above can be weakened by taking into account ε-transitions and possible decompositions of durations. From a TTS $\mathcal{T} = (L, S, s_0, E)$, the transition relation $\Rightarrow \subseteq S \times (\Sigma \cup \mathbb{T}) \times S$ is defined for $a \in \Sigma$ and $d \in \mathbb{T}$ by:

$- s \xRightarrow{d} s'$ if there exists a run of $\mathcal{T}$ from s to s' of duration d, with only ε-transitions;

$- s \xRightarrow{a} s'$ if there exists a run of $\mathcal{T}$ from s to s' of duration 0, with only a as visible action.

DEFINITION 4.11 *A binary relation $\mathcal{R}$ on $S_1 \times S_2$ is a* weak t-simulation *of $\mathcal{T}_1$ by $\mathcal{T}_2$ if (s_0^1, s_0^2) belongs to $\mathcal{R}$ and if, for each transition $s_1 \xRightarrow{\ell} s_1'$ in E_1, with $\ell \in \Sigma \cup \mathbb{T}$, such that $s_1 \mathcal{R} s_2$, there exists s_2' in S_2 such that $s_2 \xRightarrow{\ell} s_2'$ is in E_2 and $s_1' \mathcal{R} s_2'$.*

The TTS $\mathcal{T}_2$ weakly t-simulates $\mathcal{T}_1$ if there exists a weak t-simulation of $\mathcal{T}_1$ by $\mathcal{T}_2$. As above, if the inverse relation $\mathcal{R}^{-1}$ is also a weak t-simulation of $\mathcal{T}_2$ by $\mathcal{T}_1$, this relation is called a weak t-bisimulation. The systems $\mathcal{T}_1$ and $\mathcal{T}_2$ are then said to be *weakly t-bisimilar*.

This notion is well suited to timed systems and was used in the comparisons of expressive power of timed models, for instance in [ČER 93, BÉR 05b, BÉR 08a].

Other equivalences   Other simulations can be defined, for instance to express that a timed system is "faster" than another. Furthermore, the equivalences can again be weakened by abstracting time, replacing all delay transitions by an abstract "time-successor" transition. Although this operation seems to remove quantitative information, it can be defined as explained in the beginning of this chapter, so that verification can still be performed on the quotient [LAR 97b]. Finally, by adding acceptance conditions, language inclusion (and language equality) can also be defined. Time Petri nets and timed automata have been compared for this relation [BÉR 05b]. Note, however, that language inclusion is undecidable for timed automata [ALU 94], so that a bounded version was later proposed [OUA 09].

4.5. Conclusion

In this chapter, we illustrated how several notions can be taken from the untimed to the timed framework. For models such as finite automata, Petri nets or Kripke structures, the mechanism consists of adding timing constraints to the transitions, by adding time intervals or guards to variables. We also presented timed logics and timed bisimulation. This represents a very small part of the tremendous work accomplished in the last 20 years in formal methods, which were a breakthrough for the design, modeling, and verification of systems where real-time constraints must be taken into account. The theoretical work resulted in many efficient tools, which were successfully applied to numerous industrial case studies, leading to the detection of errors related to delays and parameter synthesis.

Beyond these results, open questions still remain, both on theoretical aspects and on the scalability of the methods for the verification of very large systems. The size of the resulting model is significantly increased not only with the number of components, but also with the addition of time [LAR 00]. Thus, design and analysis of large timed systems remain a challenge.

4.6. Bibliography

[ABD 01] ABDULLA P. A., NYLÉN A., "Timed Petri nets and BQOs", *Proc. 22nd International Conference on Application and Theory of Petri Nets (ICATPN'01)*, vol. 2075 of *Lecture Notes in Computer Science*, Springer, p. 53–70, 2001.

[ABD 07] ABDULLA P. A., MAHATA P., MAYR R., "Dense-timed Petri nets: checking Zenoness, token liveness and boundedness", *Logical Methods in Computer Science*, vol. 3, p. 1–61, 2007.

[ACE 02] ACETO L., LAROUSSINIE F., "Is your model checker on time? On the complexity of model checking for Timed Modal Logics", *Journal of Logic and Algebraic Programming*, vol. 52-53, p. 7-51, Elsevier Science Publishers, 2002.

[ACE 03] ACETO L., BOUYER P., BURGUEÑO A., LARSEN K. G., "The power of reachability testing for timed automata", *Theoretical Computer Science*, vol. 300, p. 411–475, 2003.

[ALU 90] ALUR R., DILL D., "Automata for modeling real-time systems", *Proc. of ICALP'90*, vol. 443 of *Lecture Notes in Computer Sciences*, Springer, p. 322-335, 1990.

[ALU 91] ALUR R., HENZINGER T., "Logics and models of real time: a survey", *Real-time: Theory in Practice, Proc. REX Workshop*, vol. 600 of *Lecture Notes in Computer Science*, Springer, p. 74-106, 1991.

[ALU 93] ALUR R., COURCOUBETIS C., DILL D., "Model-checking in dense real-time", *Information and Computation*, vol. 104, p. 2–34, Academic Press, 1993.

[ALU 94] ALUR R., DILL D., "A theory of timed automata", *Theoretical Computer Science*, vol. 126, p. 183-235, 1994.

[ALU 95] ALUR R., COURCOUBETIS C., HALBWACHS N., HENZINGER T. A., HO P.-H., NICOLLIN X., OLIVERO A., SIFAKIS J., YOVINE S., "The algorithmic analysis of hybrid systems", *Theoretical Computer Science*, vol. 138, p. 3–34, 1995.

[ALU 96] ALUR R., FEDER T., HENZINGER T. A., "The benefits of relaxing punctuality", *Journal of the ACM*, vol. 43, p. 116–146, ACM, 1996.

[ALU 97] ALUR R., HENZINGER T. A., "Real-time system = discrete system + clock variables", *Software Tools for Technology Transfer*, vol. 1, p. 86–109, 1997.

[ANN 01] ANNICHINI A., BOUAJJANI A., SIGHIREANU M., "TReX: a tool for reachability analysis of complex systems", *Proc. of 13th International Conference on Computer Aided Verification (CAV'01)*, vol. 2102 of *Lecture Notes in Computer Science*, Springer, p. 368-372, 2001.

[ASA 95] ASARIN E., MALER O., PNUELI A., "Reachability analysis of dynamical systems having piecewise-constant derivatives", *Theoretical Computer Science*, vol. 138, p. 35-65, 1995.

[ASA 97] ASARIN E., CASPI P., MALER O., "A Kleene theorem for timed automata", *Proc. of LICS'97*, IEEE Comp. Soc. Press, p. 160–171, 1997.

[ASA 02] ASARIN E., CASPI P., MALER O., "Timed regular expressions", *Journal of the ACM*, vol. 49, p. 172–206, 2002.

[ASA 07] ASARIN E., SCHNEIDER G., YOVINE S., "Algorithmic analysis of polygonal hybrid systems, part I: reachability", *Theoretical Computer Science*, vol. 379, p. 231-265, 2007.

[BAE 01] BAETEN J. C. M., MIDDELBURG C. A., "Process algebra with timing: real time and discrete time", BERGSTRA J. A., PONSE A., SMOLKA S. A., Eds., *Handbook of process algebra*, Chapter 10, p. 627–684, Elsevier, 2001.

[BEH 10] BEHRMANN G., DAVID A., LARSEN K. G., PETTERSSON P., YI W., "Developing UPPAAL over 15 years", *Proceedings of the Workshop on Tool Building in Formal Methods, ABZ 2010*, February 2010.

[BEL 05] BEL MOKADEM H., BÉRARD B., BOUYER P., LAROUSSINIE F., "A new modality for almost everywhere properties in timed automata", *Proc. 16th Int. Conf. on Concurrency Theory (CONCUR'05)*, vol. 3653 of *Lecture Notes in Computer Science*, Springer, p. 110–124, 2005.

[BER 91] BERTHOMIEU B., DIAZ M., "Modeling and verification of time dependent systems using time Petri nets", *IEEE Transactions on Software Engineering*, vol. 3, p. 259-273, 1991.

[BÉR 00] BÉRARD B., PICARONNY C., "Accepting Zeno words: a way toward timed refinements", *Acta Informatica*, vol. 37, p. 45–81, 2000.

[BÉR 05a] BÉRARD B., CASSEZ F., HADDAD S., LIME D., ROUX O., "Comparison of different semantics for time Petri nets", *Proc. 3rd Int. Symp. on Automated Technology for Verification and Analysis (ATVA'05)*, vol. 3707 of *Lecture Notes in Computer Science*, p. 293–307, 2005.

[BÉR 05b] BÉRARD B., CASSEZ F., HADDAD S., ROUX O., LIME D., "Comparison of the expressiveness of timed automata and time Petri nets", *Proc. 3rd Int. Conf. on Formal Modeling and Analysis of Timed Systems (FORMATS'05)*, vol. 3829 of *Lecture Notes in Computer Science*, Springer, p. 211–225, 2005.

[BER 06] BERTHOMIEU B., VERNADAT F., "Time Petri nets analysis with TINA", *Proceedings of 3rd International Conference on the Quantitative Evaluation of Systems (QEST 2006)*, IEEE Computer Society Press, p. 123-124, 2006.

[BÉR 08a] BÉRARD B., CASSEZ F., HADDAD S., LIME D., ROUX O. H., "When are timed automata weakly timed bisimilar to time Petri nets?", *Theoretical Computer Science*, vol. 403, p. 202-220, 2008.

[BÉR 08b] BÉRARD B., GASTIN P., PETIT A., "Timed substitutions for regular signal-event languages", *Formal Methods in System Design*, vol. 31, p. 101–134, 2008.

[BER 09] BERTRAND N., PINCHINAT S., RACLET J.-B., "Refinement and consistency of timed modal specifications", *Proc. of 3rd International Conference on Language and Automata Theory and Applications (LATA'09)*, vol. 5457 of *Lecture Notes in Computer Science*, Springer, p. 152-163, 2009.

[BOR 97] BORNOT S., SIFAKIS J., "Relating time progress and deadlines in hybrid systems", *Proc. Int. Workshop Hybrid and Real-Time Systems (HART'97)*, vol. 1201 of *Lecture Notes in Computer Science*, Springer, p. 286–300, 1997.

[BOR 98a] BORNOT S., SIFAKIS J., "On the composition of hybrid systems", *Proc. of Hybrid Systems: Computation and Control*, vol. 1386 of *Lecture Notes in Computer Science*, Springer, p. 49–63, 1998.

[BOR 98b] BORNOT S., SIFAKIS J., TRIPAKIS S., "Modeling urgency in timed systems", *Proc. Int. Symp. Compositionality: The Significant Difference (COMPOS'97)*, vol. 1536 of *Lecture Notes in Computer Science*, Springer, p. 103–129, 1998.

[BOR 00] BORNOT S., GÖSSLER G., SIFAKIS J., "On the construction of live timed systems", *Proc. of TACAS'00*, vol. 1785 of *Lecture Notes in Computer Science*, Springer, p. 109–126, 2000.

[BOU 99] BOUYER P., PETIT A., "Decomposition and composition of timed automata", *Proc. 26th Int. Coll. Automata, Languages, and Programming (ICALP'99)*, vol. 1644 of *Lecture Notes in Computer Science*, Springer, p. 210–219, 1999.

[BOU 01] BOUYER P., PETIT A., THÉRIEN D., "An algebraic characterization of data and timed languages", *Proc. 12th Int. Conf. Concurrency Theory (CONCUR'2001)*, vol. 2154 of *Lecture Notes in Computer Science*, Springer, p. 248–261, 2001.

[BOU 02] BOUYER P., PETIT A., "A Kleene/Büchi-like theorem for clock languages", *Journal of Automata, Languages and Combinatorics*, vol. 7, p. 167–186, 2002.

[BOU 04] BOUYER P., BRINKSMA E., LARSEN K. G., "Staying alive as cheaply as possible", *Proc. 7th Int. Conf. on Hybrid Systems: Computation and Control (HSCC'04)*, vol. 2993 of *Lecture Notes in Computer Science*, Springer, p. 203-218, 2004.

[BOU 08] BOUYER P., HADDAD S., REYNIER P.-A., "Timed Petri nets and timed automata: on the discriminating power of Zeno sequences", *Information and Computation*, vol. 206, p. 73-107, Elsevier Science Publishers, 2008.

[BOY 08] BOYER M., ROUX O. H., "On the compared expressiveness of arc, place and transition time Petri nets", *Fundamenta Informaticae*, vol. 88, p. 225-249, 2008.

[BRI 04] BRIHAYE T., BRUYÈRE V., RASKIN J., "Model-checking for weighted timed automata", *Proc. Joint Conference on Formal Modelling and Analysis of Timed Systems and Formal Techniques in Real-Time and Fault Tolerant System (FORMATS+FTRTFT'04)*, vol. 3253 of *Lecture Notes in Computer Science*, Springer, p. 277–292, 2004.

[BRI 10] BRIHAYE T., BRUYÈRE V., RENDER E., "Formal language properties of hybrid systems with strong resets", *Rairo - Theoretical Informatics and Applications*, vol. 44, p. 79-11, 2010.

[BRU 03] BRUYÈRE V., DALL'OLIO E., RASKIN J., "Durations, parametric model-checking in timed automata with Presburger arithmetic", *Proc. 20th Annual Symposium on Theoretical Aspects of Computer Science (STACS'03)*, vol. 2607 of *Lecture Notes in Computer Science*, Springer, p. 687–698, 2003.

[CAM 95] CAMPOS S., CLARKE E., "Real-time symbolic model checking for discrete time models", *Theories and Experiences for Real-Time System Development*, vol. 2 of *AMAST Series in Computing*, World Scientific, p. 129–145, 1995.

[CAS 00] CASSEZ F., LAROUSSINIE F., "Model-checking for hybrid systems by quotienting and constraint solving", *Proc. of 12th International Conference on Computer Aided Verification (CAV 2000)*, vol. 1855 of *Lecture Notes in Computer Science*, Springer, p. 373-388, 2000.

[ČER 93] ČERĀNS K., "Decidability of bisimulation equivalence for parallel timer processes", *Proc. 4th Int. Workshop on Computer Aided Verification (CAV'92)*, vol. 663 of *Lecture Notes in Computer Science*, Springer, p. 302–315, 1993.

[COR 99] CORRADINI F., D'ORTENZIO D., INVERARDI P., "On the relationships among four timed process algebras", *Fundamenta Informaticae*, vol. 38, p. 377–395, 1999.

[COR 03] CORRADINI F., DI COLA D., "The expressive power of urgent, lazy and busy-waiting actions in timed processes", *Mathematical Structures in Computer Science*, vol. 13, p. 619–656, 2003.

[DAW 96] DAWS C., OLIVERO A., TRIPAKIS S., YOVINE S., "The tool KRONOS", *Proc. Hybrid Systems III: Verification and Control (1995)*, vol. 1066 of *Lecture Notes in Computer Science*, Springer, p. 208–219, 1996.

[DIL 89] DILL D. L., "Timing assumptions and verification of finite-state concurrent systems", *Proc. Int. Workshop Automatic Verification Methods for Finite State Systems (CAV'89)*, vol. 407 of *Lecture Notes in Computer Science*, Springer, p. 197–212, 1989.

[DIM 00] DIMA C., "Real-time Automata and the Kleene algebra of sets of real numbers", *Proc. 17th Symp. on Theoretical Aspects of Computer Science (STACS'2000)*, vol. 1770 of *Lecture Notes in Computer Science*, Springer, p. 279–289, 2000.

[EME 92] EMERSON E. A., MOK A. K., SISTLA A. P., SRINIVASAN J., "Quantitative temporal reasoning", *Real-Time Systems*, vol. 4, p. 331–352, 1992.

[FRE 05] FREHSE G., "PHAVer: algorithmic verification of hybrid systems past HyTech", *Proc. of 8th International Workshop on Hybrid Systems: Computation and Control (HSCC 2005)*, vol. 3414 of *Lecture Notes in Computer Science*, Springer, p. 258-273, 2005.

[FRE 09] FREHSE G., RAY R., "Design principles for an extendable verification tool for hybrid systems", *Proc. of 3rd IFAC Conference on Analysis and Design of Hybrid Systems (ADHS'09)*, vol. 3, part 1, 2009.

[FRU 00] DE FRUTOS ESCRIG D., VALERO RUIZ V., MARROQUÍN ALONSO O., "Decidability of properties of timed-arc Petri nets", *Proc. of the 21st International Conference on Application and Theory of Petri nets (ICATPN'00)*, Lecture Notes in Computer Science, Springer, p. 187–206, 2000.

[GAR 05] GARDEY G., LIME D., MAGNIN M., ROUX O. H., "Roméo: a tool for analyzing time Petri nets", *Proc. of 17th International Conference on Computer Aided Verification (CAV 2005)*, vol. 3576 of *Lecture Notes in Computer Science*, Springer, p. 418-423, 2005.

[GRO 95] GROSSMAN R., LARSON R., "An algebraic approach to hybrid systems", *Theoretical Computer Science*, vol. 138, p. 101–112, 1995.

[HAN 95] HANSEN M., PANDYA P., ZHOU C., "Finite divergence", *Theoretical Computer Science*, vol. 138, p. 113–139, 1995.

[HEN 92] HENZINGER T. A., MANNA Z., PNUELI A., "What good are digital clocks?", *Proc. 19th Int. Coll. Automata, Languages, and Programming (ICALP'92)*, vol. 623 of *Lecture Notes in Computer Science*, Springer, p. 545–558, 1992.

[HEN 94a] HENZINGER T. A., MANNA Z., PNUELI A., "Temporal proof methodologies for timed transition systems", *Information and Computation*, vol. 112, p. 273–337, 1994.

[HEN 94b] HENZINGER T., NICOLLIN X., SIFAKIS J., YOVINE S., "Symbolic model checking for real-time systems", *Information and Computation*, vol. 111, p. 193-244, 1994.

[HEN 95] HENZINGER T. A., HO P., WONG-TOI H., "HYTECH: the next generation", *Proc. 16th IEEE Real-Time Systems Symposium (RTSS'95)*, IEEE Computer Society Press, p. 56–65, 1995.

[HEN 96] HENZINGER T., "The theory of hybrid automata", *Proc. of LICS'96*, New Brunswick, New Jersey, p. 278 -292, 1996, Invited tutorial.

[HEN 98a] HENZINGER T. A., KOPKE P. W., PURI A., VARAIYA P., "What's decidable about hybrid automata?", *Journal of Computer and System Sciences*, vol. 57, num. 1, p. 94-124, 1998.

[HEN 98b] HENZINGER T. A., RASKIN J.-F., SCHOBBENS P.-Y., "The regular real-time languages", *Proc. 25th Int. Coll. Automata, Languages, and Programming (ICALP'98)*, vol. 1443 of *Lecture Notes in Computer Science*, Springer, p. 580–591, 1998.

[JAF 91] JAFFE M., LEVESON N., HEIMDAHL M., MELHARD B., "Software requirements analysis for real-time process-control systems", *IEEE Trans. Software Eng.*, vol. 17, p. 241–258, 1991.

[JON 77] JONES N., LANDWEBER L., LIEN Y., "Complexity of some problems in Petri nets", *Theoretical Computer Science*, vol. 4, p. 277–299, 1977.

[KOY 90] KOYMANS R., "Specifying real-time properties with metric temporal logic", *Real-Time Systems*, vol. 2, p. 255–299, 1990.

[LAB 98] LABROUE A., Conditions de vivacité dans les automates temporisés, Report num. LSV-98-7, Lab. Specification and Verification, ENS de Cachan, Cachan, France, 1998.

[LAF 01] LAFFERRIERE G., PAPPAS G. J., YOVINE S., "Symbolic reachability computations for families of linear vector fields", *Journal of Symbolic Computation*, vol. 32, p. 231–253, 2001.

[LAR 95] LAROUSSINIE F., LARSEN K. G., WEISE C., "From timed automata to logic – and back", *Proc. 20th Int. Symp. on Mathematical Foundations of Computer Science (MFCS'95)*, vol. 969 of *Lecture Notes in Computer Science*, Springer, p. 529–539, 1995.

[LAR 97a] LARSEN K. G., PETTERSSON P., YI W., "UPPAAL in a nutshell", *Journal of Software Tools for Technology Transfer (STTT)*, vol. 1, p. 134-152, Springer, 1997.

[LAR 97b] LARSEN K. G., WANG YI, "Time-abstracted bisimulation: implicit specifications and decidability", *Information and Computation*, vol. 134, p. 75–101, 1997.

[LAR 00] LAROUSSINIE F., SCHNOEBELEN PH., "The state explosion problem from trace to bisimulation equivalence", *Proc. 3rd Int. Conf. Foundations of Software Science and Computation Structures (FOSSACS'2000)*, vol. 1784 of *Lecture Notes in Computer Science*, Springer, p. 192–207, 2000.

[LAR 02] LAROUSSINIE F., MARKEY N., SCHNOEBELEN PH., "On model checking durational Kripke structures (extended abstract)", *Proc. 5th Int. Conf. on Foundations of Software Science and Computation Structures (FoSSaCS'02)*, vol. 2303 of *Lecture Notes in Computer Science*, Springer, p. 264–279, 2002.

[LEG 10] LE GUERNIC C., GIRARD A., "Reachability analysis of linear systems using support functions", *Nonlinear Analysis: Hybrid Systems*, vol. 4, p. 250-262, 2010.

[MAL 91] MALER O., MANNA Z., PNUELI A., "From timed to hybrid systems", *Real-Time: Theory in Practice, Proc. REX Workshop*, vol. 600 of *Lecture Notes in Computer Science*, Springer, p. 447–484, 1991.

[MER 74] MERLIN P. M., A study of the recoverability of computing systems, PhD thesis, UCI, University of California, 1974.

[NIC 91a] NICOLLIN X., SIFAKIS J., "An overview and synthesis on timed process algebras", *Real-Time: Theory in Practice, Proc. REX Workshop*, vol. 600 of *Lecture Notes in Computer Science*, Springer, p. 526–548, 1991.

[NIC 91b] NICOLLIN X., SIFAKIS J., YOVINE S., "From ATP to timed graphs and hybrid systems", *Real-time: Theory in practice, Proc. REX workshop*, vol. 600 of *Lecture Notes in Computer Science*, Springer, p. 549-572, 1991.

[NIC 92] NICOLLIN X., SIFAKIS J., YOVINE S., "Compiling real-time specifications into extended automata", *IEEE Trans. Software Eng.*, vol. 18, p. 794–804, 1992.

[NIC 93] NICOLLIN X., SIFAKIS J., YOVINE S., "From ATP to timed graphs and hybrid systems", *Acta Informatica*, vol. 30, num. 2, p. 181–202, 1993.

[OUA 03] OUAKNINE J., WORRELL J., "Timed CSP = closed timed epsilon-automata", *Nordic Journal of Computing*, vol. 10, 2003.

[OUA 05] OUAKNINE J., WORRELL J., "On the decidability of metric temporal logic", *Proc. 20th IEEE Symposium on Logic in Computer Science (LICS'05)*, 2005.

[OUA 06] OUAKNINE J., SCHNEIDER S., "Timed CSP: a retrospective", *Proc. of the Workshop on Algebraic Process Calculi: The First Twenty Years and Beyond*, vol. 162 of *Electronic Notes in Computer Science*, Elsevier Science B.V., 2006.

[OUA 09] OUAKNINE J., RABINOVITCH A., WORRELL J., "Time bounded verification", *Proc. of CONCUR 2009*, vol. 5710 of *Lecture Notes in Computer Science*, 2009.

[PNU 77] PNUELI A., "The temporal logic of programs", *Proc. 18th IEEE Symp. Foundations of Computer Science (FOCS'77)*, p. 46–57, 1977.

[REE 86] REED G. M., ROSCOE A. W., "A timed model for communicating sequential processes", *Proc. 13th International Colloquium on Automata, Languages, and Programming (ICALP'86)*, Lecture Notes in Computer Science, Springer, p. 314-323, 1986.

[REY 09] REYNIER P.-A., SANGNIER A., "Weak time Petri nets strike back!", *Proc. of the 20th International Conference on Concurrency Theory (CONCUR'09)*, vol. 5710 of *Lecture Notes in Computer Science*, Springer, p. 557-571, 2009.

[SIF 96] SIFAKIS J., YOVINE S., "Compositional specification of timed systems", *Proc. 13th Annual Symposium on Theoretical Computer Science (STACS'96)*, vol. 1046 of *Lecture Notes in Computer Science*, Springer, p. 347–359, 1996.

[SRB 05] SRBA J., "Timed-arc Petri nets vs. networks of timed automata", *Proc. 26th International Conference Application and Theory of Petri Nets (ICATPN'05)*, vol. 3536 of *Lecture Notes in Computer Science*, Springer, p. 385–402, 2005.

[VAL 99] VALERO RUIZ V., DE FRUTOS ESCRIG D., CUARTERO GÓMEZ F., "On nondecidability of reachability for timed-arc Petri nets", *Proc. 8th Int. Workshop on Petri Nets and Performance Models (PNPM'99)*, IEEE Computer Society Press, p. 188–196, 1999.

[YI 91] YI W., "CCS + time = an interleaving model for real-time systems", *Proc. 18th International Colloquium on Automata, Languages, and Programming (ICALP'91)*, vol. 510 of *Lecture Notes in Computer Science*, Springer, 1991.

Chapter 5

Architecture Description Languages

5.1. Introduction

This chapter presents an overview of architecture description languages (ADLs). After introducing the motivation for ADLs and their benefits (section 5.1), we study their general concepts and underlying principles (section 5.2). We then take a deeper look into ADL from two different viewpoints. We first study more abstract and formal languages, dedicated to the analysis of composite systems, mainly software systems (section 5.3). Further, in a second step, we present more concrete languages designed to help in the actual implementation of applications (section 5.4).

A major issue when designing a distributed system is its complexity. Complexity is, of course, not specific to distributed systems, and it stems first from the size of the system. Distributed systems present features that increase complexity. First, complexity may arise from the fact that several entities have to be taken into account. Further, in a distributed system, these entities do not exist independently from one another. Their interactions are an important part of the problem as they can lead to both benefits (achieving some form of collaboration or cooperation) or to major drawbacks (deadlocks, starvation, or incorrect multiple access to resources, etc.). To solve these complexity issues, approaches based on the decomposition of a system into subsystems can be put into practice, whether is it for design, verification, or implementation.

Underlying this decomposition, is an important concept: *structuring*. It has been instantiated several times in the past years with approaches based on modules [PAR 72], objects/classes [DAH 66, MEY 97], software components [SZY 98], services [PAP 03],

---

Chapter written by Pascal POIZAT and Thomas VERGNAUD.

aspects [FIL 05], or software product lines [POH 05]. Software components make the functionalities provided by some reusable entity explicit, as modules and classes/objects did. However, software components go further by also making the required functionalities explicit. Having both provided and required functionalities explicit supports the definition of software components independently from a specific usage context.

This makes, in theory, software components more reusable than modules or objects/classes where requirements are hidden in the code. Services are the basic entities that underpin the development of service-oriented architectures (SOA) and service-oriented computing (SOC). However, for differences in description languages and underlying middleware, services can be seen as a kind of software component. Aspect-orientation[1] is a more asymmetric approach, where some first-class entity, the base business model or code, is extended with the integration of one or several second-class entities called aspects. Software product lines are another modern application of structuring, where products are the result of the integration of core assets and variation-related ones.

The abovementioned approaches lead to new software design processes with two distinct tasks[2]:

– *designing in-the-large*, the structuring of the system as a set of subsystems linked by dependency or interaction relations, a kind of structural blueprint of the system. In an analogy to building construction where buildings are constructed using an assembly plan for subparts (ground, walls, roof), such a blueprint can be referred to as the *architectural plan* of the system, and the person in charge of its definition can be called a *software architect*;

– *designing in-the-small*, the design, verification, and implementation or reuse of subsystems satisfying a subset of the system's functionalities or corresponding to deployment units.

In the following, rather than focusing on a specific application domain (modules, classes, software components, services, aspects, products, etc.), we will adopt the generic term of *component* for such a subsystem that can be assembled with others to build bigger systems.

The development of ADLs [PER 92, GAR 93, MED 00] is the application of the principle stating that different languages should be used for different activities. ADLs are domain specific languages (DSL), which support the software architect in specifying, designing, and implementing a system with an architectural viewpoint. Towards

---

1. We refer here to the mainstream aspect-oriented approach, i.e. following the Aspect-J vision.

2. The terms "designing in-the-large" and "designing in-the-small" are variations inspired from the terms "programming in-the-large" and "programming in-the-small" first introduced by De Remer and Kron in [DER 75].

this objective, ADLs enable the definition of base architectural elements, the definition of relations between base architectural elements, and the definition of *architectural models* as the composition of architectural elements and their relations.

To master complexity, ADLs enable the description of a system's architectural model (i.e. its decomposition into elements and relations) at different abstraction levels, possibly going from a very abstract functional architecture (functionalities and dependency relations) to a concrete implementation architecture (deployed and communicating subsystems). At some given abstraction level, it is also possible to describe a system under different and complementary viewpoints, such as the functional viewpoint (e.g. base elements provide some functionalities, possibly requiring some other), the quality of service viewpoint (e.g. base elements perform operations in less than x seconds), and the robustness (e.g. base elements are fault-tolerant), etc. These principles are important principles of software engineering, and can be found also in the UML for example. However, while the unified modeling language (UML) promotes the use of different diagrams, hence different underlying concepts in the meta-model, ADLs promote simpler meta-models with possible extensions (such as the UML stereotypes).

Further, ADLs integrate in a rigorous development process. Hence they also provide a well-founded semantics for the architectural definitions, and are not only restricted to a "box-and-line" notation. Building on this semantics, ADLs support architectural analysis, i.e. the analysis of architectural models. Examples include checking structural constraints (e.g. limits on the kind of components, the number of components, and/or the kind of relations between them), performing qualitative analysis (e.g. is the architecture deadlock free?), or performing qualitative analysis (e.g. does the system reply in less than x seconds to requests?). The semantics is also the support for the automatic retrieval of parts of a system's implementation from its architectural model.

The development of ADLs was undertaken in two steps. Initially, academics became interested in the definition of ADLs dedicated to qualitative verification (of software architectures) and/or to automatic or guided implementation (from software architectures). This leads to an important number of first-generation ADL being defined in the 1990s (Aesop, C2/SADL, Darwin, OLAN, MetaH, Rapide, UniCon, Wright, to cite only some). The need for interchange meta-models and formats rapidly emerged, the main solution being Acme [ABL 10], an interchange language between ADLs, and its toolbox, AcmeStudio, was developed at Carnegie Mellon. More recently, ADLs research has addressed the extension of properties taken into account in architectural analysis (e.g. with performance analysis), new kinds of systems (e.g. services-oriented architectures, software product lines), or relations between ADL and mainstream design notations such as the UML [MED 02]. It should be noted that since UML 2.0 [OMG 10b], methods for architectural description have been more widely supported in the standard notation (i.e. not extended with profiles and/or stereotypes).

A major research direction on ADL now is the support for systems with a dynamic/evolving architecture [ORE 08, KRA 09] or where mobility is crucial [MED 10]. Meanwhile, the industry has become interested in the application of ADL, mainly within the context of embedded systems. A major outcome of this is architecture analysis and design language (AADL), which defines a standard for the description of architectural models of real-time embedded systems.

In this chapter we first present, in section 5.2, the common principles and concepts behind most ADLs. The following two sections are dedicated to the presentation of ADLs with complementary viewpoints. Section 5.3 introduces two representative instances of the formal first-generation ADLs. They are abstract ADLs, based on fewer concepts, and tackle architectures with a design perspective. These concepts, being well-founded, enable the analysis and verification of architectural models. Section 5.4 introduces a type of ADL dedicated to the implementation of distributed systems. In this field, we focus mainly on AADL. Finally, we conclude noting the benefits of ADL and showing how these two kinds of ADL can meet with the formal developments around AADL.

5.2. Concepts

Numerous ADLs have been proposed, whether multi-purpose abstract ADLs, or dedicated to some specific application domain. There currently does not yet exist a consensus on the "good" abstraction and description level of an ADL. Indeed, this is also one of the reasons why ADLs can be used in very different contexts. However, there is an emerging agreement on the core concepts that should be found in an ADL. This *ADL ontology* has led to the definition of meta-models and interchange formats, such as Acme [ABL 10] or xADL [DAS 01]. This underlies the reference study and survey on ADL by Medvidovic and Taylor [MED 00].

5.2.1. *Elements of an ADL description*

A simple meta-model for ADLs is presented in Figure 5.1.

The basic elements of an architectural model are *components* and *connectors*. Components and connectors have *interfaces* that are the support for the definition of relations or *bindings*. Altogether, a set of components, a set of connectors, and bindings between their interfaces define an *architectural configuration* (or simply, configuration).

Components

A component is the basic architectural entity that abstracts some information that is available or some piece of code that is reusable. To quote [MED 00], "A component

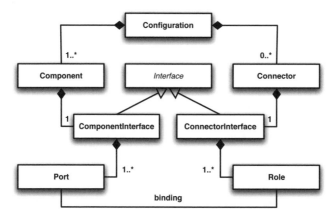

Figure 5.1. *ADL meta-model (UML class diagram notation)*

is a unit of computation or a data store [...]. Components may be as small as a single procedure or as large as an entire application". The basic motivations that trigger the encapsulation of some information or piece of code as a component are the decomposition of a complex system into small subsystems – the system components – and their interactions, or the desire to enable reuse, following the definition of Szyperski [SZY 98]: "A (software) component is a unit of composition with contractually specified interfaces and explicit context dependencies only. A (software) component [...] is subject to composition by third-parties". The former case (decomposition) integrates perfectly in a top-down vision of the software engineering process (decompose to simplify), while the later case corresponds to a bottom-up vision (building value-added systems from simpler ones).

Connectors

A connector is the basic architectural entity that abstracts some type of interaction between components. A shared variable in a threaded Java program, a Unix pipe between two commands, a socket between a client and a server, a JDBC connection between a Java program and some database, a HTTP connection between a browser and a Web server, the SOAP connections between an orchestration and basic Web services, tuple spaces, etc. are all examples connectors in every-day life. Whether there should be any (explicit) connectors at all is a matter of discussion. Some ADLs have no explicit connectors. It is particularly relevant when there are few kinds of interactions between components, e.g. in Web service compositions[3]. Other ADLs advocate that if connectors are complex they should be defined as components, having again only simple bindings between "component" components and "connector" components.

---

3. Web services can interact in different ways, but we stress out that the standard is SOAP over HTTP.

Interfaces

If we refer to the Oxford online dictionary definition [Oxf 10], an interface is "a point where two systems, subjects, organizations, etc. meet and interact". From a software point of view, the interface of an entity is both the *operational mechanism* through which this entity interacts with its environment (e.g. a protocol information, an IP address, and a port, such as http://127.0.0.1:8080/), and the *contractual specification* of the entity functionalities (e.g. "this service provides you with the possibility to buy a holiday package provided you supply the departure and return dates/-places, and for this it will require facilities to plane ticket and hotel booking available"). As we saw before, an important benefit with reference to earlier approaches is that this specification explicits both the functionalities provided by the entity (here the holiday package) and those it requires (here online services for plane and hotel booking). The first interpretation of interfaces is mandatory to enable implementability of software architectures. It gives an answer to the question "Where can I access this entity?". However, ADL go further by using the second interpretation and associated information extensively, and giving an answer to the question "What and how can this entity do something for me? – What and how should I do for this entity?".

Many ADL refine interfaces as a set of interaction points that correspond to the first interpretation. An entity has then *one* interface, made up of *one or several* interaction points. This is depicted in our meta-model, in Figure 5.1. In the component interfaces, these interaction points are called *ports*, while in the connector interfaces, they are called *roles*. *Provided ports* describe the services a component provides, while *required ports* describe the assumptions a component assumes from its environment, such as the services it should provide to the component. Taking our example, above, the trip component has one provided port (for booking a holiday package) and two required ports (respectively used by the component to buy plane tickets and to book hotel rooms). Roles describe the different roles (hence the name) that components can play in some interaction. Taking for example a Unix pipe-and-filter architecture, the pipe connectors have two roles: producer (or data source) and consumer (or data sink).

An alternative to entities having one interface with several interaction points, is to consider entities that have *several* interfaces and then these are not decomposed into several interaction points (both notions coinciding). Web services for example take the first interpretation. Let us take a composite Web service written in the BPEL orchestration language [OAS07]. It has different partners that it will communicate with. These can correspond to end-users, programs, or other services that will fulfill some functionality for the composite. For each of these partners there is a port, called partner link, which is described using the WSDL [W3C01].

Usually, ports are detailed into sets of operations (the operation being the element being called, while the port – or partner link in Web services – being the place where the call is issued) [POI 06, HAD 07, BAR 09]. Indeed, many different kinds of information can be associated with an interface (or, respectively, to ports and roles). These are often classified using four *interface description levels* and accordingly *interface description languages* (IDLs) [CAN 06].

1) *Signature level.* This is the state of the art for mainstream components and service middleware, e.g. CORBA or SOA such as Web services. Interface descriptions at this level specify the methods or services that an entity offers (as in object IDLs, like CORBA-IDL, or the public interface of a Java class). Sometimes, they also describe its external dependencies (as in component IDLs like CCM-IDL for OMG's component model, or WSDL for Web Services). Typically, these interfaces specify the name of the service, the type of its arguments and return values, and the possible exceptions raised, that is, the full signature of the entity behind the interface.

2) *Behavioral level.* Interfaces at this level specify the protocol describing the interactive behavior that a component follows, and possibly the behavior that it expects from its environment. Behavioral descriptions are required for entities with state, providing non-uniform services that are not available at any time, but that depend for example on the internal state of the entity. There are numerous proposals for extending interfaces with behavior, either for components with protocols, e.g. [PLÁ 02, POI 06, BAR 09, BRA 05, CAN 08, TIV 08], or for services with conversations, e.g. [Ben 07, MAT 08, BER 10]. We will detail formal ADLs that use behavioral interfaces in section 5.3 (*e.g.*, Wright or Darwin) but some ADLs briefly presented in section 5.4 may also have this kind of information in interfaces (e.g. SOFA or Fractal). ADLs with behavioral interfaces rely, for description and analysis, on formal behavioral model such as (labeled) transition systems (LTS), Petri nets, or process algebras.

3) *Semantic level.* This level describes what the entity actually does, not only the methods it offers or the messages it exchanges. Such specification is particularly interesting for component mining (e.g. automatic service discovery). In the field of Web services, this level of description is related to the Semantic Web, e.g. using ontologies or description logics, and languages such as OWL/OWL-S or WSMO [TOÖ]. An alternative approach consists of using formal functional descriptions for specifying functionality, e.g. preconditions and postconditions for the signature level operations.

4) *Service (non-functional) level.* Numerous non-functional properties such as temporal requirements (discrete or real-time), security, reliability, accuracy, cost, etc. are important to take into account when composing entities altogether, especially for some application domains such as real-time embedded systems. These properties are tackled by the non-functional interface description level. It is usually highly customizable, and the possible descriptions include mean values, standard deviations, and a set of quantiles characterizing the distribution of any self-defined quality metric. AADL, which we present in section 5.4 is a typical example of an ADL providing this interface description level and associated analysis techniques.

It is important to stress that, if most ADLs associate with interfaces only a subpart of these four levels, the genericity and extensibility principle of interfaces in ADLs states that anything that eases the specification, analysis, and/or implementation can be included in the description of an interface.

Configurations

An (architectural) configuration is the description of an assembly of components (i.e. a set of identified instances of component types) and connectors (i.e. a set of identified instances of connector types). The relations between components (exchanging provided/required functionalities) is achieved through connectors and the binding of component ports to the different roles of the connectors.

Configurations represent an architectural viewpoint of a system. Different abstractions or constraints of a system (e.g. whether during the design process, or at deployment where deployment constraints are highly relevant) can lead to different configurations. Configurations enable the designer to check the system's architecture (see below, *ADLs and analysis*). Further, once a deployment scheme has been chosen (e.g. if, for each component, an address is given) then ADLs enable the automatic deployment of the system.

Regarding systems complexity, an important benefit of configurations in ADL is the possibility to build *composite components*, i.e. to treat a configuration as a component and (re-)use it in further configurations. For this, it must be possible to relate the ports of the composite components to the ports of its subcomponents (see an example of this, below, in *Examples*). Composite components enable a divide-and-conquer strategy where, for example, a first decomposition level of a system can be made based on deployment issues (e.g. having three high-level components in the system corresponding to three Web services deployed on three application servers), while in a second step each of these three components can be refined as a composite using a configuration made up of functional (business) subcomponents (e.g. implemented using Java classes). The service component architecture (SCA) [Ope 07] is an example of a recent framework that is highly reliant on composite components.

Composite components raise the *compositionality* issue. An ADL is compositional if, not only is it possible to define composite components, but also the semantics of the configuration in the composite component can be related to the semantics of a component. Interestingly, this is the case for most formal ADLs with behavioral signatures: given the behaviors (e.g. some LTS) of all the components (and connectors, if not implicit) in a configuration, it is possible to retrieve the behavior (again, e.g. an LTS) for the configuration. The compositionality of the ADL raises the possibility of compositional verification of the architectures, i.e. verify a composite component without really computing the global behavior, but taking into account only the subcomponents' behaviors and their connections. Reasoning on composite components is not restricted to behavioral descriptions but it also applies to non-functional service descriptions, e.g. to retrieve the value of quality of service attributes for composite components being given the value of these attributes for the subcomponents.

Examples

In Figure 5.2, we illustrate an example of an architectural description, namely a client-server configuration with two components (a client and a server) and one connector (a remote procedure call (RPC) interaction) [ABL 10]. Each component has one port, respectively, Request for the client and Service for the server. The RPC connector has two roles: Callee for the service being called and Caller for the client calling it.

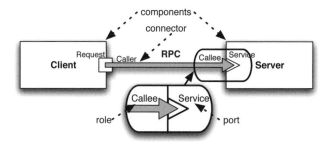

Figure 5.2. *A client-server configuration [ABL 10] (ACME notation)*

A second example is illustrated in Figure 5.3 and demonstrates that ADLs can be used to model different kinds of structured systems, and, using the connector abstraction, refine architectures depending on the distribution choice and related interaction technique(s). Here, we have a Unix pipe-and-filter architecture to find out definitions in C source files, i.e. corresponding to:

```
grep "#define" | cut -d ' ' -f 2,3 | sort.
```

It is made up of three components and two connectors. It is important to note that the configuration strictly adheres to some implicit rules constraining what is a "correct" pipe-and-filter architecture (we will see later that such rules can be made explicit): the only component types are filters, while the only connector types are pipes[4]. Each component has three ports: in (aka stdout, or &0), out (aka stdout, or &1), and err (aka stderr, or &2). Pipes have one input role (source) and one output

---

4. Actually, pipe-and-filter architectures also contain data sources and data sinks; however, we restrict them here for simplicity.

role (sink). While the previous example was a closed one, here the configuration as a whole can be seen as an open system component, with three ports (input, output, and error). Binding can be used not only to bind ports and roles, but also to bind internal component ports to the composite component ports. Refining such a system into a distributed one is eased by the architectural notation, e.g. we can replace pipe connectors by RPC connectors.

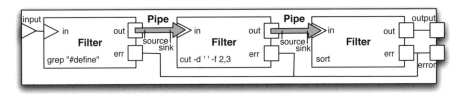

Figure 5.3. *A pipe-and-filter configuration (ACME notation)*

Our last example, in Figure 5.4, demonstrates the use of ADLs to model another kind of system, namely a centralized composite Web service (*i.e.*, an orchestration). Here we demonstrate a typical example where connectors are abstracted away (see discussion in *Connectors*, above). ADLs enable us to focus additionally on the operations corresponding to service functionalities provided or required at ports (signature level interfaces). Note that the set of operations required at a required port may be a subset of those provided at the corresponding provided port. In such a case, UML component diagrams [OMG 10b] complemented with class diagram(s) for interfaces may be a valuable alternative regarding the graphical representation of the configuration.

These examples will serve as a basis in the sequel to present representatives of the formal ADL in section 5.3. Behavioral interfaces will be demonstrated there too, while non-functional interfaces will be demonstrated in section 5.4.

5.2.2. *ADLs and analysis*

The use of ADLs gives the software architect the possibility to analyze architectural descriptions in an architectural design step that takes place between the requirement analysis and implementation. Further, when the properties or descriptions that are associated with components' and connectors' interfaces are formally grounded (i.e. they have a formal model) then automatized verification and analysis becomes possible.

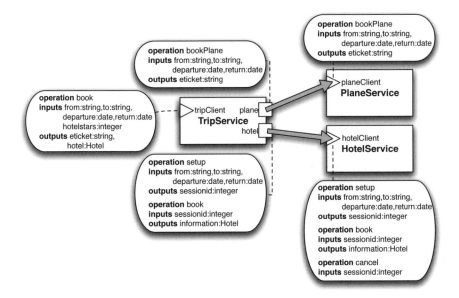

Figure 5.4. *An orchestration configuration (extended ACME notation)*

Architectural styles and their verification

The notion of *(architectural) style* is only present in some ADLs. It enables the definition of structural constraints over configurations that can be verified by tools such as AcmeStudio. This includes:

– *typing constraints.* A style can limit the types of the components and connectors that are used. An example we saw is the pipe-and-filter architectures where the only components are filters, data sources and data sink, while the only connectors are pipes;

– *binding constraints.* A style can limit the types of bindings between component ports and connector roles. Again, in the pipe-and-filter architecture, the source role of a pipe can only be bound to the output of a component, and the sink role can only be bound to the input of a component. Additionally, both roles can only be bound once (it is not possible to bind two component ports on a single connector role);

– *occurrence constraints.* A style can limit the number of components and/or connectors in configurations, e.g. for efficiency issues, or, the other way round, impose that some/all components are duplicated, e.g. for safety reasons.

Behavioral analysis, composition, and adaptation

Associating formal behavioral descriptions to components and connectors provides numerous benefits to the software architect [BER 03, POI 04, BEE 07]. Among these we may cite:

– *animation*. Using the operational semantics of behavioral descriptions, it is possible to *animate* the specifications of components and connectors. Further, when the ADL is compositional, the specification of whole configurations may be animated. Most process algebras come with animation tool facilities, which provide a basic prototype means for architectural descriptions;

– *checking behavioral equivalences, pre-orders, and refinement relations*. Checking equivalence relations between two components enables verification of whether one can replace the other. Sometimes, equivalence is too strong an assumption as the replacement component may do more than the replaced component without a problem. In such a case, a pre-order relation would be used. Finally, refinement relations, enable verification of whether some configuration is a correct implementation (or refinement in general) of a component. In ADLs, these relations are more particularly used to check whether components (their ports) fulfill the conditions specified in the connectors (their roles) they are bound to. Regarding Web service applications, a specific notion of equivalence which takes into account the direction of exchanged messages is used, namely *compatibility*;

– *checking behavioral properties*. Different kinds of properties can be checked against a component, connector, or configuration specification. These include deadlock freedom and availability properties. It is also possible to check that undesired properties are not satisfied (and, when it is the case, to get a counter example).

Rich interfaces including semantics foster *automatic composition*, where the issue is to retrieve configurations from available components (to be reused) and composition requests (to be fulfilled). This area has particularly been studied in the Web service domain [PEE 05, DUS 05, CHA 07, BER 10], but not only [MOR]. While components and services are often designed by different third-parties, they may present mismatch (e.g. deadlocks) which makes it impossible to reuse them. To complement analysis techniques enabling *problem detection*, there is the need for solutions for *problem solving*. This is the objective of *(behavioral) software adaptation* [CAN 06, SEG 08][5] which enables the building of new pieces of code, called *adaptors*, to proceed automatically. These act between mismatched components in a non-intrusive way, i.e. without changing their code but only by reordering, deconstructing, and reconstructing messages. Software adaptation can be related to controller synthesis (presented in Chapter 10) with the (important) difference that adaptation is able to perform message reordering and relabeling to avoid deadlocks. Depending on the context, an adaptor can be either seen as a kind of connector[6] dedicated to solving behavioral interoperability issues (mismatch), e.g. [BRA 05, CAN 08, TIV 08, AAL 09, SEG 10], or as

---

5. Software adaptation in this sense is following the seminal work by Yellin and Strom [YEL 97] and should not be confused with adaptive middleware [ada02] or architectural adaptation [ORE 08, KRA 09].

6. One should note that this does not prescribe the way the adaptor is implemented, in the middleware or as a standalone component.

a kind of component when adaptors are used to ensure some behavior from a set of components, e.g. for automatic service composition [MAT 08, POI 10].

Non-functional analysis

Beyond the behavioral information associated with components and connectors, and associated behavioral analysis, ADLs may support the analysis of quantitative or non-functional properties of architectures. The Wright ADL, presented in the next section, has been extended to take non-functional properties into account [VAN 05], but still no formal grounding (hence reasoning) is provided. The AEmilia [BER 02] ADL, built on top of a stochastic process algebra (EMPA) enables performance analysis of architectures. Finally, AADL, which is presented in the last section, has numerous possibilities for the specification of non-functional properties and their verification.

5.3. Formal ADLs

To present all formal ADLs in detail would be a long process; indeed the basic idea behind most formal ADLs is to enable the specification and verification of architectures for a given application domain (architectures from an abstract design perspective or closer to some implementation framework, e.g. Web services) or properties of interest (deadlock freedom, temporal properties, mobility, etc.). We focus in this section on two of the main approaches for the formal specification of architectures (i.e. formal ADLs): Wright and the approach that stems from the Darwin ADL. For more details (on other formal ADLs), we refer the reader to [BER 03, POI 04] for example.

5.3.1. *Wright*

The main objective of Wright [ALL 97a, ALL 97b] is the specification of software architectures together with the formal verification of behavioral properties or architectural styles. To achieve this goal, Wright is based on a language that can be translated into the CSP process algebra and on the FDR tool to undertake verification. Wright does not support code generation but simulation is possible using (and in the limits of) CSP and dedicated tools. One commonly referred to drawback of Wright is that it can be difficult to apprehend. However, this is the price you pay to benefit in an ADL from the expressiveness and verification means provided by a process algebra (here, CSP). While the examples we present here are simple, more complex and realistic architectures have been defined and verified using Wright [ALL 97b].

Connectors

A connector in Wright is defined as a set of roles together with a *glue*. Each role specifies the behavior that is expected from any port that will be bound to this role. The glue extends this (role-based) local specification by a global specification that prescribes how events occurring at different roles should synchronize or interleave, the possible sequences of these events, etc.

The behaviors are described in a syntax that is close to the CSP syntax, but where events are overlined when they are to be initiated by the object (role, glue) being defined. Operators include: $\rightarrow$ for prefixing, STOP for a void behavior (cannot do anything), $\sqrt{}$ for success (correct termination), § which is defined as $\sqrt{}\rightarrow$STOP, $\Box$ for external choice (the choice between branches is from the environment and the defined object has to follow it), and $\sqcap$ for non-deterministic internal choice (the choice is made by the object being defined; it is technically a way to model and if-then-else with an internal condition). Further, the notation enables modeling a reception event (ev?x), an emission event (ev!x), and parametrized behaviors ($P_v = \text{ev!v}.P_{v+1}$).

A remote procedure call (RPC) is a connector with two roles: one for the caller, performing a call and receiving a result, and one for the callee, receiving the call and returning a result. This may be defined in Wright as follows [ALL 97b]:

```
Connector RPC
  Role Caller = c̅a̅l̅l̅  →  return  →  Caller ⊓ §
  Role Callee  = call  →  r̅e̅t̅u̅r̅n̅  →  Callee □ §
  Glue = Caller.call  →  C̅a̅l̅l̅e̅e̅.̅c̅a̅l̅l̅  →  Glue
         □  Caller.return  →  C̅a̅l̅l̅e̅r̅.̅r̅e̅t̅u̅r̅n̅  →  Glue
         □  §
```

In this example note that one component can play two roles with reference to this connector: callee or caller. The caller has the decision to initiate the process or not (use of internal choice), while the callee proposes the procedure call option but it is others (here, the caller) that decide whether a call will take place or not. The glue part is used to specify temporal constraints over the two roles. For this, the glue relies on prefixing the events by the role it refers to (i.e. Caller.call refers to the call event in the Caller role). While roles correspond to local specifications, the glue is used to give a global semantics to the RPC connector.

Components

Similarly to connectors, components are defined by a formal specification of their ports and optionally by a description of the interactions between ports (*computation*).

In a client-server architecture, on top of RPC connectors, we also have two kinds of components: clients and servers. A client has a unique request port through which it outputs calls and gets results. In the same way, a server has a unique service port through which it gets calls and returns results. In Wright, we get [ALL 97b]:

```
Component Client
   Port Request = call‾ → return → Request ⊓ §
   Computation = Request.call‾ → Request.return → Computation ⊓ §
Component Server
   Port Service = call → return‾ → Service □ §
   Computation = Service.call → internal_computation
                  → Service.return‾ → Computation □ §
```

Configurations

Following the general definition of a configuration in an ADL presented earlier, a configuration in Wright is given as a set of (types of) components, a set of (types of) connectors, instances of these component and connector types and bindings between ports and roles.

Let us take the pipe-and-filter architecture presented in section 5.1 (simplified not to deal with errors). In Wright, this results in a configuration made up of three instances of one type of component, and two instances of one type of connector. Bindings relate the component ports to the connector roles.

```
Configuration DefinitionFinder
     Component Filter
       Port in = [...]
       Port out = [...]
       Computation = [...]
     Connector Pipe
       Role source = [...]
       Role sink = [...]
       Glue = [...]
  Instances
    grep:Filter
    cut:Filter
    sort:Filter
    p1:Pipe
    p2:Pipe
  Attachments
    grep.out as p1.source
    cut.in as p1.sink
    cut.out as p2.source
    sort.in as p2.sink
  End DefinitionFinder
```

Specific features

Wright enables the specification of composite components. The computation part of a components or the glue part of a connector can be defined using an architectural description, and bindings are used to connect the subcomponent ports to the composite port.

Suppose that we want to reuse our configuration that finds the definitions (see above) as a component, we can make a composite component from it as follows:

```
Component DefinitionFinderComponent
  Port in = [...]
  Port out = [...]
  Computation
      Configuration DefinitionFinder
      // see above
      End DefinitionFinder
      Bindings
        in = grep.in
        out = sort.out
  End Bindings
```

Wright also supports the definition of interface types that define generic patterns of interaction. These can be later on used in ports and roles [ALL 97b]:

```
Interface Type DataInput = [...]
Interface Type DataOutput = [...]
Component Filter
  Port in = DataInput
  Port out = DataOutput
  Computation = [...]
```

Architectural style constraints can also be specified in Wright. An example is the pipe-and-filter architectural style where only connectors are pipes and where components have only input or output data ports [ALL 97b]:

```
Style Pipe-and-Filter
    Interface Type DataInput = [...]
    Interface Type DataOutput = [...]
```

```
    Component Filter = [...]
    Connector Pipe = [...]
Constraints
    ∀ c:Connectors . Type(c) = Pipe
    ∧ ∀ c:Components; p:Port | p∈ Ports(c) . Type(p) = DataInput
    ∨ Type(p) = DataOutput
    ...
```

Wright also supports more advanced concepts such as data associated with events or parametrized components and connectors. We refer the reader to [ALL 97b] for more details. It should also be noted that Wright has been extended to take into account configuration dynamicity [ALL 98] or non-functional properties [VAN 05].

Verification

Wright supports the verification of software architectures using the transformation of definitions into the finite subset of the CSP process algebra (the number of processes has to be finite) and then the use of the FDR tool. Possible verifications in Wright include:

– for a component: consistency between the definition of its ports and its computation;

– for a connector: deadlock freedom (of the whole connector), deadlock freedom of a role;

– for a configuration (set of bound components and connectors): consistency between the definitions of bound ports-roles, respect of architectural style constraints;

– for an architectural style: consistency of its definition (bindings are consistent).

Some other verification techniques are unique to Wright (unique initiators for events, verification on the parameters, and the intervals used, etc.).

5.3.2. *Darwin and FSP*

Darwin [MAG 96] is an ADL mainly targeted at the description of (dynamic) configurations. While Wright is a text-only notation, Darwin presents both a textual and a graphical notation used in the software architect assistant tool. Darwin served as a basis for the development of Koala [OMM 00], which has been used in an industrial context.

Configurations in Darwin

Darwin supports dynamicity in the topology of architectural descriptions, such as adding/removing components or changing binding, which is increasingly required in new systems, such as ubiquitous service-based systems where the user is mobile. To support this feature, while the semantics of Wright has been given in a simple process algebra (CSP), the semantics for Darwin has been given in a more expressive process algebra, namely the π-calculus [MAG 95].

Let us take an example where n filters are serialized to achieve some composite component (Figure 5.3 was a simple example of this). In Darwin we get (combined from [MAG 95] and [MAG 96] [7]):

```
1  component filter {
2    provide in<stream char>;
3    require out<stream char>, err<stream char>;
4  };
5
6  component pipeline(char) {
7    provide input;
8    require output, error;
9    array F[n]:filter;
10   forall k:0..n-1 {
11     inst F[k]@k+1;
12     bind F[k].err -- error;
13     when k < n-1
14       bind F[k].out -- F[k+1].in;
15   }
16   bind
17     input -- F[0].in;
18     F[n-1].out -- output;
19 }
```

Listing 5.1: Components and configurations in DARWIN

As one may note, Darwin descriptions are at a lower description level than Wright (*e.g.*, with C/C++ types being used in configuration definitions). Indeed, Darwin relies on syntactic elements to relate to Regis [MAG 94], a framework, written in C++, enabling the construction and execution of distributed programs specified in Darwin. Thus, in the previous example, <stream char> denotes a port for character streams. Darwin allows components to be instantiated using the inst primitive (@ enabling to state on which machine). The dynamic binding between ports (of two components, or of a composite and one of its subcomponents) is achieved with the bind primitive. Finally, Darwin does not introduce explicit connectors (with reference to Figure 5.3,

---

7. The "inputs" of a component can be either considered as provided [MAG 96] or required [MAG 95] ports (conversely for the "outputs" and "errors"). Both interpretations are sensible as these inputs are provided by another component while usually corresponding to some operation that is provided by the component. We take the first interpretation here.

there are no "pipe" connectors in the example, above). Instead, Darwin relies on a pre-defined set of connectors between ports (hence they are bindings rather than connectors).

Component behaviors with FSP

The main objective of Darwin is implementation. However, the Darwin approach was extended in project TRACTA [GIA 99, MAG 99] to take into account the behavior of components thanks to labeled transition systems and, later on, using the FSP process algebra, a dialect of CSP. A Darwin architectural description, which is extended with FSP, may then been verified using the LTSA toolbox, a rich toolbox for the specification and verification of FSP.

Let us take again our RPC example and model it in FSP. Here, | corresponds to external choice, -> is prefixing/sequence, and @ enables the definition of a component external interface.

```
1 range T = 0..1
2 RPC = (caller.call[x:T]->callee.call[x]->RPC
3       |callee.return[x:T]->caller.return[x]->RPC
4       )@{caller.call,callee.call,
5           callee.return,caller.return}.
```
Listing 5.2: Component behavior in FSP

Note here the use of a "connector" component (see discussion in section 5.2). It is used to define complex connectors as Darwin has no explicit connector constructor. The specification of an architectural configuration consists of composing in parallel the components (including "connector" ones) using the concurrent (| |), renaming (/{new-name/old-name}), and hiding (\{hidden ports}) FSP operators [8]:

```
1 range T = 0..1
2
3 RPC = ... (see above)
4
5 CLIENT = (request[0]->response[x:T]->CLIENT).
6
7 SERVER = (query[x:T]->reply[(x+1)%2]->SERVER).
8
9 ||CLIENTSERVER = (caller : (CLIENT
10                               /{call/request, return/response})
11              || callee : (SERVER
```

---
14 ————————————

8. With reference to our example above, we have changed the names of the actions undertaken by caller and callee in order to demonstrate the use of renaming to enable correspondence between port names.

```
12                        /{call/query, return/reply})
13           || RPC)
15           \{ caller.call,caller.return,
16             callee.call,callee.return}.
```

Listing 5.3: Configuration behavior in FSP

Verification

Using the LTSA tool, the verification of FSP specifications is possible. FSP is an executable specification language. Hence, a first verification mean uses animation, where the designer can interact with the ports of architectural descriptions (configurations seen a composite components). This is particularly relevant for prototyping an architecture. LTSA also enables verification of whether an architecture is deadlock-free. In the case where it is not, a sequence of port interactions (event trace), called witness, is presented. Further, LTSA enables a particular automaton to be defined, called *property automaton*. This automaton enables legal traces (that one wants to find in the architecture) and illegal traces (that one wants to avoid) to be defined. The latter is achieved using ERROR states. The property automaton is composed in parallel with the automaton corresponding to the architectural description. Reachability analysis of ERROR states is used to ensure that illegal traces (ending in these states) are not possible. Trace equivalence can also be used to ensure that correct traces are present in the architecture. This technique enables safety and liveness properties to be checked. More recently, the techniques developed in the Darwin/FSP approach have been extended to take into account a specific architecture, Web services. Using the WS-Engineer toolbox [FOS 10],configurations where components are services can be analyzed. Similar to Wright, where it was possible for example to check configurations for port-role compatibility, it is possible to check whether services respect the role they play in a choreography (decentralized composite service specification). More generally, it is also possible to perform behavioral analysis (animation, equivalence checking, property verification) on service orchestrations.

5.3.3. *Synthesis*

By promoting an abstract architectural description level, formal ADLs enable the formal specification and the verification of architectural descriptions. They are mainly based on formal behavioral languages, more specifically process algebras such as the π-calculus, CSP, or FSP, due to their conciseness with reference to automata for example. These languages provide the ADLs with a rich and expressive framework for the description and verification of components, connectors, configurations, and styles. As a drawback, formal ADLs are often more complex to master and are sometimes considered to be too abstract when it comes to architectural descriptions close to implementation. We believe that recent applications of FSP to Web service architectures demonstrate that formal ADL are of real use in an implementation context too. However, in the next section, we will see more concrete ADLs that can complement the formal ADLs for lower-level architectural descriptions.

5.4. ADLs for actual implementation

In the previous section, we studied formal ADLs. We now present a few languages designed to help in the configuration or the generation of executable systems. They are based on the definition and composition of components, and rely on a run-time that allows the execution of the described architecture. We first outline dedicated languages, then study AADL in more detail, as it provides a very interesting approach. We finish with some considerations about UML.

5.4.1. *Specific ADLs*

Some ADLs are specific to a given execution platform; they are used as configuration languages for this platform. In this section, we present a brief overview of some of them.

ArchJava

ArchJava [ALD 01] is an extension of the Java programming language which is meant to associate architectural information with source code. The architecture information is thus bound to the functional description.

ArchJava adds notions of components and ports to structure applications: each component defines ports; these ports consist of interfaces that provide or require methods or variables. ArchJava thus allows the construction of applications by connecting component ports. It eases the design of applications. As it is associated with Java, it cannot be used to integrate components written using other programming languages. The main benefit of this approach is that it is rather easy to use.

Fractal ADL

Fractal [BRU 04b, BRU 04a] defines a way of creating component assemblies; it is defined by the ObjectWeb consortium. It is based on the notion of containers that encapsulate component code. Fractal consists of descriptions of assemblies of application components that allow reconfiguration (i.e. dynamic evolution of component assemblies). Such assemblies can be described using a specialized language.

Fractal consists of a run-time and an application programming interface (API) for different languages. In addition to these elements, there is a configuration language. Fractal does not define a concrete syntax for the configuration language: Fractal is a set of concepts rather than an actual language.

SOFA

SOFA [PLÁ 98] is an architecture that targets the assembly of reusable components while allowing their dynamic evolution. SOFA provides a component definition language (CDL) to describe components, interfaces, connectors, etc. Components are deployed in *SOFAnodes*. These SOFAnodes are assembled within a canvas, called a *SOFAnet*. The active components are associated with an execution environment called DCUP (Dynamic Component UPdating) that provides an environment to each SOFAnode.

DCUP enables the separation of the functional part and the command part. On each node, the command part can update the component, controls its execution, and manages the interface between the component and the other nodes.

Synthesis

Fractal, ArchJava, and SOFA are actually frameworks to build applications. They rely on a given run-time environment, either generic (a Java virtual machine for ArchJava) or specific (for SOFA and Fractal).

These configuration languages rely on the concepts of ADLs. In all situations, the application design relies on an assembly of components, specified using an associated ADL. The dedicated ADL describes the interfaces of the components and their connections. Connectors are not systematically involved: SOFA has the notion of connector, but ArchJava does not, as it is close to programming languages; communications in Fractal are implemented by components.

5.4.2. *AADL*

The AADL) comes from studies carried out by the Society of Automotive Engineers (SAE). It is an evolution of an older ADL called MetaH [FEI 00]. The first version of AADL was issued in 2004 [SAE04], and has matured to provide a second version in 2009 [SAE09b]. The core language is now stable; work now focuses on annexes. AADL is explicitly targeted at the description of embedded real-time systems. Its initial scope was avionics and space, but it now attracts attention from other domains.

The AADL standard defines several syntaxes: a textual syntax and a graphical syntax. An annex of the MARTE standard also exists for AADL v1[Car 10, OMG 10a]. The AADL is also defined as a meta-model. The AADL was designed to ease the interoperability between different tools; which is why the reference syntax is the textual one, which is similar to a programming language. The graphical notation can be used as a complement to ease the representation of architectures, as it provides more understandable descriptions, using less information.

AADL implements the usual ADL concepts: components, interfaces, connectors, but, some of them are more developed than others. Here we describe the main aspects of the language–we do not intend to provide a comprehensive description of the language. We will use the textual syntax, as it is the more convenient. We illustrate the different aspects of the language with examples to show an iterative way to define a simple system made of a pressure sensor connected to a processor.

Components

An AADL model consists of a hierarchy of components connected to one another. An AADL description is the declaration of these components. AADL introduces a distinction between the specifications of a component and its realization: each component has an interface (named *component type*), which corresponds to zero, one of several implementations (*component implementation*). The AADL defines several categories of components.

Software components define the application part of an architecture; there are six categories of software components. *Threads* correspond to active software elements. They correspond to system threads of operating systems. *Thread groups* are used to gather threads in order to create hierarchies or thread pools. *Processes* are memory partitions in which threads execute; a process must contain at least one thread. *Data* correspond to data structures that may be stored or exchanged between components. *Subprograms* model programming language procedures; they do not have return types, but can have in and/or out parameters. *Subprogram groups* can be used to represent libraries as sets of functionalities.

Platform components represent the hardware elements; there are six categories of platform components. *Processors* represent the combination of microprocessors and schedulers; they thus model processors with a minimalistic operating system. *Virtual processors* represent logical resources in which processes can be deployed; they can be used to support partitioned operating systems. *Memories* represent storage devices in general: hard disks, RAM, etc. *Devices* model elements, the internal structure of which is ignored at the level of the AADL model; they can typically be sensors with only interface and external characteristics being specified. *Buses* model networks and buses in general, ranging from a simple serial cable to the Internet. Buses must be connected to processors, memories, and devices to carry communications between these components. *Virtual buses* are used to model logical network flows; for example an Internet wire can be modeled by a bus, and the TCP/IP protocol can be modeled by a virtual bus.

Besides software and platform components, the AADL standard defines *system* components, which do not correspond to actual entities; they are used to create logical hierarchies. For example, the central unit of a computer can be modeled as a system that contains a processor, a memory and a bus between them. In addition, *abstract*

```
1  thread execution_thread
2  end execution_thread;
3
4  thread implementation execution_thread.impl
5  calls
6    {call1 : subprogram a_procedure;}};
7  end execution_thread.impl;
8
9  subprogram a_procedure
10 end a_procedure;
11
12 process program
13 end program;
14
15 process implementation program.mono_thread
16 subcomponents
17   thr1 : thread;
18 end program.mono_thread;
19
20 process implementation program.mono_thread2 extends program.mono_threa
21 subcomponents
22   thr1 : refined to thread execution_thread.impl;
23 end program.mono_thread2;
```

Listing 5.4: Component types and implementations in AADL

components are defined; they have no semantics at all, and are meant to be refined into one of the other component categories. Abstract components can be used in the early steps of architecture design.

A component type defines the interface of a component while a component implementation describes its internal structure. Component implementation thus always refers to an existing component type. No declaration order is required: an implementation can be declared before the type it corresponds to. Listing 5.4 illustrates the relationship between types and implementations. A component declaration (type or implementation) can be extended to add or refine elements.

Component implementations can have *subclauses*, as shown in listing 5.4. A component implementation can contain subcomponents. A subcomponent is an instance of a component declaration (either component type or implementation). This way, an AADL architecture is a set of components contained one in another, creating a tree. The declaration of a subcomponent must be associated with a component category, and possibly with a type or an implementation, depending on the accuracy of the model.

Subprogram calls model calls to procedures in imperative programming languages. They are organized into *call sequences* within subprograms or threads. Though the syntax is similar to that used for subcomponents, the call of a subprogram is not an instance of this subprogram (as in programming languages).

Interfaces and connectors

AADL does not have a complete notion of connector, as communication media are not separate from components. The communication semantics is carried by the elements of the component interfaces.

Interface elements (*features*) of a component are declared in its type, as shown in listing 5.5. Thus, each implementation of a component type offers the same interface to other components; the different implementations can thus be interchanged. There are several types of features.

Ports correspond to communication interfaces between components. They are declared as input, output, or input/output ports. *Event ports* transmit a signal. They can be compared to signals of operating systems. They can trigger the execution of an AADL thread. *Data ports* transmit data. Unlike event ports, they do not trigger anything upon reception; they can thus model a memory register that is updated in an asynchronous way. *Event data ports* are a synthesis of the two other port kinds: they transmit data and threads are notified upon reception; they can be used to model message-based communications. Subprograms do not have ports; they have parameters. Subprogram parameters have the same semantics as data ports or event data ports.

There are four kinds of subcomponent access: for bus, for data, for subprograms, and subprogram groups. In all cases, they are declared as *provided* or *required*. In the case of a data component, an access is used to share the data; a bus access is used to connect processors, devices, or memories. A subprogram accesses model remote procedure calls. A subprogram can be direct features of a thread type. This is equivalent to a provided access to a subprogram that would be part of the thread. Accesses to subprogram groups correspond to shared libraries, and thus do not completely correspond to a communication model.

AADL defines the notion of *feature groups*, that gather several features into one structure. This allows the connection of several features without having to deal with all of them separately. For example, all the pins of a parallel cable could be modeled by event ports gathered within a feature group. This can also be used to gather a set of subprogram accesses.

```
 1 data pressure_information
 2 properties
 3   Data_Model::Data_Representation => Integer;
 4   Data_Model::Number_Representation => Unsigned;
 5   Source_Data_Size => 2 Bytes;
 6 end pressure_information;
 7
 8 thread mean_pressure_processing
 9 features
10   input : in event data port pressure_information;
11   output : out data port pressure_information;
12   mean : requires data access pressure_information;
13 end mean_pressure_processing;
14
15 process pressure_processing
16 features
17   input : in event data port pressure_information;
18   output : out data port pressure_information;
19 end pressure_processing;
20
21 process implementation pressure_processing.mono_thread
22 subcomponents
23   thr1 : thread execution_thread.impl;
24   mean : data pressure_information;
25 connections
26   event data port input -> thr1.input;
27   data access mean -> thr1.mean;
28   data port thr1.output -> output;
29 end pressure_processing.mono_thread;
```
Listing 5.5: Features and connections in AADL

Connections are used to connect the features of the subcomponents, either to the features of other subcomponents or to the features of the parent component in which the subcomponents are declared. Listing 5.5 illustrates connections of features in process implementation pressure_processing.mono_thread.

Structuring declarations

In order to structure declarations, AADL provides the notion of name space (see listing 5.7). The anonymous name space is the default name space; it can contain *packages*, which are called name spaces. They have a public part, and possibly a private part. Declarations in the public part can be referenced from the outside of a package, while declarations in the private part are only seen inside the package.

Though the naming system of the AADL packages can simulate a hierarchy, packages cannot contain other packages. Packages can be used to gather AADL declarations to create logical sets of declarations, the same way Java packages or C++ name spaces. Packages are used to structure AADL declarations while systems are used to structure AADL architectures.

Support for architecture reconfiguration and analysis

AADL architectures are completely defined at the design stage: for example, it is not possible to declare components with an undetermined number of subcomponents (that would be created at run-time), or to have undefined connections (here again, that would be managed at run-time). However, the language is not restricted to completely static architectures: *modes* are used to introduce a certain dynamism in architectures. They are defined within component implementations and correspond to execution configurations to which subcomponents, connections, etc. can be associated. Conditions of mode switching are also described, so that it is possible to define a state machine in the component implementation. An example of mode definition is provided in listing 5.7, in the implementation machine.i. We defined two modes, mono and dual, that affect the connections of the process connections. Connection cnx1 is always active, while cnx2, cnx3, and cnx4 are active or inactive, depending on the current execution mode. Modes are switched upon reception of signal switch.

An AADL description is based on a hierarchy of subcomponents connected with one another; the transmission of data is managed through point-to-point connections. In order to ease the analysis of architectures, AADL defines the notion of *flow*. Flows are carried by connections and allow the description of logical flows of data across the whole architecture.

Characterization of AADL entities using properties and annexes

Properties are a key aspect of AADL. They are used to specify characteristics of AADL elements; it is thus possible to describe constraints that apply to architectures. For example, properties are used to specify the execution time of a subprogram, the period of a thread, the queuing protocol to be used for an event data port, etc. An AADL property is defined by a name, a type, the list of elements on which it can be applied, and possibly a default value (see listing 5.6). Properties are declared in *property sets*, which are similar to packages. Sets of standard AADL properties are defined, with associated semantics. These standard properties are to be recognized the same way by all tools. There are three kinds of properties: property types, constants and property names.

```
1  property set User is
2    Compiler : aadlstring => "gcc" applies to (subprogram, thread);
3    Pressure : type units (Pa, hPa => Pa * 100);
4    Pressure_Range : range of Pressure applies to (device);
```

```
5   Version : aadlinteger applies to (all);
6 end User;
```

Listing 5.6: Property declarations

Property associations assign a value to a given property, i.e. associate a value with a property name. Property associations can be used in three situations: they can be declared in a package, in the `properties` section of a component, or be directly associated with a subclause.

If a property association is declared in a package, it applies to all the components declared in this package that are specified in the `applies to` clause of the property declaration. If it is declared within a component, it applies to this component, unless it is used with the keyword `applies to`; in this case, the property applies to the element designated by the `applies to` statement. If a property association is declared at the level of a subclause of a component, it applies to this subclause. If the keyword `applies to` is used, the property applies to the subclause of the component referenced by the `applies to` statement. It is exactly the same mechanism, but applied to a subclause instead of a component declaration.

Listing 5.7 illustrates the use of property associations. We specify the range for the propagation delay of the AADL bus `network` using a standard property. We use standard property `actual_processor_binding` to bind processes `prog1` and `prog2` to processor `comp1`. We also use `pressure_range` and `version` that we defined in listing 5.6. Properties are also used in listing 5.5 to define the semantics of data type `pressure_information`; these properties are defined in the data modeling annex of the AADL standard [SAE09a].

```
1 package Hardware
2 public
3   processor computer
4   features
5     net : requires bus access network;
6   end computer;
7
8   bus network
9   properties
10     propagation_delay => 1 ns .. 2 ms;
11   end network;
12 end Hardware;
13
14 device pressure_sensor
15 features
16   net : requires bus access Hardware::network;
```

```
17   pres : out event data port pressure_information;
18 properties
19   User::pressure_range => 10 Pa .. 2000 hPa;
20 end pressure_sensor;
21
22 system machine
23 features
24   net : requires bus access Hardware::network;
25   pres_in : in event data port pressure_information;
26   pres_out : out data port pressure_information;
27   switch : in event port;
28 end machine;
29
30 system implementation machine.i
31 subcomponents
32   prog1 : process pressure_processing {User::version => 1;};
33   prog2 : process pressure_processing {User::version => 2;};
34   comp1 : processor computer;
35 connections
36   cnx1 : event data port pres_in -> prog1.input;
37   cnx2 : event data port pres_in -> prog2.input in modes (dual);
38   cnx3 : data port prog1.output -> pres_out in modes (mono);
39   cnx4 : data port prog2.output -> pres_out in modes (dual);
40 modes
41   mono : initial mode;
42   dual : mode;
43   mono -[ switch ]-> dual;
44   dual -[ switch ]-> mono;
45 properties
46   actual_processor_binding => reference comp1 applies to prog1;
47   actual_processor_binding => reference comp1 applies to prog2;
48 end machine.i;
```

Listing 5.7: Packages

Annexes are another way to associate information with the element of a description. They allow the insertion of information written in an arbitrary syntax at the level of a component declaration. An annex can be used to specify the behavior of a component or to specify constraints.

Annexes and properties are used to add information within architecture descriptions. Annexes only apply to components, while properties can be associated with all AADL elements: components, connections, features, etc. Annexes allow the integration of elements written in syntax that is different from the AADL syntax, thus easing their processing by existing tools. Properties are more integrated to the AADL syntax, and thus more suitable to specify architecture characteristics.

Exploiting AADL models

An AADL model consists of a list of declarations; subcomponents correspond to instances of component declarations. In order to create the architectural description itself, it is necessary to instantiate the different declarations, and thus obtain a tree structure of instantiated components. To do so, a top-level component that will be the root of the tree must be defined. This component must be a system without an interface, as it describes the whole architecture. Such a system is represented in listing 5.8. We declare a system without any features, called global. The implementation of this system contains all the elements of the architecture and the connections between their features.

```
 1 system global
 2 end global;
 3
 4 device console
 5 features
 6   pres : in data port pressure_information;
 7 end console;
 8
 9 device switcher
10 features
11   switch : out event port;
12 end switcher;
13
14 system implementation global.i
15 subcomponents
16   capt : device Hardware::pressure_sensor;
17   calc : system machine.impl;
18   net : bus Hardware::network;
19   switcher1 : device switcher;
20   console1 : device console;
21 connections
22   bus access net -> capt.net;
23   bus access net -> calc.net;
24   dat_cnx : event data port capt.pres -> calc.pres_in;
25   data port calc.pres_out -> console1.pres;
26   basc : event port switcher1.switch -> calc.switch;
27 properties
28   Actual_Connection_Binding => reference net applies to dat_cnx;
29   Actual_Connection_Binding => reference net applies to basc;
```

30 `end global.i;`

Listing 5.8: A global AADL system

AADL models focus on the deployment and allocation of software resources to an execution environment (mainly a hardware topology). Thus it is a good support for code generation, analysis, etc.

Each component and feature category has its own semantics, which defines legality rules with respect to what kind of subcomponent can be nested within a given component kind, what kinds of features a component type can have, etc. AADL thus provides a wide range of possibilities to describe consistent architectures, without ambiguity.

AADL models are based on a single architectural representation (with possibly several syntaxes) of applications. Some aspects, such as behavior modeling of components, are not directly in the scope of AADL. Properties and annexes can be used to associate behavior information with components, whether by specifying source code files or by providing more formal specification. It is thus useless to specify the size of the source code if we just want to perform schedulability analysis: we will just have to specify execution time, thread periods, etc. using properties. Similarly, it is not necessary to specify the types of the subcomponents: only their categories can be sufficient. It is then easy to describe the deployment of an architecture distributed on several nodes. In addition, the AADL syntax allows for flexibility: it is not necessary to provide all the details of an architecture to process it. Declarations of features, subcomponents, and subprogram calls are generally associated with component declarations. However, it is possible to specify only the category of a subcomponent, feature or subprogram. In this case, the description is valid, though inaccurate. It is thus possible to easily describe an architecture in the first stages of design, with different level of accuracy.

Because it can gather in a single representation all the necessary information to describe architectures, AADL can be used as a central language for a design and generation process: it is possible to use different tools to test schedulability, ensure that memory constraints are met, process the behavior descriptions to simulate the application, and finally, generate the application code. AADL can be used as a support for a design approach based on prototyping [VER 05], illustrated in Figure 5.5. The first step consists of modeling an abstract architecture, which is then refined to obtain a low-level, accurate model. At each step of the refinement process, we can check the theoretical validity of the architecture by simulation or verification of the properties. These different steps lead to a complete description of the application, which can be processed to generate code in order to validate the deployment. Tests can then be performed and depending on the results, the model can be modified.

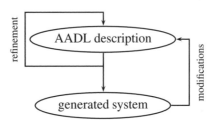

Figure 5.5. *Design process with AADL*

The generation of an executable system from its architectural description requires the use of a run-time that will support the execution of the code [VER 06]. The run-time will support the execution of the code generated from the AADL component descriptions; this component code encapsulates the functional code that was specified either using properties or annexes. Thus, the functional code is isolated from the run-time and the actual deployment issues.

Several strategies can be applied: either using a run-time based on a communication middleware (thus providing high-level communication APIs to the generated code) or relying on a minimalistic run-time based on a system thread library (thus delegating the management of communications to the generated code). Using a communication middleware eases the management of data exchange between the different nodes and requires less code generation. This approach allows an executable prototype of the application to be obtained relatively quickly; it is suitable for the first steps of the process. Using a minimalistic implies the description of the communication mechanisms in AADL: the communication mechanisms are then to be represented by a set of AADL components in the architecture. In this later case, the application designer has more work, but the description is more accurate, and more precise analysis can be performed.

5.4.3. *UML*

The UML is an OMG standard [OMG 10b]. It is designed to address as many of the modeling aspects as possible, thus aiming to be universal.

In version 2.0, the UML defines 11 syntaxes; each of which corresponds to a type of diagram. Class diagrams are well known; they are used to describe the organization of the application elements and are related to object-oriented programming languages. Package diagrams are used to structure entities into logical sets and represent dependencies between these sets. Object diagrams describe class instances. Component diagrams are at a higher level: components have ports through which they can communicate. Components can provide or require interfaces, while classes only implement (and thus provide) interfaces. Deployment diagrams describe how application elements can be installed as libraries. They can be used to represent hardware nodes on which software elements will be installed.

Composite structure diagrams describe the internal structure of a class or component and the relationships (i.e. connections) between its contained elements. They can be used as a syntactical support for architecture description languages.

Other diagrams are mostly used to describe behavior. Sequence diagrams, activity diagrams, interaction overview diagrams, and timing diagrams are used to represent the communications between the different architecture entities. State machine diagrams represent automata and thus model the evolution of the states of an entity. Use case diagrams represent roles of entities in various scenarios.

The entire UML is not an ADL, as most of the UML diagrams are not in the scope of an ADL (for example, use case diagrams, sequence diagrams, etc.). Yet, the UML can be used as an ADL: composite structure diagrams represent architectures; the other parts of UML can be used to complement this ADL aspect.

Refinement of the UML using profiles

The UML defines a set of syntaxes that can be used to describe applications. As the concept of UML is to be as general as possible, the UML in itself is often not sufficiently accurate; it is meant to be refined to fit particular modeling semantics needs. Such refinements are called *profiles*. For example, the profile for scheduling, performance and time (SPT) defines notions of quality of service associated with real-time systems (response time, queue sizes, etc.).

The MARTE [OMG 10a] also covers the embedded aspects. It integrates most of the concepts of AADL; a part of the MARTE standard describes how to model AADL architectures using the MARTE profile. Due to its versatility, the UML syntax can be used as an alternative notation for existing ADLs.

5.4.4. *Synthesis*

ADLs that target actual system implementation can take different forms. Some are associated with a specific platform (e.g. Fractal ADL). Others rely on run-time specifications, but are more general: AADL defines a precise run-time semantics, but can be used without any run-time implementation (for analysis, for example). UML covers a much wider range of usages; a part of it can be used as an ADL syntax, together with other aspects, such as behavior.

5.5. Conclusion

ADLs have now proven to be efficient solutions to cope with the complexity of systems. They can be used to support top-down analysis by allowing the decomposition of a system into inter-connected subcomponents; they can also support bottom-up analysis by allowing the reuse and combination of already existing components to create a higher-level system.

ADL reached maturity by the end of 1990s with so-called "first-generation ADLs". Such languages were developed by the academic community, and they focused on formal aspects of architecture description. The concepts involved in these languages are often simple and restricted to a small set; yet, they can support very powerful and relevant analysis. In the 2000s, new ADLs were developed with the aim of being used in industry. Some of these languages rely on an existing and well-accepted syntax (e.g. UML); others define new notations that are more adapted to the concepts of a given application domain (e.g. AADL).

Some ADLs cover a small scope, and thus ease the analysis, but are too abstract to generate code easily. Others are more expressive and close to actual implementation, and thus ease code generation, but are so complex that analysis is difficult. A good compromise would be to be able to create a link between these ADLs.

The model driven architecture (MDA) approach consists of refining abstract and formal architecture configurations into other architecture configurations of a lower level. This could help solve the ADL duality problem. Industrial approaches, based on AADL or UML/MARTE, try to enrich industrial ADLs with the advantages of academic ADLs. These methods could also bring solutions.

5.6. Bibliography

[AAL 09] VAN DER AALST W., MOOIJ A., STAHL C., WOLF K., "*Proc. of the 9th International School on Formal Methods for the Design of Computer, Communications and Software Systems: Web Services (SFM)*", vol. 5569 of *Lecture Notes in Computer Science*, Chapter Service interaction: patterns, formalization, and analysis, Springer, 2009.

[ABL 10] ABLE GROUP, "The Acme architectural description language and design environment", http://www.cs.cmu.edu/ acme/, 2010.

[ada02] "Special issue on adaptive middleware", *Communications of the ACM*, vol. 45, p. 30–64, 2002.

[ALD 01] ALDRICH J., CHAMBERS C., NOTKIN D., "Component-oriented programming in ArchJava", *OOPSLA'01*, 2001.

[ALL 97a] ALLEN R. J., GARLAN D., "A formal basis for architectural connection", *ACM Transactions on Software Engineering and Methodology*, vol. 6, p. 213–249, 1997.

[ALL 97b] ALLEN R. J., A formal approach to software architecture, PhD thesis, Carnegie Mellon University, 1997.

[ALL 98] ALLEN R., DOUENCE R., GARLAN D., "Specifying and analyzing dynamic software architectures", *Proc. of the International Conference on Fundamental Approaches to Software Engineering (FASE)*, vol. 1382 of *Lecture Notes in Computer Science*, Springer, p. 21–37, 1998.

[BAR 09] BARROS T., AMEUR-BOULIFA R., CANSADO A., HENRIO L., MADELAINE E., "Behavioural models for distributed Fractal components", *Annales des Télécommunications*, vol. 64, p. 25–43, 2009.

[BEE 07] TER BEEK M., BUCCHIARONE A., GNESI S., "Formal methods for service composition", *Annals of Mathematics, Computing & Teleinformatics*, vol. 1, p. 1–10, 2007.

[BEN07] BEN MOKHTAR S., GEORGANTAS N., ISSARNY V., "COCOA: conversation-based service composition in pervasive computing environments with QoS support", *Journal of Systems and Software*, vol. 80, p. 1941–1955, 2007.

[BER 02] BERNARDO M., DONATIELLO L., CIANCARINI P., *"Performance Evaluation of Complex Systems: Techniques and Tools"*, vol. 2459 of *Lecture Notes in Computer Science*, Chapter Stochastic process algebra: From an algebraic formalism to an architectural description lamguage, p. 236–260, Springer, 2002.

[BER 03] BERNARDO M., INVERARDI P., Eds., *Formal Methods for Software Architectures*, vol. 2804 of *Lecture Notes in Computer Science*, Springer Verlag, 2003.

[BER 10] BERTOLI P., PISTORE M., TRAVERSO P., "Automated composition of web services via planning in asynchronous domains", *Artificial Intelligence*, vol. 174, p. 316–361, 2010.

[BRA 05] BRACCIALI A., BROGI A., CANAL C., "A formal approach to component adaptation", *Journal of Systems and Software*, vol. 74, p. 45–54, 2005.

[BRU 04a] BRUNETON E., Developing with Fractal, Consortium ObjectWeb, 2004.

[BRU 04b] BRUNETON E., T. C., J.-B. S., The Fractal component model, Consortium ObjectWeb, 2004.

[CAN 06] CANAL C., MURILLO J. M., POIZAT P., "Software adaptation", *L'Objet*, vol. 12, p. 9–31, 2006.

[CAN 08] CANAL C., POIZAT P., SALAÜN G., "Model-based adaptation of behavioural mismatching components", *IEEE Transactions on Software Engineering*, vol. 34, p. 546–563, 2008.

[CAR10] CARNEGIE MELLON UNIVERSITY, "AADL predictable model-based engineering", http://www.aadl.info, 2010.

[CHA 07] CHAN K., BISHOP J., BARESI L., Survey and comparison of planning techniques for web service composition, Report , University of Pretoria, Department of Computer Science, 2007.

[DAH 66] DAHL O.-J., NYGAARD K., "SIMULA— an ALGOL-based simulation language", *Communications of the ACM*, vol. 9, p. 671–678, 1966.

[DAS 01] DASHOFY E. M., VAN DER HOEK A., N. T. R., "A highly-extensible, XML-based architecture description language", *Working IEEE / IFIP Conference on Software Architecture (WICSA)*, IEEE Computer Society, p. 103–112, 2001.

[DER 75] DE REMER F., KRON H., "Programming-in-the large versus programming-in-the-small", *International Conference on Reliable Software*, p. 114–121, 1975.

[DUS 05] DUSTDAR S. S. W., "A survey on web services composition", *International Journal of Web and Grid Services*, vol. 1, p. 1–30, 2005.

[FEI 00] FEILER P. H., LEWIS B., VESTAL S., Improving predictability in embedded real-time systems, Report num. CMU/SEI-2000-SR-011, Carnegie Mellon University, December 2000, http://la.sei.cmu.edu/publications.

[FIL 05] FILMAN R. E., ELRAD T., CLARKE S., AKŞIT M., Eds., *Aspect-oriented Software Development*, Addison-Wesley, 2005.

[FOS 10] FOSTER H., UCHITEL S., MAGEE J., KRAMER J., "An integrated workbench for model-based engineering of service compositions", *IEEE Transactions on Services Computing*, vol. 3, p. 131–144, 2010.

[GAR 93] GARLAN D., SHAW M., "*Advances in software Engineering and Knowledge Engineering*", vol. 2 of *Series on software engineering and knowledge engineering*, Chapter An introduction to software architecture, p. 1–39, World Scientific Publishing, 1993.

[GIA 99] GIANNAKOPOULOU D., KRAMER J., CHEUNG S., "Behaviour analysis of distributed systems using the Tracta approach", *Journal of Automated Software Engineering*, vol. 6, p. 7–35, 1999.

[HAD 07] HADDAD S., POIZAT P., "Transactional reduction of component compositions", *Proc. of FORTE*, p. 341–357, 2007.

[KRA 09] KRAMER J., MAGEE J., "A rigorous architectural approach to adaptive software engineering", *Journal of Computer Science and Technology*, vol. 24, p. 183–188, 2009.

[MAG 94] MAGEE J., DULAY N., KRAMER J., "Regis: a constructive development environment for distributed programs", *Distributed Systems Engineering*, vol. 1, p. 304–312, 1994.

[MAG 95] MAGEE J., DULAY N., EISENBACH S., KRAMER J., "Specifying distributed software architectures", *European Software Engineering Conference (ESEC)*, vol. 989 of *Lecture Notes in Computer Science*, Springer Verlag, p. 137–153, 1995.

[MAG 96] MAGEE J., KRAMER J., "Dynamic structure in software architectures", *ACM SIGSOFT Symposium on the Foundations of Software Engineering (FSE)*, p. 3–14, 1996.

[MAG 99] MAGEE J., KRAMER J., GIANNAKOPOULOU D., "Behaviour analysis of software architectures", *First Working IFIP Conference on Software Architecture (WICSA)*, IFIP Conference Proceedings, Kluwer, p. 35–50, 1999.

[MAT 08] MATEESCU R., POIZAT P., SALAÜN G., "Adaptation of service protocols using process algebra and on-the-fly reduction techniques", *International Conference on Service Oriented Computing (ICSOC)*, vol. 5364 of *Lecture Notes in Computer Science*, Springer, p. 84–99, 2008.

[MED 00] MEDVIDOVIC N., TAYLOR R. R., "A classification and comparison framework for software architecture description languages", *IEEE Transactions on Software Engineering*, vol. 26, p. 70–93, 2000.

[MED 02] MEDVIDOVIC N., ROSENBLUM D. S., REDMILES D. F., ROBBNS J. E., "Modeling software architectures in the unified modeling language", *ACM Transactions on Software Engineering and Methodology*, vol. 11, p. 2–57, 2002.

[MED 10] MEDVIDOVIC N., EDWARDS G., "Software architecture and mobility: a roadmap", *Journal of Systems and Software*, vol. 83, p. 885–898, 2010.

[MEY 97] MEYER B., *Object-oriented Software Construction*, Prentice Hall, 1997.

[MOR] MOREL B., ALEXANDER P., "SPARTACAS automating component reuse and adaptation".

[OAS07] OASIS, Web services business process execution language Version 2.0, 2007, http://docs.oasis-open.org/wsbpel/2.0/OS/wsbpel-v2.0-OS.html.

[OMG 10a] OMG, "The UML Profile for MARTE: modeling and analysis of real-time and embedded systems", http://www.omgmarte.org, 2010.

[OMG 10b] OMG, "Unified modeling language", http://www.uml.org, 2010.

[OMM 00] OMMERING R., LINDEN F., KRAMER J., MAGEE J., "The Koala component model for consumer electronics software", *IEEE Computer*, vol. 33, p. 78–85, 2000.

[OPE07] OPEN   SOA,   "Service   component   architecture   home", http://osoa.org/display/Main/Service+Component+Architecture+Home, 2007.

[ORE 08] OREIZY P., MEDVIDOVIC N., R.N. T., "Runtime software adaptation: framework, approaches, and styles", *ICSE Companion*, p. 899-910, 2008.

[OXF10] OXFORD UNIVERSITY PRESS,   "Oxford dictionaries online", http://oxforddictionaries.com/, 2010.

[PAP 03] PAPAZOGLOU M. P., GEORGAKOPOULOS D., "Introduction", *Communications of the ACM*, vol. 46, p. 24–28, 2003.

[PAR 72] PARNAS D. L., "On the criteria to be used in decomposing systems into modules", *Communications of the ACM*, vol. 15, p. 1053–1058, 1972.

[PEE 05] PEER J., Web service composition as AI planning – a survey, Report , University of St. Gallen, 2005.

[PER 92] PERRY D. E., WOLF A. L., "Foundations for the study of software architectures", *ACM SIGSOFT Software Engineering Notes*, vol. 17, p. 40–52, 1992.

[PLÁ 98] PLÁŠIL F., BÁLEK D., JANEČEK R., "SOFA/DCUP: architecture for component trading and dynamic updating", *ICCDS'98*, IEEE, 1998.

[PLÁ 02] PLÁŠIL F., VISNOVSKY S., "Behavior protocols for software components", *IEEE Transactions on Software Engineering*, vol. 28, p. 1056–1076, 2002.

[POH 05] POHL K., BÖCKLE G., VAN DER LINDEN F. J., Eds., *Software Product Line Engineering. Foundations, Principles and Techniques*, Springer, 2005.

[POI 04] POIZAT P., ROYER J.-C., SALAÜN G., "Formal methods for component description, coordination and adaptation", *First International Workshop on Coordination and Adaptation Techniques for Software Entities (WCAT)*, p. 89–100, 2004.

[POI 06] POIZAT P., ROYER J.-C., "A formal architectural description language based on symbolic transition systems and modal logic", *Journal of Universal Computer Science (J.UCS)*, vol. 12, p. 1741–1782, 2006.

[POI 10] POIZAT P., YAN Y., "Adaptive composition of conversational services through graph planning encoding", *International Symposium on Leveraging Applications of Formal Methods, Verification, and Validation (ISoLA), part II*, vol. 6416 of *Lecture Notes in Computer Science*, Springer, p. 35–50, 2010.

[SAE04] SAE, Architecture analysis & design language (AADL), 2004.

[SAE09a] SAE, AADL v2 Data modeling annex document, 2009.

[SAE09b] SAE, Architecture analysis & design language (AADL), version 2, 2009.

[SEG 08] SEGUEL R., ESHUIS R., GREFEN P., An overview on protocol adaptors for service component integration, BETA Working Paper Series num. WP 265, Eindhoven University of Technology, 2008.

[SEG 10] SEGUEL R., ESHUIS R., GREFEN P., "Generating minimal protocol adaptors for loosely coupled services", *International Conference on Web Services*, p. 417–424, 2010.

[SZY 98] SZYPERSKI C., *Component Software: Beyond Object-oriented Programming*, Addison-Wesley, 1998.

[TIV 08] TIVOLI M., INVERARDI P., "Failure-free coordinators synthesis for component-based architectures", *Science of Computer Programming*, vol. 71, p. 181–212, 2008.

[TOÖ] TOÖRMÄ S., VILLSTEDT J., LEHTINEN V., OLIVER I., LUUKKALA V., Semantic Web services – a survey, Report .

[VAN 05] VAN EENOO C., HYLOOZ O., KHAN K. M., "Addressing non-functional properties in software architecture using ADL", *Proc. of the 6th Australian Workshop on Software Architectures (AWSA'05)*, 2005.

[VER 05] VERGNAUD T., PAUTET L., KORDON F., HUGUES J., "Rapid development methodology for customized middleware", *RSP'05*, IEEE, 2005.

[VER 06] VERGNAUD T., ZALILA B., Ocarina, a compiler for the AADL, http://ocarina.enst.fr, 2006.

[W3C01] W3C, Web services description language (WSDL) 1.1, 2001, http://www.w3.org/TR/wsdl.

[YEL 97] YELLIN D. M., STROM R. E., "Protocol specifications and components adaptors", *ACM Trans. on Programming Languages and Systems*, vol. 19, p. 292–333, 1997.

SECOND PART

Verification Techniques for Distributed Systems

Chapter 6

Introduction to Verification

6.1. Introduction

The diversity of verification methods may be confusing for the engineer faced with issues related to the choice of appropriate techniques for the analysis of his system. This chapter aims to clarify the basis for such a choice by discussing three fundamental factors associated with the verification process:

– how to choose the formal model that will support the verification;

– how to express the requirements and expected properties of the model;

– which verification methods apply to the model.

Often the modeler is tempted to choose a very expressive formalism in order to cover all the details of his system. However, this expressiveness significantly complicates the verification process. Indeed the complexity of such a method can limit the analysis to toy systems. At worst, the property satisfaction may be an undecidable problem and requires the application of semi-algorithms. Moreover, the modeler wishes to check a property whatever the values of some parameters (number of network routers, size of buffers, etc.). This leads to parametrized models, the verification of which becomes even more untractable.

The specification of properties must address the following question: how do you specify a "good" behavior of a system? Among the different answers, the following can be suggested:

Chapter written by Serge HADDAD.

– a family of properties called *generic* expressing the behavior of the formal model independently of the system (e.g. absence of deadlocks, the finiteness, etc.);

– a language of properties adapted to dynamic systems and especially to concurrent systems (e.g. a modal logic such as linear or branching temporal logics);

– a behavioral equivalence with another model representing the specification of the expected behavior in a more abstract way (e.g. bisimulation);

– the response to a test sequence (e.g. failure tests, acceptance tests, etc).

The verification methods are generally classified according to basic criteria. To which formalisms does the method apply? Does the method work at a structural level (i.e. analyzing the model description) or at a behavioral level (i.e. building a possibly partial or abstract representation of its behaviour)? Is the verification process wholly or partially automatic? Which kinds of properties is the method able to check?

At last, in order to combine different verification methods, it is necessary to understand how one method can take into account the results of another. Furthermore, this combination also has an impact on the specification process: for instance the system can be modeled in a very abstract way such that its analysis is relatively easy and then it can be iteratively refined while keeping most of the results obtained at the previous stage at subsequent stages.

In order to illustrate our discussion and faced with the diversity of the formalisms, we will focus on Petri nets and their extensions. The rest of the chapter is organized as follows: in section 6.2 we discuss choice criteria between formalisms; then in section 6.3 we introduce several ways to express the properties of a system; in section 6.4 we examine the main categories of verification methods; lastly in section 6.5, we conclude this chapter by providing an overview of the methods presented in this part of the book.

6.2. Formal models for verification

6.2.1. *Expressiveness versus decidability and complexity*

Models devoted to verification should meet two contradictory requirements. On the one hand, they must be expressive enough to avoid over-abstraction when transforming the design model into a verification model. On the other hand, this expressiveness is necessarily limited in order to obtain efficient verification algorithms. We encourage the interested reader to read about complexity of algorithms for instance in [PAP 94].

Let us illustrate this point with the reachability problem in Petri nets: given a net, an initial marking and a final marking, we want to decide whether a firing sequence exists in the net leading from the initial marking to the final marking. As the number of markings of the net is possibly infinite, it is not *a priori* obvious that this problem is decidable. However, some properties such as the boundedness of the net and marking covering (a variant of the reachability in which we investigate whether a marking greater or equal than the final marking can be reached) are decidable using a conceptually simple construction "the covering graph" [KAR 69]. Thus it is plausible that reachability is decidable and indeed such a decision algorithm exists [MAY 84, KOS 82]. Unfortunately, this algorithm is not *primitive recursive*, otherwise stated its complexity is unpredictable, and even its implementation is relatively complicated which explains why no software completely solves this problem.

Following this result, researchers have oriented their work in two opposite direction: restricting the model with more efficient algorithms or studying the limits between decidability and undecidability. For instance in reversible nets (i.e. where the net consists of pairs of transitions each one canceling the effect of the other) reachability is EXPSPACE-complete [MAY 82] and in safe nets (i.e. where every place of a reachable marking contains at most one token), reachability is PSPACE-complete [CHE 95]. In free choice nets (i.e. where two transitions that share an input place have the same backward incidence) reachability is even NP-complete [DES 95]. At last for finite state automata viewed as particular nets (i.e. where every transition has a single input and a single output) we can solve reachability in linear time and the problem is NLOGSPACE-complete [PAP 94].

In the other direction Petri nets with inhibitor arcs have the expressive power of Turing machines and no relevant property (including reachability) is decidable. However, when there is a single inhibitor arc (or a particular pattern of inhibitor arcs), the reachability problem is still decidable [REI 08]. Reset arcs, which empty connected places during the transition firing, do not provide the expressive power of Turing machines. Thus some properties remain decidable but not reachable [DUF 98]. Finally recursive Petri nets in which a state corresponds to a dynamic tree of threads, each one with its own marking, significantly extend the expressive power of Petri nets while keeping the decidability of the reachability problem [HAD 99].

6.2.2. *Desirable characteristics of a model*

In parallel to the previous, rather theoretical, discussion, the modeller should study whether the model is adapted to the system he wants to analyze. Indeed, two equivalent models with respect to expressiveness, may be rather different with respect to the ease of the modeling. Numerous criteria can be considered: modularity, hierarchy, time representation, etc. We illustrate this point with two phenomena that are to be modeled using Petri nets: fault occurrence and time management.

Assume that a sytem has been modeled by a Petri net and the modeling is to be extended in order to represent the possibility that a fault can occur at anytime that restarts the system. If the net is bounded and a superset of the reachability space is known, such a modeling is theoretically feasable. Unfortunately, it requires the introduction of a complementary place per place of the net, and furthermore, a transition per potentially reachable marking! If the net is unbounded then it is established that such a construction does not exist. With the help of reset arcs, the modeling is now possible. Let us describe how to do it: a marked place (say `normal`) controls the standard behavior of the net which "loops" around every transition, the occurrence of the fault is represented by a transition, which empties `normal` and marks `fault`, then a second transition empties the places of the net, empties `fault`, marks `normal` and the original places of the net as in the initial marking. A similar construction is also easily undertaken using recursive Petri nets.

Time has been introduced in Petri nets in multiple ways. Here we only describe the two most prominent models, which have been the topic of numerous theoretical developments: time Petri nets (TPNs) [BER 91] and timed Petri nets (TdPNs) [FRU 00]. A time interval is associated with every transition of a TPN. When a transition becomes enabled, it may only fire occur if the time elapsed since it became enabled is within the transition interval. Moreover, time cannot elapse if the enabling duration of some transition has reached the maximal value of the interval. This semantic choice allows urgent features of a phenomenon to be modeled such as the expiration of a time-out. Meanwhile, it does not allow situations when time elapsing would disable the firing of a transition to be represented. Based on this fact, it has been proven that some timed automata are equivalent to no TPN [BÉR 08]. In TdPNs, an age is associated with every token and every arc is a multiset of intervals. In order to fire a transition, for every "input" interval a token must be chosen with an age that belongs to the interval. When tokens are produced, their initial age is fixed non deterministically but it must belong to the corresponding "output" interval. Contrary to TPNs, in TdPNs a transition can be disabled by time elapsing but these nets cannot express urgency features. From a verification point of view, all relevant properties are undecidable for unbounded TPNs while some of them remain decidable for TdPNs such as the marking covering (but not the reachability) [ABD 01].

6.2.3. *From design to verification: formal semantic*

Once the model is chosen, the modeler has to "translate" the specification of the system expressed within the design formalism. Ideally this step should be performed by an algorithm. However, this automatic process requires that the behavior of the new model is equivalent to the original one (w.r.t. some appropriate equivalence). One possible method consists of providing a formal semantic (the most often an operational one) of constructors of the design model in terms of sub-models in the verification framework.

We illustrate this point using two formalisms of high-level Petri nets: colored Petri nets [JEN 92] and the Petri box calculus [KOU 94]. Colored Petri nets are nets enlarged with color domains associated with vertices of the net and color functions associated with arcs whose domain is the color domain of the transition and range is the set of multi-set of colors where colors belong to the domain of the place. There are two equivalent semantics for such a formalism. In the first case, the firing rule is directly defined by (1) selecting a transition and a color of its domain (2) evaluating functions labeling input arcs (3) consuming the resulting multi-sets of tokens in the input places (4) evaluating functions labeling output arcs (5) producing the resulting multi-sets of tokens in the output places,

In the second case, an ordinary Petri net is defined as a net consisting of a pairing of places of the colored net and colors of their domain and whose transitions consist of pairing transitions of the colored net and colors of their domain. The valuations of the arcs of this *unfolded* net are obtained by evaluating the functions for every color of the transitions and projecting on every color of places. The behavior of the colored net is then defined as that of the unfolded net. If the latter semantic is *a priori* less appropriate than the former one, for instance regarding the simulation, it presents advantages regarding the verification. A property of the colored net is a property of the unfolded net. Moreover, the soundness of verification methods applied to colored nets is checked at the level of the unfolded net (e.g. net reductions).

Petri box calculus is a formalism based on process algebra (such as CCS [MIL 82]). one of its (equivalent) semantics consists of building a Petri net using net patterns and operational rules for every operator (sequence, choice, parallel execution, etc.). The interests of this formalism are twofold; it provides a true concurrent semantic for process algebra and verification methods of Petri nets can be applied to it. For instance, the reachability problem, which is undecidable in CCS, is here decidable due to the semantic in terms of Petri nets. Similarly the flow computation (a specific technique for Petri nets), which provide invariants of the model, is extended to the Petri box calculus.

6.3. Expression of properties

The choice of properties for Petri nets raises the same problem as the choice of the formalism. Specifying a large set of properties prevents the development of efficient specialized algorithms whilst a restricted set of properties fails to express the various properties of protocols and distributed applications.

6.3.1. *Generic properties*

If the properties are restricted then these properties must be generic in the following sense: they express the behavior of the modeled system, for a large range of interpretations. Let us examine how such an interpretation is possible. We give below a non-exhaustive list of properties that aim to be generic (still in the context of Petri nets):

– quasi-liveness: "Every transition is fired at least one time" expresses a syntactically correct design in the sense that any activity or event must occur at least once in the behavior of the net;

– deadlock-freeness: "There is no dead marking" means that a global deadlock never happens in the system;

– liveness: "Every transition is fired at least one time from any reachable marking" means that the system never looses its capacities at any time;

– boundedness: "There is a bound on the reachable marking of any place" ensures that the system will reach some stationary behavior in the long run. Let us note that multiple stationary behaviors are possible.

– home state: "A marking exists that is reachable from any other marking" denotes the possibility for the system to reinitialize itself;

– unavoidable state: "A marking exists that cannot be avoided infinitely" indicates that for the system must reinitialize itself.

6.3.2. *Specific properties*

Despite the generality of the previous properties, there will always be some features of behavior that will not be captured by a fixed set of properties. For instance, "the firing of t_1 will eventually be followed by the firing of t_2" is a useful fairness property but not one of the previous properties. Of course, it could be included, but there are many possible variants.

Thus it is better to adopt a language of properties adapted to dynamic systems and especially the concurrent ones. Among such languages, the temporal logic framework (e.g. linear time logic [PNU 77], branching time logic [EME 86], etc.) has been widely used. The reasons for this development are twofold: the most interesting properties of concurrency are expressed by simple formulas and the model checking associated with these logics can easily be implemented.

The usual temporal logics are relatively intuitive. Let us describe them in an informal way. Formulas are either state formulas or path formulas. A basic state formula only depends on the current state. In the framework of Petri nets, it could be "places p_1 and p_2 are both marked" or "the marking of p_1 is strictly greater than that of p_2". Then other state formulas can be inductively built with operators such as "for every (resp. there exists an) execution path starting from the current state, (respectively such that) a given path formula is fulfilled". Basic path formulas are state formulas which are evaluated on the first state of the path. Then path formulas can be inductively built with path operators such as "the suffix of the path obtained by deleting the first state fulfills a given path formula" or "every (resp. there exists a) suffix of the path fulfills (resp. which fulfills) a given path formula".

6.3.3. *Equivalence between models*

The framework of temporal logic is interesting if a set of properties that characterizes the expected behavior of the modeled system need to be verified. Nevertheless, starting from a global behavior, such as a set of services, requires a great deal of work to specify the correct formulas. Moreover the modeler has to build more and more complex formulas where the semantic of such formulae becomes complicated. In such cases, it is much simpler to specify the set of services by a model (e.g. a Petri net) and to compare the behavior of the net modeling the services with the behavior of the net modeling the protocol.

However, it is necessary to define what is the equivalence between nets. First, internal transitions (implementing the protocol) and external transitions (associated with the service interface) has to be distinguished. A first possible equivalence could be the language equivalence: the projection of the protocol net language onto external transitions is equal to the language of the service net. However, the language equivalence does not capture the choices offered by the model upon reaching some state. Numerous equivalences including language and choice have been proposed. The most common one is the bisimulation relation [MIL 82] which pairs states of the two models such that for every pair of states whatever the action a model can perform from its state the other can as also perform it leading to states that are also paired. Regarding verification, the interest of the bisimulations is twofold:

– bisimulation checking (on finite state systems) has a complexity similar to the one of formula satisfaction checking;

– for models such as process algebras, axiomatization of equivalence is possible at the structural level.

6.3.4. *Model testing*

Another possibility (and the last we examine here) is the response of a model to a sequence of tests. A typical test application may be described as follows:

1) it starts with a specification of expected behaviors (or failure behaviors);

2) then it generates an intermediate object, called a success tree, which takes into account the sequence of transitions and the choice offered by the states;

3) this tree is transformed into a transition system called the canonical tester;

4) the synchronous product of the Petri net and the canonical tester is built (i.e. a parallel execution synchronized on common actions);

5) the observation of deadlocks in the product provides information on the failures of the implementation specified by the model.

6.4. Verification methods

In this section, we give an overview of the different categories of verification methods emphasizing rather the principles more than the technical features. These features will be detailed in the other chapters of this part. The main dichotomy between methods consists of either representing (wholly or partially) the behavior of the model or exclusively analyzing the structure of the model in order to deduce its properties. Each approach has advantages and drawbacks and we highlight them in the following sections.

6.4.1. *Automatic verification versus manual verification*

One objective of formal models is computer-aided verification. At first sight, automatic verification may appear to be highly desirable [CLA 00]. However, there are some inherent limitations to automatic verification that the modeler should be aware of:

– there are numerous undecidable properties;

– even for decidable properties, checking is so complex that it may become untractable;

– automatic verification never takes into account the specificities of the modeled system.

Another advantage of manual verification is the insight it provides to understanding the behavior of the system [BER 04]. However, manual verification is prone to errors and a sound (and sometimes complete) axiomatization of proofs may help to develop correct proofs. The duality of the manual and automatic verification should be emphasized: for instance the reduction or the abstraction of models may be undertaken automatically whereas refinement of nets requires the participation of the designer. Yet, these are two facets of the same theory.

The automatic method may check properties given by the modeler or simply generate valid properties of the model. Both methods have their drawbacks. Checking of properties is sometimes tricky. For instance, an inductive proof a property consists (1) of checking whether it is true in the initial state, and (2) showing that if it is true in some state then it remains true in all the subsequent states. A property is inductive if there exists an inductive proof for it. Unfortunately, a valid property is not necessarily inductive whereas it would have been possible to find a stronger property which is inductive. Indeed for a large class of transition systems, a property is valid if and only if there is a stronger property that is inductive. Conversely, the automatic generation of properties is generally limited in its scope: a nonlinear invariant will never be generated by the computation of the flows in Petri nets.

6.4.2. *Structural methods*

We illustrate using Petri nets the difference between structural and behavioral method. Below are listed four methods: the first and the second ones are structural since they do not require us to apply the firing rule in order to obtain their results.

– a Petri net is a graph and the token flows must follow the arcs of this graph; structural deadlock detection is based on this feature;

– a Petri net is a linear transformation of the vector of tokens and so linear algebra-based techniques can take advantage of it (for instance computation of the flows);

– a Petri net underlies an event structure with causality and compatibility relations. Exploiting this feature, partial order methods only partially build the reachability graph;

– the colors of a domain often have the same behavior. The symmetrical-based methods also reduce the reachability graph using equivalence relations to build a quotient graph.

Let us first detail the structural methods.

Analysis of the Petri net as a graph

The examination of the graph's structure leads to two different and complementary families of methods, based either on the local structure or on the global structure. The local structure of a subnet may make it possible to investigate its behavior independently from the rest of the net. This is the key point of the reductions theory where the agglomeration of transitions corresponds to transforming a non-atomic sequence of transitions into an (atomic) transition [BER 87, HAD 06]. Even if they just simplify the net by eliminating, say a transition, their impact is considerable. Indeed, in the reachability graph they eliminate all the intermediate states between the initial firing and the final firing of the sequence. Roughly speaking, an agglomeration divides by two the reachability space and thus n agglomerations have a reduction factor of 2^n.

Analyzing the global structure of the net can be done by restricting the class of Petri nets (e.g. free-choice Petri nets [DES 95]) and developing efficient algorithms for the standard properties (liveness, boundedness, etc.). Applied on the whole class of Petri nets, similar algorithms provide necessary or sufficient conditions for the standard properties.

Linear algebra-based techniques

Linear algebra-based techniques rely on the state change equation, which states that a reachable marking is given by the sum of the initial marking and the product of incidence matrix by the occurrence vector of the firing sequence. Thus a weighting of the places whose product by the incidence matrix is null (i.e. a flow) is left invariant by any firing sequence. Similarly a vector of transition occurrences whose product by the incidence matrix is null (i.e. a rhythm) keeps any marking invariant.

So there are two goals for linear algebra-based techniques: computing a generative family of flows (resp. rhythms) and then apply the flows (resp. rhythms) to the analysis of the net. The difficulty in computing the flows depends on the constraints on flows. For instance the complexity of the computation of general flows is polynomial whereas, unfortunately, the computation of positive flows is not polynomial [KRU 87]. However, positive flows are often more useful than general flows and researchers have produced heuristics to decrease the average complexity [SIL 88]. In ordinary Petri nets, algorithms are now well known. The applications of flows and rhythms are numerous: they help to define reductions, they characterize a superset of the reachable set, they provide bounds on maximal firing rates, they make it possible to compute synchronic distances between transitions, etc.

6.4.3. *Behavioral methods*

Behavioral methods are surely the most frequently applied techniques with simulation. Thus before depicting some of them, let us explain the two main approaches to handle the combinatory explosion inherent to such methods: space management during the state graph building and the construction of an equivalent but smaller graph.

An efficient management of the graph construction has an important advantage. It is independent from the structural model generating the graph and thus can be applied to Petri nets, process algebra, etc. The two main methods of this kind are the binary decision diagram (BDD) and on-the-fly verification.

BDD

Originally the BBD technique was defined to compress the representation of boolean expressions [AKE 78]. Any Boolean expression is represented by a rooted acyclic graph where non terminal nodes are variables of the expression with two successors (depending on the valuation of the variables) and there are two terminal nodes (true and false). In order to evaluate an expression one follows the graph from the root to a terminal node choosing a successor with respect to the chosen affectation of the variable labeling the current vertex. As sub-expressions occuring more than once in the expression are factorized, the gain may be very important.

The application of the BDD technique to state graph reduction relies on the representation of a node by a bit vector and the representation of the arc relation by an expression composed of variables denoting the bits of the vectors. It can be shown that the formula of modal logics can also be represented in this way and lastly that the building of the graph and the property checking can be reduced to operations on BDDs. In a famous paper, this technique was employed to encode graphs with 10^{20} states [BUR 90]. A drawback of the method is that it is impossible to predict the compression factor even approximately.

On-the-fly verification

The on-the-fly technique is based on two ideas: state properties can be checked on each state independently and in a finite state graph there is no infinite path with different states. Thus the entire graph is not built but instead the elementary branches of this graph are developed. The only memory required is what is required for the longest elementary path of the graph [HOL 87]. In the worst case there is no gain but on average case the gain is important.

Moreover, the technique can be extended to check the properties of temporal logics [JAR 89]. In this case, the product of the state graph with an automaton (say for instance a Büchi automaton for LTL formula) can be developed and particular states [COU 90a] can be looked for. What is quite interesting with this method is its adaptation to the memory space of the machine. Indeed a cache of states can be added which remembers a number of states that are not on the current path, thus reducing the development of the branch if a cache state is encountered. Another fruitful aspect of this method is that it can be combined with other reduction methods (for instance the partial-order method discussed below).

Partial-order methods

The partial-order methods rely on structural criteria to reduce the state graph and are efficiently implemented on Petri nets. The two main methods, sleep set and stubborn set, associate a set of transitions with a state reached during the building and use this set to restrict further developments of the graph. These sets of transitions are based on a basic structural (or possibly marking-dependent) relation between transitions. Two transitions are independent if their firings are not mutually exclusive. The independence property is structural if the precondition sets do not intersect, whereas it is marking dependent if the bag sum of the preconditions do not exceed the current marking.

The sleep sets method keeps track, for every reached marking, of independent transitions fired in other branches of the graph [GOD 90]. The method ensures that if a transition of this (sleep) set is fired, an already reached marking is encountered. Thus the sleep sets method "cuts" arcs on the reachability graph but the number of states is left unchanged.

Given a marking, a stubborn set of transitions is such that any sequence built with other transitions includes only independent transitions with respect to the stubborn set [VAL 89]. Note that if the independency relation is marking-dependent then the independency must be fulfilled at the different firing markings. Then it can be shown that restricting the firing of an enabled transition being in any stubborn set preserves the possibility of the other firing sequences. The building of the reduced graph is similar to the ordinary graph except that:

– once a state is examined, the algorithm computes a stubborn set of transitions including at least one enabled transition (if the marking is not a deadlock);

– the successors of the state are those reached by the enabled transitions of the stubborn set.

An interesting consequence is the deadlock equivalence between the reduced graph and the original graph.

The stubborn set method requires more computations than the sleep set method for there is no incremental computation of the stubborn set and the computation includes disabled transitions. Conversely, the reduction factor is often more important as here states are pruned. Nevertheless, the combination of the two methods is straightforward, thus improving the reduction factor [GOD 91]. A large equivalence of properties between the reduced graph and the original one is more difficult to obtain. Safety properties may be obtained if the property is taken into account during the building process. The handling of general liveness properties is not possible and the checking of restricted liveness properties has to be performed [VAL 93].

A third partial-order method is based on unfoldings of Petri nets. An unfolding of a Petri net is an acyclic Petri net where places represent tokens of the markings of the original net and transitions represent firings of the original net. Commencing with the places corresponding to the initial marking the transitions associated with the firings of every initially enabling transition are developed linking input places to the new transition and producing (and linking) output places; then the process is iterated. Of course if the net has an infinite sequence, the unfolding would be infinite, and thus, this unfolding must be "cut". In order to produce finite unfoldings, different cut methods have been proposed [MCM 92, ESP 96]. The unfolded net is a very compact representation of the reachability set and thus safeness properties can be checked with a low order of space complexity (time complexity may also be reduced but not so significantly). The method has been extended to support linear temporal logic verification [COU 96]. The principle is to build a graph of unfolded nets where the relevant transitions for the property are always graph transitions.

High-level model analysis

In order to design verification methods for an high-level model whose semantic is provided in terms of a low-level model, two directions are possible: (1) methods for the low-level model are adapted taking into account the fact that this model has been generated by some high-level model, (2) specific methods for the high-level model are developed. We illustrate the two approaches on the model of colored Petri nets (CPN).

Color structure analysis has many theoretical applications. Here we just mention three of them. It should be emphasized that a theoretical development may be applied on colored nets and/or on *parametrized* colored nets. Parametrization means that the method does not require to fix the size of the coulour domains of it handles them as variables.

The reduction theory for colored nets is based on the following principles [HAD 90]:

1) choose a reduction for ordinary Petri net.

2) Add colored conditions to the structural conditions (i.e. conditions on the color functions valuating the arcs); these colored conditions are as weak as possible to ensure the structural conditions on the unfolded net for a set of reductions.

3) Check that there is a possible ordering of the set of reductions in the unfolded net.

4) Define the transformation by a structural transformation similar to the original reduction with complementary coloured transformations; this transformation must correspond to the successive reductions of the unfolded net.

The parametrization of the method is relatively straightforward and is obtained by substituting syntactical conditions on expressions denoting the colour functions to the original conditions [EVA 05].

The flow computation for colored nets requires deeper analysis of the color function structure. It appears that the cornerstone of the flow computation is the algebraic concept of generalized inverses. Color functions are linear transformations on a set of bags and thus this algebraic concept is sound. Moreover, a elegant algorithm adapted from Gaussian elimination rules can be developed provided that the successive generalized inverses may be computed [COU 90b]. The space and time complexity are dramatically reduced and the flows are represented in a compact way, which allows for natural interpretation.

Unfortunately, parametrization of this method is not possible, so researchers have investigated different directions: color expressions can be identified to polynomials. The idea is then to apply a Gaussian-like elimination on a ring of polynomials. The difficulty lies in the transformation (and the reciprocal transformation) from a color function to a polynomial one. Some subclasses of well-formed nets (also called symmetric nets) have been successfully studied (regular nets, ordered nets) with this technique [HAD 88]. Another way to obtain parametrized methods is not to require that the flow family be a generative family. Then simple methods can work on very general nets and give useful information anyway (even if not complete).

The symbolic reachability graph of well-formed nets exploits the symmetry of color functions with respect to the firing semantics [CHI 97]. This symmetry leads to an equivalence relation between markings and transition firings. Once canonical representation of equivalence marking (and firing transitions) classes is defined, symbolic graph building is similar to ordinary graph building. Some studies show that the comparison between the reduction factor of symmetrical methods and partial-order methods depends on the system modeled. Again these methods may be combined. Another difference between the symmetrical method and the partial-order method is that very general properties may be checked on the symbolic reachability graph. These methods have been extended in order to handle partial symmetries in the formula or in the system [BAA 05].

6.4.4. *Synthesis and control*

While verification aims to check the properties of a system, another line of research consists of starting with the requirements and automatically producing a system satisfying the requirements. In a closed system where the requirements are expressed in some logic, this problem is equivalent to the fundamental problem of satisfiability: does a model of the formula exist? It is well known that in the framework of first-order logic this problem is undecidable [BOR 01]. Therefore the logic needs to be restricted in order to obtain decidability results. Obviously, the propositional framework is insufficient to express the requirements of a dynamic systems. However, with an appropriate level of abstraction, modal propositional logics express safety, liveness, fairness, etc, in a natural way. Furthermore it appears that for most of these logics, the satisfiability problem is decidable [GRA 02].

However, distributed systems cannot been seen as closed systems. Indeed the environment plays a crucial role in such a system and should be integrated in the synthesis process. Moreover, the distribution of the system into components requires the architecture of the system to be taken into account [PNU 89b, PNU 89a]. Here the frontier between decidability and undecidability is closely related to the knowledge of the agents about the environment. On the negative side, as could be predicted, even for architecture where decidability holds, the complexity of the procedure is very high (often non-elementary). On the positive side, when the specification admits an implementation, the components can be chosen as finite-state components.

Another alternative to verification is the control approach. Given a system and a specification, the goal of the control consists of restricting the behavior of the system to satisfy the specification. In the most widely adopted approach the specification is given by a regular language and a controller is required that enables the maximal behavior of the controlled system [RAM 87]. In a distributed framework, different settings are possible depending on the information known by the local controllers, the mode of communication between controllers, etc. In general, the complexity of the control problems are simpler than the synthesis problems due to the corresponding assumptions.

6.5. Outline of Part 2

Part 2 is organized into four chapters. Chapter 7 covers the finite-state verification. Historically, it is the oldest line of research that has been developed. The main objective of finite-state verification is the reduction of complexity due to the combinatory explosion of the system. Possible approaches are structural methods, which try to avoid developing the behavior of the system and data representation which reduces the explosion by the sharing substructures or exploitation of the properties satisfied by the formalism.

Chapter 8 addresses the problem of verifying infinite-state systems. Most of the research is devoted to the design of formalisms that are slightly less expressive than Turing machine, (or equivalent computational models), and to study which properties are decidable. In this chapter, the main focus is put on extension of Petri nets and on different variants of counter machines. It emphasizes the fact that small variations lead to drastically different theories.

Chapter 9 describes timed systems. Time is a particular source of infinity. However its specificity leads to efficient verification procedures such as those developed for timed automata. Moreover, time can be combined with other sources of infinities like in time(d) Petri nets. In addition, this chapter tackles with the problem of implementing timed systems when the abstraction performed at the theoretical level (such as the perfect synchronization of the clocks) is no longer satisfied.

Chapter 10 describes the control and synthesis of distributed systems. After reviewing the centralized case, with the help of intuitive examples, it develops the specifities related to the distributed case and the different possible approaches.

6.6. Bibliography

[ABD 01] ABDULLA P. A., NYLÉN A., "Timed Petri nets and BQOs", *in Application and Theory of Petri Nets 2001, 22nd International Conference, ICATPN 2001*, vol. 2075 of *Lecture Notes in Computer Science*, Springer, p. 53-70, 2001.

[AKE 78]   AKERS S., "Binary decision diagrams", *IEEE Transactions on Computers*, vol. C-27(6), p. 509-516, June 1978.

[BAA 05]   BAARIR S., DUTHEILLET C., HADDAD S., ILIÉ J.-M., "On the use of exact lumpability in partially symmetrical well-formed nets", in *Proceedings of the 2nd International Conference on Quantitative Evaluation of Systems (QEST'05)*, Turin, Italy, IEEE Computer Society Press, p. 23-32, 2005.

[BER 87]   BERTHELOT G., "Transformations and decompositions of nets", *Advances in Petri Nets*, vol. 254 of *Lecture Notes in Computer Science*, Springer, p. 359-376, 1987.

[BER 91]   BERTHOMIEU B., DIAZ M., "Modeling and verification of time dependent systems using time Petri nets", *IEEE Trans. Software Eng.*, vol. 17, num. 3, p. 259-273, 1991.

[BER 04]   BERTOT Y., CASTÉRAN P., *Interactive Theorem Proving and Program Development Coq'Art: the Calculus of Inductive Constructions*, Texts in Theoretical Computer Science, EATCS, Springer, 2004.

[BÉR 08]   BÉRARD B., CASSEZ F., HADDAD S., LIME D., ROUX O. H., "When are timed automata weakly timed bisimilar to time Petri nets?", *Theor. Comput. Sci.*, vol. 403, num. 2-3, p. 202-220, 2008.

[BOR 01]   BORGER E., GRADEL E., GUREVITCH Y., *The Classical Decision Problem*, Springer, 2001.

[BUR 90]   BURCH J., CLARK E., MCMILLAN K., DILL D., L.J. H., "Symbolic model checking: 10^{20} states and beyond", in *Proceedings of the 5th IEEE Symposium on Logic in Computer Science*, 1990.

[CHE 95]   CHENG A., ESPARZA J., PALSBERG J., "Complexity results for 1-safe nets", *Theor. Comput. Sci.*, vol. 147, num. 1&2, p. 117-136, 1995.

[CHI 97]   CHIOLA G., DUTHEILLET C., FRANCESCHINIS G., HADDAD S., "A symbolic reachability graph for coloured Petri nets", *Theoretical Computer Science*, vol. 176, num. 1-2, p. 39-65, Elsevier Science Publishers, 1997.

[CLA 00]   CLARKE E., GRUMBERG O., PELED D. A., *Model Checking*, MIT Press, 2000.

[COU 90a]   COURCOURBETIS C., VARDI M., WOLPER P., YANNAKAKIS M., "Memory efficient algorithms for the verification of temporal properties", in *Proceedings of Computer Aided Verification 90*, vol. 30 of *DIMACS*, North-Holland, 1990.

[COU 90b]   COUVREUR J.-M., "The general computation of flows for coloured nets", in *Proc. 11th Int. Conf. Appl. and Theory Petri Nets*, Paris, France, p. 204-223, 1990.

[COU 96]   COUVREUR J., POITRENAUD D., "Model checking based on occurrence net graph", GOTZHEIN R., BREDEREKE J., Eds., in *Formal Description Techniques IX, Theory Applications and Tools, FORTE/PSTV'96*, vol. 663 of *LNCS*, Kaiserslautern, Germany, Chapman-Hall, p. 380-395, October 1996.

[DES 95]   DESEL J., ESPARZA J., *Free Choice Petri Nets*, Cambridge University Press, New York, NY, USA, 1995.

[DUF 98]   DUFOURD C., FINKEL A., SCHNOEBELEN P., "Reset nets between decidability and undecidability", *(ICALP'98) L.N.C.S*, vol. 1443, p. 103-115, July 1998.

[EME 86] EMERSON E. A., HALPERN J. Y., ""Sometimes" and "Not Never" revisited: on branching versus linear time temporal logic", *J. ACM*, vol. 33, num. 1, p. 151-178, 1986.

[ESP 96] ESPARZA J., ROMER S., VOGLER W., "An improvment of McMillan's unfolding algorithm", in *Proceedings of the Second International Workshop TACAS'96*, vol. 1055 of *LNCS*, Passau, Germany, Springer-Verlag, p. 87-106, March 1996.

[EVA 05] EVANGELISTA S., HADDAD S., PRADAT-PEYRE J.-F., "Syntactical colored Petri nets reductions", in *ATVA*, vol. 3707 of *Lecture Notes in Computer Science*, Springer, p. 202-216, 2005.

[FRU 00] DE FRUTOS-ESCRIG D., RUIZ V. V., ALONSO O. M., "Decidability of properties of timed-arc Petri nets", *ICATPN*, p. 187-206, 2000.

[GOD 90] GODEFROID P., "Using partial orders to improve automatic verification methods", in *Proceedings of Computer Aided Verification 90*, vol. 30 of *DIMACS*, North-Holland, p. 321-340, 1990.

[GOD 91] GODEFROID P., WOLPER P., "Using partial orders for the efficient verification of deadlock freedom and safety properties", in *Proceedings of Computer Aided Verification 91*, vol. 575 of *LNCS*, Springer-Verlag, 1991.

[GRA 02] GRADEL E., THOMAS W., WILKE T., Eds., *Automata, Logics, and Infinite Games*, Springer, 2002.

[HAD 88] HADDAD S., COUVREUR J.-M., "Validation of parallel systems with coloured Petri nets", COSNARD M., BARTON M. H., VANNESCHI M., Eds., in *Proceedings of the IFIP WG10.3 Working Conference on Parallel Processing (PP'88)*, Pisa, Italy, North-Holland, p. 377-390, 1988.

[HAD 90] HADDAD S., "A reduction theory for coloured nets", *European Workshop on Applications and Theory in Petri Nets*, vol. 424 of *Lecture Notes in Computer Science*, Springer, p. 209-235, 1990.

[HAD 99] HADDAD S., POITRENAUD D., "Theoretical aspects of recursive Petri nets", in *Proc. 20th Int. Conf. on Applications and Theory of Petri nets*, vol. 1639 of *Lecture Notes in Computer Science*, Williamsburg, VA, USA, Springer Verlag, p. 228-247, 1999.

[HAD 06] HADDAD S., PRADAT-PEYRE J.-F., "New efficient Petri nets reductions for parallel programs Verification", *Parallel Processing Letters*, vol. 16, num. 1, p. 101-116, 2006.

[HOL 87] HOLZMANN G., "Automated protocol validation in argos: assertion proving and scatter searching", *IEEE Transactions on Software Engineering*, vol. 13(6), p. 683-696, 1987.

[JAR 89] JARD C., JERON T., "On-line model checking for finite linear temporal logic specifications", in *Proceedings of Automatic Verification Methods for Finite State Systems*, vol. 407 of *LNCS*, Springer-Verlag, p. 189-196, 1989.

[JEN 92] JENSEN K., *Coloured Petri Nets. Basic Concepts, Analysis Methods and Practical Use. Volume 1: Basic Concepts.*, Springer-Verlag, 1992.

[KAR 69] KARP R., MILLER R., "Parallel program schemata", *Journal of Computer and System Sciences*, vol. 3, num. 2, p. 147-195, 1969.

[KOS 82] KOSARAJU S., "Decidability of reachability in vector addition systems", in *Proc. 14th ACM Symp. Theory of Computing (STOC'82)*, San Francisco, CA, p. 267-281, may 1982.

[KOU 94] KOUTNY M., ESPARZA J., BEST E., "Operational semantics for the Petri box calculus", in *CONCUR '94, Concurrency Theory, 5th International Conference*, vol. 836 of *Lecture Notes in Computer Science*, Springer, p. 210-225, 1994.

[KRU 87] KRUCKEBERG C., JAXY M., "Mathematical methods for calculating invariants in Petri nets", GOOS G., HARTMANIS J., Eds., *Advances in Petri Nets 1987*, vol. 266 of *LNCS*, Springer-Verlag, p. 104-131, 1987.

[MAY 82] MAYR E., MEYER A., "The complexity of the word problems for commutative semigroups and polynomial ideals", *Advances in Mathematics*, vol. 46, p. 305-329, 1982.

[MAY 84] MAYR E., "An algorithm for the general Petri net reachability problem", *SIAM Journal of Computing*, vol. 13, p. 441-460, 1984.

[MCM 92] McMILLAN K., "On-the-fly verification with stubborn sets", in *Proceedings of Computer Aided Verification 93*, vol. 663 of *LNCS*, Montreal, Canada, Springer-Verlag, p. 164-175, 1992.

[MIL 82] MILNER R., *A Calculus of Communicating Systems*, Springer-Verlag New York, Inc., Secaucus, NJ, USA, 1982.

[PAP 94] PAPADIMITRIOU C. M., *Computational Complexity*, Addison-Wesley, Reading, Massachusetts, 1994.

[PNU 77] PNUELI A., "The temporal logic of programs", in *18th Annual Symposium on Foundations of Computer Science, FOCS*, IEEE, p. 46-57, 1977.

[PNU 89a] PNUELI A., ROSNER A., "On the synthesis of a reactive Modules", in *Proceedings of the 16th ACM Symposium Principles of Programming Languages (POPL 1989)*, p. 179-190, 1989.

[PNU 89b] PNUELI A., ROSNER A., "On the synthesis of an asynchronous reactive module", in *Proceedings of the 16th International Colloquium on Automata, Languages, and Programming (ICALP 1989)*, vol. 372 of *Lecture Notes in Computer Science*, Springer-Verlag, p. 652-671, 1989.

[RAM 87] RAMADGE P., WONHAM W. M., "Supervisory control of a class of discrete event processes", *SIAM Journal of Control and Optimization*, vol. 25, num. 1, p. 206-230, 1987.

[REI 08] REINHARDT K., "Reachability in Petri nets with inhibitor arcs", *Electr. Notes Theor. Comput. Sci.*, vol. 223, p. 239-264, 2008.

[SIL 88] SILVA M., COLOM J. M., "On the computation of structural synchronic Invariants in P/T nets", in *European Workshop on Applications and Theory of Petri Nets*, vol. 340 of *Lecture Notes in Computer Science*, Springer, p. 386-417, 1988.

[VAL 89] VALMARI A., "Stubborn sets for reduced space generation", in *Proc. 10th Intern. Conference on Application and Theory of Petri Nets*, Bonn, Germany, 1989.

[VAL 93] VALMARI A., "On-the-fly verification with stubborn sets", in *Proceedings of Computer Aided Verification 93*, vol. 697 of *LNCS*, Springer-Verlag, p. 397-408, 1993.

Chapter 7

Verification of Finite-State Systems

7.1. Introduction

The concurrent programming paradigm is a powerful tool for the implementation of complex software. However, it may lead to applications where the interaction between threads or processes produces subtle behaviors that are difficult to predict. In this context, it is necessary to include complete and systematic verification step in the development life cycle of an application.

Two kinds of verification techniques can be used: state enumeration based methods and structural methods. The state enumeration-based methods lead to a complete verification of the modeled system but the analysis is restricted by the combinatory explosion factor (i.e. the number of control states may grown exponentially with respect to (w.r.t.) the number of thread and the size of the application). The structural methods are generally efficient but they do not ensure the complete correctness of the system. Thus an attractive trade-off is to combine both methods.

In this context, an efficient strategy is to use the structure of the model to reduce the number of execution traces that are to be analyzed. The reduction ratio obtained depends on the kind of considered properties. The more specific the properties, the greater is the reduction.

Again, two distinct approaches can be followed to obtain such a restriction. On the one hand, it is possible to apply on-the-fly techniques when building the state graph. These techniques are based on the detection that in a given state,

Chapter written by Jean-François Pradat-Peyre and Yann Thierry-Mieg.

– some enabled actions may be forgotten as they lead to an already visited state [GOD 93];

– some enabled actions may be safely delayed [VAL 93];

– some enabled actions may be executed simultaneously [VER 97].

On the other hand, the model can be simplified at the program level (or more generally at the model level) before building a reduced state graph. In this framework, a frequent approach is to merge consecutive statements into a virtual atomic one with the effect of combining the effects of these statements. Such a transformation presents the following advantages:

– the combinatory explosion is drastically reduced by the elimination of the intermediate states;

– the induced overhead computation is negligible w.r.t. the cost of the state graph building;

– this abstraction is potentially applicable to "parametrized" programs (e.g. independent of the number of instances of a process class) and this feature is not covered by the on-the-fly techniques.

In this chapter we propose to expose these techniques and we illustrate them with the help of Petri nets formalism. So, we first describe some usual definitions related to this formalism and we present useful notations. Subsequently we present some efficient structural techniques: structural reductions and linear invariants and we show how these techniques can be used to decide liveness (or deadlock freeness) for some specific classes of Petri nets.

We present then model checking techniques that are based on the analysis of the reachability graph and we provide an overview of approaches that are used to tackle the state explosion problem, which is the main limitation of these model checking techniques.

7.2. Petri net definition

DEFINITION 7.1 *A Petri net [REI 83] is four-tuple $\langle P, T, W^-, W^+ \rangle$ where: P is the set of places, T is the set of transitions, ($P \cap T = \emptyset, P \cup T \neq \emptyset$) W^- (respectively W^+) is the backward (respectively forward) incidence application from $P \times T$ to $\mathbb{N}$. We note W the incidence application defined by $W = W^+ - W^-$*

A marked Petri net is a couple $\langle N, m_0 \rangle$ where N is a Petri net and and m_0 is the initial marking (i.e. an application from P to $\mathbb{N}$).

DEFINITION 7.2 *Let $N = \langle P, T, W^-, W^+ \rangle$ be a Petri net and m_0 its initial marking.*

A vector of $\mathbb{N}^P$ is called a marking of N; $m(p)$ denotes the number of tokens contained in place p. A marking m is greater or equal that a marking m' (denoted $m \geq m'$) iff $\forall p \in P, m(p) \geq m'(p)$. A transition $t \in T$ is fireable at a marking m if and only if: $\forall p \in P, m(p) \geq W^-(p,t)$. The marking m' obtained by the firing of t is defined by: $\forall p \in P, m'(p) = m(p) - W^-(p,t) + W^+(p,t)$. We note, $m[t > m'$ which means that t is fireable at m and reaches m'. By extension, a marking m' is reachable from a marking m if there exists a sequence $s = t_0.t_1.\dots.t_n \in T^*$ and a set of markings $m_1, \dots, m_n$ such that $m[t_0 > m_1, m_1[t_1 > m_2, \dots, m_n[t_n > m'$. The set of reachable markings from m_0 is denoted by $Reach(N, m_0)$.

DEFINITION 7.3 We denote by T^* the set of finite sequences on T, by T^∞ the set of infinite sequences and $T^\omega = T^* \cup T^\infty$. ϵ denotes the empty sequence. $L^*(PN)$ denotes the set of finite firing sequences from m_0, $L^\infty(PN)$ the set of infinite firing sequences from m_0 and $L^\omega(PN) = L^*(PN) \cup L^\infty(PN)$, and $L^{max}(PN)$ the set of maximal firing sequences from m_0.

DEFINITION 7.4 For a sequence $s \in T^\omega$, a transition $t \in T$ and a set $T' \subset T$,

– $s.t$ denotes the concatenation of s and t;

– $|s|$ denotes the length of s; $|s|_t$ denotes the number of occurrences of t in s, and $|s|_{T'}$ is defined by $\sum_{r \in T'} |s|_r$;

– $\Pi_{T'}(s)$ is the sequence obtained from s by erasing the occurrences of the transitions not in T';

– $Pref(s)$ is the set of finite prefixes of s;

– $W^-(p, s.t)$, $W^+(p, s.t)$ and $W(p, s.t)$ are inductively defined by $W^-(p, s.t) = \max(W^-(p,s), W^-(p,t) - W(p,s))$, $W(p, s.t) = W(p,s) + W(p,t)$, $W^+(p, s.t) = W^-(p, s.t) + W(p, s.t)$

A *semiflow* is a natural vector $\vec{v}$ over the set of places, such that $\vec{v} \cdot W = 0$. A semiflow $\vec{v}$ induces the following linear invariant: $\forall m \in Reach(N, m_0), \vec{v} \cdot m = \vec{v} \cdot m_0$. When $\forall p \in P, \vec{v}(p) \in \mathbb{N}$ the semiflow is said to be a *positive* semiflow. We note $Supp(\vec{v}) = \|\vec{v}\| = \{p \in P | \vec{v}(p) \neq 0\}$ the *support* of the semiflow $\vec{v}$. A place p is covered by the semiflow $\vec{v}$ is $p \in \|\vec{v}\|$. By extension, a place p is covered by an invariant if there exists a semiflow $\vec{v}$ that covers p.

We sometimes consider the graph of the Petri net; given a place p (resp. a transition t) we denote $p^\bullet = \{t \in T | W^-(p,t) > 0\}$ (resp. $t^\bullet = \{p \in P | W^+(p,t) > 0\}$) and $^\bullet p = \{t \in T | W^+(p,t) > 0\}$ (resp. $^\bullet t = \{p \in P | W^-(p,t) > 0\}$)

7.3. Structural approaches

Structural approaches attempt to reduce the complexity of model-checking by simplifying the model before attempting to build its state space. Their main strength is that their complexity is related to the size of the input model, rather than to the size of the state space. These approaches are complementary of the behavioral approaches presented in section 7.4 at the end of the chapter.

7.3.1. Structural reductions

The first theoretical work concerning reduction of sequences into atomic actions for simplification purpose was performed by Lipton in [LIP 75]. Lipton focused only on deadlock property preservation. Using parallel program notations of Dijkstra he defined "left" and "right" movers. Roughly speaking, a "left" (resp. "right") mover is a local process statement that can be moved forward (resp. delayed) w.r.t. statements of other processes without modifying the halting property. Lipton then demonstrated that, in principle, the statement P(S), where S is a semaphore, is a "left" mover and V(s) is a "right" mover. Then Lipton proved that some parallel programs are deadlock free by moving the P(S) and V(S) statements and by suppressing atomic statements that have no effect on the variables.

```
integer a,b,c (a = b = c = 1);
parbegin repeat P(a); P(b); V(a); V(b); end;
         repeat P(b); P(c); V(b); V(c); end;
         repeat P(a); P(c); V(a); V(c); end; parend
```

However, two difficulties arise: the reduction preserves only deadlocks and the application conditions are difficult to check.

The result is obtained by simplifying the previous program into the following one by delaying (resp. bringing forward) some P(x) (resp. V(x)) statements and by suppressing atomic statements that have no effect on the variables. This last program obviously does not halt.

```
integer a (a = 1);
parbegin repeat P(a); V(a); end;
         repeat end;
         repeat P(a); V(a); end; parend
```

At the end of the 1990s, Cohen and Lamport [COH 98] proposed assumptions on specifications expressed by formula of temporal logic of actions (TLA) under which they defined a reduction theorem preserving liveness and safety properties. They demonstrated the usefulness of their approach by analyzing a "virtual" parallel program composed of tasks that perform transactions based on a two-phase locking policy: tasks can acquire but not release lock in the first phase and they can release but not acquire lock in the second phase (they take locks in the same order). They proved that using their theorems transactions can be considered as atomic. Note that this program can be viewed as an extension of that proposed by Lipton and discussed above.

This work fixes the reduction theorem in a "high"-level formalism, which can have clear advantages for defining specific usages. However, it is also its main drawback since it is based on the hypothesis that some actions commute, but no effective way is proposed to check whether this assumption holds.

More recently, several authors [STO 03], [FLA 03b], [FLA 03a] leveraged Lipton's theory of reduction to detect transactions in multithreaded programs (and considered these transactions as atomic actions in the model checking step). Stoller and Cohen propose in [STO 03] a reduction theorem that can be applied to models of concurrent systems using mutual exclusion for access to selected variables.

However, they use a restricted notion of "left" mover and a better reduction ratio can be obtained by applying more accurate reductions. Moreover, their reductions are justified by the correct use of "exclusive access predicates" and by the respect of a specific synchronization discipline. These predicates may be difficult to compute and no effective algorithm is given to test that the synchronization discipline is respected.

Flanagan and Qadeer noted in [FLA 03a] that the previous authors use only the notion of "left" mover and proposed an algorithm that uses both "left" and "right" mover notions to infer transactions. However, this algorithm is based on access predicates that can be automatically inferred only for specific programs using lock-based synchronization. Moreover, as they use both "left" and "right" movers to obtain a better reduction ratio and as they do not fix sufficient restrictive application conditions, their reduction theorem does not preserve deadlock.

A Petri net reduction is characterized by some application conditions, by a net transformation and by a set of preserved properties (i.e. which properties are simultaneously true or false in the original net and in the reduced one). These three characteristics are strongly interdependent: a slight modification in the application conditions may strongly modify preserved properties and, in the opposite way, a simple attempt to enlarge preserved properties will significantly restrict the application field of the reduction because of strongest conditions. Furthermore, the reduction must significantly transform the model in order to obtain a significant positive impact on the verification effort.

Different kinds of Petri net reductions exist but those that achieve the best compromise between all these constraints (simple application conditions, significant model transformation and large set of properties preservation) are the transition agglomerations. These reductions agglomerate two transitions that model two sequential actions into a single one that models the atomic corresponding action.

In Petri nets, the first work concerning reductions was performed by Berthelot [BER 80, BER 85]. The author focused the preservation on only specific Petri net properties such as liveness or boundedness. The link between transition agglomerations (the most effective reductions) and general properties, expressed in linear temporal logic (LTL) formalism, is done in [POI 00]. However, these reductions rely on "pure" structural application conditions, which is very efficient, but leads to a quite narrow application area.

Esparza and Schröter [ESP 01] simplify a point in the original pre-agglomeration conditions. However, they consider only 1-safe Petri nets (each place is bounded by 1), the application conditions remain purely structural, and as the authors focus only on infinite sequence preservation, their reductions do not even preserve the deadlock property! [1]

Orthogonally, in [SCH 00] the authors characterize reductions by means of bisimulation. The interest in this approach is that only one particular subset of the markings needs to be considered and thus, a very abstract model can be obtained. However, the applicability of these reductions is quite limited.

In order to define the most simple conditions (simple to express and simple to check) that allow the preservation of both generic properties (liveness, soundness) and more specific ones (expressed in LTL) we provide some behavioral conditions (that are simple to define but complex to check) and structural conditions that are both simple to define and simple to test, derived from the behavioral conditions.

7.3.2. *Agglomeration scheme*

We suppose in the context of agglomeration that the set of transitions of the net is partitioned as: $T = T_0 \uplus_{i \in I} H_i \uplus_{i \in I} F_i$ where I denotes a non-empty set of indices, and $\uplus$ the disjoint union. The underlying idea of this decomposition is that a pair (H_i, F_i) defines transition sets that are causally dependent: an occurrence of $f \in F_i$ in a firing sequence may always be related to a previous occurrence of some $h \in H_i$ in this sequence. Starting from this property, we develop conditions on the behavior of the net, which ensure that we can restrict the dynamics of the net to sequences where each occurrence $h \in H_i$ is immediately followed by an occurrence of some $f \in F_i$ without changing its behaviour w.r.t. a set of properties.

---

1. Note moreover that being 1-safe is not a stable characteristic regarding reductions.

This restricted behavior is the behavior of a reduced net as shown in the next definitions and propositions.

DEFINITION 7.5 (Reduced net) *The reduced Petri net* (N_r, m_0) *is defined by*

- $P_r = P, T_r = T_0 \cup_{i \in I} (H_i \times F_i)$. *We note* hf *the transition* $(h, f) \in H_i \times F_i$;
- $\forall t_r \in T_0, \forall p \in P_r, W_r^-(p, t) = W^-(p, t)$ *and* $W_r^+(p, t) = W^+(p, t)$;
- $\forall i \in I, \forall h f \in H_i \times F_i, \forall p \in P_r \; W_r^-(p, hf) = W^-(p, h.f)$ *and* $W_r^+(p, hf) = W^+(p, h.f)$.

From now on, we note $H = \cup_{i \in I} H_i$ and $F = \cup_{i \in I} F_i$. The firing rule in the reduced net is noted $\rangle_r$ (i.e. $m[s\rangle_r m'$ denotes a firing sequence in the reduced net).

As we want to compare the behavior of the reduced and the original nets and as the sets of transitions are not identical we introduce the following one-to-one homomorphism, which allows such a comparison.

DEFINITION 7.6 *We note* ϕ *the homomorphism from the monoid* T_r^* *to the monoid* T^* *defined by:* $\forall t \in T_0, \phi(t) = t$ *and* $\forall i \in I, \forall h \in H_i, \forall f \in F_i, \phi(hf) = h.f$. *This homomorphism is extended to an homomorphism from* $\mathcal{P}(T_r^*)$ *to* $\mathcal{P}(T^*)$ *and from* $\mathcal{P}(T_r^\omega)$ *to* $\mathcal{P}(T^\omega)$.

In a formal way, the next basic proposition states that the behavior of the reduced net is a subset of the original behavior.

PROPOSITION 7.7 *Let* (N, m_0) *be a marked Petri net. Then:*

1) $\forall s_r \in T_r^*, m[s_r\rangle_r m' \iff m[\phi(s_r)\rangle m'$;
2) $\forall s_r \in T_r^\omega, m[s_r\rangle_r \iff m[\phi(s_r)\rangle$;

At this point, we have proven that if a maximal or infinite sequence violates a sequence property in the reduced net then the property is also violated in the original. However, some original sequences that highlight problems may disappear in the reduced net and we have no result regarding liveness property of the Petri net (the reduced net may be live while the original is not and vice versa).

The main reason is that sequences of the original net are often not the image by ϕ of a sequence of the reduced net because a transition of H_i is not immediately followed by a transition of F_i. So we need to formalize the dependence of F_i on H_i. As we consider an abstraction that merges transitions of H_i with transitions of F_i it seems reasonable to impose that a transition of F_i must always be preceded by a transition of H_i in all sequences of the original net. We introduce this constraint with the help of a set of counting functions, denoted Γ_i.

DEFINITION 7.8 (Potential agglomerability) (N, m_0) *is potentially agglomerable (p-agglomerable for short) iff* $\forall s \in L(N, m_0)$, $\forall i \in I$, $|s|_{H_i} - |s|_{F_i} \geq 0$. *We will denote in the following* Γ_i *the mapping from* T^* *to* $\mathbb{N}$ *defined by* $\Gamma_i(s) = |s|_{H_i} - |s|_{F_i}$

In the following, we study p-agglomerable nets. The remainder of the section is devoted to the presentation of two sets of conditions that ensure the equivalence between the behaviors of the original and the reduced net. Informally stated, the pre-agglomeration scheme expresses the fact that firing the transitions of H_i is only useful for firing the transitions of F_i whereas the post-agglomeration scheme expresses the fact that the firing of transitions of F_i are mainly conditioned by the firing of the transitions of H_i.

7.3.3. *Behavioral pre-agglomeration*

We state now four conditions, which "roughly speaking" ensure that delaying the firing of a transition $h \in H_i$ until some $f \in F_i$ fires does not modify the behavior of the net w.r.t. the set of properties we want to preserve.

DEFINITION 7.9 *Let* (N, m_0) *be a p-agglomerable net.* (N, m_0) *is:*

– *H-independent iff* $\forall i \in I$, $\forall h \in H_i$, $\forall m \in Reach(N, m_0)$, $\forall s$ *such that* $\forall s' \in Pref(s)$, $\Gamma_i(s') \geq 0$, $m[h.s\rangle \Longrightarrow m[s.h\rangle$;

– *divergent-free iff* $\forall s \in L^\omega(N, m_0)$, $|s|_{T_0 \cup F} = \infty$;

– *quasi-persistent iff* $\forall i \in I$, $\forall m \in Reach(N, m_0)$, $\forall h \in H_i$,
$\forall s \in (T_0 \cup F)^*$, *such that* $m[h\rangle$ *and* $m[s\rangle$
$\exists s' \in (T_0 \cup F)^*$ *fulfilling:* $m[h.s'\rangle$, $\Pi_F(s') = \Pi_F(s)$ *and* $W(s') \geq W(s)$.
Furthermore, if $s \neq \epsilon \Longrightarrow s' \neq \epsilon$ *then the net is strongly quasi-persistent;*

– *H-similar iff* $\forall i, j \in I$, $\forall m \in Reach(N, m_0)$, $\forall s \in T_0^*$,
$\forall h_i \in H_i$, $\forall h_j \in H_j$, $\forall f_j \in F_j$
$m[h_i\rangle$ *and* $m[s.h_j.f_j\rangle \Longrightarrow \exists s' \in (T_0)^*$, $\exists f_i \in F_i$ *such that* $m[s'.h_i.f_i\rangle$ *and such that*
$s = \epsilon \Longrightarrow s' = \epsilon$;

– *HF-interchangeable iff one of these two conditions is fulfilled:*
  - $\forall m \in Reach(N, m_0)$, $\forall h, h' \in H$, $\forall f \in F$, $m[h.f\rangle \iff m[h'.f\rangle$
  - $\forall m \in Reach(N, m_0)$, $\forall h \in H$, $\forall f, f' \in F$, $m[h.f\rangle \iff m[h.f'\rangle$

The H-independence means that once a transition $h \in H_i$ is fireable it can be delayed as long as it does not need to occur in order to fire a transition of F_i. When a net is divergent-free it does not generate infinite sequences with some suffix included in H. In the pre-agglomeration scheme, we transform original sequences by permutation and deletion of transitions into sequences that can be simulated. Such an infinite sequence cannot be transformed by this way into an infinite simulateable sequence. Therefore, this condition is introduced in order to avoid this situation. The quasi-persistence ensures that in the original net the "quick" firing of transitions of H does not lead to some deadlock that could have been avoided by delaying this firing. At last, the H-similarity forbids situations where the firing of transitions of F is prevented due to a "bad" choice of a subset H_i.

Under the previous conditions (or a subset of), fundamental properties of a net are preserved by the pre-agglomeration reduction. This result is stated in the following theorem the demonstration of which is similar to that of previous theorem. Its demonstration and the proof that this reduction is a strict extension of the pre-agglomeration of Berthelot [BER 83] are provided in [HAD 04b].

THEOREM 7.10 *Let (N, m_0) be a p-agglomerable Petri net that is H-independent. If furthermore*

– (N, m_0) *is divergent-free, strongly quasi-persistent and H-similar then*

$$\Pi_{T_0 \cup F}(L^{max}(N, m_0)) = \Pi_{T_0 \cup F}(\phi(L^{max}(N_r, m_{0r})));$$

– (N, m_0) *is divergent-free then*

$$\Pi_{T_0 \cup F}(\phi(L^{\omega}(N_r, m_0))) = \Pi_{T_0 \cup F}(L^{\omega}(N, m_0));$$

– (N, m_0) *is HF-interchangeable, quasi-persistent and H-similar then*

$$(N, m_0) \text{ is live } \iff (N_r, m_0) \text{ is live.}$$

7.3.4. *Behavioral post-agglomeration*

For these reductions, we restrict I to a singleton (i.e. $I = \{1\}$ and we set $\Gamma = \Gamma_1$, $H = H_1$ and $F = F_1$). Indeed, contrary to the pre-agglomeration, we do not obtain a weakening of some application conditions when enabling a "parallel" agglomeration.

The main property that the conditions of the post-agglomeration imply is the following: in every firing sequence with an occurrence of a transition h of H followed later by an occurrence of a transition f of F, f can be immediately fired after h. From a modelling point of view, the set F represents local actions while the set H corresponds to global actions possibly involving synchronization.

DEFINITION 7.11 *Let (N, m_0) be a p-agglomerable marked net. (N, m_0) is:*

    – F-independent iff $\forall h \in H$, $\forall f \in F$, $\forall s \in (T_0 \cup H)^*$, $\forall m \in Reach(N, m_0)$, $m[h.s.f\rangle \implies m[h.f.s\rangle$;
and strongly F-independent iff $\forall h \in H$, $\forall f \in F$, $\forall s \in T^*$ s.t. $\forall s' \in Pref(s), \Gamma(s') \geq 0 \, \forall m \in Reach(N, m_0)$, $m[h.s.f\rangle \implies m[h.f.s\rangle$;

    – F-continuable iff $\forall h \in H$, $\forall s \in T^*$, s.t. $\forall s' \in Pref(s), \Gamma(s') \geq 0 \, \forall m \in Reach(N, m_0)$ $m[h.s\rangle \implies \exists f \in F$ s.t. $m[h.s.f\rangle$.

We express the dependence of the set F on the set H with three hypotheses. We first notice that, in the original net, the transitions $h \in H_i$ and $f \in F_i$ may be live whilst the sequence $h.f$ is not live. Thus the HF-interchangeability condition forbids this behavior. The F-independence means that any firing of $f \in F$ may be anticipated just after the occurrence of a transition $h \in H$ which enables this firing. The F-continuation means that an excess of occurrences of $h \in H$ can always be reduced by subsequent firings of transitions of F.

The following theorem expresses which properties are preserved by the post-agglomeration giving the required conditions in each case. The first point is related to the maximal sequences and allows the modeler to look for deadlocks for instance. The second point is related to infinite sequences, which characterize, for instance, fairness properties. More generally these two points allow any (action-based) linear time logic that does not observe transitions of F to be checked. The third point is related to the Petri net liveness as liveness cannot be specified with linear time logic. Note that we proved in [HAD 04b] that this reduction is a strict extension of the post-agglomeration of Berthelot [BER 83].

THEOREM 7.12 *Let (N, m_0) be a p-agglomerable Petri net. If furthermore*
    – (N, m_0) is F-continuable then

$$\Pi_{T_0 \cup H}(L^{max}(N, m_0)) = \Pi_{T_0 \cup H}(\phi(L^{max}(N_r, m_0)));$$

    – (N, m_0) is F-continuable and strongly F-independent then

$$\Pi_{T_0 \cup H}(L^{\omega}(N, m_0)) = \Pi_{T_0 \cup H}(\phi(L^{\omega}(N_r, m_0)));$$

    – (N, m_0) is F-continuable, F-independent and HF-interchangeable then

$$(N, m_0) \text{ is live } \iff (N_r, m_0) \text{ is live.}$$

We propose in this section sufficient structural conditions that imply the behavioral conditions presented previously and subsequently, the preservation of most properties of the net. We propose two sets of conditions: one based intensively on the use of linear invariants of the net, and one, which is more simple, which corresponds to Berthelot's initial conditions and is only based on the graph structure of the net.

First of all, we show a general methodology that enables the definition of structural conditions that characterize behaviors of the model using linear invariants of the model.

7.3.5. *Structural conditions and linear invariants of the nets*

Behavioral hypotheses defined in the previous section cannot be used directly in practice as they refer to the behavior of the model. In the worst case, verifying these hypotheses leads the reachability graph to be built before applying the reductions!

An initial method to ensure specific behavior of a net is to strictly restrict the Petri net graph in order to constrain the possible evolution of the model. For instance, the preset of a transition can be limited to a singleton. Then, the firing of the transition is only dependent on the marking of this simple place and then it can ensured that the transition is fireable as soon as this place is sufficiently marked. Generally, this kind of strategy leads to severe conditions that restrict the possible application of the transformation.

Another way to depict the behavior of a net is to use algebraical conditions based on flows and linear invariants of the net. These flows and invariants can be obtained by two means: the first one is to apply algorithms such as the Gaussian elimination or the Farkas algorithm [COL 91] when positive constraints on coefficients are required. The second is to derive already known information when nets are produced by an automatic generation from a high-level specification. We will study these algorithms in the next section.

We show now the method that can be used to define structural and algebraical conditions corresponding to the behavioral hypothesis defined in previous definitions. We illustrate these principles on the Petri net depicted in Figure 7.1 for which a simple computation leads to the following invariants:

– $\forall m \in Reach(N, m_0), m(p)+m(q)+m(u) = 1$ meaning that the sum of tokens contained in places p, q and u is always equal to 1;

– $\forall m \in Reach(N, m_0), m(r1)+m(r2) = 1$ meaning that there is always exactly one token in either $r1$ or $r2$.

Let us suppose that we want to establish the following properties:

1) when the process is in the state p (i.e. p is marked) it is never suspended (either $f1$ or $f2$ is fireable). This illustrates the F-continuation;

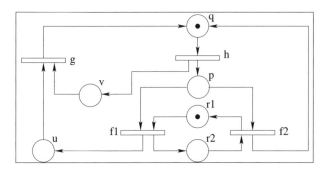

Figure 7.1. *A simple Petri net*

2) when the process is in the state p some activity is forbidden (e.g. g is not fireable). This illustrates the H-independence.

For the first property we build a linear programming problem (LP problem) in which we associate a variable x_p with each place p, which denotes the number of tokens contained in this place. Thus an assignment of the variables is equivalent to a potential marking since we introduce the linear invariants of the net to characterize a superset of the reachable markings. The constraints of this LP problem are defined by the invariants of the net, by the hypothesis that p is marked, and by the negation of the conclusion (i.e. neither $f1$ nor $f2$ are fireable). We conclude that the property is satisfied if the LP is not satisfiable (but the converse is not true).

$$
\left[
\begin{array}{l}
\forall i \in P, x_i \geq 0 \\
\left.\begin{array}{l} x_q + x_p + x_u = 1 \\ x_{r1} + x_{r2} = 1 \end{array}\right\} \\
x_p \geq 1 \\
\left.\begin{array}{l} x_{r1} = 0 \\ x_{r2} = 0 \end{array}\right\}
\end{array}
\right.
\qquad
\begin{array}{l}
\text{the markings are positive} \\[4pt]
\text{the constraints defined by the invariants are satisfied} \\[4pt]
\text{the place } p \text{ is marked} \\[4pt]
\text{neither the transition } f1 \text{ nor the transition } f2 \text{ is fireable}
\end{array}
$$

The second property is expressed similarly. Let us observe that here the negation of the conclusion leads to lower bounds for markings of places.

$$
\left[
\begin{array}{l}
\forall i \in P, x_i \geq 0 \\
\left.\begin{array}{l} x_q + x_p + x_u = 1 \\ x_{r1} + x_{r2} = 1 \end{array}\right\} \\
x_p \geq 1 \\
\left.\begin{array}{l} x_v \geq 1 \\ x_u \geq 1 \end{array}\right\}
\end{array}
\right.
\qquad
\begin{array}{l}
\text{the markings are positive} \\[4pt]
\text{the constraints defined by the invariants are satisfied} \\[4pt]
\text{the place } p \text{ is marked} \\[4pt]
\text{the transition } g \text{ is fireable}
\end{array}
$$

PROPOSITION 7.13 (Transition freezing) *Let* (N, m_0) *be a Petri net, p be a place and t be a transition. Suppose that the LP problem where:*

– the variables are $\{x_q\}_{q \in P}$*;*

– the constraints are given by the positivity of the variables, the invariants of the net and by the inequations $x_p \geq 1$ *and* $\forall q \in {}^\bullet t$, $x_q \geq W^-[q, t]$*;*

does not admit a solution. Then $\forall m \in Reach(N, m_0)$, $m(p) > 0 \Longrightarrow NOT\ m[t\rangle$. *We say that p freezes t. By extension, p freezes a set of transitions T' if $\forall t \in T'$, p freezes t.*

Since we want to prove the non-existence of a marking satisfying the linear problem, we should solve an integer linear problem (ILP). It is well-known that solving an ILP may be highly time-consuming. Thus a less accurate sufficient condition is to interpret this problem as a rational linear problem. This satisfiability checking is now processed in polynomial time. Moreover, practical experiments have shown that, for the kind of problems we solve, it seldom occurs that the ILP is unsatisfiable when the LP is satisfiable. This shows that the structural conditions are quite accurate w.r.t. the behavioral conditions.

7.3.6. *HPP structural and algebraical conditions*

Using the previous method it is possible to capture behavioral conditions stated in the previous section with the help of algebraical and structural conditions.

We now propose five structural conditions that imply the respect of the behavioral hypotheses used in the previous section. Some of them are only based on structural constraints while others use both structural and algebraical conditions.

We first provide those corresponding to the pre-agglomeration. All proofs of propositions stated in this section can be found in [HAD 04b].

The first handles the potential agglomerability. This behavioral hypothesis can be easily ensured by the following structural sufficient condition: $\forall i \in I$, $\exists p_i$ such that $m_0(p_i) = 0$, ${}^\bullet p_i = H_i$, $p_i{}^\bullet = F_i$, and $\forall h \in H_i, \forall f \in F_i, W^+(p_i, h) = W^-(p_i, f) = 1$.

The HF-interchangeable hypothesis ensures that any transitions of H_i can be replaced by any other transition of H_i or similarly that any transition of F_i can be replaced by any other transition of F_i. We propose four simple structural conditions that guarantee such a behavior. Conditions 2 and 3 are related to the F-interchangeability and conditions 1 and 4 are related to the H-interchangeability. The technical aspect of point 4 is due to the fact that if H_i and F_i are not reduced to a singleton, then the possibility to replace a transition h by a transition h' implies an equivalence in term of pre-conditions but also an equivalence in term of tokens produced by these transitions and needed for the firing of a transition of F_i.

PROPOSITION 7.14 (Structural HF-interchangeability) *A sp-agglomerable net* (N, m_0) *is HF-interchangeable if $\forall i \in I$, one of these conditions is fulfilled:*

1) $|H_i| = 1$;

2) $|F_i| = 1$;

3) $\forall f, f' \in F_i, \forall p \in P, W^-(p, f) = W^-(p, f')$;

4) $\forall h, h' \in H_i$
- $\forall p \in P, W^-(p, h) = W^-(p, h')$ *and*
- $\forall f \in F_i, \forall p \in h^\bullet \cap {}^\bullet f, W^+(p, h) = W^+(p, h')$.

In the following figure (Figure 7.2), the model on the left does not verify the structural conditions: neither H_i nor F_i are reduced to a singleton, and place $q2$ prevents from verifying point 3 or 4. In the model of the right, since $Pre(q2, f) = Pre(q2, f')$ the point 3 is fulfilled. Thus HF-interchangeability is verified.

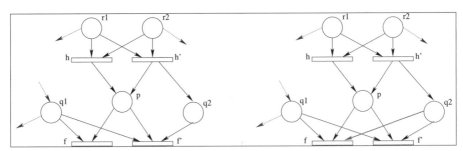

Figure 7.2. *Example of nets illustrating the structural HF-interchangeability*

In order to obtain a structural characterization of the H-independence, we require first that the tokens produced by a transition $h \in H_i$ (other than the one produced in p_i) cannot be consumed by a transition which does not belong to F_i while the place p_i is marked. Furthermore, in the case where such a token can be consumed by a transition of F_i, the transitions H_i are frozen by the place p_i.

PROPOSITION 7.15 (Structural H-independence) *A sp-agglomerable net* (N, m_0) *is H-independent if:*
$\forall i \in I$, denoting $HP_i = (H_i^\bullet \setminus \{p_i\})$;

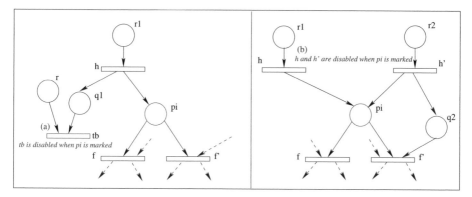

Figure 7.3. *Illustration of the structural conditions of the H-independence*

a) p_i freezes $HP_i^\bullet \setminus F_i$;

b) if $HP_i^\bullet \cap F_i \neq \emptyset$ then p_i freezes H_i.

The divergence freeness hypothesis focuses on the possibility of entering an infinite loop composed only of transitions of H. In order to structurally forbid this behavior we impose that either the places p_i are structurally bounded (point 1) or that the firing of transitions of H requires tokens that are not produced by these transitions (point 2). In both cases, the undesirable behavior is disabled.

PROPOSITION 7.16 (Structural divergence freeness) *A   sp-agglomerable   net* (N, m_0) *is divergent-free if* $\forall i \in I$,

  1) either p_i is covered by a positive flow;

  2) or $\forall h \in H_i$, $\exists q \in {}^\bullet h$ such that ${}^\bullet q \subset T_0 \cup F$.

The main idea on which the structural condition of the quasi-persistence is based is that any transition that can be in conflict with a transition h of H either has no impact on the marking (it is a neutral transition as the transition $t0$ in Figure 7.4) or such that a conflict is not effective (transition t in Figure 7.4). One more time, this last point is obtained by the expression of a linear programming problem using positive flows of the net.

PROPOSITION 7.17 (Structural quasi-persistence) *A   sp-agglomerable   net   is quasi-persistent if one of the following structural conditions are verified:* $\forall h \in H$, $\forall t \in ({}^\bullet h)^\bullet \setminus H$, *then*

1) either $t \in T_0$ is a neutral transition;

2) or the linear programming problem where
  - the variables are $\{x_q\}_{q \in P}$,
  - the constraints are defined by the positivity of the variables, the invariants of the net, and by the inequations $\forall q \in {}^\bullet h, x_q \geq W^-[q, h]$ and $\forall q \in {}^\bullet t, x_q \geq W^-[q, t]$ does not admit a solution.

If all transitions of $({}^\bullet h)^\bullet \setminus H$ verify point 2 then the net is strongly quasi-persistent.

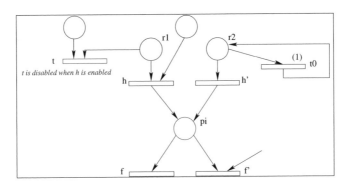

Figure 7.4. *Illustration of the structural conditions of quasi-persistence*

The H-similarity hypothesis states that when $|I| > 1$ a "bad" choice cannot be made between a transition of H_i and a transition of H_j with $i \neq j$. For instance, in Figure 7.5, $p1$ is marked and $f11$ or $f22$ is fireable implies that the firing of $f21$ or $f22$ is possible as soon as $p2$ is marked and vice-versa.

PROPOSITION 7.18 (Structural H-similarity) *A sp-agglomerable net, which is H-independent and quasi-persistent, is H-similar if:*
$\forall i, j \in I, \forall h_j \in H_j, f_j \in F_j, \forall h_i \in H_i,$
$\exists f_i \in F_i$ such that $\forall p \in {}^\bullet f_i \setminus \{p_i\}, W^-(p, h_j.f_j) \geq W^-(p, h_i.f_i).$

We now propose structural conditions for the two post-agglomeration specific behavioural properties: the F-independence and the F-continuation. We recall that $I = \{1\}$, so we abbreviate p_1 to p.

The F-independence hypothesis requires that any transition f of F can commute with sequences of $(T_0 \cup H)^*$ (or with sequences s in T^* s.t. $\forall s' \in Pref(s), \Gamma(s') \geq 0$ for the strong version). The first way to obtain this behavior is to suppose that no

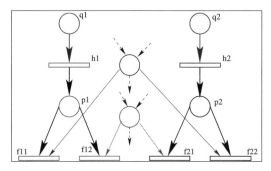

Figure 7.5. *Illustration of the structural conditions of H-similarity*

transition producing useful tokens for the firing of F can be fired when p is marked (including H for the strong version). A second method is to require that the structure of the net around concerned transitions is such that transition f commutes with other transitions.

PROPOSITION 7.19 (*F*-independence) *A sp-agglomerable net* (N, m_0) *is F-independent if* $\forall f \in F$, $\forall q \in (^{\bullet}f \setminus \{p\})$, $\forall t \in (^{\bullet}q \setminus F)$

    1) either p freezes t;

    2) or t and f fulfill conditions a) and b)

        a) $W^-(q, t) \geq min(W^+(q, t), W^-(q, f))$

        b) $W^+(q, f) \geq min(W^-(q, f), W^+(q, t))$.

A F-independent net is strongly F-independent if p freezes H.

Remark Note that if $|F| = 1$ and if the net is F-continuable then point 2.a can be suppressed.

Finally, the F-continuation condition ensures a transition of F that is fireable as soon as p is marked, always exists.

PROPOSITION 7.20 (*F*-continuation) *A sp-agglomerable net* (N, m_0) *is F-continuable if one of the three conditions is fulfilled:*

    1) $\exists f \in F$ *such that* $^{\bullet}f = \{p\}$;

    2) or $\exists F_s \subset F$ *such that:*

        a) all transitions f of F_s have only one input place p_f, which is different from
p,

b) the linear programming problem in which the variables are $\{x_q\}_{q \in P}$, the constraints are given by the positivity of the variables, the invariants of the net, and by the inequations $\forall p_f \in {}^\bullet F_s \setminus \{p\}, x_{p_f} \leq W^-[p_f, f] - 1$ and $x_p \geq 1$ does not admit a solution;

3) or $\exists\, F_s \subset F$ such that:

a) $\forall q \in {}^\bullet F_s$, q is a structural safe place (e.g. is covered by a binary positive semiflow);

b) $\forall f \in F_s, \forall q \in {}^\bullet f, W^-(q, f) = 1$;

c) the linear programming problem in which the variables are $\{x_q\}_{q \in P}$, the constraints are given by the positivity of the variables, the invariants of the net and by the inequations $\forall f \in F_s \sum_{q \in {}^\bullet f \setminus \{p\}} x_q \leq |{}^\bullet f| - 2$ and $x_p \geq 1$, does not admit a solution.

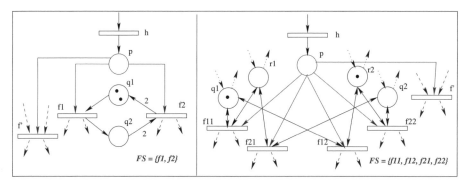

Figure 7.6. *Illustration of the structural conditions of the F-continuation*

In the left model of Figure 7.6 the invariant $\forall m, m(q1) + m(q2) = 2$ ensures that a marking m such that $m(q1) = 0$ and $m(q2) \leq 1$ cannot exist. So, as soon as p is marked one of the transition $f1$ or $f2$ is fireable. In the right model, let us suppose that there exist two invariants $m(q1) + m(q2) = 1$ and $m(r1) + m(r2) = 1$ (which may correspond to the fact that places $q1$ and $q2$ model the two possible values of a variable q when places $r1$ and $r2$ model the two possible values of a variable r). These invariants ensure that one of the four transitions $f11$ to $f22$ is fireable as soon as p is marked. Obviously, the place p may have other output transitions in both cases.

7.3.7. *Application examples*

Consider the following fragment of a Petri net (modeled in the left-hand side of Figure 7.7) modeling the access to data protected by locks (modeled by places Lock1 and Lock2) by two threads. These locks could be those associated with each Java object when Java is used in a multithreaded context. Let us note that the two processes take these locks in a different order but that these actions are performed under the protection of a mutual exclusion mechanism. Note that this construction follows some well-known guidelines used to prevent deadlocks [HAB 69].

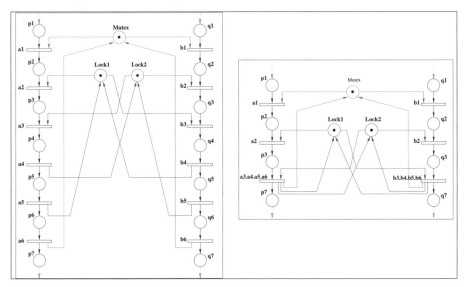

Figure 7.7. *Taking two locks under the protection of a mutex*

In this net there exist different binary places invariants (i.e. the corresponding vectors $\vec{v} \in \{0,1\}^P$) ensuring that when place $p2$ is marked then all transitions that have the place $Lock1$ as a pre-condition cannot be fired and, symmetrically, that, when place $q2$ is marked all transitions that have the place $Lock2$ as a pre-condition cannot be fired.

We now describe the reduction process. First of all, we post-agglomerate transitions $a3$ with $a4$. Then this new transition $a3.a4$ can be post-agglomerated with $a5$ and then with $a6$. We also apply a similar sequence of post-agglomerations on transitions $b3$ to $b6$ and we obtain then the model on the right-hand side of Figure 7.7.

However, using algebraic part of the conditions enables in net reduction to go further. Indeed, if we consider $H = \{a2\}$ and $F = \{a3.a4.a5.a6\}$ we immediately note that the net is p-agglomerable around place $p3$. Let us prove that the five hypotheses of the pre-agglomerations are fulfilled:

– HF-interchangeability: since $|H| = |F| = 1$ this point is obviously satisfied;

– H-independence since $a2^{\bullet} \setminus \{p3\} = \emptyset$ the set of transitions that the firing of $a2$ may enable is $a3.a4.a5.a6$. Thus, a sequence s, fireable after the firing of $a2$ from a marking m ($m[a2.s\rangle$) and such that its prefixes s' verify $\Gamma(s') > 0$, is also fireable before the firing of $a2$ ($m[s\rangle$). Let $q \neq p3 \in {}^\bullet a2$. As $a2^\bullet = \{p3\}$, $W^+(q, a2) = 0$. By hypothesis, $m(q) \geq W^-(q, a2.s) = Max(W^-(q, a2), W^-(q, s) - W(q, a2))$. So, $m(q) \geq W^-(q, a2) + W^-(q, s)$ and $m(q) \geq W^-(q, a2) + W^-(q, s) - W^+(q, s)$. It comes $m(q) + W(q, s) \geq W^-(q, a2)$. As, $m[s\rangle$, $m[s.a2\rangle$;

– divergence freeness: as the place $Lock1$ belongs to ${}^\bullet a2 \setminus a2^\bullet$, $a2$ cannot be infinitely fired and this point is also fulfilled;

– quasi-persistence: Let $S = Lock1^\bullet \setminus \{a2\}$. By construction, this net satisfies the invariant $\forall m \in Reach(N, m_0), m(Mutex) + m(p2) + m(p3) + m(q2) + m(q3) = 1$. So, when $p2$ is marked, transition $b3.b4.b5.b6 \in S$ is not fireable. So this point is also fulfilled;

– H-similarity: As here H is a singleton this point is obviously fulfilled.

We obtain the net depicted in the left-hand side of Figure 7.8. Now, symmetrically, we perform a pre-agglomeration around place $q3$. This leads to the model at the top right of Figure 7.8.

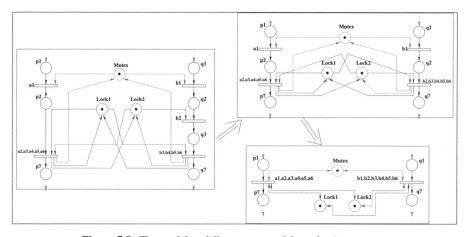

Figure 7.8. *The model at different stages of the reduction process*

At last, we can apply a "parallel" pre-agglomeration of $a1$ with $a2.a3.a4.a5.a6$ and of $b1$ with $b2.b3.b4.b5.b6$ ($H_1 = \{a1\}$ and $F_1 = \{a2.a3.a4.a5.a6\}$, $H_2 = \{b1\}$ and $F_2 = \{b2.b3.b4.b5.b6\}$) to this model. Note that it is also possible to first suppress places $Lock1$ and $Lock2$ (that are now implicit places [2]) and then apply two post-agglomerations. This reduction is interesting since no reduction with I reduced to a singleton is possible.

In the final model, the two threads atomically operate on the locks.

7.3.8. *Linear invariants and applications*

Flows, semi-flows and P and T invariants.

A shown previously, it is possible to use the structure of the model to simplify its analysis by reducing it while maintaining its properties. We show in this section that the structure of the net can be used to directly obtain results about some properties of the model. Again, as we use only the structure of the model, we can perform a parametrized analysis and we do not need to build part or whole of the reachability graph.

Let $X \in \mathbb{Z}^P$ be a natural vector indexed by P, the set of places of the net. If we denote by $W(t)$ the tth column of the incidence matrix, we can note the state equation rule as:

$$^tX.M' = {}^tX.M + {}^tX.W(t)$$

If we suppose now that $^tX.W(t) = 0$ then we can state that $^tX.M' = {}^tX.M$, and particularly $^tX.M' = {}^tX.M_0$. This last equation states that the weighted sum of tokens in places defined by the support of X, $Supp(X)$, remains constant whatever the evolution of system is. For all $t \in T$,

$$\sum_{p \in P} X(p).M(p) = \sum_{p \in P} X(p).M'(p).$$

Thus, integer solutions of the equation $^tX.W = 0$ will characterize *linear invariants* of the studied model.

These invariants can be computed using either the Gauss' algorithm, cases in which positive constraints on weights not put, or with the Farkas' algorithm, case in which positive invariants are sought. Note that the use of positive invariants leads to more complex calculus but simplifies the interpretation of found invariants w.r.t. the model semantic.

Example 7.1 Let us suppose that we want to analyze the following net (Figure 7.9), which models the mutual exclusion of two processes on a common resource. Note that the place Counter imposes that process b accesses the critical section a number of times less or equal than the process a does.

---

2. An implicit place is a place that never disables the firing of any transition by itself; this kind of places can be characterized using structural and algebraic conditions.

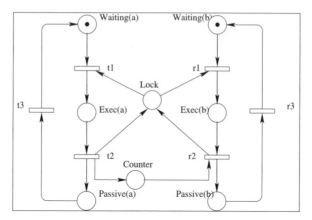

Figure 7.9. *A model for a bi-partite mutual exclusion*

In order to prove that this model defines an effective mutual exclusion between process a and process b, the first method consists of building the reachability graph and verifying that for each state, when a process i is in the critical section (place Exec(i) is marked) then the other process is not in the critical section (place Exec(j), $j \neq i$ is not marked). While this model is quite simple, it is not bounded, and so, its reachability graph is infinite and then this property cannot be proved using this strategy.

However, a set of generative positive invariants of the model can be generated (the complexity of which does not depend on the reachability graph). Applying the Farkas' algorithm on this model gives three positive flows:

1) $Waiting(a) + Exec(a) + Passive(a) = cst(M_0) = 1;$
2) $Waiting(b) + Exec(b) + Passive(b) = cst(M_0) = 1;$
3) $Exec(a) + Exec(b) + Lock = cst(M_0) = 1.$

The two first invariants state that the net models two processes that are in one of their three possible states. The last allows us to state the mutual exclusion since either the Resource is free (place Lock is marked) or one process is in the Exec state (place Exec(a) or Exec(a) is marked).

Before giving an efficient version of the Farkas' algorithm we precisely define a minimal generative family of flows or of positive flows.

DEFINITION 7.21 (Generative Family) *Let A be an integer matrix where rows are indexed by a finite set P and columns are indexed by a finite set T. A generative family in $\mathbb{Q}$ (resp. Q^+) of the equation $^tX.A = 0$ is a finite family $\{V_1, \ldots, V_m\}$ of non-null vectors in $(Q^+))$ (resp. $(Q^+)^P$) s.t.:*

$- \forall \ V_i, \ {}^tV_i.A = 0;$

$- \forall \ V \ \in \ (Q^+) \ (resp. \ (Q^+)^P) \ with \ {}^tV.A = 0,$
$\exists \lambda_1, \ldots, \lambda_m \in Q \ (resp.Q^+) \ s.t. \ V = \lambda_1.V_1 + \ldots + \lambda_m.V_m.$

The family is a minimal generative family if removing one item of this family leads to a non-generative family.

The rows of the matrix corresponds to variables of the system while columns represent equations that link variables.

The principle of the Farkas' algorithm consists of building a generative family of invariants of the system reduced to its first i equations from a generative family of the system reduced to its first $i - 1$ equations as follows: giving the equation (column) i, keep all vectors that satisfy this equations (0 in the column), and combine two-by-two vectors for which the equation i leads to a positive (positive number in the column) result with those for which the equation i leads to a negative result (negative number in the column).

The most important difficulty of this algorithm is that it may compute useless solutions (in sense that they are linear combinations of other solutions) which may lead to a possible "explosion" of the number of solutions. In order to quickly eliminate these useless solutions, a characterization of a minimal generative family based on the support of solutions can be used.

PROPOSITION 7.22 *Let $F = \{V_1, \ldots, V_m\}$ be a family of non-null vectors in $(Q^+)^P$ s.t. $\forall i, {}^tV_i.A = 0$. F is a minimal generative family if:*

1) $\forall \ V \in (Q^+)^P$ s.t. ${}^tV.A = 0$ and $V \neq 0, \exists \ V_i$ s.t. $Supp(V_i) \subseteq Supp(V)$;

2) $\forall \ V \neq V' \in F$ we have not $Supp(V') \subseteq Supp(V)$.

Using this proposition we can propose an efficient version of the Farkas' algorithm (algorithm 1):

Note that some improvements may be performed on this algorithm:

– Do not randomly choose equation t to solve but choose one that minimizes some objectives;

– only compare support of solutions of the i steps with those obtained at the $i - 1$ steps (and not with those obtained at the i); this may replace a bidirectional test with a unidirectional test and is very efficient in practice [COL 91].

1) $S := \{\overrightarrow{p}/p \in P\}$ % S is the canonical basis of $E = (\mathbb{Q}^+)^P$

2) For t taking value in T DO

% *Separate vectors of S w.r.t. the sign of their projection on the equation t*

    a) $S^0 \leftarrow \{s \in S/^t s.A_t = 0\}$

    b) $S^+ \leftarrow \{s \in S/^t s.A_t > 0\}$

    c) $S^- \leftarrow \{s \in S/^t s.A_t < 0\}$

    % *now, we perform linear combinations*

    d) For (s^+, s^-) in $S^+ \times S^-$ DO

        $S \leftarrow S \bigcup \{(^t s^+.A_t).s^- - (^t s^-.A_t).s^+\}$

    End For

    % *we suppress non minimal solutions*

    e) For (s, s') in $S \times S, s \neq s'$ DO

        If $Supp(s') \subseteq Supp(s)$ Then

            $S \leftarrow S \setminus \{s\}$

        End If

    End For

End For

S is a minimal generative family of the system $^t X.W = 0, X \in \mathbb{Q}^+$.

Let us consider the following model (Figure 7.10), which corresponds to a reduced model of the well known "swimming pool" model: swimmers enter the swimming pool (transition $t0.t1$). Then they choose a cubicle to undress in, take a basket and change into a swimsuit and go swimming (transition $t2.t3$). They end by leaving the swimming pool and releasing granted resources (transition $t5.t6$). Let us apply the previous algorithm in this model.

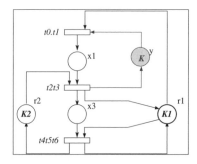

Figure 7.10. *An abstract version of the swimming pool model*

The original incidence matrix is:

$$W = \begin{array}{c} \\ \vec{y} \\ \vec{x1} \\ \vec{x3} \\ \vec{r1} \\ \vec{r2} \end{array} \overset{\begin{array}{ccc} t0.t1 & t2.t3 & t4.t5.t6 \end{array}}{\left(\begin{array}{ccc} -1 & 1 & 0 \\ 1 & -1 & 0 \\ 0 & 1 & -1 \\ -1 & 1 & 0 \\ 0 & -1 & 1 \end{array}\right)}$$

We first nullify the transition t2.t3.t4 (which is not a judicious choice but as it makes non minimal solutions appear, it enables the illustration of an important part of the algorithm). For this transition, the set S^0 is empty, $S^+ = \{\vec{y}, \vec{x3}, \vec{r1}\}$ and $S^- = \{\vec{x1}, \vec{r2}\}$. The combination of items of these two last sets leads to the following system:

$$W_1 = \begin{array}{c} \vec{y}+\vec{x1} \\ \vec{y}+\vec{r2} \\ \vec{x3}+\vec{x1} \\ \vec{x3}+\vec{r2} \\ \vec{r1}+\vec{x1} \\ \vec{r1}+\vec{r2} \end{array} \overset{\begin{array}{ccc} t0.t1 & t2.t3 & t4.t5.t6 \end{array}}{\left(\begin{array}{ccc} 0 & 0 & 0 \\ -1 & 0 & 1 \\ 1 & 0 & -1 \\ 0 & 0 & 0 \\ 0 & 0 & 0 \\ -1 & 0 & 1 \end{array}\right)}$$

We can then nullify t0.t1 by combining $\vec{x3}+\vec{x1}$ with $\vec{y}+\vec{r2}$ and $\vec{r1}+\vec{r2}$ and we obtain the matrix

$$W_1 = \begin{array}{c} \vec{y}+\vec{x1} \\ \vec{x3}+\vec{r2} \\ \vec{r1}+\vec{x1} \\ \vec{y}+\vec{r2}+\vec{x3}+\vec{x1} \\ \vec{r1}+\vec{r2}+\vec{x3}+\vec{x1} \end{array} \overset{\begin{array}{ccc} t0.t1 & t2.t3 & t4.t5.t6 \end{array}}{\left(\begin{array}{ccc} 0 & 0 & 0 \\ 0 & 0 & 0 \\ 0 & 0 & 0 \\ 0 & 0 & 0 \\ 0 & 0 & 0 \end{array}\right)}$$

At this step, the matrix is the null matrix, so the computed set is a generative family. However, the two last solutions are not minimal solutions as $Supp(\vec{y}+\vec{x1}) \subseteq Supp(\vec{y}+\vec{r2}+\vec{x3}+\vec{x1})$ and $Supp(\vec{x3}+\vec{r2}) \subseteq Supp(\vec{r1}+\vec{r2}+\vec{x3}+\vec{x1})$

These two solutions can then be suppressed while maintaining a generative family, which is done in the second part of the algorithm.

A minimal generative family of positive flows of the model of Figure 7.10 is:

$$\{(\vec{y}+\vec{x1}), (\vec{x3}+\vec{r2})(\vec{r1}+\vec{x1})\}$$

leading to the three invariants: $\forall m \in Acc(R, m_0)\ m(y) + m(x1) = K$, $m(x3) + m(r2) = K2$ and $m(r1) + m(x1) = K1$, which represent the state of the different resources of the model.

Liveness, traps, and sinks

Another way to check a property of a model is to deduce its behavior with the help of structural patterns used to guide the modeling or find by analysis the structure of the model. The most cited works in this area are those that focus on deducing liveness or weakly-liveness (deadlock freeness) from necessary or sufficient conditions on some specific sets of places called siphons. We can cite [COM 72, BAR 89, BAR 90, ESP 92b, KEM 92, COL 86, TER 93, BAR 97]. Indeed, liveness, which is an important behavioral property of nets, is closely related to the satisfiability of some predicates on siphons.

In order to simply our presentation, we restrict some propositions to *ordinary* Petri nets, i.e. Petri nets for which all valuations equal 1; see [BAR 97] for a generalization to Petri nets.

DEFINITION 7.23 *Let N be a Petri net. Let $A \subseteq P, A \neq \emptyset$.*

– A is called a siphon if and only if $^\bullet A \subseteq A^\bullet$. The siphon A is minimal if and only if it contains no other siphon as a proper subset and A is maximal if and only if none other siphon includes it.

– A is called a trap if and only if $A^\bullet \subseteq {}^\bullet A$. The trap A is minimal if and only if it contains no other trap as a proper subset and A maximal if and only if none other trap includes it.

The following propositions formalize the main characteristics of siphons and traps: as soon as a siphon becomes empty, it will remain empty forever, and, as soon as a trap is marked, it remains marked forever.

PROPOSITION 7.24 *Let (N, m_0) be an marked Petri net and S a siphon of N. Then $\forall m \in Reach(N, m_0), |m(S) = 0 \Rightarrow \forall m' \in Reach(N, m), m'(S) = 0$*

PROPOSITION 7.25 *Let (N, m_0) be marked Petri net and R a trap of N. Then $\forall m \in Reach(N, m_0), |m(R) > 0 \Rightarrow \forall m' \in Reach(N, m), m'(R) > 0$*

So, using these characteristics, it is easy to obtain the following result, which links liveness and markings of siphons:

PROPOSITION 7.26 *If an ordinary marked Petri net (N, m_0) is live then each minimal siphon remains marked for all reachable markings.*

Ensuring that each siphon remains marked is then a necessary condition for liveness; however, in the general case, ensuring that siphons remain marked is not sufficient to ensure liveness.

PROPOSITION 7.27 *Given an ordinary marked Petri net* (N, m_0) *if every minimal siphon remains marked for all reachable markings then* (N, m_0) *is weakly-live.*

So in order to build weakly-live Petri nets we have to ensure that all siphons remain marked. This can be achieved with the help of structural or algebraic conditions based on the existence of traps or places semiflows (see for instance [BAR 96]). We recall here a main proposition known as the Commoner's property.

PROPOSITION 7.28 (Commoner's property) *Given an ordinary marked Petri net* (N, m_0) *if every siphon of* N *contains a marked trap (for* m_0*) then* (N, m_0) *is weakly-live.*

Let us illustrate the use of these results on the following model (Figure 7.11) of a manufacturing system composed of two assembly lines using robots and resources for building some pieces:

This net contains five minimal siphons: $D_1 = \{p_{11}, p_1, p_{12}, p_{22}, p_{13}, p_{23}, p_{14}, p_{24}\}$, $D_2 = \{p_{21}, p_1 + p_{12}, p_{22}, p_{13}, p_{23}, p_{14}, p_{24}\}$, $D_3 = \{robot, p_{12}, p_{22}, p_{14}, p_{24}\}$, $D_4 = \{resources, p_{13}, p_{23}\}$ and $D_5 = \{robot, resources, p_{14}, p_{24}\}$

The four siphons D_1, D_2, D_3, D_4 are traps; so they will remain marked as soon as they are initially marked. We can ensure that the siphon D_5 will remain marked using the two following invariants $f_1 = robot + ressources - p_1 - p_{11}$, $f_2 = robot + ressources - p_1 - p_{21}$ which state that for any reachable marking m, $m(robot) + m(resources) = m_0(robot) + m_0(resources) - m_0(p1) - min(m_0(p11) + m_0(p21)) + m(p1) + min(m(p11) + m(p21))$

So, we can ensure that as soon as $m_0(robot) + m_0(resources) > m_0(p1) + min(m_0(p11) + m_0(p21))$ and $m_0(robot) > 0$ and $m_0(resources) > 0$, the net is weakly-live.

Controlling siphons guarantees the absence of a deadlock. However, in order to decide liveness, we have to restrict the model of concurrency of our models, which also corresponds to a need to reflect the behavior of human processes. Indeed, in organizations, the business processes use often limited types of synchronizations, so we can model realistic models without using general Petri nets. Furthermore, restricting patterns to specific ones simplifies also the complexity about deciding the correct behaviors of a model. The most relevant results in this domain concern the subclass of Petri nets called *free-choice* Petri nets.

DEFINITION 7.29 *A Petri net* N *is said to be a free-choice net if* $\forall p \in P, \forall t \in T$, $p \in {}^{\bullet}t \Rightarrow {}^{\bullet}t = \{p\}$ *or* $p^{\bullet} = \{t\}$

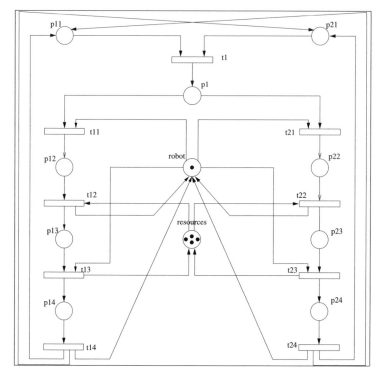

Figure 7.11. *A manufacturing system*

In other words, it is possible to model conflict and choice with the help of free-choice nets but both cannot occur at the same time.

Note that the previous definition is equivalent to the following assertion. Given two places p and q (resp. two transitions t and r) either $p^\bullet \cap q^\bullet = \emptyset$ or $p^\bullet = q^\bullet$ (resp. $^\bullet t \cap ^\bullet r = \emptyset$ or $^\bullet t = ^\bullet r$).

For this kind of Petri net, Commoner's property establishes the liveness of a model with the help of the trap control of its siphons.

PROPOSITION 7.30 (Commoner's property for free-choice nets) *A marked free-choice Petri net (N, m_0) is live if and only if each siphon of N contains a marked trap (for m_0).*

This proposition shows the main advantage of free-choice nets w.r.t. model analysis: the liveness can be stated with the help of structural characteristics, but we can go a step further with the following theorem, which links simultaneous liveness and boundedness with pure structural properties that can be checked in polynomial time.

THEOREM 7.31 (rank theorem) *A marked free-choice Petri net* (N, m_0) *is live and bounded if and only the four hypotheses hold:*

1) N is a strongly connected net: i.e. $\forall x, x' \in T \cup P$, *there exists a direct path from x to* x';

2) N is covered by states machines: i.e. there exist a decomposition of N in a set of subnets $(\{N_i\})$ *such that each sub net* N_i *is a state machine (each transition of* N_i *has a unique input place and a unique output place in* N_i);

3) $rank(W) = |\theta| - 1$ *where* θ *denotes the equivalence relation defined on T by:* $t\,\theta\,t'$ *iff* $^\bullet t = {}^\bullet t'$ *(t and* t' *are in equal conflit);*

4) each siphon of N is marked for m_0.

These four properties can be checked in a polynomial time using Tarjan's algorithm for testing the strong connectivity, the Gauss algorithm to check the rank of the incidence matrix, and by building specific siphons in a polynomial time for testing the third and fourth conditions; see [ESP 92b] for details on this result.

7.4. Formal verification by model-checking

The following sections present approaches designed for behavioral verification of finite state systems. Model-checking generally consists of an exhaustive exploration of the state space of a system, which seeks for "bad" behaviors with respect to a given property. This approach faces the combinatorial state-space explosion problem, thus requires specific algorithms and data structures to tackle the storage and exploration of the state graph.

We first define the reachability graph and explain how it can be used to check behavioral properties, focusing on properties expressed using temporal logic. We then give an overview of the most important families of approaches that have been proposed to tackle model-checking. Then we describe four of these approaches in more detail based respectively on reduced decision diagrams, partial order reductions, symmetry exploitation, and SAT-based solvers (i.e. algorithms solving the propositional satisfiability problem).

7.4.1. *Reachability graph*

This section presents the general problems raised when attempting to generate a reachability graph, and how to exploit this graph to automatically verify the properties of a system.

Model-checking consists of exploring all the possible configurations of a system. A reachability graph is a graph where vertices represent the states of the system, and edges represent the occurrence of events that induce a change of state. The principle of generation is straightforward, starting from an initial state s_0 and given a transition relation T that describes all the events that can potentially occur in the system, the graph is built inductively. Since by hypothesis the system has a finite state space, the procedure terminates.

1 Algorithm **ReachabilityGraph(M)**
   Data: Let,
   input : M : $\langle s_0, T \rangle$ a system and its initial state
   local : *todo* : initially empty, set of known states that need to be explored
   output : *graph* : the reachability graph of the system

2 **begin**
3   *todo*.push(s_0)
4   **while** *todo* $\neq \emptyset$ **do**
5          $s := todo$.pop()
6   **foreach** $t \in T$ **do**
7   **if** t *enabled in* s **then**
8                  $s' := succ(s, t)$
9   **if** $s' \notin graph$ **then**
10                     $graph$.addState(s')
11                     $todo$.push(s')
12   graph.addEdge(s,s')

13   Return graph
14 **end**

Algorithm 1: Building a state graph

The algorithm *ReachabilityGraph* presents a simple algorithm to build a reachability graph. When *todo* is a first-in, first-out (FIFO) queue, exploration order is a breadth-first search (BFS), all direct successors of a node are explored before exploring their own successors. If *todo* is a stack, the exploration order is a variant on a depth-first search (DFS), i.e. the algorithm tends to follow a path until it reaches a previously known state, before switching to the next path. A DFS can easily be implemented using a recursive function, with the call stack replacing the *todo* stack. Regardless of the exploration order chosen, the algorithm stops when all states have been explored. The graph once built can be used to look for desired (or undesirable) behaviors. Verification of behavioral properties is thus reduced to simply exploring a labeled graph.

This enumerative approach has as strength its simplicity and the fact that it can be entirely automated with ease, thus requiring less expertise from the user. In this respect, model-checking can be contrasted to theorem-proving, which meets the same goal of verifying behavioral properties of a system by assisting the user to establish a formal mathematical proof. In theorem-proving, the system is seen as a set of axioms, and properties are seen as theorems that need to be proved. Proving a property requires manual intervention of an expert, while in model-checking the whole process can be fully automated. However, model-checking cannot be easily scaled up, as the state graph explodes in size, but theorem-proving can often provide inductive proofs that scale up to the size of an arbitrary system.

The critical limitation for model-checking is the exponential blow-up of the size of the state space when the system grows. To implement the test of line (9), a hash table, which stores the nodes of the graph is typically used, but this introduces a memory complexity blow-up as all nodes are stored.

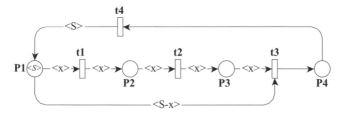

Figure 7.12. *A colored Petri net representing a resource access protocol. P1: idle, P2: requestCS, P3: wait, P4: critical ection*

For instance, consider Figure 7.12, which represents a colored Petri net modeling a simple resource access protocol among several process (see Figure2.9 and accompanying text for a presentation of this formalism). The model is parameterized by a variable $< x >$ of domain $Proc = \{pr1, pr2, \ldots\}$ the process identity. Initially, all process are idle, which is modeled by the S marker in place $P1$, representing one occurrence of each process id. Each process can autonomously decide to ask for access to the resource (thus moving to $P2$), when this request is received by the controller, the process moves to $P3$. Process $< x >$ then waits until all other process (represented by $S - x$ on arc from $P1$ to $t3$) are idle to access the resource in place $P4$.

The number of reachable states of this system can be analytically computed, since each process can be in any of three states ($P1$, $P2$ or $P3$) regardless of the other's states. An additional state where the only marked place is $P4$ represents the resource access phase for any process. Thus the state space contains $3^n + 1$ states when the system contains n processes. Table 7.1 highlights this exponential blow-up of the state space as n grows.

Processes	States		Processes	States
2	10		8	6 562
4	82		10	59 050
6	730		20	3 486 784 402

Table 7.1. *Exponential blow-up of the state space as the number of processes grow*

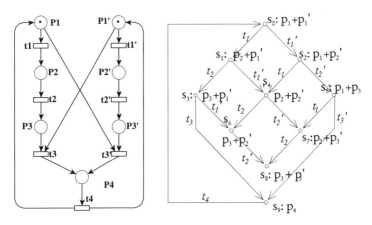

Figure 7.13. *Equivalent Petri net for two processes and its reachability graph*

Distributed and concurrent protocols often contain subtle errors, which are difficult to reproduce, but that can lead to system deadlock. Non-determinism due to the process scheduler that selects which process will progress leads to numerous possible interleaving of actions, some of which might lead to problematic situations.

For instance, the protocol described in Figure 7.12 allows a deadlock to occur. For more clarity, we show in Figure 7.13 the same protocol instantiated for just two concurrent process, and its state graph. The state $s_4 : p3 + p3'$ is a reachable deadlock state, but there are infinitely many executions that go through state $s_3 : p4$ and never deadlock. Test-based validation of such non-deterministic systems is prone to missing these tricky bad interleaving of actions.

Computing the state graph of a system allows properties that can be evaluated locally to a state, to be immediately proved or invalidated. Typically, a deadlock consists is a state with no successors, and a safety property requires that a given atomic property holds in all reachable states. An atomic property is a predicate that can be evaluated to be either true or false in any given state. More complex behavioral properties referring to execution paths or circuits in the state graph can also be verified, using standard graph algorithms. For instance, checking whether a given (nominal) situation can always be reached from any state, allows confidence that the system can repair itself to be gained.

A general framework for the verification of such behavioral properties, called the automata theoretic approach to model-checking, has been defined. In the following sections, we introduce this approach dedicated to the verification of linear-time temporal logic, then we provide an overview of the various approaches that have been proposed to improve the efficiency of model-checking techniques (section 7.5). A representative subset of these techniques is then presented in more detail. To allow easier comparison of these techniques, we will use the state graph of Figure 7.13 as a running example.

7.4.2. *Automata theoretic approach to model-checking*

To check simple reachability properties, such as the presence of deadlock states (that have no successors) or the the existence of invariants, a simple traversal of the nodes of the reachability graph is sufficient. For more complex behavioral properties reasoning on sequences of states, variants of temporal logics are used, of which the most common are linear-time temporal logic (LTL) and the branching time computation tree Logic (CTL) [CLA 86]. Verification of CTL formulas is a well-studied domain (see [VAR 01] for an overview), but it can be reduced to (nested) reachability computations, thus it is not developed in this chapter. We present here a framework for the verification of LTL formulas.

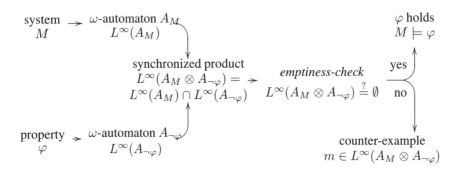

Figure 7.14. *Automata-theoretic approach to model checking*

In the automata theoretic approach to model-checking (Figure 7.14), the model M of a system is seen as an automaton A_M, composed of states and transitions, that accepts words of infinite length (called ω-words and ω-automaton). The letters of these ω-words correspond to a given configuration or state of the system. The *language* of the automaton (denoted $L^\infty(A_M)$) is the set of ω-words it accepts; it represents all possible behaviors of the system.

Furthermore, the behavioral property φ we want to check holds on M is itself expressed as an ω-automaton $A_{\neg\varphi}$ whose language is the set of all behaviors that *contradict* or invalidate property φ.

Two fundamental operations allow to decide whether $L^\infty(A_M)$ and $L^\infty(A_{\neg\varphi})$ are not disjoint, hence they share an ω-word, i.e. if there exists an execution of the system M for which φ does not hold. First the synchronized product of the two automata is built, it is itself an ω-automaton that accepts the intersection of the two languages. Then an *emptiness-check* algorithm is run on this product, allowing to decide whether its language is empty.

If the language of the product is empty, then there are no executions of M where φ does not hold. Otherwise a counter-example (or witness trace), i.e. an ω-word representing a forbidden execution of the system according to φ can be exhibited, to help the user debug his or her design.

This approach to model-checking is very general: it can be applied to any finite state system. It also allows a wide class of properties to be checked, and is easily extended to compositional models, which are defined as a synchronized product of communicating finite-state ω-automata.

7.4.3. *Automata and temporal logic*

The automata theoretic approach allows infinite sets (the languages) to be manipulated while using a finite representation (ω-automata). Many types of ω-automata exist, varying in both syntax and semantics. The most common type of ω-automata presented here is called Büchi automata.

Any property expressed by a Büchi automaton can thus be checked using the automata-theoretic approach. However, directly modeling properties as automata is a difficult and error prone task. Typically a temporal logic such as LTL is preferred as it has clearer semantics and its formula can be translated into Büchi automata [VAR 96]: In fact, Büchi automata are strictly more expressive than LTL.

LTL formulas are built from propositional Boolean variables called *atomic properties*, the usual boolean logic connectors ($\neg$, $\vee$, $\wedge$, $\Rightarrow$, ...), and *temporal operators* (F, G, U, X, ...).

Atomic properties allow states of the system to be characterized. They are Boolean variables whose value is known in any state of the system. A state s is *labeled* by atomic property ϕ if and only if ϕ holds true in s. Temporal operators allow to reason on sequences of states in a given execution of the system. Gf means the LTL subformula f must always (*Generally*) hold from this point on. Ff indicates that f must hold at some F*uture* point of this execution. Xf forces f to hold in the immediate successor (*neXt*) state. Finally fUg holds if f holds U*ntil* g does.

For instance, in Figure 7.12, atomic proposition $[P1.pr_1 + P2.pr_2]$ holds when a request of process pr_2 has been sent (in place $P2$) and simultaneously pr_1 is idle (occupying place $P1$). LTL formula $G([P1.pr_1 + P2.pr_2] \Rightarrow F[P4])$ specifies that when this situation occurs, therewill be in the future (F) necessarily an access to the critical section ($P4$). On the Petri net with two processes of Figure 7.13, $G([p_1 + p_2'] \Rightarrow F[p_4])$ expresses the same property.

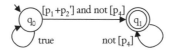

Figure 7.15. *Automaton* $A_{\neg G([p_1 + p_2'] \Rightarrow [p_4])}$

The Büchi automaton of Figure 7.15 accepts all execution sequences that invalidate the property $G([p_1 + p_2'] \Rightarrow F[p_4])$. Any ω-word accepted by this automata corresponds to an infinite sequence of states (or run), starting in the *initial* automata state (as marked by an edge with no source), and that infinitely often traverses the *acceptance state* represented by a double circle. The alphabet of this automaton is a set of atomic properties, which can be evaluated in any state of the system. An accepted word is then defined by the sequence of arc labels that are traversed to build this sequence of states.

For instance, $(true)(true)([p_1 + p_2'] \wedge \neg[p_4])(\neg[p_4])...(\neg[p_4])$ is an accepted word. The atomic proposition *true* holds in any state. For this automata, the set of accepted words can also be described by the regular expression $(true)^*([p_1 + p_2'] \wedge \neg[p_4])^1(\neg[p_4])^\infty$, where $*$ denotes an arbitrary finite number of repetitions, 1 denotes a single occurrence and ∞ an infinite number of repetitions of the letter (or arc label) in the word. Note that infinite sequences of *true* that remain on the initial state are not accepted.

7.4.4. *Automata and synchronized product*

Following the approach presented in Figure 7.14, the automaton $A_{\neg\varphi}$ corresponding to the negation of the property φ needs to be synchronized with the automaton A_M, which represents all possible behaviors of the system, to determine the existence of behaviors the contradict the formula. To relate the alphabet of $A_{\neg\varphi}$ (i.e. atomic propositions) to system states in A_M each state of the system is seen as being labeled by the truth values of each atomic property. A synchronized product is a Büchi automaton in which states are tuples $\langle s, q \rangle$ where s is a state of the system and q is a state of the Büchi automata $A_{\neg \varphi}$. For any state $\langle s_1, q_1 \rangle$ of this automaton, its successors are defined as nodes $\langle s_2, q_2 \rangle$ such that:

- s_2 is a successor of s_1 in the system;
- q_2 is a successor of q_1 in the Büchi automata;
- s_1 is labeled by the atomic propositions on the edge $q_1 \rightarrow q_2$;
- $\langle s_2, q_2 \rangle$ is accepting iff q_2 is accepting.

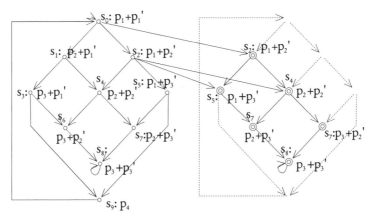

Figure 7.16. *Synchronized product with the automata* $A_{\neg G([p_1 + p_2'] \Rightarrow F[p_4])}$

Any accepted run of the synchronized product can be exhibited as a counter-example of the desired property $G([p_1 + p_2'] \Rightarrow F[p_4])$, and the property holds on the system if and only if the language of the product is empty. Note that since we only consider ω-words in this approach, deadlock states require a special treatment as they induce the existence of finite maximal runs in the system. A special atomic property *dead* is typically added to the logic, and self-loop edges bearing the label *dead* are added to any deadlock state of the system.

Figure 7.16 shows the synchronized product of the reachability graph of Figure 7.13 and the automata of Figure 7.15. The left part represents system states that are synchronized with state q_0 of the automata, while the right part represents states synchronized with q_1. Dashed lines and states are not part of the product, as they do not match the synchronized product construction rules.

In this product, we can deduce that property $\varphi : G([p_1 + p_2'] \Rightarrow F[p_4])$ does not hold, since the ω-word $\langle q_0, s_0 \rangle \langle q_0, s_1 \rangle \langle q_1, s_2 \rangle \langle q_1, s_4 \rangle (\langle q_1, s_5 \rangle)^{\infty}$ is accepted, thus the language of $A_M \otimes A_{\neg \varphi}$ is *not* empty. Through similar reasoning we could prove that $G([p_2 + p_2'] \Rightarrow \neg F[p_4])$ holds (any state in which two requests have been sent simultaneously in $P2$ leads to the critical section becoming unreachable).

Emptiness-check can be performed in linear time and memory with respect to the size of the synchronized product. However, the size of $A_{\neg \varphi}$ grows exponentially with the number of elements in the LTL formula φ, both atomic propositions and temporal operators. Fortunately, most useful LTL formulas are quite small, and typical Büchi automaton used in this procedure only have a few states. There are many variants of Büchi automata, some of which allow more compact formula representation, such as transition-based Büchi automata [GIA 02, COU 05], which carry acceptance conditions on edges rather than on states.

More troublesome, the size of the automata A_M (representing the reachability graph) grows exponentially with the size of the system. This state-space size explosion is the main hurdle to the application of this approach, thus many reduction and optimization techniques have been proposed to try to reduce this complexity. We present some of these in the next sections.

7.5. Classification of model-checking approaches

Many approaches have been proposed to allow the use of model-checking on industrial case studies. We separate them here into two categories: approaches that use a form of compression to limit the memory requirements due to storage of the state graph, and approaches that use a form of abstraction, of either states or behaviors, so that only the part of the system that is relevant to the property needs to be explored.

7.5.1. *Compression based approaches*

The automaton of the system represents the reachability graph. Its size grows exponentially with the size of the system, yet for model-checking we need to be able to test for presence of a state without performing any disk-based input-output (IO).

To allow the state space to fit in the memory, one of the approaches simply proposes that the states are compressed; clearly storing states using fewer bits allows more states to be stored in memory. Classic compression algorithms can be applied (such as zip), or bitsets can be used instead of integers to represent system variables.

A more effective approach in the specific context of model-checking, consists of using correspondence tables to encode or decode the states. The system is seen as being composed of individual components C_i, each having a finite state space. The states local to each component type are stored in local state pools H_i as they are discovered. A global system state is then represented as an array of integer variables, each variable giving the index of the state of a subcomponent in table H_i.

For instance, global state $[3, 22, 7]$ would be read: C_0 is in state $H_0[3]$, C_1 is in state $H_1[22]$, etc.

When components share their structure or type, which typically happens when a component is instantiated several times in a model, the local state tables H_i can be shared. This strategy is nearly always used, particularly when formalisms are complex and local state descriptions are much more voluminous than an integer.

This compression scheme was used in the model-checker Spin [HOL 97], and has since been largely adopted in other tools.

Another approach consists of not storing the states, but simply their presence. This approach is called *bit-state hash coding* [STE 96] and uses a single bit to represent presence of a state. This is simply an application of Bloom filters (a space-efficient probabilistic data structure, see Wikipedia) to the model-checking problem. It allows to decide whether to continue on line (9) of the reachability algorithm presented above (Figure 1). The search for bad states (deadlock, etc.) is then performed on-the-fly as the graph is not available post-construction. The only issue with this approach is the chance of collisions in the Bloom filter, which might produce false positives (i.e. we think the state has been visited when it has not). The probability of collision in the hash can be estimated as δ based on the size of the hash table and how full up it is.

To minimize this risk, several statistically uncorrelated hash functions can be used. By repeating the computation using independent hash functions, each new computation that agrees with the previous intuitively multiplies the probability of error by δ [COU 92]. For instance, if collision probability is $\delta = 1\%$, and three independent computations agree on the same result, there is only roughly a 0.0001% probability that the result is incorrect.

Finally, a very dense tree-based representation allowing efficient manipulation of sets of states has been proposed: reduced decision diagrams. *Symbolic* algorithms operating on this data structure directly work with sets of states. Decision diagrams exploit the similarity between states in a state space to share their representation. This category of techniques is detailed in section 7.6.

7.5.2. *Approaches based on equivalence relations*

A second category of approaches consists of limiting the representation of the state graph to information that is really necessary for the verification of a given property φ. A graph that is representative of the full state graph with respect to φ is built, but that can be much smaller.

Most techniques that use this approach define a specific equivalence relation on the state graph nodes, which ensures that the reduced state graph that is built preserves the existence of behaviors that are of interest for a given property or for a given dialect of temporal logic.

For instance, equivalence relations that preserve the presence or absence of deadlocks, more general reachability properties, or for preservation of stuttering invariant behaviors (such as formulas expressed in $LTL_{\setminus X}$, LTL without the neXt operator) have been proposed. They often enable an exponential reduction in the size of the state graph.

Equivalent behaviors

A class of techniques that has been very successful is based on the notion of partial ordering of events in a given execution or run. Indeed some runs can be considered equivalent up to the reordering of the occurrence of uncorrelated events. We can concentrate on specific runs that are representative of a set of runs.

For instance, run $\{a, b\}.c$ represents the runs $a.b.c$ and $b.a.c$, i.e. we know that both a and b occur before c, but a and b are incomparable (hence the name *partial order reduction*). This family of approaches preserves stuttering invariant logics, such as $LTL_{\setminus X}$. We present some *partial order reductions* in more depth in section 7.7.

Some partial order reductions are based on a partition of events (i.e. transition labels of the state graph) into observable and invisible events. Invisible events (often noted τ) do not measurably (with respect to the property φ) modify the state of the system; they can thus be abstracted away from the state graph. The notion of observability of an event can be refined depending on the property to be checked, but in general, a much smaller abstraction of the state graph can be built using this approach.

For instance, for the global property of absence of deadlocks, events local to a given component (that do not communicate with other components) can be considered unobservable. This observation-based reduction is compatible with the automata-theoretical approach to model-checking, and thus, can be applied to a wide category of systems and properties. Observability can also be exploited in the context of symbolic model-checking to considerably improve decision diagram-based techniques.

Observability of events is fundamental in the context of distributed systems, where verification by composition may allow a global property to be checked by checking some (simpler) properties on the components. When a system is defined as a set of interacting components or communicating finite state machines, compositional approaches try to tackle verification by abstracting a sub-system by a set of behaviors it is proved to uphold, allowing contract-based reasoning. This means you check whether a sub-system satisfies its contract given some constraints on its environment (the other components), then you prove the environment respects these contracts. This second proof can itself be done in a compositional way.

Equivalent states

A widespread approach consists of abstracting parts of the data describing a state, yielding both smaller states, and less of them. For instance a data abstraction such as [KES 98a], proposes to model the value of a floating point variable by one of the three symbols $\{+, -, 0\}$, which simply tell if the value is positive, negative, or zero. This information is enough to prove properties, if the program only uses floating point multiplication, and the property is not interested in the data value but only in its sign. Although the abstraction process can now be partially automated, the choice of variables to abstract and how to abstract them usually requires human expertise.

Another approach that gives good results is to exploit system symmetries to recognize states as equivalent with respect to overall system behavior. A quotient state graph can be built using such an equivalence relation, where nodes represent equivalence classes of states. Depending on the permissiveness of the equivalence relation, for systems exhibiting a large degree of symmetry, the quotient graph can be exponentially smaller than the state graph. We present a symmetry-based approach that preserves LTL in more detail in section 7.8.

To illustrate how some of these techniques work in more detail, we now show how three of them can be applied to our running example of Figures 7.12 and 7.13. We have chosen to present the symbolic approach using decision diagrams, some techniques that exploit partial order reductions, and a symmetry based reduction. These are representative examples of finite state model-checking techniques.

7.6. Decision diagram-based approaches

This section presents in more detail model-checking approaches based on reduced binary decision diagrams (BDD). Decision diagrams were initially introduced for compact representation of Boolean functions [AKE 78]. Reduced (and ordered) BDD were first defined and applied to model-checking problems on circuits by Bryant in his PhD thesis [BRY 86]. They were then made popular by the seminal paper [BUR 92], which shows how to tackle CTL model-checking using BDD, and how BDD based symbolic model-checking scales up to systems with 10^{20} states, several orders of magnitude greater than that handled by usual explicit techniques.

7.6.1. *BDD*

A BDD allows a compact representation of a Boolean function. Consider for instance the Boolean function $f = (a \lor b) \land c$ of three variables a, b and c. A decision diagram that represents this function is shown Figure 7.17 (a). This tree is read from the root to the leaves, each path in the structure leads to the truth value of f given the values of the variables a, b and c.

This decision diagram can be represented in a more compact manner by sharing subtrees, leading to a *reduced* decision diagram. A first step consists in only representing the terminal nodes 0 and 1 once, leading to Figure 7.17 (b). This reasoning can inductively be applied to all nodes of the tree, working upwards from the terminals to the root. We then obtain the diagram of Figure 7.17 (c). This reduced structure is called a reduced ordered binary decision diagram (ROBDD), or simply BDD in the following text. A BDD is reduced because subtrees are shared and linked to several parent nodes, and it is ordered because the decision variables are always encountered in the same order along any path from root to terminal (a then b then c in this example).

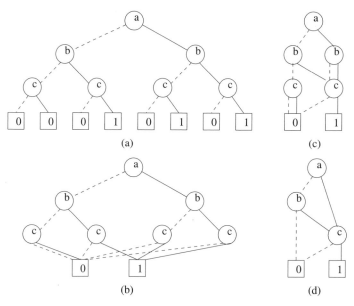

Figure 7.17. *Binary decision diagram for Boolean formula* $(a \lor b) \land c$ *and its reduced form. Full edges correspond to assigning true to the variable and dashed lines correspond to assigning false. (a) full decision diagram, not reduced; (b) with non-redundant terminal nodes; (c) with non-redundant internal nodes; (d) with no redundant tests*

Another optimization is sometimes applied to further reduce the size of the decision diagram: removal of redundant tests, as presented in Figure 7.17 (d). The variables are still encountered in a fixed order, but we allow edges to "skip" a level or variable, if the truth value of the function that is represented does not depend on the value of this variable in these decision paths. In practice this amounts to skipping nodes where both true and false arcs point to the same successor node (e.g. compare

Figure 7.17 (c) and (d)). In this last figure it is quite easy to see that this decision tree indeed represents $f = (a \vee b) \wedge c$: if a is false and b is false then (regardless of the value of c) f is false; else if a is false but b is true then f is equal to c; else if a is true, regardless of the value of b, $f = c$.

BDD techniques manipulate sets of values symbolically, since any node represents the set of paths it is the root of. The term *symbolic* model-checking is often used to refer to BDD-based approaches, by opposition to classical *explicit* approaches, where each state (or path) is represented and manipulated explicitly.

7.6.2. *BDD for finite state model-checking*

Although BDD were designed for Boolean function manipulation, they can be used to represent the state space of a system. The variables of the BDD then represent (Boolean) variables of the system, and any path that leads to the terminal 1 is interpreted as a reachable state.

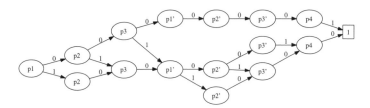

Figure 7.18. *State space of the example of Figure 7.13 represented as a BDD*

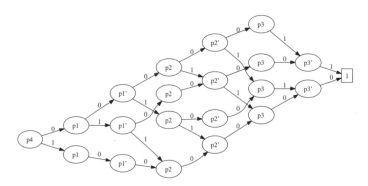

Figure 7.19. *The same state space with an unfavorable variable order*

For instance let us consider the running example for two processes described in Figure 7.13. Figure 7.18 represents its state space stored in a BDD. The variables of

Process	States	BDD nodes (contiguous order)	BDD nodes (interlaced order)
2	10	16	21
5	244	40	260
10	59050	80	13321
15	1.43489e+07	120	589838
20	3.48678e+09	160	-

Table 7.2. *Growth in number of BDD nodes as the number of process grows*

the BDD correspond to the places of the Petri net, and the values on the arcs correspond to the marking of the place in the current state. The figure is read from left to right, each state is represented by a path that starts from the root (P_0) and leads to terminal 1. For instance, the uppermost decision path in the diagram represents state where the a process is in the critical section ($P4$ is marked and all other places are empty).

Table 7.2 allows the appreciation of how BDD enable scaling up to large state spaces, when the order chosen is appropriate. Indeed, although the state space grows exponentially ($3^n + 1$ states for n process), the BDD encoding of the state space grows linearly ($8n$ nodes)! More specifically, for 20 processes, 3 billion states are represented on 160 nodes (less than 1 kilobyte of memory). Moreover, complexity of BDD operations is related to the size of the structure in number of nodes, thus computation time for this example is counted in microseconds.

BDD are an extremely efficient compression technique; they are able to store the states of the system while managing the huge volume of states. This is to in contrast to abstraction-based techniques, where equivalence classes of states are manipulated (such as the symmetry based approach presented in section 7.8), allowing the state explosion to be dealt with by representing much smaller graphs. However, the two approaches have been combined successfully, allowing large sets (as BDD) of equivalence classes [THI 04] to be stored.

Unfortunately, the size of the BDD strongly depends on the variable order chosen to build the diagram. The BDD of Figure 7.19 represents the same state space for two processes, but we have chosen to interlace the variables corresponding to each process. Instead of the variable order $p_1 > p_2 > p_3 > p'_1 > p'_2 > p'_3$ we chose to use $p_1 > p'_1 > p_2 > p'_2 > p_3 > p'_3$. With the first variable order, the places that represent the state of a given process are placed in a contiguous fashion, respecting the system structure. The interlaced order leads to a representation whose size grows exponentially, thereby nullifying the whole point of using BDD. The last column of Table 7.2 shows the growth in number of nodes with this unfavorable interlaced variable order.

The computation of the BDD did not terminate for 20 process on a machine with 3 Gb of RAM.

Thus, for a given model, we can exhibit variable orders leading to linear size BDD encodings, as well as variable orders that lead to exponential blowup of the representation. Furthermore, finding an optimal ordering of variables has been shown to be NP-complete [TAN 93]; hence BDD techniques must rely on heuristics to provide a good variable order. Even then, some boolean functions can be shown to have exponential representation size whatever the order chosen, so BDD are not a panacea.

Static variable orders can usually be deduced from the structure of the input specification, using various heuristics, as suggested as early as [BRY 86], and this is still the approach that is most often applied. Dynamic reordering of variables [RUD 93] can also be applied as the structure is being built, triggered when the representation size exceeds a certain threshold, but this is usually a complementary technique to proposing a "reasonable" initial variable order computed by some heuristic.

7.6.3. *Construction and manipulation*

In this section we present how BDD are built, how they can be manipulated to encode a transition relation, and finally, how to use them for symbolic model checking.

Canonical form and cache

Construction of a BDD relies on a unique table of existing nodes: since the decision tree is built from the terminals up to the root, when creating a node its successor nodes are already in the unique table. If a node with the same successors already exists, the existing node in the unique table is used directly. The union operation of two BDD is the fundamental construction operation, and ensures a canonical form for the resulting BDD. It is described in algorithm 2; a cache is used to result in a complexity proportional to the product of the number of nodes in the representation rather than to the number of paths (states). Line (9) of this algorithm is the critical inductive step: the union of a and b leads to a node with a 0 successor node defined as the union of the 0 successor nodes of a and b, and a 1 successor computed as the union of the 1 successors of a and b.

Thanks to use of an operation cache, BDD allow the implementation of efficient algorithms that manipulate a set of values, with a complexity linked to the number of nodes in the representation rather than to the number of values (decision paths) in the set. For instance, the set-theoretic operations (union, intersection and set difference) between two BDD a and b has a complexity proportional to the number of nodes in the representation of a and b.

Construction of a BDD node is always done by first checking if the node already exists in the unique table (it is handled by $CreateBDD$ in line (9) of union above).

```
1  bdd Union(bdd a,bdd b) :
2  begin
3  |    if  a = 0 ∨ b = 1 then
4  |    |   return b
5  |    if  b = 0 ∨ a = 1 then
6  |    |   return a
7  |    if  ⟨{a, b}, r⟩ ∈ Cache then
8  |    |   return r
9  |    bdd r := CreateBDD(0 → Union(a[0], b[0]), 1 → Union(a[1], b[1]))
10 |    Cache.add(⟨{a, b}, r⟩)
11 |    return r
12 end
```

Algorithm 2: *Algorithm to build the union of two BDD*

The unique node representation of memory allows the use of an efficient cache, the number of entries in the cache being proportional to number of nodes in the unique representation. However, as shown on our running example, this number may be exponentially smaller than the number of states in the state space.

Transition relation

For model checking, the transition relation is usually represented itself as a BDD that contains $2k$ variables when the state is represented with k variables. Variable of index $2i, i \in 0..k$ of the transition relation BDD gives the value of the variable before the transition, and variable indexed $2i + 1$ gives its resulting value(s) after the transition. Applying a BDD T representing a transition relation to a BDD representing a state space is akin to the particular synchronized product of the two BDD, and again uses a cache.

This encoding of the transition relation allows the computation of the effect of the union of two transitions as the union of their BDD representations. Hence the full transition relation T of the system can be built and manipulated symbolically, without referring directly to the individual events $t \in T$. Applying a BDD T representing a transition relation to a BDD S produces the set of states $S' = T(S)$ reachable from a state $s \in S$ by firing an event $t \in T$. States in S' are direct successors of states in S by an event in T.

The complexity of this operation is still proportional to the node sizes of T and S, but may build huge sets of successor states in a single application step. This symbolic encoding of the transition relation is, however, itself sensitive to variable ordering issues, hence many approaches [BUR 91, MIN 99] have suggested splitting T into smaller parts that are less likely to blow up in representation size.

Data:

Let $M : \langle s_0, T \rangle$ be a system, its initial state and set of transitions

$bdd\ todo$: new states to explore

$bdd\ reach$: reachable states already computed

begin

    $todo := \{ s_0 \}$

    $reach := \{ s_0 \}$

    while $todo \neq \emptyset$ **do**

        $bdd\ tmp := T(todo)$

        $todo := tmp \setminus reach$

        $reach := reach \cup tmp$

end

begin

    $todo := \{ s_0 \}$

    $reach := \{ \}$

    while $todo \neq reach$ **do**

        $reach := todo$

        $todo := todo \cup T(reach)$

end

Algorithm 3: *Two variants of BDD based algorithms to compute reachable states*

Two variants to compute the reachable states of a system are presented on algorithm 3. In the left variant, the immediate successors of states are obtained in *todo* by applying T and keeps states that were not seen before to continue the computation. The traversal of the state space is thus a strict breadth-first search (BFS). Note that we build *reach* instead of *graph* as in algorithm 1, as it is actually storing the *set* of reachable states and not the full reachability graph.

Contrarily, it is actually often more efficient to use the variant on the right, which simply adds states until a fixpoint is reached. While this is still a BFS traversal, the algorithm progressively adds states to the *graph*, removing the need for the intermediate *tmp* variable of the first algorithm, and the need for the set difference operation. Indeed, the *tmp* variable represents a BDD of a subset of states at an intermediate step of the construction, and is unlikely to contain nodes that will be part of the final state space representation. Hence nodes in *tmp* clutter the cache and unique table, whereas the successor computation on the full *graph* of the second algorithm might not be as costly as anticipated due to the cache. The BDD *todo* of the first algorithm is just as likely as *graph* to require exponential representation size at some point of the computation even though it contains less states.

Indeed, this is a critical problem for symbolic model checking approaches: sometimes, although the final representation size of the reachable state space is small, the intermediate BDD representing steps of the computation may become huge and unmanageable. This problem is described as the "peak effect", i.e. during the computation, representation size grows and falls, but often goes through a peak memory requirement that may be orders of magnitude greater than the final representation. This peak effect can be partially explained by the BFS traversal order of the state space, that discovers successor states relevant for reachability, but irrelevant with respect to the BDD representation of states.

The peak effect can sometimes be tackled by exploiting locality of actions to compute the fixpoint on parts of the transition relation, split according to the variables that are impacted by an event. The *saturation* algorithm [CIA 03] applies transition to fixpoint starting upward from the terminals of the decision diagram. A node at level k above the terminal is said to be saturated if and only if all events that impact this variable and any lower variable of index $k' < k$ have been applied until a fixpoint is reached. When a node is fully saturated the algorithm climbs to its predecessor nodes at level $k + 1$, and applies all event that concern the variables of indexes 0 to $k + 1$. If any of these events modifies a node of a lower level (thus that was saturated before, by construction) it re-saturated before allowing the computation to continue. When the algorithm reaches the root of the structure, all events have been fired to fixpoint, hence the computation is finished. This saturation algorithm often allows us to circumvent the peak effect, allowing gains of several orders of magnitude with respect to plain BFS exploration. For systems with a high degree of locality and concurrency, such as Petri nets, saturation is very successful, but it does not perform as well for highly synchronous models, such as circuits (which are controlled by a clock signal).

Symbolic model checking and temporal logic

Symbolic approaches easily answer the reachability problem, hence they allow states satisfying a given condition (invariant, deadlock...) to be found. In fact, identifying such a state once the representation of the reachable state space has been built can mostly be done in constant time and memory, by simply traversing the BDD.

Verification of properties expressed using the computational tree logic CTL can be reduced to a succession of nested fixpoint computations, using either the transition relation T, or its inverse T^{-1} [BUR 92]. Computing the inverse is not difficult given a BDD representing T, but may be quite costly. Since fixpoint algorithms must already be available to build the reachable state space, most BDD-based tools offer support for the verification of CTL.

For properties expressed in LTL, a common approach is to reduce the problem to CTL with additional fairness constraints [CLA 94]. The fairness constraints are introduced to ensure the existence of infinite runs, that cannot be adequately expressed in CTL. Other algorithms [KES 98b] propose directly model-checking properties of LTL using BDD.

For the verification of the stuttering invariant fragment of LTL, $LTL_{\setminus X}$, some hybrid approaches, such as the symbolic observation graph [HAD 04a] propose building a graph where each node contains a set of states represented as a BDD, and the edges between nodes represent observable events. The successors through invisible events of states in a node are aggregated into the node. When the number of observable events is small, the approach provides good results.

7.6.4. *BDD extensions*

To apply symbolic approaches to a given problem, the first step is to find an appropriate encoding of the system states. With classical BDD, this is an encoding using a fixed-length vector of Boolean variables. Depending on the type of model, this encoding may not be the most appropriate, which has led to various extensions of BDD, that exploit similar canonical form and cache mechanisms, some of which we present here.

BDD can be seen as representing functions $\mathbb{B}^n \longmapsto \mathbb{B}$. When the function is sparse, i.e. it is mostly false, it can be interesting to suppress decision paths leading to the zero terminal; this reduction is almost always applied. It is congruent regarding the way BDD are manipulated in model-checking to represent a set of objects (states).

When along the paths that lead to the accepting terminal 1 the variables are mostly false, the canonization rule can be amended to skip variables that only have a *false* successor edge. This version is called *Zero-suppressed BDD* (ZBDD) [MIN 93]. Depending on the input problem, this variant can be more or less efficient than the usual canonization rule (skip nodes where both edges point to the same successor node).

A major extension of BDD is the definition of a canonical form for functions $\mathbb{B}^n \longmapsto \mathbb{R}$. These are multi-terminal BDD (MTBDD [FUJ 97]) also called algebraic decision diagrams (ADD [BAH 93]). The main idea here is that although domain $\mathbb{R}$ is infinite, a given function of n variables can only have a finite number of output values, bounded by 2^n. Thus the BDD construction rules can be extended to build a terminal node for each value that is in effect an output of the function, the rest of the construction rules being the same as for BDD. For model-checking, this type of decision diagram has been used to solve stochastic problems [HER 03], where the ADD stores the probability of occurrence for each reachable state. In that context, they enable compact representations of both the state space and the probabilistic transition relation matrix.

Another extension consists of representing functions $\mathbb{N}^n \longmapsto \mathbb{B}$. These multi-valued decision diagrams (MDD) were defined by [SRI 90] through an unfolding to an equivalent BDD, but have also been implemented directly with nodes of the decision diagram having several output edges in [MIN 99]. If the domain of the variables of the MDD can be bounded a priori then there is a possible binary encoding of the problem using $\log_2(n)$ BDD variables to represent an MDD variable with n possible values.

MDD can sometimes be much more efficient than BDD, because decision paths are much shorter and their interpretation (in the transition relation) is more straightforward, as they allow system variables to be mapped to MDD variables directly. However, on some models, if the number of edges per node is excessive, the efficiency of manipulation algorithms and cache can be negatively impacted, and the storage cost for individual nodes may grow to unmanageable levels. In practice, in MDD, paths leading to the terminal 0 are always suppressed from the representation. Note that MDD can be combined with multiple terminals.

A difficulty that is common to all these decision diagram variants is the strong constraint on the variable order (remember BDD are really reduced *ordered* BDD) and the length of the decision paths. Data decision diagrams (DDD [COU 02]) allow these constraints to be relaxed in the context of MDD. In particular they allow objects with variable size such as stacks or lists to be captured even without an a priori bound on their size. Their manipulation is based on *homomorphisms*, which offer an abstract high-level mechanism to define the transition relation instead of using a $2k$ level BDD, as explained above, for classical BDD. In particular, the expression of a transition relation as a homomorphism allows decision diagram saturation algorithms to be automatically enabled [HAM 98].

7.7. Partial order reductions

Model-checking approaches that use partial order reductions address a fundamental source of state space explosion: interleaving of actions introduces a large number of intermediate steps, even when these events are, in reality, independent. For instance, in a given state suppose a system admits n independently enabled events, there are $n!$ firing sequences to consider from this state, if all possible interleavings are considered. Since the only difference between these execution sequences is the order the events are fired in, the state space can be hugely reduced by considering a subset of these sequences (or even just one sequence) that are representative of the possible interleavings.

The foundations of this theory was proposed by Mazurkiewicz in [MAZ 86], where he defined the notion of *trace* instead of considering plain executions. A trace represents an equivalence class of sequences of events, such that equivalent traces are obtained by permuting two adjacent independent events in the trace. In practice, two events are either "in conflict" if firing one deactivates the other, or are "causally related" if firing one event enables the other. Otherwise, the events are said to be "independent".

This type of techniques is generally known as partial order reduction, since the traces considered only enforce a partial order on the order of occurrence of events in a run.

Graph of traces

Most partial order-based approaches consist of reducing the state graph by removing executions which are redundant with respect to the trace-based interpretation.

There are many variants of graphs of traces; a large body of work on this subject is due to Valmari [VAL 90, VAL 93], Godefroid and Wolper [GOD 92, GOD 96], and Peled [PEL 94c, PEL 94b]. Some of the algorithms they propose are presented in more detail below.

Covering step graph

Another slightly different exploitation of the independence relation between events is the covering step graph (CSG). The CSG is a relatively recent proposition [VER 97] that aims to reduce state explosion due to interleaving issues in the state graph. The principle is to compute the set of independent transitions in a given state, and then fire this whole transition set simultaneously in a single step. This algorithm produces a new graph, the CSG, where the nodes are still states of the system, but edges represent *firing steps* of sets of events of the system. The CSG enables huge reductions with respect to the state graph, particularly when several processes evolve independently, but sometimes synchronize.

For some examples, the CSG can even be shown to be linearly better than a graph of traces. A CSG covers all possible execution sequences, hence many properties can be checked using this reduced state graph representation. For instance, absence of deadlocks and liveness (i.e. the capacity of the system to recover from perturbations) can be checked on a CSG.

The CSG is also simpler than other methods, such as persistent sets, since no proviso is necessary. Lastly, the CSG can be built to preserve the behavior as projected onto a set of observable transitions. Stuttering invariant logics over these events can then be checked, provided the CSG is restricted to contain one observable transition in each step at most. This simple condition ensures that all interleavings of observable actions are represented in the CSG. This method can also be adapted to be applicable to timed systems, and can even be combined with other partial order reductions, such as persistent sets [RIB 02].

Unfoldings

A third approach consists of directly representing the partial order of event occurrences, by using the notions of transition conflict and independence of Petri nets. This approach, proposed in [NIE 81, WIN 87], consists of translating a given Petri net into a special class of labeled Petri nets called a branching process.

This translation is called an unfolding, since a given transition (and connected places) may be represented several times in the unfolding, depending on its occurrence order in an execution. In an unfolding, independent event occurrences are represented by separate transitions, thus directly representing their possible interleavings without explicitly representing them.

Unfolding exploits the strong locality of Petri net models, i.e. the fact that a transition only modifies the state of a small set of places (those connected to it). Many variants of unfoldings have been proposed [MCM 95, ESP 92a, ESP 93, KON 96, COU 96], to offer practical algorithms to compute an unfolding and use it to verify system properties efficiently.

These partial order reduction-based methods allow a wide class of temporal logic properties to be checked. The next section presents two algorithms to build a graph of traces in more detail, the stubborn set and sleep set approaches. Due to space considerations, the CSG construction and unfolding technique will not be further detailed in this book. Our running example from Figure 7.13 will be used to exhibit the reduced state graph representations built by these algorithms.

7.7.1. *Traces and verification*

In a given run of a system, partial order regarding event occurrence is defined according to an independence relation between event occurrences, also called the diamond property: it states that two events t_1 and t_2 are independent in a state s if and only if both the sequences $t_1.t_2$ and $t_2.t_1$ are enabled in s, and they lead to the same resulting state. This independence relation can be defined locally for each state s or globally for all states. Global independence relations can usually be computed using a structural approach in the input model: typically actions local to a process (that do not update global variables or use communication channels) are independent of local actions of another process.

Given this independence relation, executions (or *runs*) of the system can be grouped into equivalence classes called traces. Two runs belong to the same trace (i.e. are considered equivalent) if one can be obtained from the other by iteratively permuting adjacent independent events in the run.

For instance, in the state space of Figure 7.13, note that (t_1, t_1') from state $p_1 + p_1'$, (t_2, t_1') from state $p_2 + p_1'$, (t_1, t_2') from state $p_1 + p_2'$ and (t_2, t_2') from state $p_2 + p_2'$ are pairs of independent events. Hence many runs from $p_2 + p_1'$ such as $t_2.t_1'.t_2'$, $t_1'.t_2.t_2'$, $t_1'.t_2'.t_2$ can be considered equivalent and represented by a single trace $[t_2.t_1'.t_2']$.

Notion of trace

In a reachability graph, the number of interleavings that need to be considered can thus be considerably reduced by only studying traces representative of the system behavior. More precisely, a trace is represented in a graph G if all the runs it represents are prefixes of runs in G or valid permutations (according to the independence relation) of these prefixes. This definition using a prefix, allows more compact state graph representations to be built, i.e. a graph of traces.

For instance, sequence $t'_1.t_2$ is a prefix of $t'_1.t_2.t'_2$, and can thus be represented by the trace $[t_2.t'_1.t'_2]$. Figures 7.20, 7.21(a) and 7.21(b) show three different trace graphs built using this definition. In these figures, the full line edges represent transitions that are considered representative, while the light grey edges are transitions that are not explored, and are represented simply to allow easier comparison of these approaches to the full state graph of Figure 7.13.

These graphs differ in the runs that are chosen as trace representatives, but they all cover the full set of traces enabled from the initial system state, i.e. the three traces: $[t_1.t_2.t'_1.t'_2]$, $[[t_1.t_2.t_3 + t'_1.t'_2.t'_3]^*.t_4.t_1.t_2.t'_1.t'_2]$ and $[[t_1.t_2.t_3 + t'_1.t'_2.t'_3].t_4]^\infty$. The best reduction for this example is obtained in Figure 7.21(b), since the graph cannot be further reduced without losing some traces.

Of course, the partial order construction must not introduce any behaviors that are incorrect with respect to the property we wish to check. The first condition enforcing this is that the trace graph be a subset of the state graph. But, this is usually not enough, because of the prefix condition used to limit the exploration: if the graph of Figure 7.21(a) is interpreted as a normal state graph, the sequence $t_1.t'_1.t'_2$ leads to a deadlock state, which is not true in the original state graph.

Many behavioral properties can be checked using a valid trace graph. For instance quasi-liveness, which states that for every transition of the system there exists a run from the initial state which contains the transition; this can be checked using a trace graph that only contains one trace per transition. Similarly, state invariants can be checked by introducing an artificial transition that is only enabled in faulty states, and then checking its quasi-liveness. For instance, the invariant "p_2 and p'_2 are never simultaneously marked" can be checked for by introducing a transition enabled when p_2 and p'_2 are simultaneously marked.

More general safety properties and liveness properties require greater interpretation effort as we need to distinguish *observable* events from *invisible* events with respect to the property. A transition is *observable* if its firing can modify the truth value of an atomic proposition of the property, and it is *invisible* if it has no direct impact on atomic propositions of the property. For Petri nets and state-based properties, a transition can be considered invisible if it is not connected to any place queried in the atomic propositions of the property.

Valid trace graph

Three key issues must be correctly handled when building a trace graph, to ensure preservation of temporal properties, which may be sensitive to the order of occurrence of certain events:

1) the set of traces built must cover all possible interleavings of observable transitions, to allow correct results when building the synchronized product with the (negation of) the formula automaton;

2) as a result, partial order reductions are limited to invisible events. This allows the preservation of safety and liveness properties that reason over infinite runs of observable events. However, infinite runs that end by a loop over invisible events need to be identified, as they might be accepted in the product automaton with the formula, but are not captured by the first condition above. These runs, called divergent runs, need to be represented in a valid trace graph, although sometimes representing a subset of them is enough;

3) the third issue to consider is the class of properties that can be checked using a trace graph. Indeed, as evidenced by point (1), if all events are observable for a given property, the trace graph is degenerated to the full state graph, hence the whole approach is useless. The property must be insensitive to finite sequences of occurrence of invisible transitions, which is not the case for general LTL where the neXt operator is used. Many works [WIL 96] thus limit the scope of the technique to the fragment $LTL_{\setminus X}$, which is known to be a *stuttering invariant*. A property is stuttering invariant if its truth value is not affected by any finite repetition of the atomic propositions it manipulates. For instance, if a formula accepts sequence $a.b.c$, all sequences of the form $a^+.b^+.c^+$ should also be accepted, where a^+ designates a finite non-empty sequence of repetitions of a. Properties that are not stuttering invariant require all transitions to be observed, since, by definition, the firing of invisible transitions (which have been abstracted away) causes this repetition of atomic proposition values.

Of course while it is possible to compute the independence relation between events by building the state graph, this would be counter-productive as the goal of the approach is to avoid building the full state graph. In practice, trace graphs are usually built on the fly, since the independence of the events enabled in a given state can usually be computed *a priori*. For Petri nets, this computation uses the notion of transition conflict described above, applied to the subset of events enabled in the current state.

One approach to building a trace graph is to only fire a subset of the enabled transitions in each state; enabled transitions that were not chosen are by definition still enabled in the successor state. For a multiprocess system, the actions of a process can be considered independent of other process actions only if they manipulate variables local to the process. The trace graph built using this algorithm is thus a reduced representation of the full state graph, however all properties of interest must be preserved.

Interpretation of a trace graph

Two issues can be problematic when some enabled events are not fired:

– the first issue is the problem of "ignored transitions", where some events might be enabled but never chosen when building the trace graph. This problem may occur when a subset of system transitions is isolated or independent from the other system transitions. Typically, consider a trace graph built for a system of with two independent process, if we always choose to fire transitions of the first process when both process could progress, the construction might miss some important behaviors;

– the second problem is called transition confusion, whereby some states might never be visited although they allow sequences to be fired that are not otherwise represented in the trace graph. On our running example in Figure 7.13, when building the trace graph of Figure 7.20, although t_1 and t'_1 are not in conflict in the initial state, both transitions should be fired. Indeed, if we only choose one of these transitions, say t_1, then all sequences containing t'_3 will be lost from the trace graph, because the state $p_1 + p'_3$ will never be reached. This is due to a conflict between t_1 and t'_3 which is not obvious in the initial state (because t'_3 is not yet enabled), but that becomes critical once the sequence $t'_1.t'_2$ has been fired. Thus a dependence between transitions can be induced by a causal relationship between events.

We present here two different algorithms to build a full valid trace graph in more detail. The first approach is based on *persistent sets*, and is a direct application of the general principles given above. The second approach called *sleep sets* allows some edges of the state graph to be discarded, but keeps all the nodes. We then show how these two techniques are complementary and can thus be combined to build a trace graph that is smaller than that produced by either technique by itself.

7.7.2. *Persistent sets*

A set of transitions T enabled in a given state s is said to be a *persistent set* if for any transition $t \in T$, and for any sequence $t.w$ fireable from s, where w is a sequence of transitions that do not belong to T, all sequences built by permuting t with an element of w are enabled in s, and lead to the same resulting state. The transitions that belong to a persistent set are thus independent of transitions that do not belong to the set. In the extreme case where all transitions depend on each other, the persistent set is thus simply the full set of enabled transitions of the system.

Based on this definition of a persistent set, the trace graph is built using the following algorithm:

– when a new state is reached, the algorithm computes a persistent set that contains at least one enabled transition (except if the state is a deadlock state);

– the state then admits a successor for every transition of the persistent set.

This technique can be seen as a linearization of the firing of independent transitions, as enabled transitions that are not chosen (those outside the persistent set) are, by definition, still enabled in the successor states. This trace graph, while smaller than the state graph, thus preserves both deadlocks and the presence of infinite firing sequences. Depending on the way the persistent sets are computed, this construction is prone to the "ignored transitions" problem mentioned above. However, for certain classes of models (such as bounded and strongly connected Petri nets [VAL 89]), the problem probably never occurs.

Proviso

In more general settings, the problem can be avoided by ensuring that a certain constraint is enforced in each state, called the *proviso*. Literally this is a "provided that" condition, i.e. a proviso is a sufficient (but not necessary) condition for correctness. In [VAL 89], a first proviso definition was proposed, based on the computation of all non-trivial strongly connected components of the state graph. If in one of these components an enabled transition is never chosen, the persistent set is enlarged to cover the missing transition. A simpler proviso was proposed in [HOL 92]. It consists of detecting states in which an enabled transition allows a circuit to be closed. The fact that no enabled transitions are perpetually ignored in the trace graph ensures preservation of deadlocks as well as state invariants. Other proviso conditions have been proposed [VAL 90], some of which are specifically adapted to ensure preservation of behaviors in the synchronized product with a property expressed as an automaton [VAL 93, PEL 94a].

Computing persistent sets

Based on structural analysis of a Petri net, several algorithms have been proposed to efficiently compute persistent sets in each visited state. The simplest forms simply search for transitions that are in conflict [GOD 94, BAU 97] while some strategies are more involved such as th

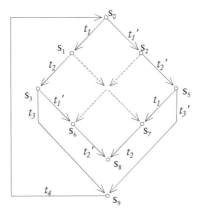

Figure 7.20. *Persistent set trace graph construction*

A simple method to compute persistent sets is the conflict-based method [GOD 91]. It is based on the following observations:

1) if we start by adding a random enabled transition to the set, and then recursively add any other enabled transition that is in conflict with a transition of the set, we have a particular case of persistent set. If some transitions that are not enabled are in conflict with a transition of the set, we can fall back to case below;

2) if in the current state there are transitions that are in conflict with a transition of the set but are not enabled, we can always use the full set of enabled transitions as our persistent set, ensuring correctness.

This simple approach thus ensures that all transitions in the persistent set are enabled and do not have any conflict with transitions that will not be fired (those outside the set). This simple approach is often less effective than the more complex stubborn set approach, because when we fall back to case 2), no reductions are obtained for the current state. The stubborn set approach improves case 2); when there exists a transition t that is not currently enabled but is in conflict with some transition(s) of the set, the algorithm selects a place whose marking is responsible for disabling t (i.e. it does not contain enough tokens). It then adds to the persistent set any enabled transition that could add tokens to this place.

The stubborn set algorithm thus always computes smaller or equal persistent sets than the basic conflict-based approach. In some cases the two algorithms coincide, such as on our running example (see Figure 7.20).

7.7.3. *Sleep set approach*

The *sleep set* approach [GOD 94] tries to exploit the absence of conflict between event occurrences. The aim is to avoid reaching the same state by many different paths, by predicting the diamond effect due to interleaving of independent events. Almost identically to the persistent set computation presented above, the *sleep set* S of a state s (noted (s, S)) represents a set of enabled transitions that will *not* be fired, because the target state they would reach will already be explored through another path. This technique thus reduces the number of edges of the state graph that need to be explored, but builds all the states of the graph.

Sleep sets are built on the fly as the construction of the graph progresses. In the initial state, the sleep set is initially empty. To build the successors of a given state (s, S), we consider the *ordered* set T of enabled transitions in s. For each transition $t \in T$, we build a successor (s', S'), where S' is defined as S augmented by all transitions that precede t in T, but where transitions that are in conflict with t in s are removed from the sleep set.

Figure 7.21(a) shows the reduced state graph that is built using this approach. As the sleep set in the initial state is empty, $T = \{t_1, t_1'\}$, and t_1 and t_1' are both explored as usual. If t_1 is fired first (remember transitions are ordered in this approach), we reach state $p_2 + p_1'$, then we reach $p_1 + p_2'$ through t_1'. The sleep set in state $p_2 + p_1'$ is still empty, but in state $p_1 + p_2'$ it contains $\{t_1\}$ since t_1 and t_1' are not in conflict, and t_1 precedes t_1' in T. Then, from $p_2 + p_1'$, all enabled transitions are explored, but

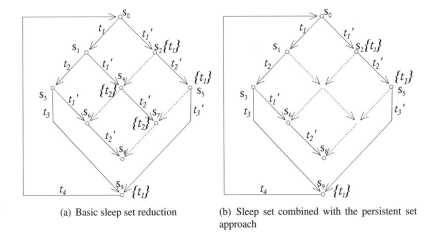

(a) Basic sleep set reduction

(b) Sleep set combined with the persistent set approach

Figure 7.21. *State graph reductions using sleep set*

in state $p_1 + p_2'$ only t_2' will be explored (because we can infer that the successor by t_1 will be explored through another path).

As we can see in this example, most states are reached by a single path, leading to drastic time reductions to explore the full state graph. This is especially true for models in which the successor computation is costly, typically because some other strategy (such as symmetry reductions) is being applied in conjunction with this approach. Regarding memory requirement, the graph built is usually larger than that built using persistent sets, this is the case for our running example (see Figures 7.20 and 7.21(a)). However, for some examples, the persistent set approach may yield no reductions because it tries to take into account "future" conflicts, whereas the sleep set may be more effective because it only considers immediate conflicts in a given state.

The fact that all states of the reachability graph are preserved allows reachability properties to be easily checked, such as invariants. All traces of the reachability graph are also preserved, as the edges that are removed from the graph are, by definition, already covered by other paths, but some traces are incomplete, e.g. $[t_1.t_1'.t_2']$ is only the prefix of trace $[t_1.t_1'.t_2'.t_2]$. Hence some properties, such as presence of deadlock states, cannot be evaluated unless it is noted that transitions of the sleep set of each state could have been fired. More generally, verification algorithms on the graph built using the sleep set method need to be adapted to provide correct results.

7.7.4. *Combining sleep and stubborn set approaches*

The sleep set approach can be combined with the stubborn set approach yielding a smaller trace graph representation: when computing the stubborn set of transitions that need to be fired, we can remove transitions of the sleep set computed using a given transition ordering. This allows the trace graph to be further reduced. Figure 7.21(b) shows the effect of combining both approaches on our running example. We can notice on this example that state $p_2 + p_3'$ is no longer reached; indeed from the initial state state $p_1 + p_3'$ is reached by firing $t_1'.t_2'$ but $\{t_1\}$ is the sleep set in this state. Since its stubborn set is limited to $\{t_1, t_3'\}$, only t_3' will be explored by this variant of the algorithm.

Verification of stuttering invariant properties is possible on this reduced trace graph, although we need to introduce a proviso condition as presented above.

7.8. Reductions exploiting symmetry

To fight the combinatorial state space explosion, a successful approach consists of exploiting system symmetries [CHI 91] to explore only representative parts of the behavior. Many distributed systems are actually built as the parallel composition of identical components. For instance, the processes of our running example (Figure 7.12) behave identically. It is thus possible to build a reduced state graph according to a given equivalence relation, called a quotient graph, where the nodes and edges represent equivalence classes of states and firing of equivalent events.

7.8.1. *Quotient graph*

The main idea of this approach is to avoid distinguishing similar occurrences of a given process. Hence instead of building a node in the reachability graph for the state where process 0 has fired t_1 and another node for the state where process 1 has fired t_1', we build a single node that represents the states where *one of the processes* has fired t_1.

Figure 7.22 and Table 7.3 illustrate the reduction in the number of states that need to be represented when building a quotient graph, with respect to the ordinary state graph. As exhibited in this example, the quotient graph can be exponentially smaller than the ordinary reachability graph. More formally, each node of the quotient graph represents an equivalence class of states, according to a given equivalence relation $\mathcal{R}$ that defines which permutations of process identities are permissible in this state.

The basic symmetry reduction approach considers a single equivalence relation that holds for the whole reachability graph, but this constraint can be partially removed

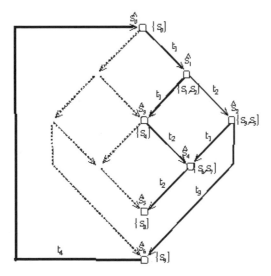

Figure 7.22. *Quotient graph when considering that both process are equivalent*

Process	States	Quotient states
2	10	7
4	82	16
6	730	29
8	6562	46
10	59050	67
20	3486784402	232

Table 7.3. *Compared evolution of the size of the reachability graph and of the quotient graph*

when considering partial symmetries, i.e. cases where the system is mostly symmetrical except for some part of the behavior, such as initial conditions. The equivalence relation that holds for a given system could be computed simply by testing on the full reachability graph which permutations of process identities leave the graph invariant; however, computing such graph isomorphisms is prohibitively costly, since it requires exponential complexity on the size of the (already huge) state graph.

Most symmetry-based approaches thus attempt to pre-compute the equivalence relation by exploiting structural information derived from the specification of the system. For instance, in high-level colored Petri net description of our running example (Figure 7.12), the set of process identities can be easily identified as being symmetric, since none of the transitions of the system act differently for a given process identity. A favorable characteristic of the symmetry reduction is that the size of the quotient state graph is bounded by the size of the ordinary state graph, since at worst the equivalence relation does not allow any permutations (i.e. it is limited to identity) and each equivalence class of states contains a single state.

Two main approaches are possible when building such a quotient graph; the first (and simplest) consists of choosing a representative for each equivalence class (i.e. an ordinary state of the state graph). While this allows less states to be built, it usually forces all possible transitions that can be fired from this state to be considered, hence a large number of edges. Another approach [CHI 91] consists in directly representing equivalence classes rather than choosing a representative for each class; this may allow the edges of the quotient graph to be *symbolically* computed, yielding a more efficient algorithm.

Consider, for instance, Figure 7.22 representing the quotient graph of our running example; the edge from $\hat{s}_0$ to $\hat{s}_1$ actually represents two equivalent edges. With a naïve algorithm that just uses state representatives, this edge would be computed twice.

The quotient graph approach allows reachability properties to be checked easily, since testing if a state belongs to an equivalence class is easy. However, for more complex behavioral properties, such as LTL, some care must be taken, since the property should itself be symmetric with respect to the equivalence relation used to build the quotient graph for the result to be correct.

7.9. Conclusion

Finite state model-checking is thus a formal approach that ensures that a given system fulfills some expected behavioral properties, even in the presence of non-determinism due to interleaving of actions. Moreover, since it is based on full state space exploration, it can be fully automated and hidden from the end-user, which is usually not the case for other approaches, such as theorem proving. Model-checking for the verification of hardware systems is now extensively adopted industrially, but is not generally in use for the development of software. The main factors that limit its more widespread adoption are first the combinatorial explosion problem which limits the size of specifications to which model-checking is applicable, and second the gap between formal specification languages (such as Petri nets) and specifications used in industry.

As more effective abstraction and reduction techniques are developed, larger systems can be tackled successfully; for decreasing the gap between models, the currently popular approach is to use model transformation to translate industrial specifications (e.g. UML or code) to formal specifications that are appropriate for model-checking tools.

7.10. Bibliography

[AKE 78] AKERS B., "Binary decision diagrams", *IEEE Transaction on Computers*, vol. 27, p. 509-516, 1978.

[BAH 93] BAHAR R. I., FROHM E. A., GAONA C. M., HACHTEL G. D., MACII E., PARDO A., SOMENZI F., "Algebraic decision diagrams and their applications", *ICCAD '93: Proceedings of the 1993 IEEE/ACM International Conference on Computer-Aided Design*, Los Alamitos, CA, USA, IEEE Computer Society Press, p. 188–191, 1993.

[BAR 89] BARKAOUI K., LEMAIRE B., "An effective characterization of minimal deadlocks and traps based on graph theory", in 10th *ICATPN*, Springer-Verlag, 1989.

[BAR 90] BARKAOUI K., MINOUX M., "Deadlocks and traps in Petri Nets as Horn satisfiability solutions and some related polynomially solvable problems", *Discrete Applied Mathematics*, vol. No. 29, 1990.

[BAR 96] BARKAOUI K., PRADAT-PEYRE J., "On liveness and controlled siphons in Petri nets", REISIG, Ed., *Petri Nets, Theory and Application*, vol. 1091 of *LNCS*, Springer-Verlag, 1996.

[BAR 97] BARKAOUI K., KAISER C., PRADAT-PEYRE J., Petri nets based proofs of Ada95 solution for preference control, Report num. 97-08, Conservatoire National des Arts et Métiers, laboratoire Cedric, ftp.cnam.fr/pub/CNAM/cedric/tech_reports/, 1997.

[BAU 97] BAUSE F., "Analysis of Petri Nets with a Dynamic Priority Method", *Proc. Int. Conf. on Applications and Theory of Petri nets*, vol. 1248 of *LNCS*, Toulouse, France, Springer Verlag, p. 215–234, June 1997.

[BER 80] BERTHELOT G., ROUCAIROL G., VALK R., "Reduction of nets and parallel programs.", BRAUER, W., Ed., *LNCS: Net Theory and Applications*, vol. 84, Berlin, Heidelberg, New York, Springer-Verlag, p. 277–290, 1980.

[BER 83] BERTHELOT G., Transformation et analyse de réseaux de Petri, applications aux protocoles, state thesis, University Pierre et Marie Curie, Paris, 1983.

[BER 85] BERTHELOT G., "Checking properties of nets using transformations", IN G. ROZENBERG, Ed., *Advances in Petri nets*, vol. No. 222 of *LNCS*, Springer-Verlag, 1985.

[BRY 86] BRYANT R., "Graph-based algorithms for Boolean function manipulation", *IEEE Transactions on Computers*, vol. 35, num. 8, p. 677–691, 1986.

[BUR 91] BURCH J., CLARKE E., LONG D., "Symbolic Model Checking with Partitioned Transition Relations", A. HALAAS, P.B. DENYER, Eds., *International Conference on Very Large Scale Integration*, Edinburgh, Scotland, North-Holland, p. 49–58, 1991.

[BUR 92] BURCH J., CLARKE E., MCMILLAN K., "Symbolic model checking: 10^{20} states and beyond", *Information and Computation*, vol. 98, num. 2, p. 153–181, 1992.

[CHI 91] CHIOLA G., FRANCESCHINIS G., "A structural colour simplification in well-formed coloured nets", *in Proc. 4th Int. Workshop on Petri Nets and Performance Models (PNPM'91)*,, Melbourne, Australia, IEEE Comp. Soc. Press, p. 144–153, 1991.

[CIA 03] CIARDO G., MARMORSTEIN R., SIMINICEANU. R., "Saturation unbound", GAR-AVEL H., HATCLIFF J., Eds., *in Proc. Tools and Algorithms for the Construction and Analysis of Systems (TACAS'03)*, Warsaw, Poland, Springer-Verlag LNCS 2619, p. 379–393, 2003.

[CLA 86] CLARKE E. M., EMERSON E. A., SISTLA A. P., "Automatic verification of finite-state concurrent systems using temporal logic specifications", *ACM Trans. Program. Lang. Syst.*, vol. 8, num. 2, p. 244–263, ACM Press, 1986.

[CLA 94] CLARKE E., GRUMBERG O., HAMAGUCHI K., "Another Look at LTL Model Checking", DAVID L. DILL, Ed., *Proceedings of the Sixth International Conference on Computer-Aided Verification CAV*, vol. 818, Stanford, California, USA, Springer-Verlag, p. 415–427, 1994.

[COH 98] COHEN E., LAMPORT L., "Reduction in TLA", in *International Conference on Concurrency Theory*, p. 317-331, 1998.

[COL 86] COLOM J., MARTINEZ J., SILVA M., "Packages for validating discrete production systems modeled with Petri nets", in *IMACS-IFAC Symposium*, Lille, France, 1986.

[COL 91] COLOM J. M., SILVA M., "Convex geometry and semiflows in P/T Nets. A comparative study of algorithms for computation of minimal P-semiflows", in *LNCS; Advances in Petri Nets 1990*, vol. 483, p. 79–112, Springer-Verlag, 1991, NewsletterInfo: 33,39.

[COM 72] COMMONER F., "Deadlocks in Petri nets", *Applied Data Inc.*, Report CA-7206-2311, 1972.

[COU 92] COURCOUBETIS C., VARDI M., WOLPER P., YANNAKAKIS M., "Memory-efficient algorithms for the verification of temporal properties", *Formal Methods in System Design*, vol. 1, p. 275–288, 1992.

[COU 96] COUVREUR J., POITRENAUD D., "Model checking based on occurrence net graph", GOTZHEIN R., BREDEREKE J., Eds., in *Proc. Formal Description Techniques IX, Theory, Application and Tools, FORTE/PSTV'96*, Kaiserslautern, Germany, Chapman and Hall, p. 380–395, 1996.

[COU 02] COUVREUR J.-M., ENCRENAZ E., PAVIOT-ADET E., POITRENAUD D., WACRE-NIER P.-A., "Data decision diagrams for Petri net analysis.", in *Proc. of ICATPN'2002*, vol. 2360 of *LNCS*, Springer Verlag, p. 101–120, 2002.

[COU 05] COUVREUR J.-M., DURET-LUTZ A., POITRENAUD D., "On-the-fly emptiness checks for generalized Büchi automata", GODEFROID P., Ed., in *Proceedings of the 12th International SPIN Workshop on Model Checking of Software*, vol. 3639 of *LNCS*, Springer-Verlag, p. 143–158, August 2005.

[ESP 92a] ESPARZA J., Model checking using net unfoldings, Report num. 14/92, Hildesheimer Informatikfachbericht, 1992.

[ESP 92b] ESPARZA J., SILVA M., "A polynomial-time algorithm to decide liveness of bounded free-choice nets", *T.C.S*, vol. N 102, p. 185-205, 1992.

[ESP 93] ESPARZA J., "Model checking using net unfoldings", GAUDEL M., JOUANNAUD J., Eds., in *Proc. TAPSOFT'93*, vol. 668 of *LNCS*, Springer Verlag, p. 613–628, 1993.

[ESP 01] ESPARZA J., SCHRÖTER C., "Net reductions for LTL model-checking", MAR-
GARIA T., MELHAM T., Eds., in *Correct Hardware Design and Verification Methods
(CHARME'01)*, vol. 2144 of *LNCS*, Springer-Verlag, p. 310–324, 2001.

[FLA 03a] FLANAGAN C., QADEER S., "Transactions for software model checking", IN BY-
RON COOK, STOLLER S., VISSER W., Eds., *Electronic Notes in Theoretical Computer
Science*, vol. 89, Elsevier, 2003.

[FLA 03b] FLANAGAN C., QADEER S., "A type and effect system for atomicity", *Proceedings of the ACM SIGPLAN 2003 Conference on Programming Language Design and Implementation*, ACM Press, p. 338–349, 2003.

[FUJ 97] FUJITA M., MCGEER P. C., YANG J. C.-Y., "Multi-terminal binary decision diagrams: an efficient data structure for matrix representation", *Formal Methods in System
Design*, vol. 10, num. 2/3, p. 149-169, 1997.

[GIA 02] GIANNAKOPOULOU D., LERDA F., "From states to transitions: improving translation of LTL formulae to Büchi automata", PELED D., VARDI M., Eds., in *Proceedings of
the 22nd IFIP WG 6.1 International Conference on Formal Techniques for Networked and
Distributed Systems (FORTE'02)*, vol. 2529 of *LNCS*, Houston, Texas, Springer-Verlag,
p. 308–326, 2002.

[GOD 91] GODEFROID P., WOLPER P., "A partial approach to model checking", in *Proc. 6th
IEEE Symposium on Logic in Computer Science*, Amsterdam, Holland, p. 406–415, July
1991.

[GOD 92] GODEFROID P., WOLPER P., "Using partial orders for the efficient verification of
deadlock freedom and safety properties", in *Proceedings of the 3rd International Workshop
on Computer Aided Verification*, Springer-Verlag, p. 332–342, 1992.

[GOD 93] GODEFROID P., WOLPER P., "Using partial orders for the efficient verification of
deadlock freedom and safety properties", *Form. Methods Syst. Des.*, vol. 2, num. 2, p. 149–
164, Kluwer Academic Publishers, 1993.

[GOD 94] GODEFROID P., Partial-order methods for the verification of concurrent systems, an
approach to the state-explosion problem, PhD Thesis, University of Liège, 1994, also in
volume 1032 of LNCS, Springer Verlag, 1996.

[GOD 96] GODEFROID P., *Partial-order Methods for the Verification of Concurrent Systems:
an Approach to the State-explosion Problem*, Springer-Verlag New York, Inc., 1996.

[HAB 69] HABERMANN A. N., "Prevention of system deadlocks", *Commun. ACM*, vol. 12,
num. 7, p. 373–ff., ACM Press, 1969.

[HAD 04a] HADDAD S., ILIÉ J.-M., KLAI K., "Design and evaluation of a symbolic and
abstraction-based model checker", in *2nd International Symposium on Automated Technology for Verification and Analysis ATVA'04*, Springer Verlag, 2004.

[HAD 04b] HADDAD S., PRADAT-PEYRE J., Efficient Reductions for LTL Formulae Verification, Report num. 634, CEDRIC, CNAM, Paris, 2004.

[HAM 98] HAMEZ A., THIERRY-MIEG Y., KORDON F., "Hierarchical set decision diagrams
and automatic saturation", in *Proc. of ICATPN'08*, vol. 5062 of *LNCS*, 1998.

[HER 03] HERMANNS H., KWIATKOWSKA M., NORMAN G., PARKER D., SIEGLE M., "On the use of MTBDDs for performability analysis and verification of stochastic systems", *Journal of Logic and Algebraic Programming: Special Issue on Probabilistic Techniques for the Design and Analysis of Systems*, vol. 56, num. 1-2, p. 23–67, 2003.

[HOL 92] HOLZMANN G., GODEFROID P., PIROTIN D., "Coverage preserving reduction strategies for the reachability analysis", LINN R., UYAR M., Eds., in *Proc. Protocol Specification, Testing and Verification XII*, Florida, USA, IFIP, North-Holland, p. 349–364, 1992.

[HOL 97] HOLZMANN G., "State compression in Spin", in *Proc. Third Spin Workshop*, Twente University, The Netherlands, 1997.

[KEM 92] KEMPER P., BAUSE F., "An efficient polynomial-time algorithm to decide liveness and boundedness of free-choice nets", *LNCS*, vol. 616, p. 263-278, Springer-Verlag, 1992.

[KES 98a] KESTEN Y., PNUELI A., "Modularization and abstraction: the keys to practical formal verification", *LNCS*, vol. 1450, p. 54–70, 1998.

[KES 98b] KESTEN Y., PNUELI A., ON RAVIV L., "Algorithmic verification of linear temporal logic specifications", *LNCS*, vol. 1443, 1998.

[KON 96] KONDRATYEV A., KISHINEVSKY M., TAUBIN A., TEN S., "A structural approach for the analysis of Petri nets by reduced unfoldings", BILLINGTON J., REISIG W., Eds., *Proc. 17th Int. Conf. on Applications and Theory of Petri nets*, vol. 1091 of *LNCS*, Osaka, Japan, Springer Verlag, p. 346–365, 1996.

[LIP 75] LIPTON R. J., "Reduction: a method of proving properties of parallel programs", *Commun. ACM*, vol. 18, num. 12, p. 717–721, ACM Press, 1975.

[MAZ 86] MAZURKIEWICZ A., "Trace theory", BRAUER W., REISIG W., ROZENBERG G., Eds., *Petri Nets: Applications and Relationships to other Models of Concurrency, Advances in Petri Nets, Part II*, vol. 255 of *LNCS*, Bad Honnef, Germany, Springer Verlag, p. 279–324, 1986.

[MCM 95] MCMILLAN K., "Trace theoretic verification of asynchronous circuits using unfoldings", WOLPER P., Ed., in *Proc. 7th Int. Conf. on Computer-Aided Verification*, vol. 939 of *LNCS*, Liège, Belgium, Springer Verlag, p. 180–195, 1995.

[MIN 93] ICHI MINATO S., "Zero-suppressed BDDs for set manipulation in combinatorial problems", *DAC '93: Proceedings of the 30th International Conference on Design Automation*, New York, NY, USA, ACM Press, p. 272–277, 1993.

[MIN 99] MINER A., CIARDO G., "Efficient reachability set generation and storage using decision diagrams", *Proc. of ICATPN'99*, vol. 1639 of *LNCS*, Springer Verlag, p. 6–25, 1999.

[NIE 81] NIELSEN M., PLOTKIN G., WINSKEL G., "Petri Nets, Events Structures and Domains, Part I", *Theoretical Computer Science*, vol. 13, num. 1, p. 85–108, 1981.

[PEL 94a] PELED D., "Combining partial order reductions with on-the-fly model-checking", in *Proc. 6th Int. Conf. on Computer-Aided Verification*, vol. 818 of *LNCS*, Stanford, USA, Springer Verlag, p. 377–390, 1994.

[PEL 94b] PELED D., PNUELI A., "Proving partial-order properties", *Theoretical Computer Science*, vol. 126, p. 143–182, 1994.

[PEL 94c] PELED D., "Combining partial order reductions with on-the-fly model-checking", in *Proceedings of the 6th International Conference on Computer Aided Verification*, Springer-Verlag, p. 377–390, 1994.

[POI 00] POITRENAUD D., PRADAT-PEYRE J., "Pre and post-agglomerations for LTL model checking", NIELSEN M., SIMPSON D., Eds., *High-level Petri nets, Theory and Application*, num. 1825LNCS, Springer-Verlag, p. 387-408, 2000.

[REI 83] REISIG W., *EATCS-An Introduction to Petri Nets*, Springer-Verlag, 1983.

[RIB 02] RIBET P.-O., VERNADAT F., BERTHOMIEU B., "On combining the persistent sets method with the covering steps graph method", *FORTE '02: Proceedings of the 22nd IFIP WG 6.1 International Conference Houston on Formal Techniques for Networked and Distributed Systems*, London, UK, Springer-Verlag, p. 344–359, 2002.

[RUD 93] RUDELL R., "Dynamic variable ordering for ordered binary decision diagrams", *ICCAD '93: Proceedings of the 1993 IEEE/ACM International Conference on Computer-aided Design*, Los Alamitos, CA, USA, IEEE Computer Society Press, p. 42–47, 1993.

[SCH 00] SCHNOEBELEN P., SIDOROVA N., "Bisimulation and the reduction of Petri nets", NIELSEN M., SIMPSON D., Eds., *High-level Petri Nets, Theory and Application*, num. 1825LNCS, Springer-Verlag, p. 409-423, 2000.

[SRI 90] SRINIVASAN A., KAM T., MALIK S., BRAYTON R. K., "Algorithms for discrete function manipulation.", in *ICCAD*, p. 92-95, 1990.

[STE 96] STERN U., DILL D., "A new scheme for memory-efficient probabilistic verification", GOTZHEIN R., BREDEREKE R., Eds., *Proc. Formal Description Techniques IX, Theory, Application and Tools*, Kaiserslautern, Germany, Chapman Hall, p. 333–348, October 1996.

[STO 03] STOLLER S. D., COHEN E., "Optimistic synchronization-based state-space reduction", GARAVEL H., HATCLIFF J., Eds., *TACAS'03*, vol. 2619 of *LNCS*, Springer-Verlag, p. 489-504, April 2003.

[TAN 93] TANI S., HAMAGUCHI K., YAJIMA S., "The complexity of the optimal variable ordering problems of shared binary decision diagrams", in *ISAAC: 4th International Symposium on Algorithms And Computation (formerly SIGAL International Symposium on Algorithms)*, ACM/IPSJ/IEICE, 1993.

[TER 93] TERUEL E., SILVA M., "Liveness and home states in equal conflict systems.", MARSAN, M. A., Ed., in *LNCS; Application and Theory of Petri Nets 1993, Proceedings 14th International Conference, Chicago, Illinois, USA*, vol. 691, Springer-Verlag, p. 415–432, 1993.

[THI 04] THIERRY-MIEG Y., ILIÉ J.-M., POITRENAUD D., "A symbolic symbolic state space", in *Proc. of the 24th IFIP WG 6.1 Int. Conf. on Formal Techniques for Networked and Distributed Systems (FORTE'04)*, vol. 3235 of *LNCS*, Madrid, Spain, Springer, p. 276–291, 2004.

[VAL 89] VALMARI A., "Stubborn sets for reduced state space generation", in *Proceedings of ATPN'89*, Springer Verlag, LNCS 483, 1989.

[VAL 90] VALMARI A., "A stubborn attack on state explosion", CLARKE E., KURSHAN R., Eds., *in Proc. 2th Int. Conf. on Computer-Aided Verification*, vol. 531 of *LNCS*, New Brunswick, NJ, USA, Springer Verlag, p. 156–165, 1990.

[VAL 93] VALMARI A., "On-the-fly verification with stubborn sets", COURCOUBETIS C., Ed., in *Proc. 5th Int. Conf. on Computer-Aided Verification*, vol. 697 of *LNCS*, Elounda, Greece, Springer Verlag, p. 397–408, 1993.

[VAR 96] VARDI M. Y., "An automata-theoretic approach to linear temporal logic", MOLLER F., BIRTWISTLE G. M., Eds., *in Proceedings of the 8th Banff Higher Order Workshop*, vol. 1043 of *LNCS*, Springer-Verlag, p. 238–266, 1996.

[VAR 01] VARDI M. Y., "Branching vs. linear time: final showdown", *LNCS*, vol. 2031, p. 1–22, 2001.

[VER 97] VERNADAT F., MICHEL F., "Covering step graphs preserving failure semantics", in *Proc. 18th Int. Conf. on Applications and Theory of Petri nets*, vol. 1248 of *LNCS*, Toulouse, France, Springer Verlag, p. 253–270, 1997.

[WIL 96] WILLEMS B., WOLPER P., "Partial-order methods for model checking: from linear time to branching time", *Proc. 11th Annual Symposium on Logic in Computer Science*, New Brunswick, NJ, USA, p. 294–303, July 1996.

[WIN 87] WINSKEL G., "Event structures", *Advances in Petri Nets 1986, Part II*, vol. 255 of *LNCS*, Springer Verlag, p. 325–392, 1987.

Chapter 8

Verification of Infinite-State Systems

8.1. Introduction

In this section, we briefly present several methods that are used for the verification of infinite-state systems. Furthermore, we show how the developments in counter systems are related to other techniques (exact methods or by approximation).

8.1.1. *From finite-state to infinite-state systems*

Model-checking is a well-known approach to verifying behavioral properties of computing systems; which has been very successful in the verification of finite-state systems, see e.g. [MCM 93, CLA 00b, BER 01]. The assumption that programs are finite-state is usually too restrictive; which is why, model-checking techniques for infinite-state systems have flourished over the last 20 years. However, dealing with infinity or unboundedness of computational structures has dramatic consequences computationally. The source of infinity of infinite-state systems is not unique and it can be caused by at least the following factors. Programs manipulate local or global variables interpreted in infinite domains such as the set of integers or the set of real numbers. Similarly, dynamic data structures are considered in programs which is another source of infinity. Programs contain procedure/method calls, leading to an unbounded context stack to handle the control. The size of the stack can be arbitrarily large depending on the number of nested calls, in which recursive calls may induce unbounded control structures. Similarly, process creation can be the source of infinity (see section 8.3). Furthermore, the behavior of programs depends on input data values (parameters).

Chapter written by Stéphane DEMRI and Denis POITRENAUD.

Similarly, systems may be parameterized by the number of subsystems that are synchronized, etc. Parameterized systems can therefore represent an infinite number of specific systems, depending on the parameter values. Note, for instance, to verify a property automatically regardless of the number of processes is a great challenge. Among the jungle of infinite-state systems, there are many interesting classes that have been used for modeling computer systems and for undertaking formal verification. Here are a few of them: Petri nets, see e.g. [REI 98]; timed systems (see Chapter 9); pushdown systems, see e.g. [FIN 97]; counter systems (see section 8.2) and systems with lossy channels [ABD 96].

8.1.2. *Decision problems for infinite-state systems*

Decision problems related to verification for infinite-state systems can be roughly divided into two categories. Firstly, numerous decision problems are essential for finite-state and for infinite-state systems such as reachability problems (including control state repeated reachability problem), model-checking temporal formulae or checking behavioral equivalences with respect to a finite-state system. Nevertheless, specific methods or adaptations of existing methods are required in order to deal with infinity. In this chapter, we shall mainly focus on reachability problems since their resolution often enables much more complex problems to be solved. Secondly, decision problems also exist that are more specific to infinite-state systems. This includes decision problems related to boundedness (for instance, checking whether a counter in a counter automaton takes a bounded amount of values) and those related to model-checking temporal formulae in which atomic formulae can state properties about unbounded values (a typical example is to replace control states in the temporal language by constraints on counter values).

8.1.3. *Techniques for verifying infinite-state systems*

Techniques for the verification of infinite-state systems stem from exact methods in which potentially infinite sets of configurations are finitely represented symbolically to semi-algorithms that are designed to behave well in practice (of course these latter procedures may not terminate). When exact methods provide decision procedures, this is mainly due to the identification of an underlying finite structure in the verification problem. For instance, the set of reachable configurations can be effectively represented symbolically, for instance by a formula in Presburger arithmetic for which satisfiability is known to be decidable [PRE 29] (see section 8.4). The use of Presburger arithmetic for formal verification has been advocated in [SUZ 80]. Finiteness can also occur in a more subtle way as in well-structured transition systems [FIN 01] for which termination is guaranteed thanks to underlying well quasi-orderings, see also [HEN 05] for a classification of symbolic transition systems. Section 8.4 presents exact methods to decide reachability problems for subclasses of counter systems by taking advantage of decision procedures for Presburger arithmetic. Similarly, section 8.3 introduces the class of recursive Petri nets, an extension of Petri nets with recursion, and it shows how standard proof techniques for Petri nets (that are already common and often studied class of infinite-state systems) can be extended in presence of recursion. As there are methods to verify finite systems that can be extended to infinite-state systems (for instance the automata-based approach), specific methods for infinite-state systems need to be developed too, for instance those based on well quasi-orderings.

8.1.4. *Automata-based symbolic representations*

A major problem for the verification of infinite-state systems consists of computing the set of configurations reachable from a set of configurations. This requires a well-suited symbolic representation for such (potentially infinite) sets and techniques to compute the transitive closure of transition relations. Regular model-checking is an approach that represents sets of configurations by regular sets of finite words (or infinite words, or trees) and transducers encode the transition relations of the systems. Regularity is typically captured by finite-state automata. This automata-based approach has been developped for several types of systems including systems for integers and reals [BOI 98], pushdown systems [FIN 97] or systems with lossy channels [ABD 96] (see also a similar approach by automatic structures in [BLU 00]); recent developments can be found in [LEG 08]. Regular sets of trees are for instance considered in [BOU 06b] in order to verify programs with dynamic data structures. In section 8.4, we shall illustrate how sets of reachable configurations can be represented by finite-state automata accepting finite words.

8.1.5. *Approximations*

An important difficulty in the approach with regular model-checking is the state-explosion problem since the number of states of the built automata (representing sets of configurations) can be huge. This is partly due to the fact that the automata are constructed regardless of the properties to be shown. By contrast, approximation methods may over-approximate the exact set of reachable configurations so that in case of termination, non-reachability can be deduced. The aim is to reduce the verification of such systems to the verification of finite-state systems with the hope of using known and efficient methods. For instance, predicate abstraction produces Boolean programs (program variables are Boolean) but the crux of the method relies on the ability to automatically produce a precise enough abstraction that allows the desired property to be checked. Indeed, the inacurracy of the abstraction should not induce the production of spurious counter examples. The method CEGAR (counter-example guided abstraction refinement) [CLA 00a] aims to automatically derive more and more refined abstractions in order to check the desired properties. Many tools successfully use this method, including BLAST [HEN 03].

8.1.6. *Counter systems*

Despite numerous symbolic representations having been proposed to deal with infinite-state systems (see e.g. timed automata [ALU 94] in Chapter 9), their formal verification remains a difficult problem. Many general formalisms referring to infinite-state systems have an undecidable model-checking problem. Sometimes, decidability can be regained by considering subproblems of the general problem. The class of counter systems is an example of such a formalism. Counter systems have many applications in formal verification. Their ubiquity stems from their use as operational models of numerous infinite-state systems, including for instance broadcast protocols [FIN 02], programs with pointer variables (see [BOU 06a]) and logics for data words. However, numerous model-checking problems for counter systems, such as reachability, are known to be undecidable. Many subclasses of counter systems admit a decidable reachability problem such as reversal-bounded counter automata [IBA 78] and flat counter automata [BOI 98, COM 98, FIN 02]. These two classes of systems admit reachability sets effectively definable in Presburger arithmetic (assuming some additional conditions, unspecified herein). In general, computing the transitive closures of integer relations is a key step to solve verification problems on counter systems, see e.g. [BOZ 10].

In this chapter, we consider

– the class of sequential recursive Petri nets in order to illustrate how recursion can be handled by adapting adequately techniques for Petri nets;

– subclasses of counter systems in order to illustrate the use of Presburger arithmetic to solve verification problems on such systems.

8.1.7. *Structure of the chapter*

In section 8.2, we present the class of counter systems that are essentially finite-state automata equipped with program variables (counters) interpreted by non-negative integers. To do so, we first present Presburger arithmetic, since the update functions on counters are governed by constraints expressed in Presburger arithmetic. Several subclasses of counter systems are also introduced, including the vector addition systems with states that are known to be equivalent to Petri nets. The subsequent sections are dedicated to subclasses of counter systems in which verification tasks can be done effectively. In section 8.3, we present the class of recursive Petri nets that extend Petri nets by adding recursion in a controlled way. Verification techniques for this enriched computational model are described by emphasizing how the proof techniques for Petri nets can be indeed extended adequately to this more expressive model. This includes the resolution of the reachability problem as well as the computation of linear invariants. In section 8.4, we introduce subclasses of counter systems for which reachability questions can be solved in Presburger arithmetic viewed as a means to symbolically represent sets of tuples of natural numbers. Unlike section 8.3, the new feature is not recursion but rather the possibility to perform zero-tests (and more sophisticated updates that can be expressed in Presburger arithmetic) but at the cost of making further restrictions, for example on the control graphs. Concluding remarks can be found in section 8.5.

8.2. Counter systems

In this section, we present Presburger arithmetic, the class of counter systems as well as remarkable subclasses, including VASS that are known to be equivalent to Petri nets (models of greater practical appeal).

8.2.1. *Presburger arithmetic in a nutshell*

Roughly speaking, Presburger arithmetic is the first-order theory of the structure $(\mathbb{N}, +)$ shown decidable in [PRE 29] (which contrasts with Peano arithmetic that also admits multiplication). This logical formalism is used to define sets of tuples of natural numbers. Moreover, it will serve several purposes. Firstly, in the definition of counter systems, Presburger arithmetic is used as a language to define guards and actions (updates on counter values) on transitions. Secondly, each formula from Presburger arithmetic defines a set of tuples (related to the set of assignments that make true the formula) and Presburger arithmetic is therefore a means to represent and symbolically manipulate infinite sets of tuples of natural numbers. Thirdly, formulae from Presburger arithmetic will serve as symbolic representations for semilinear sets (see section 8.3). This section is dedicated to the basics of Presburger arithmetic and to the main properties we shall use in the chapter.

Basics on tuples of natural numbers

We write $\mathbb{N}$ [resp. $\mathbb{Z}$] for the set of natural numbers [resp. integers] and $[m, m']$ with $m, m' \in \mathbb{Z}$ to denote the set $\{j \in \mathbb{Z} : m \leq j \leq m'\}$. Given a dimension $n \geq 1$ and $a \in \mathbb{Z}$, we write $\vec{a}$ to denote the vector with all values equal to a. For $\vec{x} \in \mathbb{Z}^n$, we write $\vec{x}(1), \ldots, \vec{x}(n)$ for the entries of $\vec{x}$. For $\vec{x}, \vec{y} \in \mathbb{Z}^n$, $\vec{x} \preceq \vec{y} \overset{\text{def}}{\Leftrightarrow}$ for $i \in [1, n]$, we have $\vec{x}(i) \leq \vec{y}(i)$. We also write $\vec{x} \prec \vec{y}$ when $\vec{x} \preceq \vec{y}$ and $\vec{x} \neq \vec{y}$.

Definition

Let VAR $= \{x, y, z, \ldots\}$ be a countably infinite set of *variables*. *Terms* are defined by the grammar $t ::= 0 \mid 1 \mid x \mid t+t$, where $x \in$ VAR and 0 and 1 are distinguished constants (interpreted by zero and one respectively). For $k \geq 1$, we write kx instead of $x + \cdots + x$ (k times). Similarly, for $k \geq 1$, we write k instead of $1 + \cdots + 1$ (k times). *Presburger formulae* are defined by the grammar $\varphi ::= t \equiv_k t \mid t < t \mid \neg\varphi \mid \varphi \wedge \varphi \mid \exists x\, \varphi \mid \forall x\, \varphi$, where $k \geq 2$. The atomic formula $x \equiv_2 y$ holds true whenever the difference between x and y is even (equality modulo 2). As usual, an occurrence of the variable x in the formula φ is *free* if it does not occur in the scope of either $\exists$x or $\forall$x. Otherwise, the occurrence is *bound*. For instance, in $x_1 < x_2$, all the occurrences of the variables are free.

A *valuation* **v** is a map VAR $\to \mathbb{N}$ and it can be extended to the set of all terms as follows: $\mathbf{v}(0) = 0$, $\mathbf{v}(1) = 1$ and $\mathbf{v}(t + t') = \mathbf{v}(t) + \mathbf{v}(t')$. The satisfaction relation for Presburger arithmetic is equipped with a valuation witnessing that Presburger formulae are interpreted over the structure $(\mathbb{N}, +)$.

- $\mathbf{v} \models t \equiv_k t'$ $\overset{\text{def}}{\Leftrightarrow}$ there is $n \in \mathbb{Z}$ such that $kn + \mathbf{v}(t) = \mathbf{v}(t')$;
- $\mathbf{v} \models t < t'$ $\overset{\text{def}}{\Leftrightarrow}$ $\mathbf{v}(t) < \mathbf{v}(t')$;
- $\mathbf{v} \models \neg\varphi$ $\overset{\text{def}}{\Leftrightarrow}$ $\mathbf{v} \not\models \varphi$;
- $\mathbf{v} \models \varphi \wedge \varphi'$ $\overset{\text{def}}{\Leftrightarrow}$ $\mathbf{v} \models \varphi$ and $\mathbf{v} \models \varphi'$;
- $\mathbf{v} \models \exists x\, \varphi$ $\overset{\text{def}}{\Leftrightarrow}$ there is $n \in \mathbb{N}$ such that $\mathbf{v}[x \mapsto n] \models \varphi$ where $\mathbf{v}[x \mapsto n]$ is equal to $\mathbf{v}$ except that x is mapped to n;
- $\mathbf{v} \models \forall x\, \varphi$ $\overset{\text{def}}{\Leftrightarrow}$ for every $n \in \mathbb{N}$, we have $\mathbf{v}[x \mapsto n] \models \varphi$.

As usual, the Boolean connectives $\vee$ (disjunction) and $\Rightarrow$ (implication) can be defined from negation and conjunction in the standard way. Equality between two terms, written $t = t'$, can be expressed by $\neg(t < t' \vee t' < t)$. Similarly, we write $t \leq t'$ to denote the formula $(t = t') \vee (t < t')$. Observe also that $t \equiv_k t'$ is equivalent to $\exists x\, (t = kx + t' \vee t' = kx + t)$ (x is a variable that does not occur in t and t'). We invite the reader to check that 0 and 1 can be removed from the above definitions without changing the expressive power of the formulae.

In the chapter, we assume that the variables in VAR are linearly ordered by their indices. So, any valuation restricted to $n \geq 1$ variables can be viewed as a tuple in $\mathbb{N}^n$. Any formula with $n \geq 1$ free variables $x_1, \ldots, x_n$ defines a set of n-tuples (n-ary relation) as follows:

$$\text{REL}(\varphi) \overset{\text{def}}{=} \{(\mathbf{v}(x_1), \ldots, \mathbf{v}(x_n)) \in \mathbb{N}^n : \mathbf{v} \models \varphi\}.$$

For instance, $\text{REL}(x_1 < x_2) = \{(n, n') \in \mathbb{N}^2 : n < n'\}$. Similarly, the set of odd natural numbers can be defined by the formula $\exists y\, x = y + y + 1$. A set $X \subseteq \mathbb{N}^n$ is said to be *Presburger-definable* iff there is a Presburger formula φ such that $X = \text{REL}(\varphi)$. Sets that are Presburger-definable are known to correspond exactly to semilinear sets [GIN 66].

A formula φ is *satisfiable* (in Presburger arithmetic) whenever there is a valuation **v** such that $\mathbf{v} \models \varphi$. Similarly, a formula φ is *valid* (in Presburger arithmetic) when for all valuations **v**, we have $\mathbf{v} \models \varphi$. When φ has no free variables, satisfiability and validity are equivalent notions. Two formulae are *equivalent* (in Presburger arithmetic) whenever they define the same set of tuples.

THEOREM 8.1 *[PRE 29] (I) The satisfiability problem for Presburger arithmetic is decidable. (II) Every Presburger formula is equivalent to a Presburger formula without first-order quantification.*

Theorem 8.1(II) takes advantage of atomic formulae of the form $t \equiv_k t'$ that contain an implicit quantification. Removing atomic formulae of the form $t \equiv_k t'$ does not change the expressive power but the equivalence in theorem 8.1(II) would not hold in that case. Moreover, in (II) above, the equivalent formula can be effectively built witnessing the quantifier elimination property. In subsequent developments, we mainly consider quantifier-free Presburger formulae, which does not restrict the expressive power but may modify complexity issues. It is worth noting that the first-order theory of $(\mathbb{N}, \times)$ is decidable too (known as *Skolem arithmetic*) whereas the first-order theory of $(\mathbb{N}, \times, +)$ is undecidable (see e.g. [TAR 53]). Observe also that $(\mathbb{Z}, <, +)$ is decidable [PRE 29] as well as the first-order theory of $(\mathbb{R}, \times, +)$ [TAR 51].

Satisfiability problem for Presburger arithmetic can be solved in triple exponential time [OPP 78] by analyzing the quantifier elimination procedure described in [COO 72]. Besides, satisfiability problem for Presburger arithmetic is shown 2EXPTIME-hard in [FIS 74] and in 2EXPSPACE in [FER 79]. An exact complexity charaterization is provided in [BER 80] (double exponential time on alternating Turing machines with linear amount of alternations). Due to the wide range of applications for Presburger arithmetic, computational complexity of numerous fragments has been also characterized, see e.g. [GRÄ 88]. Moreover, its restriction to quantifier-free formulae is NP-complete [PAP 81] (see also [BOR 76]).

8.2.2. *Classes of counter systems*

A counter system $\mathcal{S}$ is defined below as a finite-state automaton equipped with counters, i.e. program variables interpreted by non-negative integers. In full generality, the counters are governed by constraints that can be expressed by Presburger formulae (this generality is mainly useful for section 8.4.1). Minsky machines [MIN 67] form a special class of counter systems and therefore most interesting problems on counter systems happen to be undecidable since Minsky machines can simulate Turing machines [MIN 67]. However, we shall study important subclasses of counter systems for which decidability can be regained for various decision problems.

DEFINITION 8.2 *A counter system $\mathcal{S} = (Q, n, \delta)$ is a structure such that*
  – Q is a nonempty finite set of control states *(a.k.a.* locations*);*
  – $n \geq 1$ is the dimension *of the system, i.e. the number of counters; we assume that the counters are represented by the variables $x_1, \ldots, x_n$;*

 – δ *is the* transition relation *defined as a finite set of triples of the form* (q, φ, q'), *where* q, q' *are control states and* φ *is a Presburger formula whose free variables are among* $x_1, \ldots, x_n, x'_1, \ldots, x'_n$.

Elements $t = (q, \varphi, q')$ are called *transitions* and are often represented by $q \xrightarrow{\varphi} q'$. As usual, by convention, prime variables are intended to be interpreted as the next values of the unprimed variables. Moreover, observe that a counter system has no initial control state and no final control state but in the chapter we shall introduce such control states on demand. It is certainly possible to propose an alternative definition without control states and to encode them by new counters, for instance. However, when infinite-state transition systems arise in the modeling of computational processes, there is often a natural factoring of each system state into a control component and a memory component, where the set of control states is typically finite.

Figure 8.1 contains a counter system (augmented with an initial control state). It is related to the famous Collatz problem. The role of control state q_0 is to compute an arbitrary counter value before reaching the control state q_1. At the control state q_1, if the counter value is even, then divide by two the counter value. Otherwise, multiply by 3 and add 1. It is open whether whenever the system enters in the control state q_1, eventually it reaches the counter value 1.

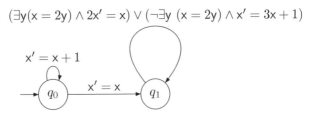

$$(\exists y(x = 2y) \wedge 2x' = x) \vee (\neg \exists y\ (x = 2y) \wedge x' = 3x + 1)$$

$$x' = x + 1$$

$$x' = x$$

Figure 8.1. *An example of counter system*

The class of counter systems is quite general and it very often makes sense to label the transitions by Presburger formulae that can be decomposed by a *guard* (constraints on the current counter values) and an *update function* (constraints on the way the new counter values are computed from the previous ones).

A *configuration* of the counter system $\mathcal{S} = (Q, n, \delta)$ is defined as a pair $(q, \vec{x}) \in Q \times \mathbb{N}^n$. Given two configurations $(q, \vec{x})$, $(q', \vec{x'})$ and a transition $t = q \xrightarrow{\varphi} q'$, we write $(q, \vec{x}) \xrightarrow{t} (q', \vec{x'})$ whenever $\mathbf{v}_{\vec{x}, \vec{x'}} \models \varphi$ and for $i \in [1, n]$, $\mathbf{v}_{\vec{x}, \vec{x'}}(x_i) \overset{\text{def}}{=} \vec{x}(i)$ and $\mathbf{v}_{\vec{x}, \vec{x'}}(x'_i) \overset{\text{def}}{=} \vec{x'}(i)$. The operational semantics of counter systems updates configurations, and runs of such systems are essentially sequences of configurations. Every counter system $S = (Q, n, \delta)$ induces a (possibly infinite) graph made of configurations. Indeed, all the interesting problems on counter systems can be formulated on its *transition system*.

DEFINITION 8.3 *Given a counter system* $S = (Q, n, \delta)$, *its* transition system $T(S) = (S, \rightarrow)$ *is a graph such that* $S = Q \times \mathbb{N}^n$ *and* $\rightarrow \subseteq S \times S$ *such that* $((q, \vec{x}), (q', \vec{x'})) \in \rightarrow$ $\overset{\text{def}}{\Leftrightarrow}$ *there exists a transition* $t \in \delta$ *such that* $(q, \vec{x}) \overset{t}{\rightarrow} (q', \vec{x'})$. *As usual,* $\overset{*}{\rightarrow}$ *denotes the reflexive and transitive closure of the binary relation* $\rightarrow$.

Given a counter system S, a *run* ρ is a non-empty (possibly infinite) sequence $\rho = (q_0, \vec{x_0}), \ldots, (q_k, \vec{x_k}), \ldots$ of configurations such that two consecutive configurations are in the relation $\rightarrow$ from $T(S)$. $(q_0, \vec{x_0})$ is called the *initial* configuration of ρ.

Standard decision problems

Below, we enumerate a list of standard decision problems for counter systems. They are mainly related to reachability questions. The list is certainly not exhaustive but it contains the main problems related to verification and model-checking.

Reachability problem:

– *Input*: a counter system S and two configurations $(q, \vec{x})$ and $(q', \vec{x'})$;
– *Question*: is there a finite run with initial configuration $(q, \vec{x})$ and final configuration $(q', \vec{x'})$?

Control state reachability problem:

– *Input*: a counter system S, a configuration $(q, \vec{x})$ and a control state q_f;
– *Question*: is there a finite run with initial configuration $(q, \vec{x})$ and whose final configuration has control state q_f?

Covering problem:

– *Input*: a counter system S and two configurations $(q, \vec{x})$ and $(q', \vec{x'})$;
– *Question*: is there a finite run with initial configuration $(q, \vec{x})$ and whose final configuration is $(q', \vec{x''})$ with $\vec{x'} \preceq \vec{x''}$?

Boundedness problem:

– *Input*: a counter system S and a configuration $(q, \vec{x})$;
– *Question*: is the set $\{(q', \vec{x'}) \in Q \times \mathbb{N}^n : (q, \vec{x}) \overset{*}{\rightarrow} (q', \vec{x'})\}$ finite?

Termination problem:

– *Input*: a counter system S and a configuration $(q, \vec{x})$;

– *Question*: is there an infinite run with initial configuration $(q, \vec{x})$?

Control state repeated reachability problem:

    – *Input*: a counter system $\mathcal{S}$, a configuration $(q, \vec{x})$ and a control state q_f;

    – *Question*: is there an infinite run with initial configuration $(q, \vec{x})$ such that the control state q_f is repeated infinitely often?

Most standard verification problems on counter systems reduce to one of the above mentioned decision problems. For instance, model-checking over linear-time temporal logic (LTL) in which atomic formulae are restricted to control states amounts to questions on control state repeated reachability problem. Hence, designing algorithms for such decision problems can be helpful for instance to verify computer systems such as programs with pointers [BOU 06a], broadcast protocols [ESP 99], or replicated finite-state programs [KAI 10] (Boolean programs with a finite set of configurations but can be executed by an unknown number of threads), to quote but a few.

In the forthcoming subsections, we introduce several subclasses of counter systems by restricting the general definition provided above. Additional requirements can be of distinct nature: restriction on syntactic ressources (number of counters, Presburger formulae etc.), restriction on the control graph (e.g. flatness), and semantical restrictions (reversal-boundedness, etc.)

Succinct counter automata

In the chapter, we adopt the convention that a counter automaton is a counter system in which the instructions are either zero-tests, increments, or decrements, possibly encoded succinctly. A *succinct counter automaton* is a counter system (Q, n, δ) in which the transitions are of the form either $q \xrightarrow{\mathrm{inc}(\vec{b})} q'$ with $\vec{b} \in \mathbb{Z}^n$ or $q \xrightarrow{\mathrm{zero}(\vec{b'})} q'$ with $\vec{b'} \in \{0, 1\}^n$ where:

    – $\mathrm{inc}(\vec{b})$ is a shortcut for $\bigwedge_{i \in [1,n]} x'_i = x_i + \vec{b}(i)$;

    – $\mathrm{zero}(\vec{b'})$ is a shortcut for $\bigwedge_{i \in [1,n] \text{ s.t. } \vec{b'}(i)=1} x_i = 0 \wedge \bigwedge_{i \in [1,n]} x'_i = x_i$ (as usual, empty conjunction is understood as $\top$).

In succinct counter automaton, each transition either performs zero-tests on a subset of counters or updates counters by adding a vector in $\mathbb{Z}^n$. All the counters are tested or updated simultaneously.

Standard counter automata

A *standard counter automaton* is a counter system (Q, n, δ) in which the transitions are of the form either $q \xrightarrow{\mathrm{inc}(i)} q'$ or $q \xrightarrow{\mathrm{dec}(i)} q'$ or $q \xrightarrow{\mathrm{zero}(i)} q'$ ($i \in [1, n]$) where

    – $\mathrm{inc}(i)$ is a shortcut for $(x'_i = x_i + 1) \wedge (\bigwedge_{j \neq i} x'_j = x_j)$ (also written $x_i{+}{+}$);

– dec(i) is a shortcut for $(x'_i = x_i - 1) \wedge (\bigwedge_{j \neq i} x'_j = x_j)$ (also written x_i- -);
– zero(i) is a shortcut for $(x_i = 0) \wedge (\bigwedge_j x'_j = x_j)$ (also written $x_i = 0$?).

By contrast to succinct counter automata, transitions in standard counter automata can perform a simple operation at once (otherwise, a succession of transitions is needed). Indeed, standard counter automata and succinct counter automata are very similar but when it comes to complexity issues, exponential blow-up may occur when passing from one model to another. In the sequel, unless otherwise stated, by a counter automaton we mean a standard one. It is easy to check that Minsky machines (with two counters) form a subclass of standard counter automata.

8.2.2.1. *Vector addition systems with states*

A *vector addition system with states* (VASS) [KAR 69] is a succinct counter automaton without zero-tests, i.e. all the transitions are of the form $q \xrightarrow{\text{inc}(\vec{b})} q'$ with $\vec{b} \in \mathbb{Z}^n$. In the sequel, a VASS is represented by a tuple $\mathcal{V} = (Q, n, \delta)$ where Q is the finite set of control states and δ is a finite subset of $Q \times \mathbb{Z}^n \times Q$. Standard counter automata can be naturally viewed as VASS augmented with zero-tests by simulating transitions of the form $q \xrightarrow{\vec{b}} q'$ by sequences of increments and decrements. Additionally, VASS are known to be equivalent to Petri nets that are models of greater practical appeal. Figure 8.2 presents an example of VASS. One can show that for all $\vec{x} \in \mathbb{N}^4$, the set $\{\vec{y} \in \mathbb{N}^4 : (q_0, \vec{x}) \xrightarrow{*} (q_0, \vec{y})\}$ is finite. Moreover, for $\vec{x} \in \mathbb{N}^2$, $\{k \in \mathbb{N} : k \leq \vec{x}(1) \times \vec{x}(2)\} = \{\vec{y}(4) : (q_0, \vec{y_0}) \xrightarrow{*} (q_0, \vec{y}), \vec{y_0}(1) = \vec{x}(1), \vec{y_0}(2) = \vec{x}(2), \vec{y_0}(3) = \vec{y_0}(4) = 0\}$.

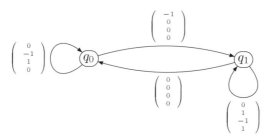

Figure 8.2. *A VASS weakly computing multiplication*

THEOREM 8.4 *(see e.g. [MAY 84, KOS 82]) The reachability problem for VASS is decidable.*

The exact complexity of the reachability problem is open: we know it is EX-PSPACE-hard [LIP 76] and no primitive recursive upper bound exists. By contrast, the covering problem and boundedness problems seem easier since they are Ex-PSPACE-complete [LIP 76, RAC 78]. Observe also that the covering problem can express the thread-state reachability problem for replicated finite-state programs, see e.g. [KAI 10]. Similarly, the boundedness problem for asynchronous programs has been considered in [GAN 09].

8.2.2.2. *Relationships with Petri nets*

In this section, we briefly recall how Petri nets (see e.g. [REI 98]) are related to VASS . First, let us recall that a *Petri net* N is a structure (P, T, W^-, W^+, m_I) such that P is a finite set of *places*, T is a finite set of *transitions*, $W^- : (P \times T) \to \mathbb{N}$ and $W^+ : (P \times T) \to \mathbb{N}$ are *weight functions*. A *marking* m is a map of the form $P \to \mathbb{N}$: for each place, we specify a number of *tokens* (possibly none). In the Petri net N, $m_I : P \to \mathbb{N}$ is the initial marking (initial distribution of tokens). We assume that the reader is familiar with the semantics of this model (otherwise see e.g. [PET 81, REI 98]). We just recall below a few definitions. A transition $t \in T$ is *m-enabled*, written $m \xrightarrow{t}$, whenever for all places $p \in P$, $m(p) \geq W^-(p, t)$. An m-enabled transition t may fire and produce the marking m', written $m \xrightarrow{t} m'$, with for all places $p \in P$, $m'(p) = m(p) - W^-(p, t) + W^+(p, t)$. A marking m' is *reachable* from m whenever there is a sequence of the form $m_0 \xrightarrow{t_0} m_1 \xrightarrow{t_1} \cdots \xrightarrow{t_{k-1}} m_k$ with $m_0 = m$ and $m_k = m'$ (also written $m \xrightarrow{t_0 \cdots t_{k-1}} m'$).

Here are standard problems for Petri nets.

Reachability problem for Petri nets:

– *Input*: a Petri net (P, T, W^-, W^+, m_I) and a marking m;
– *Question*: is m reachable from m_I?

Covering problem for Petri nets:

– *Input*: a Petri net (P, T, W^-, W^+, m_I) and a marking m;
– *Question*: is there a marking m' reachable from m_I such that for all $p \in P$, we have $m'(p) \geq m(p)$?

Boundedness problem for Petri nets:

– *Input*: a Petri net (P, T, W^-, W^+, m_I);
– *Question*: is the set of markings reachable from m_I infinite?

Petri nets and VASS are known to be equivalent models as far as the reachability problem, the covering problem, and the boundedness problem are concerned, see e.g. [REU 90]. By way of example, let us show how to simulate a VASS using a Petri net. Let $\mathcal{V}$ be a VASS (Q, n, δ) and $(q_I, \vec{x_I})$ be a configuration. We can build a Petri net $N_\mathcal{V}$ that simulates $\mathcal{V}$, by using a standard translation from VASS to Petri nets.

For every control state q in $\mathcal{V}$, we introduce a place p_q in $N_\mathcal{V}$ and for $i \in [1, n]$, we introduce a place p_i. An initial marking m_I contains one token in the place p_{q_I} and for $i \in [1, n]$, $m_I(p_i) = \vec{x}_I(i)$. From this marking, we only obtain markings where a unique token belongs to a place of the form p_q ($q \in Q$) which means that a unique control state is active for every marking. For every transition in $\mathcal{V}$, say $t = q \xrightarrow{\vec{b}} q'$, we consider a transition $\mathbf{t}$ in $N_\mathcal{V}$ that consumes a token in p_q, produces a token in $p_{q'}$ and produces [respectively consumes] $\vec{b}(i)$ tokens in the place p_i when $\vec{b}(i) \geq 0$ [respectively when $\vec{b}(i) < 0$].

In the rest of this chapter, we shall consider two types of extensions of Petri nets, namely recursive Petri nets in section 8.3; which adds recursion to Petri nets and subclasses of counter systems in which zero-tests are allowed in section 8.4 (presented as extensions of VASS with zero-tests or with more complex Presburger-definable update functions). Methods to handle verification problems for such extensions will be of a different nature. As far as recursive Petri nets are concerned, extensions of techniques for standard Petri nets are considered. In contrast, in section 8.4, the decidability of verification problems is established by reduction into the satisfiability problem for Presburger arithmetic.

8.3. Recursive Petri nets

The recursive Petri net formalism (RPN) has been introduced to model dynamic systems for which the creation of processes (or threads) is required [EL 95, EL 96]. In this formalism, a process is characterized by a Petri net in which particular transitions (called *abstract*) allow the creation of processes and sets of markings from which the process is allowed to terminate. More precisely, termination of a process is possible when the current marking belongs to a given semilinear set, i.e. to a set defined by a Presburger formula. All the processes share the same control structure (i.e. the same RPN) but the initial marking of each process depends on the abstract transition which has created it. In consequence, the state of a process is completely characterized by a marking (a distribution of tokens over places) of the RPN and by the abstract transition that has created the process. Parallelism, which is a fundamental feature of Petri nets, is allowed between a process and its father. Termination of a process induces the update of the current marking of the father process (mainly by adding tokens to places). In this way, the relationships between processes and their fathers is encoded in the global state of the RPN. Hence, the global state of a recursive Petri net can be viewed as a finite tree whose nodes are markings (in the usual sense for Petri nets) and each edge is labeled by the abstract transition that has created the child process.

It has been shown in different papers [HAD 99, HAD 00, HAD 01] that RPN form a strict extension of Petri nets in terms of expressive power. It has also been shown that the reachability problem remains decidable for RPN. It is important to note that this property is essential for the design of verification tools. However, in [HAD], the authors have established that the verification of linear-time temporal formulae is an undecidable problem whereas it is decidable for the standard class of Petri nets (limited to event-based formulae).

In this section, we focus on a particular subclass of RPN called *sequential recursive Petri nets* (SRPN) [HAD 01]. In such a net, a father process creating a child process is blocked until the child process terminates. Consequently, parallelism is only allowed within the unique active process, if any. The global state of a sequential recursive Petri net can be viewed as a finite stack of processes, the topmost process being the active one. Moreover, each process can be represented by a marking (in the usual sense for Petri nets) and by the abstract transition that has created it (if any), the father process being just below on the stack. This formalism is less expressive than RPN but it is a strict extension of Petri nets. Moreover, the verification of (event-based) linear-time temporal formulae remains a decidable problem for SRPN.

8.3.1. *Definitions*

Similar to an ordinary Petri net, a SRPN has *places* and *transitions*. The transitions are split into two categories: *elementary transitions* and *abstract transitions*.

The semantics of such a net may be informally explained as follows. In an ordinary net, a process plays the token game by firing a transition and by updating the current marking (its internal state). In an SRPN, there is a stack of processes (each one with its current marking) where the only active process is on top of the stack. A *step* of an SRPN is thus a step of this process. The enabling rule of the transitions is specified by the *backward incidence matrix*.

When a process fires an elementary transition, it consumes the tokens specified by the backward incidence matrix and produces tokens defined by the *forward incidence matrix* (as in ordinary Petri nets).

When a process fires an abstract transition, it consumes the tokens specified by the backward incidence matrix and creates a new process (called its son) put on top of the stack which consequently becomes the active process. Such a process begins its token game with an *initial marking* that depends on the abstract transition.

Termination of an active process is possible when the current marking belongs to a given set of markings that is effectively semilinear. Herein, effective semilinearity is guaranteed by using Presburger formulae whose free variables refer to places of the net (see section 8.2.1). So, a family of effective representations of semilinear sets of *final markings* is defined in order to describe the termination of processes. This family is indexed by a finite set whose items are called *termination indices*. When a process reaches a final marking, it may terminate its token game (i.e. it is popped out of the stack). Then, it produces in the token game of its father (the new top of the stack) and for the abstract transition which created it, the tokens specified by the forward incidence matrix. Unlike ordinary Petri nets, this matrix depends also on the termination index of the semilinear set which the final marking belongs to. Such a firing is called a *cut step* (or equivalently a *return step*). When a cut step occurs in a stack reduced to a single process, this results to the empty stack.

The next definitions are helpful to define what are the configurations (global states) of an SRPN. Below, such configurations are called *extended markings*.

DEFINITION 8.5 (SRPN) *An SRPN is defined by a tuple* $N = \langle P, T, I, W^-, W^+, \texttt{Init}, \Upsilon \rangle$ *where:*

- $P = \{p_1, \ldots, p_\alpha\}$ *is a finite set of places;*
- T *is a finite set of transitions such that* $P \cap T = \emptyset$;
- *A transition of* T *can be either elementary or abstract. The sets of elementary and abstract transitions are respectively denoted by* T_{el} *and* T_{ab};
- I *is a finite set of indices;*
- W^- *is the pre function defined from* $P \times T$ *to* $\mathbb{N}$;
- W^+ *is the post function defined from* $P \times [T_{el} \cup (T_{ab} \times I)]$ *to* $\mathbb{N}$;
- $\texttt{Init}$ *is a labeling function* $T_{ab} \to (P \to \mathbb{N})$ *which associates an ordinary marking called the starting marking of* t *with each abstract transition;*
- $\Upsilon = (\varphi_i)_{i \in I}$ *is a family of Presburger formulae with free variables among* $x_1, \ldots, x_\alpha$. *Each formula* φ_i *defines the set of ordinary markings* $\{m : P \to \mathbb{N} \mid \mathbf{v} \models \varphi_i$, *for* $1 \leq j \leq \alpha$, $\mathbf{v}(x_j) = m(p_j)\}$. *By abuse of notation, we say that a marking* m *belongs to* $\text{REL}(\varphi_i)$ *to mean that it belongs to the above set. For instance,* '$x_1 = x_2$' *would be interpreted as a symbolic way to represent the set of markings such that the number of tokens in the place* p_1 *is equal to the number of tokens in the place* p_2.

In the chapter, we distinguish two kinds of markings. As usual for Petri nets, an *ordinary marking* is a map from P to $\mathbb{N}$. By contrast, an *extended marking* corresponds to a global state of the SRPN that can be viewed as a finite stack of ordinary markings augmented with abstract transitions. When no confusion is possible, we simply use the term "marking".

DEFINITION 8.6 (Extended marking) *An extended marking* em *for a SRPN* $N = \langle P, T, I, W^-, W^+, \texttt{Init}, \Upsilon \rangle$ *is either the empty stack* $\perp$ *or a sequence* $(m_d, t_d), \ldots, (m_2, t_2), m_1$ *for some* $d \geq 1$ *such that*

- d *is the* depth *of* em *and* $\{1, \ldots, d\}$ *is the set of* levels;

– $m_1, \ldots, m_d$ *are ordinary markings;*
– $t_2, \ldots, t_d$ *are abstract transitions. The intention is that a process* (m_i, t_i) *has been created by the abstract transition* t_i *and its current marking is* m_i. *Whenever* $d \geq 2$, *the* active *process is* (m_d, t_d). *When* $d = 1$, *the* active *process is* m_1.

Obviously, an extended marking different from $\perp$ can be viewed as a tree reduced to a single path where nodes are indexed by levels and labeled by ordinary markings and edges are labeled by abstract transitions. The root of this tree corresponds to the bottom of the stack and the single leaf to its top (for instance, see Figure 8.6). A *marked* SRPN (N, em_0) is an SRPN N together with an initial extended marking em_0. According to the presentation, the size of the stack corresponding to an extended marking em is d and the ordinary markings associated with the processes of the stack are $m_1, \ldots, m_d$. Since the effect of cut steps depends on the abstract transition which created a process, the transitions $t_2, \ldots, t_d$ are stored in the extended marking.

Given a SRPN, we can define its corresponding *reachability graph* whose nodes are made of extended markings and edges are labelled by *actions*. Three types of actions can be distinguished:

1) firing an elementary transition $t \in T \setminus T_{ab}$, corresponding to an *internal step*;
2) firing an abstract transition $t \in T_{ab}$, corresponding to a *gosub step*;
3) terminating the active process with the current marking in $\mathrm{REL}(\varphi_i)$ for some $i \in I$ and possibly returning to the father process, corresponding to a *return step* (also called *cut step*).

An *elementary step* corresponds to performing a single action. Hence, the semantics of a SRPN, completely determined by its corresponding reachability graph, is based on the notions of *enabled actions* and *firing of steps*.

DEFINITION 8.7 *Let* $em = (m_d, t_d), \ldots, (m_2, t_2), m_1$ *be an extended marking (different from* $\perp$*) for the SRPN N.*

1) A transition $t \in T$ *is enabled in* em, *denoted by* $em \xrightarrow{t}$ *iff for all* $p \in P$, *we have* $m_d(p) \geq W^-(p, t)$;

2) Return step τ_i *with* $i \in I$ *is enabled in* em, *denoted by* $em \xrightarrow{\tau_i}$, *iff* $m_d \in \mathrm{REL}(\varphi_i)$.

DEFINITION 8.8 *Let* $em = (m_d, t_d), \ldots, (m_2, t_2), m_1$ *and* $em' = (m'_{d'}, t'_{d'}), \ldots, (m'_2, t'_2), m'_1$ *be two extended markings for the SRPN N.*

– *For* $t \in T \setminus T_{ab}$, $em \xrightarrow{t} em'$ *iff*
1) t *is enabled in* em,

2) $d = d'$ *and, em and em' differ at most on their active process,*
3) $t_d = t'_d$ *and for all* $p \in P$, $m'_d(p) = m'_d(p) - W^-(p, t) + W^+(p, t)$;
– *For* $t \in T_{ab}$, $em \xrightarrow{t} em'$ *iff*
   1) t *is enabled in em,*
   2) $d' = d + 1$,
   3) $(m'_{d'}, t'_{d'}) = (\mathtt{Init}(t), t)$,
   4) *for all* $p \in P$, $m'_d(p) = m_d(p) - W^-(p, t)$,
   5) $t_d, (m_{d-1}, t_{d-1}), \ldots, (m_2, t_2), m_1 = t'_d, (m'_{d-1}, t'_{d-1}), \ldots, (m'_2, t'_2), m'_1$;
– *For* $i \in I$, $em \xrightarrow{\tau_i} em'$ *iff*
   1) τ_i *is enabled in em,*
   2) $d' = d - 1$,
   3) *if* $d' \geq 1$, *then for all* $p \in P$, $m'_{d'}(p) = m_{d'}(p) + W^+(p, t_d, i)$,
   4) *We have the equality below:*

$$t_{d'}, (m_{d'-1}, t_{d'-1}), \ldots, (m_2, t_2), m_1 = t'_{d'}, (m'_{d'-1}, t'_{d'-1}), \ldots, (m'_2, t'_2), m'_1.$$

A *firing sequence* σ is a sequence of the form $em_1 \xrightarrow{a_1} em_2 \xrightarrow{a_2} em_3 \cdots \xrightarrow{a_{n-1}} em_n$ such that for every $i \in [1, n-1]$, $em_i \xrightarrow{a_i} em_{i+1}$ is a single step. In the sequel, for the sake of simplicity, σ will be often denoted by $\sigma = a_1 \ldots a_{n-1}$. When multiple SRPNs are involved, we denote by $em_1 \xrightarrow{\sigma}_N em_n$ a firing sequence σ in an SRPN N. In a marked SRPN (N, em_0), an extended marking em is *reachable* iff there exists a firing sequence $em_0 \xrightarrow{\sigma}_N em$. The *reachability graph* of (N, em_0) is defined as follows: the nodes are the reachable extended markings and the edges are labeled by actions.

8.3.2. *Expressive power*

This section illustrates both the syntax and the semantics of SRPN with the help of relevant examples. Furthermore, we simultaneously demonstrate the expressive power of the model and its suitability with respect to standard discrete event system patterns [CAS 99].

Modeling of interrupts and exceptions. SRPNs are illustrated by integrating an interrupt mechanism step by step in an existing net. Then, the treatment of exceptions is added. The SRPN modeling the abstraction of the original system is given in Figure 8.3. This net can be understood as a standard Petri net and it can realize a unique behavior where the transition $t_{correct}$ is systematically fired. It is important to note that any Petri net can be interpreted as a SRPN without abstract transitions and extended markings are reduced to ordinary markings.

When an (software or hardware) interrupt is handled, the context of the system must be saved and the control given to the interrupt handler. If different levels of

Figure 8.3. *An abstraction of a system*

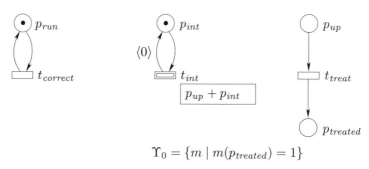

$$\Upsilon_0 = \{m \mid m(p_{treated}) = 1\}$$

Figure 8.4. *Integration of an interrupt mechanism*

interrupts have to be taken into account, an interrupt can mask some others. Moreover, when the handler returns, the execution context must be restored.

The SRPN presented in Figure 8.4 adds an interrupt mechanism to the net from Figure 8.3. Contrary to ordinary nets, SRPNs are often disconnected since each connected component may be activated by the firing of different abstract transitions. As the initial extended marking is reduced to a single node, we have directly described the ordinary marking associated with this node by putting tokens in places. We will follow the same convention in the sequel. The new elements are:

– the transition t_{int}: this transition is an abstract one (represented by a double line rectangle) and represents the trigger point of the interrupt. Here, we consider that the interrupt can always occur and in consequence, the unique input place (p_{int}) of the abstract transition is initially marked. The firing of t_{int} creates a new process on top of the stack and freezes the execution of the father process until the child process terminates. The child process starts its execution with the marking $p_{up} + p_{int}$ (indicated in the frame near the abstract transition). Because, p_{int} will be still marked, a new interrupt may occur during its execution. The firing of t_{int} consumes also a token from its input place p_{int} but produces no token. This step is delayed until the end of the new process and depends on its type (index) of termination;

– the set Υ_0: In this example, a unique set characterizes the final markings from which a return step is possible. Υ_0 represents the set of markings where the interrupt has been treated (the place $p_{treated}$ is marked). The index 0 associated with this set is used to indicate the type of termination (here, there is a unique type);

– the valuation $\langle 0 \rangle$ labels the arc linking the transition t_{int} to the place p_{int}: when a process terminates (its current marking should belong to Υ_0), the marking of the father process is modified depending on the index of the semilinear sets used for termination of the active child process. Then, the post-condition of an abstract transition is conditioned by the index associated to the termination set. In this example, the firing of a cut step will always produce a token in the place p_{int}.

The initial extended marking of the SRPN of Figure 8.4 is composed of a unique process in which only the places p_{run} and p_{int} both contain a unique token. It is clear that this net can reach an infinite number of configurations. Indeed, taking into account an interrupt does not mask those that can occur during its handling (the place p_{int} is marked in the starting marking of t_{int}). We can remark that this infinite state space can occur whatever the boundedness of the places (all the places may contain at most a unique token).

The integration of a mechanism for exceptions is illustrated in Figure 8.5. In this example, an exception can occur (the firing of the abstract transition t_{ex}) only if the main process runs (witnessed by the presence of a token on the place p_{run}). Its treatment can recover the error (place $p_{recover}$) or leads to a fatal situation (place p_{fatal}). The two termination sets Υ_1 and Υ_2 allow to distinguish both cases and the output arcs of the abstract transition t_{ex} are labeled consecutively.

Modularity is a natural feature of SRPNs. Indeed, if the system does not include the interrupt mechanism, the designer simply deletes the corresponding elements in the figure.

Figure 8.6 presents a subgraph of the reachability graph of the SRPN. The right part of the figure illustrates the interrupts and the left the exceptions. Interrupt cannot occur during the treatment of exception. On the contrary, if an exception leads to a fatal situation and when this error has been transmitted to the main process, the behavior of this last process will be limited to the treatment of interrupts (the unique enabled transition – not represented in the figure – from the state where the main process reaches the marking $p_{stop} + p_{int}$, is t_{int}).

The example of Figure 8.5 shows the ability of SRPN to implicitly keep the context of suspended processes. This kind of formalization in terms of Petri net requires an explicit representation of each context. By using this feature, it has been shown in [HAD 00] that SRPN include the family of algebraic languages. On the other hand, it has been also shown that the language of palindromes (a well-known algebraic language) cannot be recognized by a (labeled) Petri net [JAN 79]. Thus, the family of

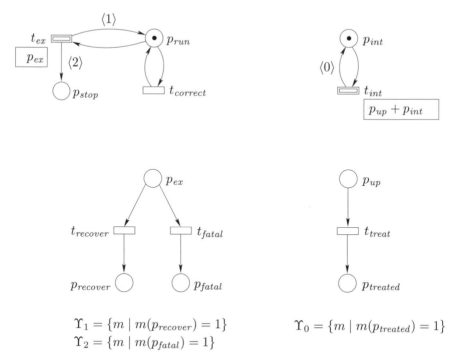

$$\Upsilon_1 = \{m \mid m(p_{recover}) = 1\} \qquad \Upsilon_0 = \{m \mid m(p_{treated}) = 1\}$$
$$\Upsilon_2 = \{m \mid m(p_{fatal}) = 1\}$$

Figure 8.5. *An exception mechanism*

languages recognized by SRPNs strictly includes the family of languages recognized by ordinary Petri nets.

Modeling of fault tolerance. In order to analyse fault-tolerant systems, the engineer may start by a nominal system and then introduces the faulty behavior as well as repairing mechanisms. We limit ourselves to an abstract view for such a system since this pattern can be simply generalized. This abstraction is given in the right part of Figure 8.7. The nominal system infinitely executes instructions (elementary transition t_{count}). The marking of place p_{count} represents the number of instruction executions.

The complete SRPN is obtained by adding the left part of Figure 8.7. Its behavior can be described as follows. There are only two reachable extended markings reduced to a single node: the initial global state (em_{start}) where a token in p_{start} indicates that the system is ready to start and the repairing state (em_{repair}) where a token in the place p_{repair} indicates that the system is being repaired. Starting from the initial state, the abstract transition t_{start} is fired and the execution of instructions is "played" by the new process. If this process terminates, meaning that a crash occurs, the repairing state

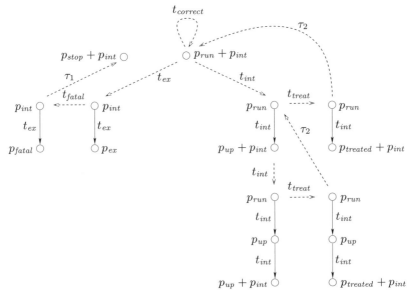

Figure 8.6. *Subgraph of the reachability graph of the SRPN of Figure 8.5*

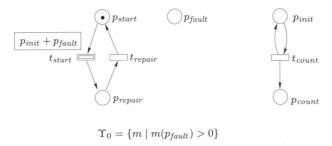

$$\Upsilon_0 = \{m \mid m(p_{fault}) > 0\}$$

Figure 8.7. *A fault-tolerant system*

is reached. The place p_{fault} represents the possibility of a crash. As p_{fault} is always marked in the correct system and from the very definition of Υ_0, the occurrence of a fault is always possible. We assume that no crash occurs during the repairing stage. With additional places and by modifying Υ_0, we could model more complex fault occurrences (e.g. conditioned by software execution).

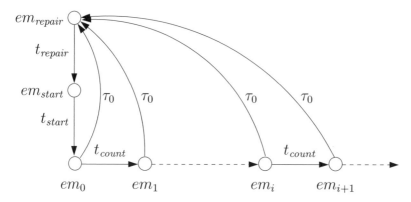

Figure 8.8. *(Infinite) reachability graph of the SRPN of the figure 8.7*

The reachable extended markings either consist of a single node or an initial node and its son. However, the number of reachable markings in this latter node is infinite (the place p_{count} is unbounded). In other words, the repairing state can be reached from an infinite number of extended marking which means that *the transition system associated with an SRPN may have some states with an infinite in-degree*. This situation cannot occur with standard Petri nets or with process algebras. In particular, in a reachability graph obtained from a Petri net, for each marking/node, its in-degree is bounded by the number of transitions. Moreover allowing unobservable transitions does not solve the problem. Indeed, it has been proven that the transition system shown in Figure 8.8 cannot be generated by a standard Petri net with unobservable transitions.

Otherwise stated, the modeling of crash for a nominal system with an infinite number of states is impossible with Petri nets. In the restricted case where the nominal system has a finite number of reachable configurations, theoretically it is possible to model it with a standard Petri net. However, the modeling of a crash requires a number of transitions proportional to the number of reachable configurations, which leads to an intricate net. The SRPN designed herein does not depend on this number and leads to a quite compact representation.

8.3.3. *Verification*

A distinguished feature of Petri nets is the decidability of the reachability problem, even though the best known decision procedure does not lead to a primitive recursive complexity, see e.g. [REU 90]. Many safety properties (specifying that nothing bad will happen) can be reduced to instances of the reachability problem. Then, a decision procedure for the reachability problem can be viewed as a building block in larger verification tools.

It is possible to decide whether a Petri net is bounded. Because, the reachability graph of a bounded net is finite (by definition), the methods presented in Chapter 7 can be applied. Moreover, the membership problem with a language specified by a labeled Petri net is also a decidable problem. This allows verification that an expected behavior can be effectively realized by the system. Finally, the verification of a temporal property is possible but limited to the event-based linear-time temporal formula (an LTL formula can express the firing of transitions but not constraints on reached markings). The work in [ESP 94] gives a large synthesis of the decidability results concerning Petri nets.

These problems remain decidable for SRPN. Hence, even if it is a strict extension of Petri nets, the verification of numerous behavioral properties is still possible. In this section, we limit ourselves to the study of the reachability problem.

Another important feature of Petri net concerns the structural verification technique presented in Chapter 7. We present an algorithm for the computation of linear invariants of SRPN.

Behavioral verification. Given a marked SRPN, the reachability problem consists of checking whether an extended marking can be reached from the initial extended marking (through a sequence of successive firings). The decision procedure, informally presented below, is inspired from a more complex one that is dedicated to the larger class of RPNs. The idea consists of reducing an instance of the problem to several instances of the reachability problem for ordinary Petri nets.

The decision procedure can be divided into different stages:

– the first one is independent of the initial and final extended markings. It consists of determining whether a process created by a given abstract transition can reach a marking belonging to a termination set (those termination sets are specified by Υ in a SRPN). Such an abstract transition is said to be *closable* with respect to this termination set. This verification should be done for each abstract transition and for each termination set; thus it should be done at most $\mathrm{card}(T_{ab}) \times \mathrm{card}(I)$ times;

– the second stage aims to predict the behavior of processes composing the initial extended marking and, hence, the nature of the processes composing the extended marking to be reached. Indeed, a process of the initial extended marking can either be terminated during the firing sequence or can persist modifying its marking. The processes of the final extended marking, which do not correspond to processes of the initial extended marking, must be created by the firing sequence. Even if each prediction must satisfy some constraints (e.g. if a child process must be created by the firing sequence, its child processes must be created as well), many different predictions are generally possible. Figure 8.9 presents such a prediction. The two processes

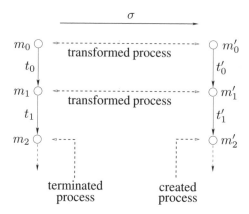

Figure 8.9. *A coherent prediction of the behavior of processes*

of the initial extended marking labeled by the markings m_0 and m_1 must evolve to the respective markings m'_0 and m'_1. On the contrary, the process labeled by m_2 must terminate during the sequence and, consequently, its child processes must also terminate. Finally, it is expected that the process labeled m'_2 in the reached extended marking will be created by the sequence. It is clear that the number of distinct and coherent predictions is bounded by the number of processes composing the initial and final extended markings.

All the steps of the decision procedure are based on the same principle: the construction of an ordinary Petri net and a reachability problem equivalent to the elementary problem to be decided. We now focus on the determination of *closable* abstract transitions.

Note that it is decidable to determine whether a marking from a semilinear set can be reached in a Petri net equipped with an initial marking (even if the semilinear set is infinite).

An abstract transition is said *closable* in a termination set if a process (created by this abstract transition) can realize a return step from this termination set. This amounts to checking an instance of the reachability problem and, when an abstract transition is closable, it induces a corresponding firing sequence. When an abstract transition is fired in a given process, the execution of this process is suspended until the child process created by the abstract transition terminates. Consequently, in the associated firing sequence, the firing corresponding to the root level can only involve some closable abstract transitions.

This leads to an iterative computation of the set $F \subseteq T_{ab} \times I$ of closable abstract transitions. F_0 is the subset of F where the associated firing sequence contains no firing of abstract transitions. When new elements are added to F, this indicates that these transitions can be used.

The elements of F_0 are determined by testing if the ordinary net obtained by suppressing all the abstract transitions can reach a marking from a termination set from the initial marking of a given abstract transition (specified by Init in a SRPN). In order to compute the set F_1, the abstract transitions belonging to F_0 are now simulated by ordinary transitions having the same pre-conditions and post-conditions (for a given termination set). The aim of these transitions is to simulate the creation of child processes that are able to terminate (in this termination set).

Assuming that F_i is defined, F_{i+1} is defined as the set of closable abstract transitions, excluding those from F_i, such that we consider the SRPN in which the abstract transitions belonging to F_i are now simulated by ordinary transitions having the same pre-conditions and post-conditions. Observe that there is $J \leq (\text{card}(T_{ab}) \times \text{card}(I)) + 1$ such that $F_J = \emptyset$ and whenever F_i is empty, this implies that for all $j > i$, we have that F_j is empty too. Knowing that the set of abstract transitions is finite as well as the number of final marking sets demonstrate the termination of the decision procedure. Hence, $F \stackrel{\text{def}}{=} \bigcup_i F_i$.

We are now in position to describe the procedure for the decision of the reachability problem. Let src be the initial extended marking and $dest$ be the destination extended marking. If $src = \bot$ (the empty state) then it is sufficient to test if $dest = \bot$. Assume that $src \neq \bot$ and $dest = \bot$. This problem is similar to decide whether an abstract transition is closable except that the initial state is not necessarily composed by a unique process. Hence, the child processes must also be successively closed. This leads to a set of termination problems.

Finally, when $src \neq \bot$ and $dest \neq \bot$, the principle consists of testing the possible predictions one by one. The main difference comes from the fact that some processes of $dest$ can be predicted as created. Here again, the decision can be reduced to instances of the reachability problem in an ordinary Petri net. By way of example, let us consider the two extended markings below:

$$em_1 = (m_{d+d_1}, t_{d+d_1}), \ldots, (m_{d+1}, t_{d+1}), (m_d, t_d), \ldots, (m_2, t_2), m_1$$

$$em_2 = (m'_{d+d_2}, t'_{d+d_2}), \ldots, (m'_{d+1}, t'_{d+1}), (m_d, t_d), \ldots, (m_2, t_2), m_1$$

with $d_1, d_2 \geq 1$ and $d \geq 2$ (they share a common bottom of the stack). Assuming that these extended markings are defined with respect to the SRPN N, let N^- be the standard Petri net obtained from N by deleting the non-closable abstract transitions, and each closable abstract transition in F is replaced by an ordinary transition having the same pre-condition and post-condition. We can show that em_2 is reachable from em_1 in N iff there exists $i_1, \ldots, i_{d_1} \in I$ such that:

1) there exists a marking m in $\text{REL}(\varphi_{i_{d_1}})$ such that $m_{d+d_1} \xrightarrow{*} m$ in N^-;

2) for $j \in [1, d_1 - 1]$, there exists a marking m in $\text{REL}(\varphi_{i_j})$ such that $m_{d+j} + W^+(\cdot, t_{d+j+1}, i_{j+1}) \xrightarrow{*} m$ in N^-. As usual, $m_{d+j} + W^+(\cdot, t_{d+j+1}, i_{j+1})$ denotes the marking m' such that for every place $p \in P$, $m'(p) = m_{d+j}(p) + W^+(p, t_{d+j+1}, i_{j+1})$. A similar notation is used below;

3) $\text{Init}(t'_{d+d_2}) \xrightarrow{*} m'_{d+d_2}$ in N^-;

4) For $j \in [1, d_2 - 1]$, $\text{Init}(t'_{d+j}) \xrightarrow{*} m'_{d+j} + W^-(\cdot, t'_{d+j+1})$.

Predictions (indeed non-determinism) are witnessed by the sequence of termination indices $i_1, \ldots, i_{d_1}$. Moreover, observe that (3) and (4) are instances of the reachability problem for Petri nets whereas (1) and (2) are instances of the reachability problem into a semilinear set, this latter problem being easily reducible to plain reachability.

Structural verification. Among the structural method presented in Chapter 7, we focus on the computation of linear invariants that we adapt to SRPN. The computation shown here is an adaptation of the one dedicated to RPN.

The incidence matrix W of a SRPN is defined as follow. Rows are indexed by the places and by the abstract transitions. The intended meaning of a variable indexed by a place is its number of tokens while the interpretation of a variable indexed by an abstract transition is the current number of processes created by its firing.

The columns of the matrix are indexed by the transitions and by the pairs (t, i) where t is an abstract transition and $i \in I$ is an index corresponding to a termination set. A column indexed by a transition represents its firing while a pair (t, i) indicates the firing of a cut step related to the termination set $\text{REL}(\varphi_i)$ in a child process initiated by the abstract transition t.

The incidence matrix is defined by:

– for all $p \in P$, for all $t \in T_{el}$ and for all $t' \in T_{ab}$,
$\quad W(p, t) = W^+(p, t) - W^-(p, t)$ and $W(t', t) = 0$;

– for all $p \in P$, for all $t, t' \in T_{ab}$ with $t' \neq t$,
$\quad W(p, t) = -W^-(p, t)$ and $W(t, t) = 1$ and $W(t', t) = 0$;

– for all $p \in P$, for all $t, t' \in T_{ab}$, for all $i \in I$ with $t' \neq t$,
$W(p, (t, i)) = W^+(p, t, i)$ and $W(t, (t, i)) = -1$ and $W(t', (t, i)) = 0$.

Figure 8.10 illustrates the definition of the matrix W. The matrix is divided into six blocks depending on the type of rows and columns. Let us look at some items of the row indexed by place p: the elementary transition t_{el} consumes one token from p and produces 4 tokens for it, thus the corresponding value in the matrix is 3; firing the abstract transition t_{ab} consumes 2 tokens thus the corresponding item is -2 and the cut step associated with t_{ab} and index 0 (resp. 1) produces 1 token (resp. 4 tokens)

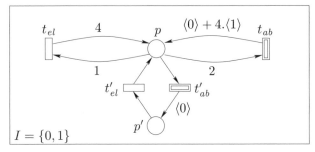

(a) A SRPN (only relevant elements are represented)

	t_{el}	t'_{el}	t_{ab}	t'_{ab}	$(t_{ab}, 0)$	$(t_{ab}, 1)$	$(t'_{ab}, 0)$	$(t'_{ab}, 1)$	
p	3	1	-2	-1	1	4	0	0	$\Big\} P$
p'	0	-1	0	0	0	0	1	0	
t_{ab}	0	0	1	0	-1	-1	0	0	$\Big\} T_{ab}$
t'_{ab}	0	0	0	1	0	0	-1	-1	

$$\underbrace{}_{T_{el}} \quad \underbrace{}_{T_{ab}} \quad \underbrace{}_{T_{ab} \times I}$$

(b) Its incidence matrix W

Figure 8.10. *A SRPN and its incidence matrix*

thus the corresponding item is 1 (resp. 4). Let us have a look at the row indexed by the abstract transition t_{ab}: firing t_{ab} creates one more process initiated by t_{ab}, thus the corresponding item is 1 while firing any of the two cut steps corresponding to t_{ab} terminates one such process yielding an item -1.

Given a process pr in an extended marking em, we denote by $fire(pr)^{em}$ the vector, indexed on T_{ab}, such that for any abstract transition t, $fire(pr)^{em}(t)$ is equal to one if a child process initiated by t has been created by pr and is not already terminated and equal to zero otherwise. We are now in position to justify the choice of W as incidence matrix.

Let em' be an extended marking of an SRPN; which is reachable from a given state em via a firing sequence σ. Assume the existence of a process pr in both em and em' (and then in all the extended markings visited by σ). We note $m(pr)^{em}$ the marking of the process pr in the state em. Let x be a solution of $x \cdot W = 0$, then:

$$x \cdot (m(pr)^{em'}, fire(pr)^{em'}) = x \cdot (m(pr)^{em}, fire(pr)^{em})$$

As for ordinary Petri nets, when em is the initial state of the SRPN, this equation is called a linear invariant. In order to obtain linear invariants, we can compute a generative family of solutions $\{x_1, \ldots, x_n\}$ of this equation. For a process pr of the initial extended marking em_0, we obtain a superset of the reachable "states" of this process by the set of equations: for $i \in [1, n]$, $x_i \cdot (m(pr)^{em}, fire(pr)^{em}) = x_i \cdot (m(pr)^{em_0}, fire(pr)^{em_0})$.

The same overestimation can be done for the reachable ordinary marking space of a process pr dynamically created by the firing of an abstract transition t: for all $i \in [1, n]$, $x_i \cdot (m(pr)^{em}, fire(pr)^{em}) = x_i \cdot (\text{Init}(t), \vec{0})$ (where $\text{Init}(t)$ corresponds to the starting marking associated with t).

The fact that depending on the initial marking $\text{Init}(t)$ some transitions are dead may lead to additional sources of overestimation. Since this last factor often happens in practical cases, we describe now an iterative method that tackles this problem. In fact, the method is also applicable to Petri nets but it is of limited interest in this case since usually the transitions of a Petri net are not dead.

Algorithm 4 simultaneously computes a set of linear invariants fulfilled by markings reachable from m, an ordinary marking, and a superset of the transitions enabled at least once from m. More precisely, it initialises T_{live} as the empty set. Then it computes the positive invariants for the recursive Petri net whose transitions are reduced to T_{live}. In the algorithm 4, the function *Invariant* returns a generative family of invariants (see [COL 90] for efficient computation of such families). For each transition that does not belong to T_{live}, it builds a linear problem with the invariants and the firing conditions of this transition. If this problem admits a solution, it is possibly enabled and so, it adds it to T_{live}. This process is iterated until T_{live} is saturated.

Finally, we describe how the linear invariants can be used to obtain information about the structure of the reachable extended markings. We build a graph whose nodes are the abstract transitions. There is an edge from t to t' if starting from the marking $\text{Init}(t)$ a process may fire t'. In order to determine such an edge, we compute the invariants associated with $\text{Init}(t)$ by a call to *structReach*. If t' belongs to the set returned by this call then an edge is added. This graph is a skeleton for the dynamic structure of the extended markings. For instance, if it is acyclic, then any reachable extended marking has a bounded depth.

8.3.4. *Related work*

We have seen that Petri nets can be extended while preserving the decidability status of numerous problems (reachability problems, etc.). However, it is important to note that minor extensions can lead to undecidability results. For instance, the reachability problem is undecidable for Petri nets with two inhibitor arcs (a computational

input : an ordinary marking m
output: a set of invariants and a set of transitions

1 $T_{live} = \emptyset$;
2 $New = \emptyset$;
3 $In = \emptyset$;
4 **repeat**
5      $New = \emptyset$;
6      $In = Invariant(N, m, T_{live})$;
7   **foreach** $t \in T \setminus T_{live}$ **do**
8   Build a linear problem Pb in $\mathbb{N}^P$ with In and $W^-(-, t)$;
9   **if** Pb *has a solution* **then**
10             $New = New \cup \{t\}$;
11   **end**
12   **end**
13     $T_{live} = T_{live} \cup New$;
14 **until** $(New == \emptyset)$;
15 **return** $\langle In, T_{live} \rangle$;

Algorithm 4: *structReach*

model similar to Minsky machines) while it becomes decidable with one inhibitor arc (or a particular nested structure of inhibitor arcs). The self-modifying nets introduced by R. Valk have (like Petri nets with inhibitor arcs) the power of Turing machines and thus many properties including reachability are undecidable [VAL 78a, VAL 78b]. Moreover, these extensions do not offer a practical way to model the dynamic creation of objects.

In order to tackle this problem, A. Kiehn introduced a model called net systems [KIE 89] that are Petri nets with special transitions whose firing starts a new token game of one of these nets. A *call* to a Petri net, triggered by such a firing, may return if this net reaches a final marking. All the nets are required to be safe and the constraints associated with the final marking ensure that a net may not return if it has pending calls. It is straightforward to simulate a net system by an RPN. Moreover, as the class of languages recognized by Petri nets is not included in the class of languages recognized by net systems, the class of languages recognized by net systems is strictly included in the family of RPN languages.

Process algebra nets (PANs), introduced by R. Mayr [MAY 97], are a model of process algebra including the sequential composition operator as well as the parallel operator. The left term of any rule of a PAN may use only the parallel composition of variables whereas the right side is a general term. This model includes Petri nets and context-free grammars. In [HAD 00], the authors demonstrate that RPNs also include PANs. However, it is not known whether the inclusion of the PAN languages by the

RPN languages is strict. Moreover, PANs as well as process rewrite systems (a more expressive model) cannot represent a transition system with an infinite in-degree.

A verification technique, which is not treated in this section, concerns the equivalence relations between two nets. This approach is essential when the design is realized by successive refinements. In [HAD 07], it has been shown that checking bisimulation between an SRPN (satisfying some additional constraints) and a finite automaton is a decidable problem.

8.4. Presburger arithmetic as symbolic representation

In section 8.3, we have seen how verification problems for SRPNs can be solved by using techniques for standard Petri nets, at the cost of adequately adapting standard methods. Typically, an instance of the reachability problem for SRPNs (involving extended markings) is transformed into a finite number of instances of the reachability problem for Petri nets. By contrast, in this section, we consider other extensions of VASS by allowing for instance zero-tests, but in a controlled manner. In this section, decidability of the reachability problem is obtained by reduction into instances of the satisfiability problem for Presburger arithmetic. More precisely, in this section, we consider subclasses of counter systems for which the reachability sets of the form $\{\vec{x} \in \mathbb{N}^n : (q_0, \vec{x_0}) \xrightarrow{*} (q, \vec{x})\}$ are effectively Presburger-definable ($(q_0, \vec{x_0})$ and q are fixed). By decidability of Presburger arithmetic, this allows us to solve problems restricted to such counter systems such as the reachability problem, the control state reachability problem, the boundedness problem, or the covering problem. Indeed, suppose that given $(q_0, \vec{x_0})$ and q, we can effectively build a Presburger formula φ_q such that $\mathrm{REL}(\varphi_q) = \{\vec{x} \in \mathbb{N}^n : (q_0, \vec{x_0}) \xrightarrow{*} (q, \vec{x})\}$. We can then easily show the properties below:

1) $\{\vec{x} \in \mathbb{N}^n : (q_0, \vec{x_0}) \xrightarrow{*} (q, \vec{x})\}$ is infinite iff the formula below is satisfiable:

$$\neg \exists y \, \forall x_1, \ldots, x_n \, \varphi_q(x_1, \ldots, x_n) \Rightarrow (x_1 \leq y \wedge \cdots \wedge x_n \leq y);$$

2) $(q_0, \vec{x_0}) \xrightarrow{*} (q, \vec{z})$ iff the formula below is satisfiable:

$$\varphi_q(x_1, \ldots, x_n) \wedge x_1 = \vec{z}(1) \wedge \cdots \wedge x_n = \vec{z}(n),$$

where any constant $k > 0$ is encoded by the term $\overbrace{1 + \cdots + 1}^{k \text{ times}}$;

3) control state q can be reached from $(q_0, \vec{x_0})$ iff the Presburger formula $\varphi_q(x_1, \ldots, x_n)$ is satisfiable.

Below, we consider the class of reversal-bounded counter automata and the class of admissible counter systems. However, other types of counter systems with Presburger-definable reachability sets exist, see numerous examples in [PAR 66, ARA 77, HOP 79,

ESP 97, COM 98, FIN 00, LER 03] (see also the generalizations presented in [LER 05, BOZ 10]). Besides, let us briefly recall below why reachability sets for VASS (succinct counter automata without zero-tests) may not be semilinear, witnessing the fact that semilinearity is not always guaranteed even for harmless VASS. In Figure 8.11, we present a slight variant of the VASS described in Figure 8.2 by adding two components to store counter values just before entering in the control state q_0 for the first time. We can show that

$$\{(\vec{x}(1), \vec{x}(2), \vec{x}(6)) : (q_0, \vec{0}) \xrightarrow{*} (q_1, \vec{x})\} = \{(n_1, n_2, n_3) \in \mathbb{N}^3 : n_3 \leq n_1 \times n_2\}$$

Now, suppose that there is a Presburger formula $\varphi(x_1, \ldots, x_6)$ such that $REL(\varphi) = \{\vec{x} : (q_0, \vec{0}) \xrightarrow{*} (q_1, \vec{x})\}$. We can build from it a Preburger formula $\chi(x)$ such that $REL(\chi(x)) = \{n^2 : n \geq 0\} (= Y)$:

$$\exists x_1, \ldots, x_5 \, \varphi(x_1, \ldots, x_5, x) \wedge x_1 = x_2 \wedge (\forall x'(x' > x) \Rightarrow \neg \exists x_3, x_4, x_5 \, \varphi(x_1, \ldots, x_5, x'))$$

Since Y is infinite, there are $b \geq 0$ and $p_1, \ldots, p_m > 0$ $(m \geq 1)$ such that $(Z =)\{b + \sum_{i=1}^{m} n_i p_i : n_1, \ldots, n_m \in \mathbb{N}\} \subseteq Y$. Let $N \in \mathbb{N}$ be such that $N^2 \in Z$ and $(2N + 1) > p_1$. The value N always exists since Z is infinite. Since Z is a linear set, we also have $(N^2 + p_1) \in Z$. However $(N + 1)^2 - N^2 = (2N + 1) > p_1$. Hence $N^2 < N^2 + p_1 < (N + 1)^2$, which leads to a contradiction.

By contrast, the reachability sets for VASS of dimension 2 can be shown to be effectively Presburger-definable [HOP 79].

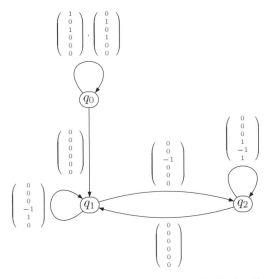

Figure 8.11. *A VASS weakly computing multiplication (bis)*

8.4.1. *Presburger-definable reachability sets*

Reversal-bounded counter automata

A *reversal* for a counter occurs in a run when there is an alternation from non-increasing mode to non-decreasing mode and vice versa. Figure 8.12 presents schematically the behavior of a counter with five reversals.

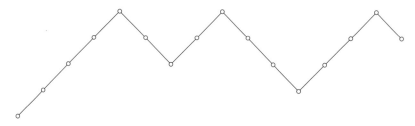

Figure 8.12. *Five reversals in a row*

A counter automaton is *reversal-bounded* whenever there is $r \geq 0$ such that for any run from a given initial configuration, every counter makes no more than r reversals. This class of counter automata has been introduced and studied in [IBA 78]. A formal definition will follow, but before going any further, it is worth pointing out a few peculiarities of this subclass. Indeed, reversal-boundedness is defined for initialized counter automata (a counter automaton augmented with an initial configuration) and the bound r depends on the initial configuration. Secondly, this class is not defined from the class of counter automata by imposing syntactic restrictions but rather semantically. Its very definition is motivated by technical and theoretical considerations rather than by constraints from case studies.

Let $\mathcal{S} = (Q, n, \delta)$ be a standard counter automaton. Let us define the auxiliary (succinct) counter automaton $\mathcal{S}_{rb} = (Q', 2n, \delta')$ such that $Q' = Q \times \{\text{DEC}, \text{INC}\}^n$ and $(q, \vec{mode}) \xrightarrow{\varphi'} (q', \vec{mode}') \in \delta' \stackrel{\text{def}}{\Leftrightarrow}$ there is $q \xrightarrow{\varphi} q' \in \delta$ such that if φ does not deal with the jth component, then $\vec{mode}(j) = \vec{mode}'(j)$ and for every $i \in [1, n]$, one of the conditions below is satisfied:

- $\varphi = \text{zero}(i)$, $\vec{mode}(i) = \vec{mode}'(i)$, $\varphi' = \varphi \wedge \bigwedge_{j \in [1,n]} x'_{n+j} = x_{n+j}$;
- $\varphi = \text{dec}(i)$, $\vec{mode}(i) = \vec{mode}'(i) = \text{DEC}$ and $\varphi' = \varphi \wedge \bigwedge_{j \in [1,n]} x'_{n+j} = x_{n+j}$;
- $\varphi = \text{dec}(i)$, $\vec{mode}(i) = \text{INC}$, $\vec{mode}'(i) = \text{DEC}$ and

$$\varphi' = \varphi \wedge (x'_{n+i} = x_{n+i} + 1) \wedge \bigwedge_{j \in [1,n] \setminus \{i\}} x'_{n+j} = x_{n+j};$$

- $\varphi = \text{inc}(i)$, $\vec{mode}(i) = \vec{mode}'(i) = \text{INC}$ and $\varphi' = \varphi \wedge \bigwedge_{j \in [1,n]} x'_{n+j} = x_{n+j}$;

$- \varphi = \text{inc}(i)$, $\vec{mode}(i) = \text{DEC}$, $\vec{mode}'(i) = \text{INC}$ and

$$\varphi' = \varphi \wedge (\mathsf{x}'_{n+i} = \mathsf{x}_{n+i} + 1) \wedge \bigwedge_{j \in [1,n] \setminus \{i\}} \mathsf{x}'_{n+j} = \mathsf{x}_{n+j}.$$

Essentially, the n new components in $\mathcal{S}_{rb}$ count the number of reversals for each component from $\mathcal{S}$. Moreover, the above construction could be easily adapted so that to control $\mathcal{S}$ by imposing that each counter does not perform more than r reversals, for some fixed bound r. Observe that $\mathcal{S}_{rb}$ is succinct because two counters may be updated in one step. Initialized counter automaton $(\mathcal{S}, (q, \vec{x}))$ is *reversal-bounded* [IBA 78] $\overset{\text{def}}{\Leftrightarrow}$ for every $i \in [n+1, 2n]$, $\{\vec{y}(i) : \exists \text{ run } (q_{rb}, \vec{x}_{rb}) \overset{*}{\to} (q', \vec{y}) \text{ in } \mathcal{S}_{rb}\}$ is finite with $q_{rb} = (q, \text{INC})$, $\vec{x}_{rb}$ restricted to the n first components is $\vec{x}$ and $\vec{x}_{rb}$ restricted to the n last components is $\vec{0}$. When $r \geq \max(\{\vec{y}(i) : \text{ run } (q_{rb}, \vec{x}_{rb}) \overset{*}{\to} (q', \vec{y}) \text{ in } \mathcal{S}_{rb}\} : i \in [n+1, 2n])$ $\mathcal{S}$ is said to be *r-reversal-bounded* from $(q, \vec{x})$.

A counter automaton $\mathcal{S}$ is *uniformly reversal-bounded* iff there is $r \geq 0$ such that for every initial configuration, the initialized counter automaton is r-reversal-bounded. We can check that the counter automaton in Figure 8.13 is not uniformly reversal-bounded.

Figure 8.13 contains a counter automaton $\mathcal{S}$ such that any initialized counter automaton of the form $(\mathcal{S}, (q_1, \vec{x}))$ with $\vec{x} \in \mathbb{N}^2$ is reversal-bounded. Let $\vec{x} \in \mathbb{N}^2$ and φ be the Presburger formula

$$\varphi = (\mathsf{x}_1 \geq 2 \wedge \mathsf{x}_2 \geq 1 + \vec{x}(2) \wedge (\mathsf{x}_2 - \vec{x}(2)) + 1 \geq \mathsf{x}_1) \vee$$

$$(\mathsf{x}_2 \geq 2 \wedge \mathsf{x}_1 \geq 1 + \vec{x}(1) \wedge (\mathsf{x}_1 - \vec{x}(1)) + 1 \geq \mathsf{x}_2)$$

We can show that $\text{REL}(\varphi)$ is precisely equal to the reachability set $\{\vec{y} \in \mathbb{N}^2 : (q_1, \vec{x}) \overset{*}{\to} (q_9, \vec{y})\}$.

Reversal-boundedness for counter automata is very appealing because reachability sets are Presburger-definable as stated below.

THEOREM 8.9 *[IBA 78] Let $r \geq 0$ and $(\mathcal{S}, (q, \vec{x}))$ be an initialized counter automaton that is r-reversal-bounded. For each control state q', the set $\{\vec{y} \in \mathbb{N}^n : \exists \text{ run } (q, \vec{x}) \overset{*}{\to} (q', \vec{y})\}$ is effectively Presburger-definable.*

This means that we can compute a Presburger formula that characterizes the reachable configurations whose control state is q'. The original proof for reversal-boundedness can be found in [IBA 78].

As a consequence of theorem 8.9, we get:

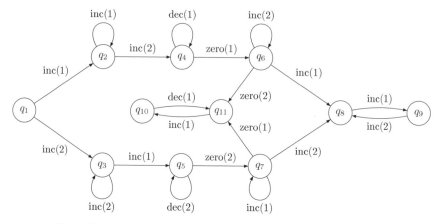

Figure 8.13. *A counter automaton that bounds the numbers of reversals*

COROLLARY 8.10 *The reachability problem for reversal-bounded counter automata is decidable.*

Moreover, the control state repeated reachability problem for reversal-bounded counter automata is decidable too by reduction into the reachability problem, see e.g. [DAN 01].

Let us consider another problem that can be shown decidable even though it takes as input a standard counter automaton without any further restriction.

Reachability problem with bounded number of reversals:

 – *Input*: a counter automaton $\mathcal{S}$, a bound $r \in \mathbb{N}$, an initial configuration $(q_0, \vec{x_0})$ and a final configuration $(q, \vec{x})$;
 – *Question*: is there a finite run of $\mathcal{S}$ with initial configuration $(q_0, \vec{x_0})$ and final configuration $(q, \vec{x})$ such that each counter has at most r reversals?

Observe that when $(\mathcal{S}, (q_0, \vec{x_0}))$ is r'-reversal-bounded for some $r' \leq r$, we get an instance of the reachability problem with initial configuration $(q_0, \vec{x_0})$.

COROLLARY 8.11 *The reachability problem with bounded number of reversals is decidable.*

By using [GUR 81], the problem can be solved in non-deterministic exponential time.

Affine counter systems with finite monoids

We shall define the class of *affine counter systems* that slightly generalizes the class of succinct counter automata (roughly speaking, a counter value can be multiplied by a factor different from 1). To do so, we start by proposing a few definitions.

A *binary relation of dimension n* is a relation $R \subseteq \mathbb{N}^{2n}$. R is *Presburger-definable* $\overset{\text{def}}{\Leftrightarrow}$ there is a Presburger formula $\varphi(x_1, \ldots, x_n, x'_1, \ldots, x'_n)$ with $2n$ free variables such that $R = \text{REL}(\varphi)$. A partial function f from $\mathbb{N}^n$ to $\mathbb{N}^n$ is *affine* $\overset{\text{def}}{\Leftrightarrow}$ there exist a matrix $A \in \mathbb{Z}^{n \times n}$ and $\vec{b} \in \mathbb{Z}^n$ such that for every $\vec{a} \in \text{dom}(f)$, we have $f(\vec{a}) = A\vec{a} + \vec{b}$. f is *Presburger-definable* $\overset{\text{def}}{\Leftrightarrow}$ the graph of f is a Presburger-definable relation.

A counter system $\mathcal{S} = (Q, n, \delta)$ is *affine* when for every transition $q \overset{\varphi}{\to} q' \in \delta$, $\text{REL}(\varphi)$ is affine. In the sequel, each formula φ labeling a transition in an affine counter system is encoded by a triple $(A, \vec{b}, \psi)$ such that

1) $A \in \mathbb{Z}^{n \times n}, \vec{b} \in \mathbb{Z}^n$;
2) ψ has free variables $x_1, \ldots, x_n$;
3) $\text{REL}(\varphi) = \{(\vec{x}, \vec{x'}) \in \mathbb{N}^{2n} : \vec{x'} = A\vec{x} + \vec{b} \text{ and } \vec{x} \in \text{REL}(\psi)\}$.

The formula ψ can be viewed as the guard of the transition and the pair $(A, \vec{b})$ as the (deterministic) update function. Such a triple $(A, \vec{b}, \psi)$ is called an *affine update* and we also write $\text{REL}((A, \vec{b}, \psi))$ to denote $\text{REL}(\varphi)$. Furthermore, succinct counter automata are affine counter systems in which the matrices are equal to the identity matrix. Moreover, in succinct counter automata the guards are reduced to the truth constant or to a zero-test. This class of counter systems has been introduced in [FIN 02].

Lemma 8.12 roughly states that the composition of affine updates is still an affine update, which shall be helpful to show that the accessibility relation for admissible counter systems is Presburger-definable.

LEMMA 8.12 *Let* $(A_1, \vec{b_1}, \psi_1)$ *and* $(A_2, \vec{b_2}, \psi_2)$ *be two affine updates. There exists an affine update* $(A, \vec{b}, \psi)$ *such that*

$$\text{REL}((A, \vec{b}, \psi)) =$$

$$\{(\vec{x}, \vec{x'}) \in \mathbb{N}^{2n} : \exists \vec{y} \in \mathbb{N}^n \ (\vec{x}, \vec{y}) \in \text{REL}((A_1, \vec{b_1}, \psi_1)) \text{ and } (\vec{y}, \vec{x'}) \in \text{REL}((A_2, \vec{b_2}, \psi_2))\}$$

In the forthcoming class of admissible counter systems, we shall assume that the control graph is flat. A counter system is *flat* whenever every control state belongs to at most one simple cycle, i.e. with no repeated vertex, in the control graph. Moreover,

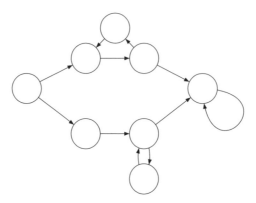

Figure 8.14. *A flat control graph*

we require that there is at most one transition between two control states. An example of flat control graph can be found in Figure 8.14.

Hence, it becomes essential to symbolically represent the effect of loops on counter values. This sounds a necessary condition to establish that a reachability relation is Presburger-definable. We already know by Lemma 8.12 that transitions in affine counter systems are closed under bounded compositions.

Let R be a binary relation of dimension n. The *reflexive and transitive closure* of R, written R^*, is a subset of $\mathbb{N}^{2n}$ such that $(\vec{y}, \vec{y'}) \in R^*$ iff there are $\vec{x_1}, \dots \vec{x_k} \in \mathbb{N}^n$ such that $\vec{x_1} = \vec{y}$, $\vec{x_k} = \vec{y'}$ and for $i \in [1, k-1]$, we have $(\vec{x_i}, \vec{x_{i+1}}) \in R$. If R is Presburger-definable, then this does not imply that R^* is Presburger-definable too. For instance, if $R = \{(k, 2k) \in \mathbb{N}^2 : k \in \mathbb{N}\}$ then $R^* = \{(k, 2^{k'}k) \in \mathbb{N}^2 : k, k' \in \mathbb{N}\}$ is not Presburger-definable. By contrast, if $S = \{(k, k+1) \in \mathbb{N}^2 : k \in \mathbb{N}\}$ then $S^* = \{(k, k') \in \mathbb{N}^2 : k < k', k, k' \in \mathbb{N}\}$ is Presburger definable. Counter systems of dimension n induce naturally one-step binary relations of dimension n that are Presburger-definable; the question of deciding whether their reflexive and transitive closure of is Presburger-definable would directly answer whether the reachability relations in such systems are Presburger-definable or not.

Indeed, consider the following loop with $q_1 = q_k$:

$$q_1 \xrightarrow{\varphi_1(x_1,\dots,x_n')} q_2 \xrightarrow{\varphi_2(x_1,\dots,x_n')} \cdots \xrightarrow{\varphi_{k-1}(x_1,\dots,x_n')} q_{k-1} \xrightarrow{\varphi_k(x_1,\dots,x_n')} q_k.$$

The effect of the loop can be represented by the Presburger formula below:

$$\psi(\vec{x}, \vec{x'}) \stackrel{\text{def}}{=} \exists \, \vec{y_1}, \dots, \vec{y_k} \; \varphi_1(\vec{x}, \vec{y_1}) \wedge \varphi_2(\vec{y_1}, \vec{y_2}) \wedge \cdots \wedge \varphi_k(\vec{y_k}, \vec{x'})$$

The effect of visiting the loop a finite (but unbounded) number of times amounts to represent symbolically the reflexive and transitive closure of $\text{REL}(\psi(\vec{x}, \vec{x'}))$. The best we can hope for is that $\text{REL}(\psi(\vec{x}, \vec{x'}))^*$ is Presburger-definable.

Given $A \in \mathbb{Z}^{n \times n}$, we write A^* to denote the monoid generated from A with $A^* = \{A^i : i \in \mathbb{N}\}$. The identity element is naturally the identity matrix $A^0 = I$. Given a matrix $A \in \mathbb{Z}^{n \times n}$, checking whether the monoid generated by A is finite, is decidable [MAN 77].

A loop in an affine counter system has the *finite monoid property* $\overset{\text{def}}{\Leftrightarrow}$ its corresponding affine update $(A, \vec{b}, \psi)$, possibly obtained by composition of several affine updates, satisfies that A^* is finite. Let us introduce below the class of admissible counter systems.

DEFINITION 8.13 *A counter system $\mathcal{S}$ is admissible if $\mathcal{S}$ is an affine counter system, its control graph is flat, and each loop has the finite monoid property.*

THEOREM 8.14 *[BOI 98, FIN 02] Let $\mathcal{S}$ be an admissible counter system and $q, q' \in Q$. We can compute a Presburger formula φ such that for every valuation $\mathbf{v}$, we have $\mathbf{v} \models \varphi$ iff $(q, (\mathbf{v}(\mathsf{x}_1), \ldots, \mathbf{v}(\mathsf{x}_n))) \overset{*}{\rightarrow} (q', (\mathbf{v}(\mathsf{x}'_1), \ldots, \mathbf{v}(\mathsf{x}'_n)))$.*

As a corollary, the reachability problem for admissible counter systems is decidable. This result can be pushed a bit further by showing that model-checking over an extension of the temporal logic CTL* with arithmetical constraints for admissible counter systems is decidable too [DEM 06]. Indeed, theorem 8.14 states that the reachability relation is indeed Presburger-definable.

If we give up the assumption on the finite monoid property, the reachability problem is undecidable for flat affine counter systems [COR 02]. However, theorem 8.14 still holds true if we relax the notion of admissibility a bit for instance by allowing that between two control states for which no transition belongs to a cycle, more than one transitions are allowed. Giving up the flatness condition in admissible counter systems also leads to undecidable reachability problems since this new class would capture the class of counter automata.

As observed in [COM 98, FIN 02, LER 03], flatness is very often essential to get effective Presburger-definable reachability sets (but of course this is not a necessary condition, see e.g. [PAR 66, HOP 79, ESP 97]). However, flat counter systems are seldom natural in real-life applications. Therefore, a relaxed version of flatness has been considered in [LER 05, DEM 06] so that an initialized counter system $(\mathcal{S}, (q, \vec{x}))$ is *flattable* whenever there is a partial unfolding of $(\mathcal{S}, (q, \vec{x}))$ that is flat and has the same reachability set as $(\mathcal{S}, (q, \vec{x}))$. In that way, reachability questions on $(\mathcal{S}, (q, \vec{x}))$ can still be decided even in the absence of flatness but in general properties on finite traces are not preserved. For the sake of completeness, let us provide below basic definitions about flattable counter systems.

Let L be a finite union of bounded languages of the form

$$u_1(v_1)^* u_2(v_2)^* \cdots (v_k)^* u_{k+1},$$

where $u_i \in \Sigma^*$, $v_i \in \Sigma^+$, $\Sigma = \delta$ is the set of transitions from $\mathcal{S}$ such that in the expression $u_1(v_1)^* u_2(v_2)^* \cdots (v_k)^* u_{k+1}$, two consecutive transitions share an intermediate control state. So, $(\mathcal{S}, (q, \vec{x}))$ is *initially flattable* [LER 05] if there is some language L of the above form such that the configurations reachable from $(q, \vec{x})$ are those reachable by firing the sequences of transitions from L (not every such sequence leads to a run, partly because counter values should be non-negative). So, there is some language L of the above form such that

$$\{(q', \vec{x'}) : (q, \vec{x}) \xrightarrow{*} (q', \vec{x'})\} = \{(q', \vec{x'}) : (q, \vec{x}) \xrightarrow{u} (q', \vec{x'}), u \in L\}$$

For instance, the initialized counter system $(\mathcal{S}, (q_1, \vec{0}))$ in Figure 8.15 is initially flattable (see e.g. further explanations about the phone controller in [COM 00]). Indeed, whenever the control state q_1 is visited, the counters are reset. So, by deleting the transition from q_1 to q_6, we obtain a flat counter system without modifying the reachability set from $(q_1, \vec{0})$.

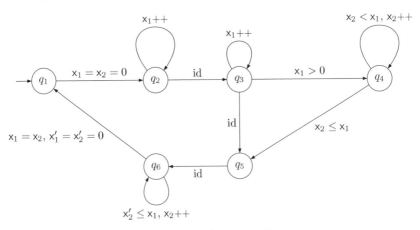

Figure 8.15. *Phone controller*

Similarly, $\mathcal{S}$ is *uniformly flattable* [LER 05] iff there is some language L of the above form such that the reachability relation $\xrightarrow{*}$ is equal to $\{((q, \vec{x}), (q', \vec{x'})) : (q, \vec{x}) \xrightarrow{u} (q', \vec{x'}), u \in L\}$, which means that reachability can be restricted to sequences of transitions from a bounded language. Surprisingly, standard classes of counter automata contain already flattable counter systems, see many examples in [LER 05].

THEOREM 8.15 *[LER 05] Uniformly reversal-bounded counter automata are uniformly flattable, reversal-bounded initialized counter automata are initially flattable, and the finite unions of bounded languages can be effectively computed.*

This provides an alternative proof for the effective semilinearity of the reachability relation. Indeed, an initialized counter automaton and a finite union of bounded languages can be simulated by an admissible counter system.

8.4.2. *Automata-based approach for Presburger arithmetic*

In the previous sections, we have seen that the satisfiability problem for Presburger arithmetic is decidable and many verification problems for subclasses of counter systems can be reduced to this problem. In this section, we shall informally describe the decidability of satisfiability problem for Presburger arithmetic by translation into the non-emptiness problem for finite-state automata. The use of automata for logical decision problems goes back to [BÜC 60a] and we shall provide below the approach by automatic structures developed in [BOU 96, BLU 00] (see also [WOL 95]). The seminal paper [BÜC 60b] describes how to use the automata-based approach to deal with Presburger arithmetic. Of course, other decision procedures exist for Presburger arithmetic: for instance, quantifier elimination method from [RED 78] improves the method developed in [COO 72].

Before presenting the principles of the automata-based approach for Presburger arithmetic, let us mention that in general, the automata-based approach consists in reducing logical problems into automata-based decision problems in order to take advantage of known results from automata theory. Alternatively, this can be viewed as a means to transform declarative statements (typically formulae) into operational devices (typically automata with sometimes rudimentary computational power). The most standard target problems in automata used in this approach is the non-emptiness problem that checks whether an automaton admits at least one accepting computation. A pioneering work by Büchi [BÜC 60a] show that Büchi automata are equivalent to formulae in monadic second-order logic (MSO) over $(\mathbb{N}, <)$; models of a formula built over the second-order variables $P_1, \ldots, P_N$ are ω-sequences over the alphabet $\mathcal{P}(\{P_1, \ldots, P_N\})$. In full generality, the following are a few desirable properties of the approach:

– the reduction should be conceptually simple, apart from being semantically faithful;

– the computational complexity of the automata-based target problem should be well-characterized. In that way, a complexity upper bound is obtained to solve the source logical problem;

– last but not least, the reduction should preferably allow the optimal complexity for the source logical problem to be obtained.

We have seen that each Presburger formula φ with $n \geq 1$ free variables defines a subset of $\mathbb{N}^n$, namely $\text{REL}(\varphi) \subseteq \mathbb{N}^n$, that corresponds to the set of variable valuations that make φ true. For instance, $\text{REL}(x = y+z) = \{(k_1, k_2, k_3) \in \mathbb{N}^3 : k_1 = k_2+k_3\}$. The automata-based approach for Presburger arithmetic consists of representing the tuples in $\text{REL}(\varphi)$ by a regular language that can be effectively defined, for instance with the help of a finite-state automaton. In that way, satisfiability of φ, which is equivalent to the non-emptiness of $\text{REL}(\varphi)$, becomes equivalent to the non-emptinesss of a finite-state automaton (which is an easy problem to solve once the automaton is built). In order to define regular languages, first we need to specify how natural numbers and tuples of natural numers are encoded by words over a finite alphabet. Numerous options are possible (see e.g. [LER 03, KLA 04b]) and below we adopt a simple and standard encoding in which natural numbers are viewed as finite words over the alphabet $\{0,1\}$ by using a binary representation in which the least significant bit is first. We adopt a representation of natural numbers that is not unique, for instance the number five can be encoded by 101 or by 101000. Tuples of natural numbers of dimension n are represented by finite words over the alphabet $\{0,1\}^n$ by using an equal length representation for each number. Typically, the pair $\left(\begin{smallmatrix} 5 \\ 8 \end{smallmatrix}\right)$ can be represented by the word $\left(\begin{smallmatrix} 1 \\ 0 \end{smallmatrix}\right)\left(\begin{smallmatrix} 0 \\ 0 \end{smallmatrix}\right)\left(\begin{smallmatrix} 1 \\ 0 \end{smallmatrix}\right)\left(\begin{smallmatrix} 0 \\ 1 \end{smallmatrix}\right)\left(\begin{smallmatrix} 0 \\ 0 \end{smallmatrix}\right)$ over the alphabet $\{0,1\}^2$. So, we introduce the map $f : \mathbb{N} \to \mathcal{P}(\{0,1\}^*)$ such that $f(0) \stackrel{\text{def}}{=} 0^*$ and for $k > 0$, $f(k) \stackrel{\text{def}}{=} b_k \cdot 0^*$ where b_k is the shortest binary representation of k (least significant bit first). The map f is extended to subsets of $\mathbb{N}$ in the obvious way as well as to n-tuples of natural numbers with alphabet $\{0,1\}^n$ such that $f(\vec{x}) \subseteq \mathcal{P}((\{0,1\}^n)^*)$ with $\vec{x} \in \mathbb{N}^n$ and $\vec{b} \in f(\vec{x})$ iff for $i \in [1, n]$, the projection of $\vec{b}$ on the ith row belongs to $f(\vec{x}(i))$. The map f is typically a state-encoding schema in the sense of [BOI 98, LEG 08].

Given a Presburger formula φ with $n \geq 1$ free variables and a finite-state automaton $\mathcal{A}$ over the alphabet $\{0,1\}^n$, we write $\varphi \approx \mathcal{A}$ whenever $\text{L}(\mathcal{A}) = f(\text{REL}(\varphi))$.

THEOREM 8.16 (see e.g. [BOU 96]) Given a Presburger formula φ, we can build a finite-state automaton $\mathcal{A}_\varphi$ such that $\varphi \approx \mathcal{A}_\varphi$.

We also have $\text{REL}(\varphi) \subseteq \text{REL}(\psi)$ iff $\text{L}(\mathcal{A}_\varphi) \subseteq \text{L}(\mathcal{A}_\psi)$ (see e.g., [LEG 08, theorem 3.22]).

The finite-state automaton $\mathcal{A}_\varphi$ can be built recursively over the structure of φ. For instance, conjunction is handled by the product construction, existential quantifier is handled by projection, negation is handled by the complement construction, see details below. Nevertheless, a crude complexity analysis of the construction of $\mathcal{A}_\varphi$ reveals a non-elementary worst-case complexity. Indeed, for every negation, a complementation needs to be operated. However, developments related to the optimal size of automata can be found in [KLA 04a].

The recursive definition is based on the following properties. Let φ and ψ be Presburger formulae with free variables $x_1, \ldots, x_n$.

conjunction If $\varphi \approx \mathcal{A}$ and $\psi \approx \mathcal{B}$, then $\varphi \wedge \psi \approx \mathcal{A} \cap \mathcal{B}$ where $\cap$ is the product construction computing intersection;

negation If $\varphi \approx \mathcal{A}$, then $\neg \varphi \approx \overline{\mathcal{A}}$ where $^{-}$ performs complementation, which may cause an exponential blow-up;

quantification If $\varphi \approx \mathcal{A}$, then $\exists\, x_n\, \varphi \approx \mathcal{A}'$ where $\mathcal{A}'$ is built over the alphabet $\{0,1\}^{n-1}$ by forgetting the nth component. Typically, $q \xrightarrow{\vec{b}} q'$ in $\mathcal{A}'$ whenever there is a transition $q \xrightarrow{\vec{b'}} q'$ in $\mathcal{A}$ such that $\vec{b}$ and $\vec{b'}$ agree on the $n - 1$ first bit values.

In the above construction, we assumed that φ and ψ share the same set of free variables, which does not always hold true for arbitrary formulae. If it is not the case, $\varphi \approx \mathcal{A}$ and $\psi \approx \mathcal{B}$, then we perform an operation that consists of adding dummy bits. For instance, suppose that φ contains the free variables $x_1, \ldots, x_n$. We can build the automaton $\mathcal{A}'$ over the alphabet $\{0,1\}^{n+1}$ obtained by adding the $n+1$th component. Typically, $q \xrightarrow{\vec{b}} q'$ in $\mathcal{A}'$ whenever there is a transition $q \xrightarrow{\vec{b'}} q'$ in $\mathcal{A}$ such that $\vec{b}$ and $\vec{b'}$ agree on the n first bit values. It remains to deal with atomic formulae to achieve the inductive building of the automaton.

The proof of theorem 8.16 is clearly based on the above constructions but we need to complete the argument in order to deal with atomic formulae. Without any loss of generality, we can restrict ourselves to equalities of the form $x = y + z$ (at the cost of introducing new variables in order to deal with sums made of more than two variables). Such a restriction is only helpful to simplify the presentation of the method but it makes sense to consider the full language with linear constraints in order to optimize the reduction to automata, see e.g. [BOI 02, BOU 96]. The variables in $x = y + z$ are not necessarily distinct.

The automaton for $x_1 = x_2 + x_3$ is described in the left part of Figure 8.16 where q_1 is the initial state as well as the final state. The state q_1 represents a carry-over of 0 whereas the state q_2 represents a carry-over of 1. We can check that $(x_1 = x_2 + x_3) \approx \mathcal{A}$. The right part of Figure 8.16 describes the automaton for $x_1 = x_2 + x_2$.

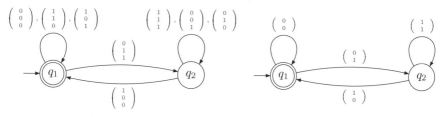

Figure 8.16. *Finite-state automata for* $x_1 = x_2 + x_3$ *and* $x_1 = x_2 + x_2$

The automata-based approach for Presburger arithmetic can be extended to richer theories such as $(\mathbb{R}, \mathbb{Z}, +, \leq)$, see e.g. [BOI 02], or can be refined by providing other reductions, see e.g. [LER 03, KLA 04a, SCH 07]. An overview of automata-based decision procedures for Presburger arithmetic and related formalisms can be found in [KLA 04a].

8.4.3. *A selection of tools for Presburger arithmetic*

So far, we have seen how to reduce verification problems into the satisfiability problem for Presburger arithmetic. Then, we presented the principle of an automata-based decision procedure for Presburger arithmetic by viewing sets of tuples defined in Presburger arithmetic as regular languages. Below, we provide a (non-exhaustive) list of tools that can handle first-order logics with linear arithmetic. In that way, we have provided the natural set of steps to perform formal verification of infinite-state systems dealing with counters:

– LIRA implements decision procedures based on automata-theoretic techniques for the first-order theory of $(\mathbb{Z}, +, <)$ and for other related logics with linear arithmetic [BEC 07]. It is closely related to MONA [BIE 96], LASH [BOI 01] and PRESTAF [COU 05]. Contrary to numerous SMT solvers, LIRA can handle quantifiers (this is also true for MONA and LASH very briefly described below);

– the MONA tool provides an implementation for the automata-based decision procedure for weak monadic second-order logic WS1S [BIE 96]. The logic WS1S is known to be strongly related to Presburger arithmetic, see e.g. [BÜC 60b];

– LASH is an automata library that provides the implementation of standard constructions on automata [BOI 01] as well as constructions for linear inequations. Comparisons of data structures used in MONA and LASH can be found in [KLA 04a, Chapter 5]. As an application domain, LASH has been used successfully to verify properties on counter systems, see e.g., [BOI 98];

– TAPAS is a suite of libraries [LER 09] dedicated to first-order logics of linear arithmetic. The application programming interface GENEPI for such logics encapsulate many standard solvers such as LIRA or MONA. FAST [BAR 06] is a tool over TAPAS that is designed to verify reachability properties of counter systems; this is a client application in TAPAS;

– the tool CVC3 is an automatic theorem prover for Satisfiability Modulo first-order Theories (SMT), see e.g., [BAR 08], [BAR 07]. CVC3 is the last offspring of a series of popular SMT provers, which originated at Stanford University with the SVC system. In particular, it builds on the code base of CVC Lite, its most recent predecessor. The automatic theorem prover CVC3 (and the new version CVC4) is a tool that can prove the validity of first-order formulae in a large number of built-in logical theories, including rational and integer linear arithmetic, arrays, tuples, bit vectors, etc;

– Z3 is an efficient SMT solver, see e.g., [MOU 08], that can deal with linear real and integer arithmetic. This is an SMT solver developed by Microsoft Research that is freely available for academic research. Z3 is designed to tackle problems that arise in software verification and software analysis.

8.5. Concluding remarks

The verification of infinite-state systems is a very tough problem for which decision procedures do not always exist. In this chapter, we have illustrated the verification methods for such systems on recursive Petri nets and on subclasses of counter systems.

As far as SRPNs are concerned, we have seen that the addition of recursion to Petri nets increases the expressive power of the computational model even though some of the verification problems remain decidable, such as the reachability problem. The decidability proof for that problem on SRPNs uses a solver for the reachability problem for standard Petri nets as a blackbox. Similarly, the computation of linear invariants for Petri nets can be adapted to SRPNs as shown in section 8.3.

As far as counter systems are concerned, we have shown how to reduce a verification problem in a subclass of counter systems (for instance for the reversal-bounded counter automata) into satisfiability in some first-order theory. In order to solve the instances of the logical problem, one option consists of eliminating quantifiers and then using dedicated SMT solvers such as Z3 or CVC3. Alternatively, a Presburger formula can be effectively transformed into a finite-state automaton such that satisfiability is equivalent to the non-emptiness of the language recognized by the automaton. This allows the use of tools dedicated to decision procedures for automata such as LIRA or LASH. Alternatively, the formula can be given to a suite of libraries such as TAPAS and then satisfiability can be checked with any standard solver that is plugged in.

At some abstract level, similar ideas can be found to verify timed systems with real-time constraints (timed automata, timed Petri nets, see e.g. Chapter 9) or pushdown systems even though the methods are undertaken differently. The wealth of infinite-state systems as well as the diversity of properties that require verification has induced the development of numerous methods and tools even though two central problems always need to be solved in order to run verification tools:

1) how do you symbolically represent an infinite set (configurations, processes, data)?

2) which data structures allow you to represent concisely such sets (when possible) in order to effectively manipulate the symbolic representations in verification tools?

8.6. Bibliography

[ABD 96] ABDULLA P., JONSSON B., "Verifying programs with unreliable channels", *Information and Computation*, vol. 127, num. 2, p. 91–101, 1996.

[ALU 94] ALUR R., DILL D., "A theory of timed automata", *Theoretical Computer Science*, vol. 126, p. 183–235, 1994.

[ARA 77] ARAKI T., KASAMI T., "Decidability problems on the strong connectivity of Petri net reachability sets", *Theoretical Computer Science*, vol. 4, p. 99–119, 1977.

[BAR 06] BARDIN S., LEROUX J., POINT G., "FAST extended release", in *CAV'06*, vol. 4144 of *Lecture Notes in Computer Science*, Springer, p. 63–66, 2006.

[BAR 07] BARRETT C., TINELLI C., "CVC3", in *CAV'07*, vol. 4590 of *Lecture Notes in Computer Science*, Springer, p. 298–302, 2007.

[BAR 08] BARRETT C., SEBASTIANI R., SESHIA S., TINELLI C., "*Satisfiability modulo theories*", vol. 185 of *Frontiers in Artificial Intelligence and Applications*, Chapter 26, p. 825–885, IOS Press, 2008.

[BEC 07] BECKER B., DAX C., EISINGER J., KLAEDTKE F., "LIRA: handling constraints of linear arithmetics over the integers and the reals", in *CAV'07*, vol. 4590 of *Lecture Notes in Computer Science*, Springer, p. 307–310, 2007.

[BER 80] BERMAN L., "The complexity of logical theories", *Theoretical Computer Science*, vol. 11, p. 71–78, 1980.

[BER 01] BERARD B., BIDOIT M., FINKEL A., LAROUSSINIE F., PETIT A., PETRUCCI L., SCHNOEBELEN P., *Systems and Software Verification, Model-checking Techniques and Tools*, Springer, 2001.

[BIE 96] BIEHL M., KLARLUND N., RAUHE T., "Mona: decidable arithmetic in practice", in *FTRTFT'96*, vol. 1135 of *Lecture Notes in Computer Science*, Springer, p. 459–462, 1996.

[BLU 00] BLUMENSATH A., GRÄDEL E., "Automatic structures", in *LICS'00*, p. 51–62, 2000.

[BOI 98] BOIGELOT B., Symbolic methods for exploring infinite state spaces, PhD thesis, University of Liège, 1998.

[BOI 01] BOIGELOT B., JODOGNE S., WOLPER P., "On the use of weak automata for deciding linear arithmetic with integer and real variables", in *IJCAR'01*, vol. 2083 of *Lecture Notes in Artificial Intelligence*, Springer, p. 611–625, 2001.

[BOI 02] BOIGELOT B., WOLPER P., "Representing arithmetic constraints with finite automata: an overview", in *ICLP'02*, vol. 2401 of *Lecture Notes in Computer Science*, Springer, p. 1–19, 2002.

[BOR 76] BOROSH I., TREYBIG L., "Bounds on positive integral solutions of linear diophantine equations", *AMS*, vol. 55, p. 299–304, 1976.

[BOU 96] BOUDET A., COMON H., "Diophantine equations, Presburger arithmetic and finite automata", in *CAAP'96*, vol. 1059 of *Lecture Notes in Computer Science*, Springer, p. 30–43, 1996.

[BOU 06a] BOUAJJANI A., BOZGA M., HABERMEHL P., IOSIF R., MORO P., VOJNAR T., "Programs with lists are counter automata", in *CAV'06*, vol. 4144 of *Lecture Notes in Computer Science*, Springer, p. 517–531, 2006.

[BOU 06b] BOUAJJANI A., HABERMEHL P., ROGALEWICZ A., VOJNAR T., "Abstract tree regular model checking of complex dynamic data structures", *SAS'06*, vol. 4134 of *Lecture Notes in Computer Science*, Springer, p. 52–70, 2006.

[BOZ 10] BOZGA M., IOSIF R., KONEČNÝ F., "Fast acceleration of ultimately periodic relations", in *CAV'10*, vol. 6174 of *Lecture Notes in Computer Science*, Springer, p. 227–242, 2010.

[BÜC 60a] BÜCHI J., "On a decision method in restricted second-order arithmetic", *in Logic, Methodology, and Philosophy of Science*, p. 1–11, 1960.

[BÜC 60b] BÜCHI R., "Weak second-order arithmetic and finite automata", *Zeitschrift für Mathematische Logik und Grundlagen der Mathematik*, vol. 6, p. 66–92, 1960.

[CAS 99] CASSANDRAS C. G., LAFORTUNE S., *Introduction to Discrete Event Systems*, Kluwer Academic Publishers, 1999.

[CLA 00a] CLARKE E., GRUMBERG O., JHA S., LU Y., VEITH H., "Counter-example-guided abstraction refinement", in *CAV'00*, vol. 1855 of *Lecture Notes in Computer Science*, Springer, p. 154–169, 2000.

[CLA 00b] CLARKE E., GRUMBERG O., PELED D., *Model Checking*, The MIT Press Books, 2000.

[COL 90] COLOM J. M., SILVA M., "Convex geometry and semiflows in P/T nets. A comparative study of algorithms for computation of minimal P-semiflows", *in Advances in Petri Nets*, vol. 483 of *Lecture Notes Computer Science*, Springer-Verlag, p. 79–112, June 1990.

[COM 98] COMON H., JURSKI Y., "Multiple counters automata, safety analysis and Presburger arithmetic", in *CAV'98*, vol. 1427 of *Lecture Notes in Computer Science*, Springer, p. 268–279, 1998.

[COM 00] COMON H., CORTIER V., "Flatness is not a weakness", in *CSL'00*, vol. 1862 of *Lecture Notes in Computer Science*, Springer, p. 262–276, 2000.

[COO 72] COOPER D., "Theorem proving in arithmetic without multiplication", *Machine Learning*, vol. 7, p. 91–99, 1972.

[COR 02] CORTIER V., "About the decision of reachability for register machines", *Theoretical Informatics and Applications*, vol. 36, num. 4, p. 341–358, 2002.

[COU 05] COUVREUR J., "A BDD-like implementation of an automata package", in *CIAA'04*, vol. 3317 of *Lecture Notes in Computer Science*, Springer, p. 310–311, 2005.

[DAN 01] DANG Z., IBARRA O., SAN PIETRO P., "Liveness verification of reversal-bounded multicounter machines with a free counter", in *FST&TCS'01*, vol. 2245 of *Lecture Notes in Computer Science*, Springer, p. 132–143, 2001.

[DEM 06] DEMRI S., FINKEL A., GORANKO V., VAN DRIMMELEN G., "Towards a model-checker for counter systems", in *ATVA'06*, vol. 4218 of *Lecture Notes in Computer Science*, Springer, p. 493–507, 2006.

[El 95] EL FALLAH SEGHROUCHNI A., HADDAD S., "A Formal model for coordinating plans in multiagents systems", in *Proceedings of Intelligent Agents Workshop*, Oxford, United Kingdom, Augusta Technology Ltd, Brooks University, 1995.

[El 96]   EL FALLAH SEGHROUCHNI A., HADDAD S., "A recursive model for distributed planning", *Second International Conference on Multi-Agent Systems*, Kyoto, Japan, 1996.

[ESP 94]   ESPARZA J., NIELSEN M., "Decidability issues for Petri nets - a survey", *Bulletin of the European Association for Theoretical Computer Science*, vol. 52, p. 245–262, 1994.

[ESP 97]   ESPARZA J., "Petri nets, commutative context-free grammars, and basic parallel processes", *Fundamenta Informaticae*, vol. 31, num. 13, p. 13–26, 1997.

[ESP 99]   ESPARZA J., FINKEL A., MAYR R., "On the verification of broadcast protocols", in *LICS'99*, p. 352–359, 1999.

[FER 79]   FERRANTE J., RACKOFF C., *The Computational Complexity of Logical Theories*, vol. 718 of *Lecture Notes in Mathematics*, Springer, 1979.

[FIN 97]   FINKEL A., WILLEMS B., WOLPER P., "A direct symbolic approach to model checking pushdown systems", in *INFINITY'97*, vol. 9 of *Electronic Notes in Theoretical Computer Science*, Elsevier Science Publishers, 1997.

[FIN 00]   FINKEL A., SUTRE G., "Decidability of reachability problems for classes of two counter automata", in *STACS'00*, vol. 2256 of *Lecture Notes in Computer Science*, Springer, p. 346–357, 2000.

[FIN 01]   FINKEL A., SCHNOEBELEN P., "Well-structured transitions systems everywhere!", *Theoretical Computer Science*, vol. 256, num. 1–2, p. 63–92, 2001.

[FIN 02]   FINKEL A., LEROUX J., "How to compose Presburger accelerations: applications to broadcast protocols", in *FST&TCS'02*, vol. 2256 of *Lecture Notes in Computer Science*, Springer, p. 145–156, 2002.

[FIS 74]   FISCHER M., RABIN M., "Super-exponential complexity of Presburger arithmetic", in *Complexity of Computation*, vol. 7 of *SIAM-AMS proceedings*, American Mathematical Society, p. 27–42, 1974.

[GAN 09]   GANTY P., MAJUMDAR R., RYBALCHENKO A., "Verifying liveness for asynchronous programs", in *POPL'09*, ACM, p. 102–113, 2009.

[GIN 66]   GINSBURG S., SPANIER E., "Semigroups, Presburger formulas and languages", *Pacific Journal of Mathematics*, vol. 16, num. 2, p. 285–296, 1966.

[GRÄ 88]   GRÄDEL E., "Subclasses of Presburger arithmetic and the polynomial-time hierarchy", *Theoretical Computer Science*, vol. 56, p. 289–301, 1988.

[GUR 81]   GURARI E., IBARRA O., "The complexity of decision problems for finite-turn multicounter machines", in *ICALP'81*, vol. 115 of *Lecture Notes in Computer Science*, Springer, p. 495–505, 1981.

[HAD]   HADDAD S., POITRENAUD D., Decidability and undecidability results for recursive Petri nets, Report , University.

[HAD 99]   HADDAD S., POITRENAUD D., "Theoretical aspects of recursive Petri nets", *in Proc. of the 20th Int. Conf. on Applications and Theory of Petri nets*, vol. 1639 of *Lecture Notes in Computer Science*, Williamsburg, VA, USA, Springer-Verlag, p. 228–247, 1999.

[HAD 00] HADDAD S., POITRENAUD D., "Modelling and analyzing systems with recursive Petri nets", in *Proc. of the 5th Workshop on Discrete Event Systems - Analysis and Control*, Gand, Belgique, Kluwer Academics Publishers, p. 449–458, 2000.

[HAD 01] HADDAD S., POITRENAUD D., "Checking linear temporal formulas on sequential recursive Petri nets", in *Proc of the 8th International Symposium on Temporal Representation and Reasonning*, Cividale del Friuli, Italy, IEEE Computer Society Press, 2001.

[HAD 07] HADDAD S., POITRENAUD D., "Recursive Petri nets – theory and application to discrete event systems", *Acta Informatica*, vol. 44, num. 7–8, p. 463–508, Springer, December 2007.

[HEN 03] HENZINGER T., JHALA R., MAJUMDAR R., SUTRE G., "Software verification with BLAST", in *SPIN'03*, vol. 2648 of *Lecture Notes in Computer Science*, Springer, p. 235–239, 2003.

[HEN 05] HENZINGER T., MAJUMDAR R., RASKIN J., "A classification of symbolic transitions systems", *ACM Transactions on Computational Logic*, vol. 6, num. 1, p. 1–32, 2005.

[HOP 79] HOPCROFT J., PANSIOT J., "On the reachability problem for 5-dimensional vector addition systems", *Theoretical Computer Science*, vol. 8, p. 135–159, 1979.

[IBA 78] IBARRA O., "Reversal-bounded multicounter machines and their decision problems", *Journal of the Association for Computing Machinery*, vol. 25, num. 1, p. 116–133, 1978.

[JAN 79] JANTZEN M., "On the hierarchy of Petri net languages", *RAIRO*, vol. 13, num. 1, p. 19–30, 1979.

[KAI 10] KAISER A., KROENING D., WAHL T., "Dynamic cutoff detection in parameterized concurrent programs", in *CAV'10*, vol. 6174 of *Lecture Notes in Computer Science*, Springer, p. 645–659, 2010.

[KAR 69] KARP R. M., MILLER R. E., "Parallel program schemata", *Journal of Computer and System Sciences*, vol. 3, num. 2, p. 147–195, 1969.

[KIE 89] KIEHN A., "Petri nets systems and their closure properties", in *Advances in Petri Nets 1989*, vol. 424 of *Lecture Notes in Computer Science*, Springer-Verlag, p. 306-328, 1989.

[KLA 04a] KLAEDTKE F., Automata-based decision procedures for weak arithmetics, PhD thesis, Institut für Informatik, Albert-Ludwigs-University, Freiburg, February 2004.

[KLA 04b] KLAEDTKE F., "On the automata size for Presburger arithmetic", in *LICS'04*, IEEE, p. 110–119, 2004.

[KOS 82] KOSARAJU R., "Decidability of reachability in vector addition systems", in *STOC'82*, p. 267–281, 1982.

[LEG 08] LEGAY A., Generic methods for the verification of infinite-state systems, PhD thesis, University of Liège, 2008.

[LER 03] LEROUX J., Algorithmique de la vérification des systèmes à compteurs. approximation et accélération. implémentation de l'outil FAST., PhD thesis, ENS de Cachan, France, 2003.

[LER 05] LEROUX J., SUTRE G., "Flat counter systems are everywhere!", in *ATVA'05*, vol. 3707 of *Lecture Notes in Computer Science*, Springer, p. 489–503, 2005.

[LER 09] LEROUX J., POINT G., "TaPAS: the Talence Presburger arithmetic suite", in *TACAS'09*, vol. 5505 of *Lecture Notes in Computer Science*, Springer, p. 182–185, 2009.

[LIP 76] LIPTON R. J., The reachability problem requires exponential space, Report num. 62, Department of Computer Science, Yale University, 1976.

[MAN 77] MANDEL A., SIMON I., "On finite semigroups of matrices", *Theoretical Computer Science*, vol. 5, num. 2, p. 101–111, 1977.

[MAY 84] MAYR E., "An algorithm for the general Petri net reachability problem", *SIAM Journal of Computing*, vol. 13, num. 3, p. 441–460, 1984.

[MAY 97] MAYR R., "Combining Petri nets and PA-processes", in *Proc. of the 3rd Int. Symposium on Theoretical Aspects of Computer Software*, vol. 1281 of *Lecture Notes in Computer Science*, Sendai, Japan, Springer-Verlag, p. 547–561, 1997.

[MCM 93] MCMILLAN K., *Symbolic Model Checking*, Kluwer Academic Publishers, 1993.

[MIN 67] MINSKY M., *Computation: Finite and Infinite Machines*, Prentice Hall, Englewood Cliffs, NJ, 1967.

[MOU 08] DE MOURA L., BJÖRNER N., "Z3: An efficient SMT solver", in *TACAS'08*, vol. 4963 of *Lecture Notes in Computer Science*, Springer, p. 337–340, 2008.

[OPP 78] OPPEN D., "A $2^{2^{2pn}}$ upper bound on the complexity of Presburger arithmetic", *Journal of Computer and System Sciences*, vol. 16, num. 3, p. 323–332, 1978.

[PAP 81] PAPADIMITRIOU C., "On the complexity of integer programming", *Journal of the Association for Computing Machinery*, vol. 28, num. 4, p. 765–768, 1981.

[PAR 66] PARIKH R., "On context-free languages", *Journal of the Association for Computing Machinery*, vol. 13, num. 4, p. 570–581, 1966.

[PET 81] PETERSON J., *Petri Net Theory and the Modelling of Systems*, Prentice-Hall, 1981.

[PRE 29] PRESBURGER M., "Über die vollständigkeit eines gewissen systems der arithmetik ganzer zahlen, in welchem die addition als einzige operation hervortritt", *Comptes Rendus du premier congrès de mathématiciens des Pays Slaves, Warsaw*, p. 92–101, 1929.

[RAC 78] RACKOFF C., "The covering and boundedness problems for vector addition systems", *Theoretical Computer Science*, vol. 6, num. 2, p. 223–231, 1978.

[RED 78] REDDY C., LOVELAND W., "Presburger arithmetic with bounded quantifier alternation", in *STOC'78*, ACM press, p. 320–325, 1978.

[REI 98] REISIG W., ROZENBERG G., Eds., *Lectures on Petri Nets I: Basic Models*, vol. 1491 of *Lecture Notes in Computer Science*, Springer, 1998.

[REU 90] REUTENAUER C., *The Mathematics of Petri Nets*, Masson and Prentice, 1990.

[SCH 07] SCHUELE T., SCHNEIDER K., "Verification of data paths using unbounded integers: automata strike back", in *HVC'06*, vol. 4383 of *Lecture Notes in Computer Science*, Springer, p. 65–80, 2007.

[SUZ 80] SUZUKI N., JEFFERSON D., "Verification decidability of Presburger array programs", *Journal of the Association for Computing Machinery*, vol. 27, num. 1, p. 191–205,
1980.

[TAR 51] TARSKI A., *A Decision Method for Elementary Algebra and Geometry*, University
of California Press, 1951.

[TAR 53] TARSKI A., *Undecidable theories*, Studies in Logic and the Foundations of Mathematics, North-Holland, 1953, In collaboration with A. Mostowski. and R. Robinson.

[VAL 78a] VALK R., "On the computational power of extended Petri nets", in *Proceedings
of the 7th Int. Symposium on Mathematical Foundations of Computer Science*, vol. 64 of
Lecture Notes Computer Science, Zakopane, Poland, Springer-Verlag, p. 526–535, 1978.

[VAL 78b] VALK R., "Self-modifying nets, a natural extension of Petri nets", in *Proc. of the
5th Int. Colloquium on Automata, Languages and Programming*, vol. 62 of *Lecture Notes
Computer Science*, Udine, Italy, Springer-Verlag, p. 464–476, 1978.

[WOL 95] WOLPER P., BOIGELOT B., "An automata-theoretic approach to Presburger arithmetic constraints", in *SAS'95*, vol. 983 of *Lecture Notes in Computer Science*, Springer,
p. 21–32, 1995.

Chapter 9

Verification of Timed Systems

9.1. Introduction

This chapter is devoted to the presentation of verification techniques for systems involving quantitative time constraints. Different ways of modeling such systems have been presented in Chapter 4. In this chapter, we present different results ranging from well established techniques (such as the region graph construction for timed automata) to more advanced issues (such as the implementability of timed automata).

Main methods to tame timed systems

Timed systems are a particular type of infinite-state systems in which the state space involves dense time variables. A general introduction on the verification techniques used to infinite-state systems can be found in Chapter 8. The most standard tool used to analyze timed systems is the symbolic representation of configurations, i.e. the identification of a framework that enables the finite representation of infinitely many configurations.

For some classes of timed systems, we can even use such a symbolic representation to transform the timed system into a finite-state system on which the property can be decided. In this chapter, we present such symbolic representations for several classes of timed systems. The first presentations of such constructions are the *state-class graph* for time Petri nets [BER 83], and the *region graph* for timed automata [ALU 94].

Chapter written by Pierre-Alain REYNIER.

These reductions to finite-state systems are usually based on an equivalence relation between configurations that admits a finite number of equivalence classes. However, it can also be the case that this equivalence admits an infinite number of classes, and still yields decidability results, for instance if there exists a well quasi-order on the equivalence classes.

From decidability to efficient procedures

Although the previously mentioned techniques allow decidability results to be proved, the algorithms resulting from them are not always the most efficient. For instance, for the class of timed automata, while the region graph construction is comonly used to prove decidability, it is never computed in practice. As an alternative, the symbolic representation of *zones* is considered which, though not always theoretically optimal, often yields much better algorithms in practice.

In this chapter we are mainly interested in decidability results, and thus we do not present such algorithms. However, most of the positive results presented here have been turned into efficient procedures.

Implementability of timed systems

Implementing mathematical models on physical machines is an important step for applying theoretical results to practical examples. This step is well-understood for many untimed models that have been studied (e.g. finite automata, pushdown automata). In the timed setting, while timed automata are widely-accepted as a framework for modeling real-time aspects of systems, it is known that they cannot be faithfully implemented on finite-speed central processing units (CPUs) [CAS 02]. Studying the "implementability" of timed automata is thus a challenging problem which has obvious theoretical and practical interest.

Structure of the chapter

Section 9.2 is elaborated around the standard region graph construction for timed automata. After describing it precisely, we will present other models with a finite-state abstraction of their state space, and decidability results for temporal logics resulting from these abstractions.

When considering extensions of Petri nets with time, we obtain models that are infinite "in two directions". We present in section 9.3 the setting of timed Petri nets, for which an equivalence relation with an infinite number of equivalence classes can be used to prove decidability results.

Finally, we discuss in section 9.4 implementability issues in timed automata, and present a recent approach based on a parametric semantics for timed automata.

9.2. Construction of the region graph

To decide reachability properties in timed systems, many positive results are based on the construction of a finite-state automaton that abstracts the timed system. The construction ensures that checking whether a configuration (or a set of configurations) is reachable in the timed system is equivalent to checking whether a state (or a set of states) is reachable in the finite automaton. More precisely, this construction often yields a finite state automaton that precisely accepts all the untimed words that can be obtained from the timed words accepted by the timed automaton by dropping out the time components. The standard way to obtain such an abstraction is the construction of an equivalence relation of finite index (i.e. with finitely many equivalence classes) over the configurations. To be compatible with reachability checking, this equivalence must ensure that from two equivalent configurations, the same behaviors will be possible. In timed systems, there are two types of transitions, time elapsing, and discrete firing of a transition: if from a configuration, it is possible to delay (respectively to take a transition), then this can occur from an equivalent configuration, and the two configurations resulting from the two moves are then also equivalent. However, precise delays need not to be respected, and thus the equivalence will only be a *time-abstract bisimulation* (unlike timed bisimulations defined in Chapter 4).

9.2.1. *Timed automata*

We describe a notion of regions initially presented in [ALU 90, ALU 94] for the decision of the reachability of a location in a timed automaton.

The equivalence relation

For timed automata, an equivalence relation (with finite index) verifying the above properties always exists, and it can be defined as follows. Let $\mathcal{A}$ be a timed automaton with set of clocks X and maximal constant M. Without loss of generality, we assume that all constants of $\mathcal{A}$ are integers, this can be obtained by multiplying all the constants by the same value. Two configurations (q, v) and (q', v') are equivalent if $q = q'$ and $v \equiv_M v'$, where the relation $v \equiv_M v'$ holds whenever for each clock $x \in X$,

1) $v(x) > M \iff v'(x) > M$;

2) if $v(x) \leq M$, then[1] $\lfloor v(x) \rfloor = \lfloor v'(x) \rfloor$, and $\langle v(x) \rangle = 0 \iff \langle v'(x) \rangle = 0$, and for each pair of clocks (x, y);

3) if $v(x) \leq M$ and $v(y) \leq M$, then $\langle v(x) \rangle \leq \langle v(y) \rangle \iff \langle v'(x) \rangle \leq \langle v'(y) \rangle$.

As M is defined as the maximal constant appearing in $\mathcal{A}$, the two first conditions imply that two equivalent valuations satisfy exactly the same clock constraints of the

---

1. $\lfloor v(x) \rfloor$ (resp. $\langle v(x) \rangle$) denotes the integral part of $v(x)$ (resp. its fractional part).

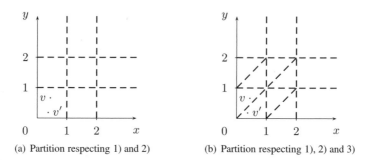

(a) Partition respecting 1) and 2)   (b) Partition respecting 1), 2) and 3)

Figure 9.1. *Partitions of the upper-right quarter of the plane*

timed automaton. The third condition ensures that from two equivalent configurations, letting time elapse will lead to the same integral values for the clocks, in the very same order. The equivalence $\equiv_M$ is called the *region equivalence*, and an equivalence class is then called a *region*. We denote the set of regions obtained in this way as $\mathcal{R}_M(X)$. More formally, we have, given two clock valuations $v, v' \in \mathbb{R}_+^X$,

$$v \equiv_M v' \Rightarrow \begin{cases} \text{for any constraint } g \text{ in } \mathcal{A}, \ v \models g \iff v' \models g \\ \forall d \in \mathbb{R}_+, \exists d' \in \mathbb{R}_+ \text{ s.t. } v + d \equiv_M v' + d' \end{cases} \tag{9.1}$$

We can verify that the number of regions is bounded by $n! \cdot 2^n \cdot (2M + 2)^n$, where n denotes the number of clocks. Indeed, a region is characterized by specifying:

(i) a mapping from clocks to the set of so-called one-dimensional regions $\{[0, 0],]0, 1[, [1, 1], \ldots,]M - 1, M[, [M, M],]M, +\infty[\}$;

(ii) for each pair of clocks x and y such that, according to point (i), both clocks have non-nul fractional parts and are bounded by M, whether $\langle x \rangle$ is less than, equal to, or greater than $\langle y \rangle$.

Point (i) yields $(2M+2)^n$ choices as there are $2M+2$ one-dimensional regions. Point (ii) is characterized by a subset of representative clocks (thus at most 2^n choices) and an order on clocks (at most $n!$ choices). Indeed, we can obtain the strict/non-strict order on fractional values clocks from the order on clocks by collapsing it on the representative clocks.

To illustrate this definition, we consider the case of two clocks x and y, with maximal constant 2. A valuation can then be understood as a point in the quarter of the plan depicted in Figure 9.1(a). The partition depicted in Figure 9.1(a) respects all constraints defined with integral constants smaller than or equal to 2, but the two valuations v and v' are not equivalent due to time elapsing (item 3 above): indeed, if we

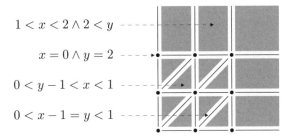

$1 < x < 2 \wedge 2 < y$

$x = 0 \wedge y = 2$

$0 < y - 1 < x < 1$

$0 < x - 1 = y < 1$

Figure 9.2. *The 44 regions in two dimensions with maximal constant* 2

let some time elapse from the valuation v, we will first satisfy the constraint $y = 1$ and then $x = 1$, while it will be the converse from the valuation v'. Hence, the possible behaviors from v and v' are different. More precisely, property (9.1) is not satisfied: there exists a delay d such that $v + d$ satisfies the constraint $x < 1 \wedge y = 1$, while there exists no such delay for valuation v'. To handle time elapsing constraints induced by time-elapsing, condition 3) refines the partition of Figure 9.1(a) by adding diagonal lines. The resulting partition is given in Figure 9.1(b) and is a time-abstract bisimulation.

Following the above characterization of regions, they can be represented by the linear equalities and inequalities satisfied by the valuations they represent. All the regions of our example are represented in Figure 9.2. Note that there are different types of regions: regions reduced to a single element (corners), regions composed of a segment, regions composed of a half-line, regions composed of a triangle, etc. Examples of constraints associated with regions are given in this figure.

Construction of the region automaton

We present now how regions allow a finite-state automaton to be built that accepts the untimed language of the timed automaton. States of this automaton are pairs (q, R) composed of a control state of $\mathcal{A}$ and of a region of $\mathcal{R}_M(X)$. There exists a transition $(q, R) \xrightarrow{a} (q', R')$ if, and only if, there exists a transition $q \xrightarrow{g,a,r} q'$ in $\mathcal{A}$, a valuation v in the equivalence class R, and a non-negative duration $t \in \mathbb{R}_+$ such that $v + t \models g$ and $v' = (v + t)[r \leftarrow 0]$ belongs to the equivalence class R'. Note that in this definition, a transition in the region automaton represents an action transition preceded by a delay transition. We could also define transitions in the region automaton to explicitly represent delay transitions in the timed automaton in order to express qualitative properties on time elpasing. We denote by $\mathcal{R}(\mathcal{A})$ the resulting finite-state automaton, which we call *the region automaton*. Recall that operator *Untime* projects a timed language on its untimed component. We can easily prove the following property:

PROPOSITION 9.1 *Let $\mathcal{A}$ be a timed automaton. We have:*

$$\mathcal{L}(\mathcal{R}(\mathcal{A})) = Untime(\mathcal{L}(\mathcal{A}))$$

As a consequence, we obtain:

THEOREM 9.2 ([ALU 94]) *The two following problems are PSPACE-complete:*
- *Checking the emptiness of the language of a timed automaton;*
- *Checking the reachability of a location in a timed automaton.*

These problems are already PSPACE-hard for a fixed number k of clocks, with $k \geq 3$.

These two problems can be reduced to each other by considering accepting locations. PSPACE-membership can be deduced from the construction of the region automaton of a timed automaton, considering the bound given above on the number of regions. Indeed, the number of locations of the region automaton is exponential in the size of the timed automaton, and can thus be stored in polynomial space. Then, an NPSPACE procedure simply guesses the path allowing the location to be reached, and checks that the path is correct with polynomial space. As there are exponentially many locations in the region automaton, the length of this path is at most exponential, and can thus also be stored in polynomial space. We conclude with Savitch's theorem. To prove the PSPACE-hardness, one can encode the behavior of a linearly space bounded Turing machine on a given input. In this encoding, clock values are used to represent the content of the tape during the execution of the Turing machine.

To conclude this section, we illustrate the construction of the region automaton with an example. Consider the timed automaton depicted on Figure 9.3, which has two clocks x and y. The region automaton resulting from the previous definitions is depicted on Figure 9.3(b). In each of its location, the location of the timed automaton and the constraint corresponding to the region are given. The language of this automaton is a^*a^2b. In particular, this shows that in order to reach the accepting location in the timed automaton, the loop should be fired twice around location ℓ_1.

9.2.2. *Other timed models with finite-state abstractions*

Region construction is a very standard tool for proving decidability results in timed systems. In the chapter, we sketch other region constructions for extensions of timed automata or for other timed models.

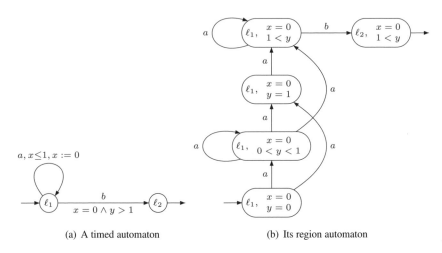

(a) A timed automaton   (b) Its region automaton

Figure 9.3. *A timed automaton and its region automaton*

Extensions of timed automata

Timed automata constitute an extension of finite-state automata equipped with clocks, in which transitions are labeled by conditions on clock values, and by operations of updates on clock values. In the original model of Alur and Dill, conditions are Boolean combinations of comparisons of a clock with a constant and updates are simply resets to zero.

These two aspects can be extended in different ways, and several works have studied such extensions. We briefly present here some of the results established in [BOU 04].

In this work, conditions are extended with so-called *diagonal constraints*. Such constraints are of the form $x - y \sim c$, where x and y are clock variables and $\sim \in \{\leq, <, =, >, \geq\}$. They are called diagonal as they involve the difference between two clocks.

Regarding updates, they consider several extensions of the standard zero reset:
– reset to a constant value different from zero: $x := c$;
– reset to the value of another clock: $x := y$;
– incrementation: $x := x + 1$;
– decrementation: $x := x - 1$;

$\mathcal{U}_0(X)\cup$	Diagonal free constraints	General constraints
$x := c, x := y$	PSPACE-complete	PSPACE-complete
$x := x + 1$		Undecidable
$x := x - 1$	Undecidable	

Table 9.1. *Decidability status of extensions of timed automata*

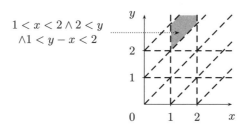

$$1 < x < 2 \wedge 2 < y$$
$$\wedge 1 < y - x < 2$$

Figure 9.4. *Partition compatible with the presence of diagonal constraints*

Denoting $\mathcal{U}_0(X)$ as the standard set of updates allowed in timed automata, some of the results of [BOU 04] are summarized in Table 9.1. Among them, it is interesting to note that while adding decrementation to updates always leads to undecidability, it is possible to allow incrementation if diagonal constraints are not allowed.

To obtain the decidability results presented in this table, the authors exhibit different conditions of compatibility of a set of regions with a set of updates and/or a set of clock conditions. In some cases, it is possible to explicitly build regions verifying these compatibility conditions. We describe such a case below. However, in more involved cases, the author expresses the existence of compatible regions as the solution of a system of diphantine equations, and prove that this sytem always admits a solution. Note that to prove some of these results, we could also reduce the problem to standard timed automata by using automata translations. For instance, this can be done for diagonal constraints [BÉR 98].

Regions in presence of diagonal constraints. We describe here a construction of regions for a system composed of two clocks x and y, containing diagonal constraints, and whose maximal constant is 2. A possible partition of the set of clock valuations is described on Figure 9.4. We can easily verify that this partition ensures property (9.1), and that it is compatible with the reset operation (the result of a region by a reset is still a region). In the general case of a set of clocks X and a maximal constant M, in addition to the constraints defined in section 9.2.1, we have to consider constraints of the form $x - y \leq c$, for any pair of clocks x, y and any $c \in \{0, 1, \ldots, M\}$.

Figure 9.5. *An interrupt timed automaton*

Interrupt timed automata

The model of *interrupt timed automata* has recently been introduced in [BÉR 09] to model multi-task systems with interruptions.

We recalled in Chapter 4 that the class of hybrid automata is undecidable. An interesting subclass is the class of stopwatch automata, which extends timed automata by allowing clock variables to be frozen. However, the reachability problem is also undecidable for this class.

Interrupt timed automata form a subclass of stopwatch automata, where the real valued variables (with rate 0 or 1) are organized along priority levels. As proved in [BÉR 09], untiming languages accepted by these models yields regular languages with the effective construction of a region automaton.

We will not precisely describe the model, but will indicate on how it operates and comment on the proof of decidability. In an interrupt timed automaton, the set of locations is partitioned into interrupt levels, denoted by integers $1, \ldots, n$. In addition, a unique clock is associated with each level, denoted by x_i for level i, and in a location of level i, only clock x_i is active (*i.e.* evolves when time elapses). The clocks from lower levels are suspended, as stopwatches, and those from higher levels are not relevant. Regarding transitions, the guard of a transition leaving a location of level k can be any linear constraint involving clocks $x_1, \ldots, x_k$. Finally, concerning updates, if the transition enters a location of level k' with $k < k'$, then the new clocks $x_{k+1}, \ldots, x_{k'}$ are simply reset to zero. Other clocks can reset using linear constraints involving clocks from *strictly lower* levels. If the transition does not strictly increase the level, then only clocks $x_1, \ldots, x_k$ can be reset, using linear constraints involving clocks from strictly lower levels.

As an example, an interrupt timed automaton considered in [BÉR 09] is depicted in Figure 9.5. In this figure, the level of locations is indicated beside its name. Location q_0 is the initial location with level 1. Locations q_1 and q_2 are on level 2, and location q_2 is the final location. As there are two levels, there are thus two interrupt clocks x_1 and x_2. Consider an execution in this model. The constraint $x_1 < 1$ on the transition labeled by a implies that it is fired after a delay $1 - \tau$, with $0 < \tau \leq 1$, reaching a configuration (q_1, v) where v is the clock valuation defined by $v(x_1) = 1 - \tau$ and $v(x_2) = 0$. Then, the second transition is fired after a delay τ' which must satisfy $(1 - \tau) + 2\tau' = 1$. This yields $\tau' = \frac{\tau}{2}$ and thus the timed language accepted by this interrupt timed automaton is $L = \{(a, 1 - \tau)(b, 1 - \frac{\tau}{2}) \mid 0 < \tau \leq 1\}$. Note in particular that this language *cannot* be accepted by a timed automaton.

The construction of the region automaton for interrupt timed automata extends the construction of [ALU 94] as follows. For timed automata, we defined regions as partitions of the set of clock valuations that respect constraints appearing in the timed automaton, and that are compatible with time elapsing and reset. In the setting of interrupt timed automata, clock constraints are more general as they involve linear constraints on interrupt clocks. Similarly, updates are also more general. Thus, we define here the set E_k of linear constraints for each level k, which can be built in the interrupt timed automaton on level k (this includes guards of level k, but also combinations with updates of higher levels). Then, regions associated with location q are characterized by a total preorder on E_k, for each $1 \leq k \leq \lambda(q)$, where $\lambda(q)$ denotes the level of q. Intuitively, this is used to ensure that two clock valuations belonging to the same region give the same order to all the linear constraints in which they could be evaluated. This implies that the same time elapsing and the same discrete transitions are possible. This can be used to prove the correctness of the construction of a region automaton for interrupt timed automata. As for timed automata, this automaton is time-abstract bisimilar to the original model, and thus it recognizes the untiming of the language of the interrupt timed automaton. The complete description of this procedure, and its application on the example of Figure 9.5 can be found in [BÉR 09].

Time Petri nets

We conclude this subsection with the setting of *time Petri nets*, a model presented in Chapter 4. Note that the set of states of a time Petri net may be infinite for two reasons: on one hand because it can admit an unbounded number of (untimed) markings and, on the other hand, because its semantics is a timed transition system which involves unbounded (and dense) clock valuations.

Most verification problems are undecidable for time Petri nets, and thus for verification issues of this model, one considers *bounded* time Petri nets, i.e. time Petri nets that admit a finite number of (untimed) reachable markings. We will present in the next section decidability results for timed Petri nets, which, however, also have an infinite state space "for two reasons".

Decidability results for bounded time Petri nets rely on the construction of the so-called *state class graph* [BER 83, BER 91], which can be seen as the construction of a region graph. This construction preserves the reachable markings and the LTL properties. Other graph constructions have been proposed that decide the reachability of a configuration of the time Petri net, or that decide whether a CTL property is satisfied [BER 03].

Let $\mathcal{N} = (P, T, \Sigma_\varepsilon, Pre, Post, M_0, \lambda, I)$ be a time Petri net. A *state class* is a pair (M, D) composed of a marking M on places P, and a firing domain D. The firing domain should give, for each enabled transition t, the set of delays after which the timing constraint of t is satisfied. Formally, it is given by a system of linear inequalities involving one variable per enabled transition. Two state classes (M, D) and (M', D') are said *equivalent*, denoted $(M, D) \cong (M', D')$, whenever $M = M'$ and D and D' have equal solution sets.

Notations. Let $t \in T$ be a transition. By definition $I(t)$ gives the interval of firing of t. We denote by $eft(t)$, which stands for the earliest firing time, (resp. $lft(t)$, which stands for the latest firing time) the left-bound (resp. the right-bound) of $I(t)$. In the sequel, we denote by x_t a variable associated with transition t.

The construction of the state class graph proceeds as follows:
Initialization: the initial state class is (M_0, D_0) where D_0 is defined by the following set of inequations: $\{eft(t) \leq x_t \leq lft(t) \mid {}^\bullet t \leq M_0\}$;
New Successor: let (M, D) be a state class built by the procedure. Transition t is firable from (M, D) if and only if the two following conditions are satisfied:

(i) ${}^\bullet t \leq M$ (discrete enabledness), and

(ii) the system $D \wedge \{x_t \leq x_{t'} \mid t' \neq t \wedge {}^\bullet t' \leq M\}$ admits a solution.

Let t be a transition satisfying these conditions, then we build a new state class, denoted (M', D'), which is the successor of (M, D) by the transition t. This state class is defined by $M' = M - {}^\bullet t + t^\bullet$, and D' is obtained by:

(a) $D := D \wedge \{x_t \leq x_{t'} \mid t' \neq t \wedge {}^\bullet t' \leq M\}$;

(b) for each transition u enabled at M', a new variable x'_u is introduced, obeying:
$\qquad x'_u = x_u - x_t$ if the predicate [2] $\uparrow enabled(u, M, t)$ evaluates to false,
$\qquad eft(u) \leq x'_u \leq lft(u)$ otherwise;

(c) variables x_v for $v \in T$ are eliminated by considering an existential quantification for these variables (this is possible in linear arithmetic over real numbers).

In this construction, when a new state class is built, if an equivalent state class (with respect to relation $\cong$ defined above) exists in the graph, then the two nodes of the graph are merged. The equivalence $\cong$ can be checked by transforming the systems of linear inequalities into canonical forms. Indeed, these systems are conjunctions of inequalities on differences of variables. Thus, a canonical form can be obtained by the computation of the strongest constraints, what can be obtained by a "shortest paths" algorithm, for instance the Floyd-Warshall algorithm. Note that while the time complexity of the general Floyd-Warshall algorithm is $O(n^3)$ where n denotes the number of variables, the computation of a canonical form after the above operations can be performed in time $O(n^2)$ if the previous constraints were in canonical form.

---

2. See Chapter 4 for the definition of this predicate.

Then, we can state the following theorem:

THEOREM 9.3 ([BER 83]) *Let $\mathcal{N}$ be a bounded time Petri net, then the state class graph of $\mathcal{N}$ is finite and recognizes the language $Untime(\mathcal{L}(\mathcal{N}))$.*

To conclude this section, we illustrate this construction with an example. We consider the time Petri nets depicted in Figure 4.12 of Chapter 4. The state class graph obtained by the procedure described above applied on this time Petri net is depicted in Figure 9.6. In this figure, we represent the marking and the constraints defining the firing domain in each node state class. On each transition, we write both the name of the transition from the original time Petri net and its label. Note that variable x_i refers to transition t_i. When no transition is enabled in a marking, we denote by $\perp$ the firing domain. Consider the transition labeled by a between markings $p_1 + p_2 + p_3$ and $p_2 + 2p_3$. This corresponds to the firing of transition t_1 of the net. The firing of this transition from this marking does not newly enable transition t_3, but it newly enables transition t_2. As a consequence, the constraint associated with t_3 has been modified, since it is deduced from the fact that at least one time-unit has elapsed to allow the firing of t_1. On the contrary, the constraint associated with t_2 is fresh, as t_2 is newly enabled. Note also that the discrete structure of the graph is different from that of the reachability of the underlying Petri net. Indeed, marking p_3 is represented twice with different constraints.

9.2.3. *Application to the decision of temporal logics*

The region construction of timed automata also has consequences on the decidability results of model checking. We present here two model-checking algorithms for timed automata based on the region automaton construction.

Model checking LTL

The model checking of LTL properties for finite-state systems was presented in subsection 7.4.2. It relies on the construction of a Büchi automaton for the LTL formula, and of its synchronized product with the automaton of the model. Following Proposition 9.1, which states that the untimed language is preserved by the region automaton construction, the same process can be applied on the region automaton, yielding the decidability of the LTL model checking for timed automata.

Model checking TCTL

The timed logic TCTL has been presented in Chapter 4. It constitutes a timed extension of the branching logic CTL. We present here an adaptation of the region automaton construction which allows to decide whether a timed automaton satisfies a property expressed as a TCTL formula.

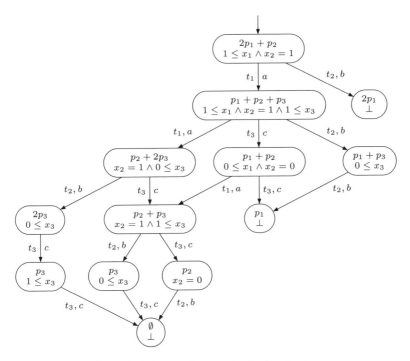

Figure 9.6. *A state class graph of a time Petri net*

THEOREM 9.4 ([ALU 93]) *Model checking TCTL over timed automata is decidable and the problem is PSPACE-complete.*

The model checking of TCTL formulas on timed automata can be reduced to the model checking of a CTL formula on a modified region automaton. We describe here how this procedure works. The central property of the equivalence used above to define the regions of a timed automaton is its consistency with TCTL formula: let $\mathcal{A} = (\Sigma, X, Q, q_0, \Delta)$ be a timed automaton, $\equiv_M$ the associated equivalence relation, $q \in Q$ a state and $v \equiv_M v'$ two equivalent valuations. Then for each formula ϕ of TCTL, $(q, v) \models \phi \iff (q, v') \models \phi$. The proof of this property relies on a notion of equivalence between runs, extending the equivalence between valuations. Then, for model checking, a construction similar to that for the region automaton is performed, which additionally takes into account the formula ϕ that $\mathcal{A}$ must satisfy:

– a new clock z_ϕ (not in X) is added to measure delays associated with subformulas of ϕ. We set $X^* = X \cup \{z_\phi\}$;

– recall that M is the maximal constant associated with $\mathcal{A}$. In order to take into account the constants appearing in the time constraints of the subformulas, we denote the largest of these constants as M_ϕ and we set $M' = \max(M, M_\phi)$.

Then a region automaton $H_\mathcal{A}$ is built from $\mathcal{A}$ with X^* as set of clocks and M' as maximal constant. States are thus elements of the form (q, R), where q is a location of $\mathcal{A}$ and $R \in \mathcal{R}_{M'}(X^*)$ is a region involving one more component than regions on X, corresponding to the values of the special clock z_ϕ. In this construction, the case of boundary regions must also be handled by modifying some transitions (we omit these technical details here). The last step before applying the CTL labeling algorithm is to add atomic propositions $p \sim c$ to label the states of $H_\mathcal{A}$: a state (q, R) is labeled by $p \sim c$ if the value of z_ϕ in the region R satisfies the constraint $z_\phi \sim c$. For instance, to handle a formula like $\phi : AF_{<3}P$, meaning that atomic proposition P will hold on all runs before three time units, we transform the condition for a configuration $(q, v) \models \phi$ into $(q, [v, 0]) \models AF(P \wedge p < 3)$ in $H_\mathcal{A}$.

In other words, from a state where the value of z_ϕ is equal to 0, a state can always be reached where P holds and at the same time the value of z_ϕ is less than 3. The construction is illustrated on the timed automaton of Figure 9.3. This timed automaton has two clocks x and y and 1 as maximal constant 1. We also choose 1 for M_ϕ, so we can deal with formulas using 0 or 1 as constants. The region automaton $H_\mathcal{A}$ is thus built with $M = 1$. For the sake of simplicity, consider only formulas with one level (no nested formulas). Then the clock z is never reset (as clock y in this example) and thus the region automaton $H_\mathcal{A}$ is obtained from the region automaton depicted in Figure 9.3(b) by letting z be equal to y in all regions.

To conclude this section, note that this technique can be adapted to obtain a proce-dure for the model checking of the timed logic L_ν [LAR 95].

9.3. Handling infinite abstractions

The different settings presented in the previous section share the property of admit-ting an equivalence relation of a finite index. This yields a finite number of regions and thus allows decidability results to be deduced. We present here a setting in which the number on regions is infinite, but still yields a decidability result, through additional techniques of infinite state systems (here, well quasi orders). This setting concerns the model of timed Petri nets, an extension of Petri nets which model timed systems. We do not recall here the model as it was presented in Chapter 4.

A lazy semantics

As for the model of time Petri nets, the set of reachable states of a time Petri net may be infinite for two reasons: on the one hand because it can admit an unbounded number of (untimed) markings and, on the other hand, because its semantics involves unbounded (dense) clock valuations. However, as we will see, several problems are decidable for this model. This positive property partly follows from the fact that the semantics of time Petri nets is urgent, while the semantics of timed Petri nets is lazy. In time Petri nets, when a transition is enabled, it cannot get disabled by time elapsing. On the opposite, in timed Petri nets, one can miss the firing of a transition by time elapsing. This induces a monotony property for timed Petri nets, not satisfied by time Petri nets, that is central in the decidability results we present in this section.

9.3.1. *A symbolic representation for timed Petri nets*

Let $\mathcal{N} = (P, T, \Sigma_\varepsilon, Pre, Post, M_0, \Lambda)$ be a timed Petri net where the bounds of intervals are in $\mathbb{N}_{\geq 0} \cup \{\infty\}$. There is no loss of generality in assuming that finite bounds of the net are integers (otherwise we refine the granularity of the regions).

Definition of the Coverability problem. Let N be a finite set of markings with integral ages (again, we could pick rational numbers and refine the granularity). By $N^\uparrow$, we denote the upward closure of N, *i.e.*, the set $\{\nu \mid \exists \nu' \in N, \ \nu' \leq \nu\}$ (where the order is the standard order of $Bag(P \times \mathbb{R}_+)$). The *coverability problem* for $\mathcal{N}$ and set of configurations N asks whether there exists a path in $\mathcal{N}$ from ν_0, the initial configuration of $\mathcal{N}$, to some $\nu \in N^\uparrow$. We prove the following result.

THEOREM 9.5 (Coverability Problem [ABD 01]) *The coverability problem is decidable for timed Petri nets.*

In order to prove this theorem, we introduce the notion of region for timed Petri nets. Such a construction has been done for example in [MAH 05] for timed Petri nets, and has been used recently in several other contexts [OUA 04, OUA 05, LAS 05], and extended to timed Petri nets with read-arcs in [BOU 08a]. By max we denote the maximal integer appearing in the bounds of intervals of the net and in the ages of the tokens in the configurations of N.

DEFINITION 9.6 *A region R for $\mathcal{N}$ is a sequence $a_0 a_1 \ldots a_n a_\infty$ where $n \in \mathbb{N}_{\geq 0}$, for all $0 \leq i \leq n$, $a_i \in Bag(P \times \{0, 1, \ldots, \max\})$ with $size(a_i) \neq 0$ if $i \neq 0$, and $a_\infty \in Bag(P \times \{\infty\})$.*

We first informally explain the semantics of a region. Given the bag of tokens defining a configuration, we obtain its associated region as follows. We put in a_∞ all the tokens whose ages are strictly greater than max and forget their ages. We then put in a_0 the tokens with integral ages and add the information about their ages. Finally, we order the remaining tokens depending on the fractional part of their ages in $a_1, \ldots, a_n$, forget their fractional part, and only store the integral part of their ages. Hence n is the number of different positive fractional values for ages of the remaining tokens. For instance, consider the bag of tokens $(p, 1) + (p, 2.8) + (q, 0.8) + (q, 5.1) + (r, 1.5)$. Then, if the maximal constant is 4, its region encoding will be $a_0 a_1 a_2 a_\infty$ where $a_0 = (p, 1)$ (because there is a single token with integral age), $a_\infty = (q, \infty)$ (because the age of token $(q, 5.1)$ is 5.1, hence above the maximal constant), $a_1 = (r, 1)$ (among all fractional parts, 0.5 is the smallest one), and $a_2 = (p, 2) + (q, 0)$ (all tokens with fractional part 0.8).

We now define more formally the semantics of the regions. Let ϕ be the mapping from $\mathbb{R}_+$ to $\{0, 1, \ldots, \max, \infty\}$ defined by: if $x > \max$ then $\phi(x) = \infty$ else $\phi(x) = \lfloor x \rfloor$. We extend ϕ to $P \times \mathbb{R}_+$ by $\phi((p, x)) = (p, \phi(x))$ and to $Bag(P \times \mathbb{R}_+)$ by linearity. Let us recall the order defined on finite multisets (also called bags). An element $m \in Bag(Z)$ is a mapping with finite domain from Z to $\mathbb{N}$. Given $m, m' \in Bag(Z)$, $m \leq m'$ holds if, and only if, for all $z \in Z$, we have $m(z) \leq m'(z)$. To ease the reading, given $z \in Z$ and $m \in Bag(Z)$, we may also write $z \leq m$ whenever $m(z) \geq 1$.

Let $R = a_0 a_1 \ldots a_n a_\infty$ be a region. Then $[R]$ is a set of configurations ν such that there exist $\nu_1, \nu_2, \ldots, \nu_n, \nu_\infty$ belonging to $Bag(P \times \mathbb{R}_+)$ with:

$- \nu = a_0 + \nu_1 + \nu_2 + \ldots + \nu_n + \nu_\infty$;
$- \forall 1 \leq i \leq n, \phi(\nu_i) = a_i$, and $\phi(\nu_\infty) = a_\infty$;
$- \forall 1 \leq i \leq n, \forall (p, x) + (q, y) \leq \nu_i, 0 < x - \lfloor x \rfloor = y - \lfloor y \rfloor$;
$- \forall 1 \leq i < j \leq n, \forall (p, x) \leq \nu_i, (q, y) \leq \nu_j, x - \lfloor x \rfloor < y - \lfloor y \rfloor$.

Note that every configuration ν belongs to a single region, that we write $R(\nu)$. Conversely, according to the hypothesis, elements of N have integral ages, for any $\nu \in N$, we have $[R(\nu)] = \{\nu\}$. The original coverability problem thus reduces to the coverability problem for finitely many regions, which itself reduces to solve the coverability problem for a single region R.

9.3.2. Coverability of timed Petri nets

We first notice that, given two regions $R = a_0 a_1 \ldots a_n a_\infty$ and $R' = a'_0 a'_1 \ldots a'_{n'} a'_\infty$, we can check whether $[R]^\uparrow \subseteq [R']^\uparrow$: the necessary and sufficient conditions are $a_0 \geq a'_0$, $a_\infty \geq a'_\infty$ and the existence of a strictly increasing mapping ψ from $\{1, \ldots, n'\}$ into $\{1, \ldots, n\}$ such that for every $1 \leq i \leq n'$, $a_{\psi(i)} \geq a'_i$.

We define a partial order between regions by $R \leq R'$ iff $[R']^\uparrow \subseteq [R]^\uparrow$. Then, using Higman's lemma [HIG 52], we can show that this is a well quasi-order, i.e., for every infinite sequence of regions $\{R_i\}_{i \in \mathbb{N}}$ there exist $i < j$ such that $R_i \leq R_j$. Indeed, each region R is a finite sequence of bags over a finite set, hence applying [ABD 01, theorem 1], the above mentioned partial order is a well quasi-order.

The algorithm for solving the coverability problem for the upward closure of a single region R then consists of iteratively computing the predecessors (by time elapsing and by discrete steps) of $[R]^{\uparrow}$. As we will see, each such predecessor is a finite union of upward closures of regions. We stop exploring the predecessors of an upward closure of a region when it is larger (for partial order $\leq$) than an already computed region. Note that all configurations reachable from $[R_2]^{\uparrow}$ are also reachable from $[R_1]^{\uparrow}$ whenever $R_1 \leq R_2$. The computation can then be seen as a finitely branching tree. To prove that it terminates, it is sufficient to prove that this tree is finite. Suppose it is not. By applying König lemma, this tree has an infinite branch. However, as $\leq$ is a well quasi-order, we will eventually obtain a region that is larger than a previous one. This leads to a contradiction. Hence, the computation tree is finite, and the computation terminates. The set of configurations N is covered by the timed Petri net $\mathcal{N}$ if and only if its initial configuration ν_0 occurs in the upward closure of some region of the tree.

Finally we explain how we compute the time and discrete predecessors of the upward closure of a region $R = a_0 a_1 \ldots a_n a_\infty$.

Time predecessors

If a_0 contains a token $(p, 0)$, there is no strict time predecessor of $[R]^{\uparrow}$. Otherwise if $size(a_0) \neq 0$, then the time predecessor is $[R']^{\uparrow}$ with $R' = a'_0 a_1 \ldots a_n a'_{n+1} a_\infty$ where a'_0 is the empty bag and a'_{n+1} is obtained from a_0 by decrementing by 1 the (integral) age of each token. Informally, this operation represents a (reverse) small time elapse such that no token of a_1 reaches an integral value and no token of a_∞ reaches back max.

Otherwise (i.e. $size(a_0) = 0$) we need to choose if tokens of a_1 will first reach an integral value or some tokens of a_∞ will first reach max. It could be the tokens of a_1, a bag of tokens $b_\infty \leq a_\infty$, or both. We only illustrate this last case (which assumes $n \geq 1$). The above mentioned time predecessor is $[R']^{\uparrow}$ where $R' = a'_0 a'_1 \ldots a'_{n-1} a'_\infty$ is obtained as follows.

- $a'_\infty = a_\infty - b_\infty$;
- $a'_0 = a_1 + c_\infty$ where c_∞ is obtained from b_∞ by setting the age of each token to max;
- $\forall 1 \leq i \leq n - 1, a'_i = a_{i+1}$.

Discrete predecessors

We pick a transition t. Recall that in the syntax of a timed Petri net, there exist two mappings Pre and $Post$ from $T \times P$ to the set $\mathcal{I}$ of closed intervals with a lower bound in $\mathbb{N}$ and an upper bound in $\mathbb{N} \cup \{\infty\}$ (we assume that the constants are integers instead of rational numbers, this can be achieved by multiplying all the constants of the system). In addition, the fact that place p is not an input place of transition t corresponds to the case where $Pre(t, p)$ is the empty interval. We introduce an alternative notation for pre- and postconditions. We define $Pre(t) = \sum\limits_{p \mid Post(t,p) \neq \emptyset} (p, Post(t, p))$, and similarly for $Post(t)$. For instance, a transition t consuming a token in place p_1 with interval $[0, 1]$, no token in p_2 and p_3, and a token in place p_4 with interval $[2, 3]$ verifies $Pre(t) = (p_1, [0, 1]) + (p_4, [2, 3])$.

Note that given an interval I of the net and a token (p, x) belonging to some a_i for $i \in \{0, 1, \ldots, n, \infty\}$, we can compute whether, given a configuration belonging to that region, the corresponding token belongs to I. According to the property of the regions, this is independent of the choice of the configuration. We then write $(i, x) \models I$.

We consider the upward closure of the region $a_0 a_1 \ldots a_n a_\infty$, and want to compute its preimage by transition t. Transition t produces a bag of tokens as defined by $Post(t)$. These tokens may appear in one of the a_i's, but this is not required, they may only be in the upward closure. This constitutes an important difference with standard reachability analysis, and comes from the fact that we are interested in a coverability problem. Hence, we choose bags of tokens $\mathsf{post}_i \in Bag(P \times \{0, 1, \ldots, \max\} \times \mathcal{I})$ for every $i \in \{0, 1, \ldots, n\}$ and $\mathsf{post}_\infty \in Bag(P \times \{\infty\} \times \mathcal{I})$ such that [3]

- for all $(p, x, I) \leq \mathsf{post}_i$, $(i, x) \models I$;
- for all $i \in \{0, 1, \ldots, n, \infty\}$, $\pi_{1,2}(\mathsf{post}_i) \leq a_i$;
- $\sum_i \pi_{1,3}(\mathsf{post}_i) \leq Post(t)$.

The bag post_i represents the tokens produced by t which "belong" to a_i. However, there may be additional tokens produced that do not appear in one of the a_i's (this is possible as we consider the upward closure of the region), which is why the two last conditions are inequalities and not equalities. Figure 9.7 illustrates the decomposition. The first condition states that the values of x, i and I in a bag (p, x, I) of post_i are coherent. The second condition states that post_i constitutes a subset of a_i. The third condition states that post_i constitutes a subset of $Post(t)$ (in the second and third conditions, projections are used as a_i contains integral values while $Post(t)$ contains intervals).

Applying this first decomposition, we build an intermediate region $R' = a_0' a_1' \ldots a_n' a_\infty'$ by substracting $\pi_{1,2}(\mathsf{post}_i)$ from a_i for every i and deleting the item in the resulting sequence if its size is null (for $1 \leq i \leq n$).

---

3. $\pi_{1,2}$ (resp. $\pi_{1,3}$) projects bags onto the two first components (resp. onto the first and the third).

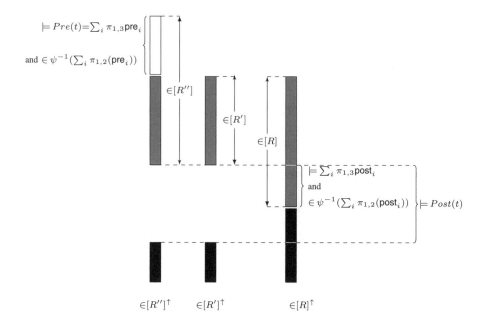

$\models Pre(t)=\sum_i \pi_{1,3}\mathsf{pre}_i$

and $\in \psi^{-1}(\sum_i \pi_{1,2}(\mathsf{pre}_i))$

$\in [R'']$

$\in [R']$

$\in [R]$

$\models \sum_i \pi_{1,3}\mathsf{post}_i$

and

$\in \psi^{-1}(\sum_i \pi_{1,2}(\mathsf{post}_i))$ $\models Post(t)$

$\in [R'']^\uparrow$ $\qquad$ $\in [R']^\uparrow$ $\qquad$ $\in [R]^\uparrow$

Figure 9.7. *Decomposition of the set of tokens for the discrete predecessor computation*

Then, to really simulate the discrete transition t, we need to initially have all to-kens that are consumed by the pre-arcs. We set bags of tokens $\mathsf{pre}_i \in Bag(P \times \{0,1,\ldots,\max\} \times \mathcal{I})$ for every $i \in \{0,1,\ldots,n''\}$ for some integer n'', $\mathsf{pre}_\infty \in Bag(P \times \{\infty\} \times \mathcal{I})$ and a strictly increasing mapping ψ from $\{1,\ldots,n'\}$ into $\{1,\ldots,n''\}$ such that:

– for all $(p,x,I) \leq \mathsf{pre}_i$, $(i,x) \models I$;
– $a_0'' = a_0' + \pi_{1,2}(\mathsf{pre}_0)$;
– $a_\infty'' = a_\infty' + \pi_{1,2}(\mathsf{pre}_\infty)$,
– for every $i \in \{1,\ldots,n''\}$, if there exists j such that $\psi(j) = i$ then $a_i'' = a_j' + \pi_{1,2}(\mathsf{pre}_i)$, otherwise $a_i'' = \pi_{1,2}(\mathsf{pre}_i)$;
– $\sum_i \pi_{1,3}(\mathsf{pre}_i) = Pre(t)$.

The bags pre_i are the tokens required by the pre-arcs of the transition. See Figure 9.7 for an illustration of the construction.

Under those conditions, the region $R'' = a_0'' a_1'' \ldots a_{n''}'' a_\infty''$ is a predecessor by t of $[R]^\uparrow$. Note that the constructed region R'' depends on the various choices we have made (all bags post_i, pre, and also the indices n', n'', the mapping ψ). For each of these (finitely many) choices, it gives a region that is in the preimage of R by t (indeed, take any configuration $\nu'' \in [R'']^\uparrow$, then quite straightforwardly, any configuration image of ν by t is in $[R]^\uparrow$), and all regions in the preimage by t can, of course, be obtained in that way.

Hence, time predecessors and discrete predecessors of regions are finite unions of regions, and can be effectively computed, which concludes the proof of the theorem.

9.3.3. *Survey of decidable properties for timed Petri nets*

We have presented in the previous sections how a region construction with infinitely many regions can be used to prove the decidability of the coverability problem for timed Petri nets. It is worth noticing that this model, which combines dense-time with an unbounded control structure (represented here by the tokens), is very difficult to analyze. In this section, we will present several decidability results, which, for most of them, relies on the techniques presented previously. These results are taken from [ABD 07, BOU 08a].

Token liveness

As the semantics of timed Petri nets is lazy, we can miss the firing of a transition. As a consequence, it may happen that a token can no longer be used in the firing of a transition, in which case we say that the token is not live anymore. More formally, a marking is composed of a finite set of tokens, and each token is characterized by the place p in which it lies and by its age, given as a non-negative real number x (a token is thus represented by the pair (p, x)). Let M be a marking, and (p, x) a token in M. The token (p, x) is called *live* from marking M in a timed Petri net $\mathcal{N}$ if there exists a sequence of transitions in $\mathcal{N}$, starting from M, which eventually consumes the token. Conversely, if a token is not live, then we say that it is a *dead* token. Formally, we say that the token (p, x) can be consumed in M if there exists a transition t satisfying the following properties:

– t is enabled in M; and

– $x \in Post(t, p)$.

Given a timed Petri net $\mathcal{N}$, a marking M; and a token (p, x) in M, the problem of token liveness consists of deciding whether (p, x) is live or not. This problem is called the semantic liveness of tokens. Without loss of generality, we assume that the ages of tokens composing the marking M are all integers.

THEOREM 9.7 ([ABD 07]) *The semantic liveness of tokens is decidable in timed Petri nets.*

The proof of this result is proceeded by a direct reduction to (several instances of) the coverability problem. As we have seen that this problem is decidable for timed Petri nets, the result follows. We briefly describe how the reduction works.

We define the timed Petri net $\mathcal{N}'$ as follows. The set of places is obtained by substituting of place p with a new place p', not connected to any transition. The initial marking is the marking $M_{init} = M - (p, x) + (p', x)$. Finally, the set of target markings N is defined as follows. Let t be a transition such that p is an input place of t. Then we write $Pre(t) = \sum_{i=1}^{n}(p_i, I_i) + (p, I)$. We define the set of markings N_t as:

$$N_t = \left\{ \sum_{i=1}^{n}(p_i, \tau_i) + (p', x') \mid \forall i, \tau_i \in I_i \wedge x' \in I \right\}$$

This set can be represented as a finite union of regions. We then define the set N as the union of sets N_t over the transitions t having p as input place. In this construction, we move the token from place p to a fictive place p' where it cannot be used, it will only get older as time elapses. Then, we look for markings, composed of tokens with integral ages, that allow a transition involving place p to be fired. We can easily prove that the token (p, x) is live if, and only if, the set of markings N can be covered.

Boundedness

We say that an untimed Petri net is bounded if, and only if, there exists a bound $k \in \mathbb{N}$ such that all its reachable markings have at most k tokens in each place. In particular, a bounded Petri net has a finite reachability set. For timed Petri nets, we will also be interested by bounding the number of tokens. However, this will not yield a finite reachability set because of the ages of the tokens.

Two notions of boundedness are distinguished, whether dead tokens are counted or not:

– syntactic boundedness: does a bound $k \in \mathbb{N}$ exist such that all reachable markings are composed of at most k tokens?

– semantic boundedness: does a bound $k \in \mathbb{N}$ exist such that all reachable markings are composed of at most k *alive* tokens?

The following theorem is stated in [ABD 07]:

THEOREM 9.8 ([ABD 07]) *The syntactic boundedness is decidable for timed Petri nets. The semantic boundedness is undecidable for timed Petri nets.*

The undecidability result is proven by a reduction in the problem of space boundedness for lossy counter machines. Details can be found in [MAH 05]. For the decidability result, we consider an algorithm similar to the Karp-Miller algorithm [KAR 69] to solve the boundedness problem for Petri nets. This algorithm builds a tree labeled by markings and, when a new marking is added, checks whether one of the ancestors is strictly dominated. If this is the case, then the number of reachable markings is unbounded. We can consider a similar algorithm, in which nodes of the trees are labeled by regions. The termination of the algorithm is guaranteed due to the fact that the inclusion ordering on regions is a well-quasi-ordering (see subsection 9.3.2).

Zenoness

Zeno behaviors are executions that perform an infinite number of actions in a finite amount of time. Such time-convergent behaviors are unrealistic in practice. For timed automata, the existence of such behaviors can be decided using the region graph. One can also consider this problem for timed Petri nets:

– zenoness: given a timed Petri net $\mathcal{N}$ and a marking M, does a Zeno execution in $\mathcal{N}$ exist that starts in M?

– universal zenoness: given a timed Petri net $\mathcal{N}$ and a marking M, are all infinite runs of $\mathcal{N}$ issued from M Zeno runs?

Note that the negation problem is the problem of the existence of an infinite non-Zeno execution.

The following theorem is stated in [ABD 07]:

THEOREM 9.9 ([ABD 07]) *The Zenoness is decidable for timed Petri nets. The universal Zenoness is undecidable for timed Petri nets.*

We will not give the details of the proofs of these results as they rely on sophisticated techniques of Petri nets. More precisely, the decidability result uses a characterization of the set of markings admitting an infinite computation in an extension of standard Petri nets, which is a subclass of transfer nets.

Extension to read arcs

We conclude with an extension of our first result on the coverability. The construction we have presented can be extended to the setting of timed Petri nets with read arcs. Read arcs allow a transition to test the presence of some tockens in a place, without consuming them (in particular their age is left unchanged). It can be shown that read arcs allow the expressiveness of timed automata to subsumed (see [BOU 08a]).

THEOREM 9.10 ([BOU 08a]) *The coverability problem is decidable for timed Petri nets with read arcs.*

9.4. Robustness issues in timed systems

In this section, we present issues related to the implementation of timed systems, and more specifically a recent approach proposed for the class of timed automata.

9.4.1. *Motivations*

The verification of real-time systems is now a well-established procedure, with efficient algorithms and scalable tools. However, the timed models used suffer from mathematical idealization, which makes their implementation problematic. For instance, timed automata are governed by an idealized, theoretical semantics, and their implementation on real hardware could fail to satisfy their mathematically proved properties. More precisely, timed automata assume that clocks are continuous and infinitely precise, while CPU have a finite frequency and are digital.

A well-known difficulty is the case of so-called Zeno behaviors, in which an infinite number of actions can occur in a finite amount of time, which naturally correspond to unrealistic physical behaviors. The difficulties of implementation for timed systems are, however, not limited to the non-Zenoness property. As an illustration, we recall on Figure 9.8 a timed automaton presented in [CAS 02]. In this example, location 4 is considered to be a bad location that should be avoided. Thus, the system should be able to perform infinite executions around locations 1, 2, and 3. It can be shown that infinite executions admitted by this timed automaton must go "faster and faster". More precisely, one cycle through these three locations must last exactly one time unit because of the timing constraints on x between locations 1 and 2. In addition, before firing the last transition of the cycle (from 3 to 1), the execution must let some time elapse (because of the constraint on z). We denote this value by d_i for the i-th execution of the loop. Then, valuation v_i obtained when entering location 1 after the i-th loop is defined by $v_i(x) = \sum_{j \leq i} d_j$, $v_i(y) = 0$ and $v_i(z) = d_i$. As a consequence, in order to obtain an infinite execution, delay d_i must be choosen so as to verify the inequality $\sum_{i \geq 1} d_i < 1$. For instance, a possible execution is obtained by letting $d_i = \frac{1}{2^{i+1}}$. As a consequence, the delays between the last two transitions of the cycle must converge towards 0. In particular, no discrete-time execution can verify this property, no matter how fine the granularity. As a consequence, any implementation of such an automaton will eventually fail to satisfy that property, and will finally reach location 4.

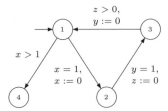

Figure 9.8. *A timed automaton admitting no discrete-time implementation*

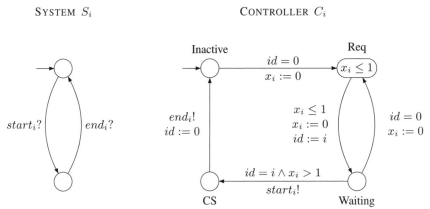

Figure 9.9. *Timed automata models for the Fischer protocol*

Consider the example of the Fischer protocol for ensuring mutual exclusion: two systems S_1 and S_2 want to access a critical section; they are supervised by two controllers in charge of ensuring that they will not simultaneously access the critical section. Figure 9.9 represents a system and its controller. We can show, using a verification tool such as Uppaal [BEH 04], HyTech [HEN 97], or Kronos [DAW 96], that mutual exclusion is ensured by these controllers. Intuitively, the protocol works as follows. A shared integer variable id is used to store the identifier of the process allowed to enter the critical section. More precisely, this variable initially has value 0. Then, when process S_i moves from location Req to location Waiting, it sets this variable to value i, and checks that $id = i$ when it enters location CS. In addition to this untimed rule, timing constraints are used to ensure that a process cannot decide to enter the critical section (by setting variable id to its identifier) when another process is already in its critical section.

However, this property greatly depends on the infinite precision (i.e. exact) of the model of timed automata. In particular, it relies on the fact that guard $x_i > 1$

is strict. Indeed, it ensures, combined with invariant $x_i \leq 1$ of location Req, that when a process S_i can reach its critical section, then no other process S_j can lie in location Req. Thus, relaxing constraing $x_i > 1$ in constraint $x_i \geq 1$ results in an incorrect system, thus proving its brittleness. For instance, if clocks are digital, or if clocks are not perfectly synchronized, or if there are some communication delays between systems, or again if delays of write/read actions slow down the system, then transitions may be performed at time stamps that are not allowed in the mathematical model. Of course, such imprecisions are unavoidable in physical devices, and thus the mutual exclusion can be violated.

9.4.2. *A parametric semantics to handle imprecisions of clock valuations*

Following the example of the Fischer protocol, some properties related to the idealization of timed models cannot be satisfied by physical devices. We list some of them:

1) perfect synchronization of the different components of the system, inputs reception without delay, output production without delay;

2) infinite precision of clocks;

3) instantaneous execution of actions (infinite speed of the system while evaluating guards, and choosing which action to fire).

A real system, when it simulates the behavior of a timed automaton, cannot fire transitions in zero time. Similarly, the variables it manipulates have a finite precision, and synchronizations between processes are not instantaneous. The standard hypothesis allowing these issues to be ignored consists of assuming that the delays related to computation times or message exchanges are negligible with respect to constants used in the guards and invariants of the timed automaton. However, this approach does not rely on any mathematical justification.

In order to handle the different imperfections of a real system, a new semantics, called the **AASAP** ("almost as soon as possible") semantics, was introduced in [DEW 05] for timed automata. This semantics relaxes the hypotheses that were too strong in the classical semantics. The **AASAP** semantics can be seen as a relaxation of the standard **ASAP** ("as soon as possible") semantics. Formally, these two semantics are defined as timed transition systems. We do not present them here, but rather describe their main characteristics. We refer the reader to [DEW 05] for a complete presentation.

The notion of timed simulation, introduced in Chapter 4 for timed transition systems, is the key tool to compare semantics. Indeed, such relations preserve safety properties, but more generally, they preserve properties expressing a universal quantification over executions, such as LTL [PNU 77] or ACTL [BRO 88].

The **ASAP** semantics requires a transition to be fired or to react to an input *as soon as possible*. In the **AASAP** semantics, a parameter Δ is given, and intuitively the system should react within Δ time units. The main characteristics of this semantics can be summarized as follows:

– an enabled transition does not need to be fired instantaneously, but must be fired within Δ time units;

– the durations of emission and reception of messages are taken into account: a distinction is made between the emission of a signal by a component and its reception by another component. The delay between these two actions is bounded by Δ;

– the precision of clocks is relaxed: guards of transitions are enlarged by Δ.

The **AASAP** semantics of $\mathcal{A}$ for parameter Δ is denoted $[\![\mathcal{A}]\!]^{AASAP}$, and verifies the following property:

PROPOSITION 9.11 ("Faster is better" [DEW 05, theorem 3]) *Let $\mathcal{A}$ be a timed automaton, and $\Delta_1, \Delta_2 \in \mathbb{Q}_{>0}$ such that $\Delta_2 \leq \Delta_1$, then the timed transition system $[\![\mathcal{A}]\!]^{AASAP}_{\Delta_2}$ is simulated by $[\![\mathcal{A}]\!]^{AASAP}_{\Delta_1}$, denoted by $[\![\mathcal{A}]\!]^{AASAP}_{\Delta_2} \sqsubseteq [\![\mathcal{A}]\!]^{AASAP}_{\Delta_1}$.*

Intuitively, this means that increasing the precision of the system reduces the set of admissible behaviors. Thus, with respect to the verification of universal path properties, if the model $[\![\mathcal{A}]\!]^{AASAP}_{\Delta_1}$ verifies the property, then so does $[\![\mathcal{A}]\!]^{AASAP}_{\Delta_2}$.

In order to build a link with the implementation of a timed automaton, a *program semantics* is introduced, representing the behavior of a real execution platform. We describe the model considered for this platform. The procedure simulating the timed automaton repeatedly executes the following cycle of instructions:

1) the current time is read in the clock register of the processor and stored in a variable T;

2) the list of input signals is updated: sensors are checked to detect whether signals have been emitted by other components;

3) timing constraints of the output transitions of the current location of the timed automaton are evaluated with the value of T. If one of these conditions is satisfied, then one of the firable transitions is taken.

The program semantics of $\mathcal{A}$ depends on two parameters Δ_P, Δ_L and is denoted by $[\![\mathcal{A}]\!]^{Prog}_{\Delta_L, \Delta_P}$. These two parameters represent the performance of the platform. More precisely, they are defined as follows:

1) the clock register is incremented every Δ_P time units;

2) the time necessary to process one cycle of instructions is less or equal than Δ_L.

The fundamental result that links the two previously introduced semantics is:

THEOREM 9.12 (Simulation [DEW 05, theorem 4]) *Let $\mathcal{A}$ be a timed automaton and $\Delta, \Delta_P, \Delta_L \in \mathbb{Q}_{>0}$ three rational parameters. Then if the inequality $3\Delta_L + 4\Delta_P \leq \Delta$ is satisfied, the associated transition systems verify:*

$$[\![\mathcal{A}]\!]^{Prog}_{\Delta_L, \Delta_P} \sqsubseteq [\![\mathcal{A}]\!]^{AASAP}_{\Delta}$$

As for any positive Δ, it is always possible to find parameters values of Δ_L and Δ_P verifying the above inequality, this result establishes that if the **AASAP** semantics is correct for some value of Δ, then there exists a correct implementation of $\mathcal{A}$.

Finally, we present a last result, stating that the **AASAP** semantics can be simulated by a syntactic transformation of timed automata, involving a parameter.

THEOREM 9.13 ([DEW 05, theorem 8]) *Let $\mathcal{A}$ be a timed automaton and $\Delta \in \mathbb{Q}_{>0}$. It is possible to build a timed automaton $\mathcal{F}(\mathcal{A}, \Delta)$ such that:*

$$[\![\mathcal{A}]\!]^{AASAP}_{\Delta} \sqsubseteq [\![\mathcal{F}(\mathcal{A}, \Delta)]\!] \text{ and } [\![\mathcal{F}(\mathcal{A}, \Delta)]\!] \sqsubseteq [\![\mathcal{A}]\!]^{AASAP}_{\Delta}$$

The main operation involved in the definition of $\mathcal{F}(\mathcal{A}, \Delta)$ is the enlargment of guards and invariants by Δ. Intuitively, this consists in replacing a constraint of the form $x \in [a, b]$ by the constraint $x \in [a - \Delta, b + \Delta]$. As the other transformations involved in $\mathcal{F}(\mathcal{A}, \Delta)$ are less important, we consider in the chapter a parametric semantics of timed automata:

DEFINITION 9.14 (Enlarged semantics) *Let $\mathcal{A}$ be a timed automaton. We define the enlarged semantics of $\mathcal{A}$ as a parametric semantics depending on a rational parameter Δ. It is defined by the timed transition system associated with the timed automaton obtained from $\mathcal{A}$ by enlarging all guards and invariants of Δ, and denoted by $[\![\mathcal{A}]\!]_{\Delta}$.*

The problem of interest is to decide whether a positive value of Δ exists for which the enlarged semantics meets a specification given by a universal property on executions.

9.4.3. *Related work*

Recently, several works have proposed approaches to ensure implementability of timed models. In this section, we present one of them, which relies on a parametric enlargment of timed automata. We present a short survey of related works:

– this approach using the **AASAP** semantics contrasts with a modeling-based solution proposed in [ALT 05], where the behavior of the platform is modelled as a timed automaton. While this approach offers a very rich framework to model the platform, it suffers from two drawbacks. First, it does not verify the "faster is better property" (if a model is implementable on an implementation, then it should also be the case on any "faster" implemention). Second, verification problems are difficult and the approach of [ALT 05] does not offer decidability results;

– other works has introduced other notions of "robustness" in order to relax the mathematical idealization of the semantics of timed automata [GUP 97, OUA 03, BAI 07b, BAI 07a]. Those approaches are different from ours, since they roughly consist of dropping "isolated" or "unlikely" executions;

– these results should also be compared with tools related to code generation from timed automata. The TIMES tool [AMN 03] automatically generates executable code from timed automata. However, it does not take into account the imprecisions, as it relies on the perfect synchrony paradigm. Henzinger *et al.* proposed in [HEN 03] a model for embedded systems, called GIOTTO, which can be seen as an intermediary step beween timed automata and real platforms.

9.4.4. *Decidability result for safety properties*

We consider here a safety property, which is given by a set of locations of the timed automaton that should be avoided and is denoted **Bad**. Thus, in the enlarged semantics, the problem we want to solve is the following: does there exist a positive value of Δ such that $Reach(\llbracket A \rrbracket_\Delta)$ does not intersect **Bad**?

This problem has been solved in [PUR 00, DEW 08], under some assumptions on timed automata that we recall here. In this subsection, we assume that the timed automata we consider satisfy the following requirements:

– all guards and invariants involve non-strict inequalities;

– all the clocks are always bounded;

– all the cycles of the region graph are *progress cycles*, i.e. do reset all clocks to zero.

The first hypothesis does not change the expressive power of the model under the enlarged semantics. The second hypothesis is not really restrictive since every timed automaton can be transformed into such a bounded timed automaton (see for example [BEH 01]). Note that it entails that any time-divergent path contains an infinite number of action transitions. As mentioned in [DEW 08], the third requirement is less restrictive than classical strong-non-Zenoness assumptions.

The proof of the decidability result relies on the following proposition:

PROPOSITION 9.15 *Let A be a timed automaton, and **Bad** be a set of locations. We have:*

$$\exists \Delta > 0 \mid Reach(\llbracket A \rrbracket_\Delta) \cap \textbf{Bad} = \emptyset \iff \left(\bigcap_{\Delta>0} Reach(\llbracket A \rrbracket_\Delta) \right) \cap \textbf{Bad} = \emptyset$$

Intuitively, this property follows from the fact that two subsets of $\mathbb{R}^n_{\geq 0}$, defined by zones [4] with integral constraints, and whose intersection is empty, are at distance at least $\frac{1}{n}$. In addition, as all guards are non-strict, we can prove that all sets involved in the proposition verify these conditions.

As a consequence, the problem is reduced to the computation of the set $Reach^*(\llbracket A \rrbracket)$ defined as $\bigcap_{\Delta>0} Reach(\llbracket A \rrbracket_\Delta)$. This set exactly contains configurations that are reachable for any *positive* value of the parameter.

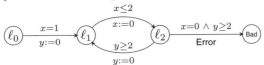

Figure 9.10. *A timed automaton A*

This set can differ from the set $Reach(\llbracket A \rrbracket)$. As an illustration, consider the timed automaton depicted in Figure 9.10, and where ρ is the simple cycle around locations ℓ_1 and ℓ_2. The two corresponding sets are depicted on Figure 9.11, together with the sets of reachable configurations after one and two executions of cycle ρ. In this example, the guard enlargment allows the first transition of the cycle (from ℓ_1 to ℓ_2) to be fired a bit after the constraint $x = 2$ is satisfied and the second transition to be fired a bit before the constraint $y = 2$ is satisfied. As a consequence, this allows location ℓ_1 to be reached, after one loop, with a clock valuation of $v(x) = 1 - 3\Delta$ and $v(y) = 0$ (see Figure 9.10). This slight perturbation can be accumulated by iterating the cycle, after a second loop, a clock valuation of $v(x) = 1 - 5\Delta$ and $v(y) = 0$ is obtained (see Figure 9.10). As a consequence, however small Δ is, any valuation of the set $Reach^*(\llbracket A \rrbracket)$ can be reached after a sufficient number of iterations of the cycle.

---

4. A zone is defined by a conjunction of lower and upper bounds on clocks and clock differences.

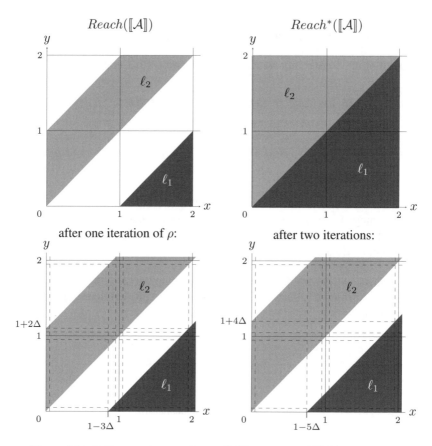

Figure 9.11. *Differences between $Reach(\llbracket \mathcal{A} \rrbracket)$ and $Reach^*(\llbracket \mathcal{A} \rrbracket)$, and intermediate computations of the reachable configurations in $\llbracket \mathcal{A} \rrbracket_\Delta$*

Algorithm 5 can be used to compute the set $Reach^*(\llbracket \mathcal{A} \rrbracket)$, which was proposed in [PUR 00]. This algorithm relies on the region graph construction presented in section 9.2. In its presentation, notation $Reach(\mathcal{R}(\mathcal{A}), J^*)$ denotes the set of reachable states from J^* in $\mathcal{R}(\mathcal{A})$. In addition, given a region R of a timed automaton, its topological closure is denoted $\overline{R}$, and this notation is extended to sets of regions.

The proof of correction of the algorithm is long and technical, and thus we only briefly describe it. The proof proceeds by double inclusion. To prove the soundness of the algorithm, i.e. the inclusion $J^* \subseteq Reach^*(\llbracket \mathcal{A} \rrbracket)$, the authors show a key lemma stating that two configurations belonging to the topological closure of a same strongly connected component can reach each other, for any postive value of Δ. For the completeness, the authors prove a bound between the distance of a run in the enlarged

Input: a timed automaton $\mathcal{A}$
Output: the enlarged reachability set $Reach^*(\llbracket \mathcal{A} \rrbracket)$

1 Compute the region graph $\mathcal{R}(\mathcal{A}) = (\Gamma, \gamma_0, \rightarrow)$
2 Compute the set $\mathcal{S}$ of strongly connected components of $\mathcal{R}(\mathcal{A})$
3 $J^* := \{\gamma_0\}$
4 $J^* := Reach(\mathcal{R}(\mathcal{A}), J^*)$
5 **while** $\exists S \in \mathcal{S}$ such that $S \not\subseteq J^*$ and $J^* \cap \overline{S} \neq \emptyset$ **do**
6 $\quad \big|\quad J^* := J^* \cup \overline{S}$
7 $\quad \big\lfloor\quad J^* := Reach(\mathcal{R}(\mathcal{A}), J^*)$
8 Return J^*;

Algorithm 5: *Computation of the set $Reach^*(\mathcal{A})$*

semantics and a run in the standard semantics, depending on the parameter Δ. Using the fact that long paths will necessarily go through strongly connected components, they prove that this bound vanishes when $\Delta \rightarrow 0$. Finally, we obtain the following theorem.

THEOREM 9.16 *Let $\mathcal{A}$ be a timed automaton and **Bad** be a subset of locations of $\mathcal{A}$. One can decide whether there exists a positive value of parameter Δ such that $Reach(\llbracket \mathcal{A} \rrbracket_\Delta) \cap \textbf{Bad} = \emptyset$. In addition, this problem is PSPACE-complete.*

Recall that the emptiness problem for timed automata is already PSPACE-complete (theorem 9.2).

9.4.5. *Other results and current challenges*

This semantical approach to the robustness and implementability of timed automata has been extended in several works in the recent years. We describe here some of these results.

Symbolic computations

First, as we mentionned in the introduction, the decidability results based on the region graph construction do not yield efficient algorithms. In [DAW 06], a symbolic algorithm is proposed for the computation of $Reach^*(\mathcal{A})$. This algorithm uses zones as a symbolic representation of clock valuations. The computation of the strongly connected components of the region graph is replaced by a notion of stable zone of a cycle, which corresponds intuitively to the set of valuations that are connected through this cycle, regardless how small the perturbation is. The authors prove that the stable zone can be computed as a greatest fixpoint. However, their approach only handles flat timed automata, as the computation of the stable zone must be done for each cycle of the system. Flat means here that the system does not contain nested cycles.

Another perturbation

In the seminal paper by Puri [PUR 00], the notion of guard enlargment is introduced, and also a notion of drift of clocks. This is formalized, given a positive rational number $\varepsilon > 0$, by modifying the semantics of the timed automaton by allowing clocks to have a rate in the interval $[1 - \varepsilon, 1 + \varepsilon]$. As a consequence, clocks may not evolve at the same speed.

This notion of perturbation is very attractive, as it intuitively corresponds to actual flaws of real systems. It turns out to be equivalent to guard enlargement. More formally, it was proved in [PUR 00, DEW 08] that a similar definition of the set $Reach^*(\mathcal{A})$ for clock drift yields the same set. The two perturbations can be combined and this still yields the same set of configurations (see [DEW 08] for a detailed proof).

Robust verification

The results presented so far concern safety properties. In [BOU 06, BOU 08b], the robust verification is considered for other properties such as temporal properties. First, it is proven that the robust model-checking of LTL properties is PSPACE-complete, as for standard model-checking. Second, an expressive fragment of the timed logic MTL is proposed, for which the robust model-checking is also decidable. This fragment encompasses the logic LTL, the bounded fragment of MTL, and can express interesting properties such as bounded response-time. Again, the complexity obtained is the same as for standard model-checking.

Quantitative robustness

Using the previous results, we can decide whether a positive perturbation exists for which the property is satisfied. In [JAU 11], a more difficult problem is tackled, which consists of computing the largest value of the parameter for the system to meet the specification. The authors propose a parametric extension of the symbolic algorithm introduced in [DAW 06], which allows the set of reachable states in the timed automaton to be computed, for all values of the parameter, which corresponds to the parametric reachability set. However, as for [DAW 06], the algorithm only applies to flat timed automata.

Current challenges

This semantical approach of robustness opens promising perspectives for research. Among them, we can mention the problem of robust control. This problem consists of synthesizing a controller, for instance from a timed game specification, which is robust, i.e. such that a positive enlargment exists for which the enlarged controller still ensures that the system under control is correct. This problem has been investigated in [CHA 08], but only for a fixed value of the enlargment.

9.5. Conclusion

Real-time aspects are central to the design of many applications, such as embedded systems. We have presented in this chapter how verification techniques can be extended to timed systems. Therefore, we have focused on the notion of region, which consists of gathering configurations of the system in equivalence classes, yielding a quotient system on which the property can be checked.

In addition to region constructions, existing tools for the verification of timed systems may also use other symbolic techniques such as zones (see Uppaal [BEH 04], Romeo [GAR 05]). Recently, several case studies have proven that these tools have reached a level of maturity that allows them to tackle relevant industrial problems.

Current works are investigating extensions to these techniques to more complex models. We have presented recent works related to the implementability of timed systems. Among other directions, let us mention two-player games, which are useful for controller synthesis problems; the extensions to weighted systems which allow variables with more complex dynamics than clock variables to modeled; and probabilistic systems, used for instance to model communication protocols.

9.6. Bibliography

[ABD 01] ABDULLA P. A., NYLÉN A., "Timed Petri nets and BQOs", in *Proc. 22nd International Conference on Application and Theory of Petri Nets (ICATPN'01)*, vol. 2075 of *LNCS*, Springer, p. 53–70, 2001.

[ABD 07] ABDULLA P. A., MAHATA P., MAYR R., "Dense-timed Petri nets: checking Zenoness, token liveness and boundedness", *Logical Methods in Computer Science*, vol. 3, num. 1, p. 1–61, 2007.

[ALT 05] ALTISEN K., TRIPAKIS S., "Implementation of timed automata: an issue of semantics or modeling?", in *Proc. 3rd International Conference on Formal Modeling and Analysis of Timed Systems (FORMATS'05)*, vol. 3829 of *LNCS*, Springer, p. 273-288, 2005.

[ALU 90] ALUR R., DILL D., "Automata for modeling real-time systems", in *Proc. 17th International Colloquium on Automata, Languages and Programming (ICALP'90)*, vol. 443 of *LNCScience*, Springer, p. 322–335, 1990.

[ALU 93] ALUR R., COURCOUBETIS C., DILL D., "Model-checking in dense real-time", *Information and Computation*, vol. 104, num. 1, p. 2–34, 1993.

[ALU 94] ALUR R., DILL D., "A Theory of timed automata", *Theoretical Computer Science*, vol. 126, num. 2, p. 183–235, 1994.

[AMN 03] AMNELL T., FERSMAN E., MOKRUSHIN L., PETTERSSON P., YI W., "TIMES: A tool for schedulability analysis and code generation of real-time systems", in *Proc. 1st International Workshop on Formal Modeling and Analysis of Timed Systems (FORMATS'03)*, vol. 2791 of *LNCS*, Springer, p. 60–72, 2003.

[BAI 07a] BAIER C., BERTRAND N., BOUYER P., BRIHAYE TH., GRÖSSER M., Almost-sure model checking of infinite paths in one-clock timed automata, Research Report num. LSV-07-29, ENS Cachan, France, 2007.

[BAI 07b] BAIER C., BERTRAND N., BOUYER P., BRIHAYE TH., GRÖSSER M., "Probabilistic and topological semantics for timed automata", in*Proc. 27th Conf. Found. Softw. Tech. & Theor. Comp. Sci. (FSTTCS'07)*, vol. 4855 of *LNCS*, Springer, p. 179–191, 2007.

[BEH 01] BEHRMANN G., FEHNKER A., HUNE TH., LARSEN K. G., PETTERSSON P., ROMIJN J., VAANDRAGER F., "Minimum-cost reachability for priced timed automata", *in Proc. 4th International Workshop on Hybrid Systems: Computation and Control (HSCC'01)*, vol. 2034 of *LNCS*, Springer, p. 147–161, 2001.

[BEH 04] BEHRMANN G., DAVID A., LARSEN K. G., "A tutorial on UPPAAL", in *Proc. 4th International School on Formal Methods for the Design of Computer, Communication and Software Systems: Real Time (SFM-04:RT)*, vol. 3185 of *LNCS*, Springer, p. 200–236, 2004.

[BER 83] BERTHOMIEU B., MENASCHE M., "An enumerative approach for analyzing time Petri nets", in *Proc. 9th IFIP Congress*, Elsevier Science Publishers, p. 41–46, 1983.

[BER 91] BERTHOMIEU B., DIAZ M., "Modeling and verification of time dependent systems using time Petri nets", *IEEE Transactions in Software Engineering*, vol. 17, num. 3, p. 259–273, 1991.

[BÉR 98] BÉRARD B., DIEKERT V., GASTIN P., PETIT A., "Characterization of the expressive power of silent transitions in timed automata", *Fundamenta Informaticae*, vol. 36, num. 2–3, p. 145–182, 1998.

[BER 03] BERTHOMIEU B., VERNADAT F., "State Class Constructions for Branching Analysis of Time Petri Nets", *Proc. 9th International Conference on Tools and Algorithms for the Construction and Analysis of Systems (TACAS'03)*, vol. 2619 of *Lecture Notes in Computer Science*, Springer, p. 442–457, 2003.

[BÉR 09] BÉRARD B., HADDAD S., "Interrupt timed automata", in *Proc. 12th International Conference on Foundations of Software Science and Computation Structures (FoSSaCS'09)*, vol. 5504 of *LNCS*, Springer, p. 197-211, 2009.

[BOU 04] BOUYER P., DUFOURD C., FLEURY E., PETIT A., "Updatable timed automata", *Theoretical Computer Science*, vol. 321, num. 2–3, p. 291–345, 2004.

[BOU 06] BOUYER P., MARKEY N., REYNIER P.-A., "Robust model-checking of linear-time properties in timed automata", in *Proc. 7th Latin American Symposium on Theoretical Informatics (LATIN'06)*, vol. 3887 of *LNCS*, Valdivia, Chile, Springer, p. 238-249, 2006.

[BOU 08a] BOUYER P., HADDAD S., REYNIER P.-A., "Timed Petri nets and timed automata: On the discriminating power of zeno sequences", *Inf. Comput.*, vol. 206, num. 1, p. 73-107, 2008.

[BOU 08b] BOUYER P., MARKEY N., REYNIER P.-A., "Robust analysis of timed automata *via* channel machines", in *Proc. 11th International Conference on Foundations of Software Science and Computation Structures (FoSSaCS'08)*, vol. 4962 of *LNCS*, Springer, p. 157-171, 2008.

[BRO 88] BROWNE M. C., CLARKE E. M., GRUMBERG O., "Characterizing finite Kripke structures in propositional temporal logic", *Theoretical Computer Science*, vol. 59, p. 115-131, 1988.

[CAS 02] CASSEZ F., HENZINGER TH. A., RASKIN J.-F., "A comparison of control problems for timed and hybrid systems", in *Proc. 5th International Workshop on Hybrid Systems: Computation and Control (HSCC'02)*, vol. 2289 of *LNCS*, Springer, p. 134–148, 2002.

[CHA 08] CHATTERJEE K., HENZINGER T. A., PRABHU V. S., "Timed parity games: complexity and robustness", in *Proc. 6th International Conference on Formal Modeling and Analysis of Timed Systems (FORMATS 2008)*, vol. 5215 of *LNCS*, Springer, p. 124-140, 2008.

[DAW 96] DAWS C., OLIVERO A., TRIPAKIS S., YOVINE S., "The tool Kronos", in *Proc. Hybrid Systems III: Verification and Control (1995)*, vol. 1066 of *LNCS*, Springer, p. 208–219, 1996.

[DAW 06] DAWS C., KORDY P., "Symbolic robustness analysis of timed automata.", in *Proc. 4th International Conference on Formal Modeling and Analysis of Timed Systems (FORMATS'06)*, vol. 4202 of *LNCS*, Springer, p. 143-155, 2006.

[DEW 05] DE WULF M., DOYEN L., RASKIN J.-F., "Almost ASAP semantics: from timed models to timed implementations", *Formal Aspects of Computing*, vol. 17, num. 3, p. 319-341, 2005.

[DEW 08] DE WULF M., DOYEN L., MARKEY N., RASKIN J.-F., "Robust safety of timed automata", *Formal Methods in System Design*, vol. 33, num. 1-3, p. 45-84, Kluwer Academic Publishers, 2008.

[GAR 05] GARDEY G., LIME D., MAGNIN M., ROUX O. H., "Romeo: A tool for analyzing time Petri nets", in *Proc. 17th International Conference on Computer Aided Verification (CAV'05)*, vol. 3576 of *LNCS*, Springer, p. 418–423, 2005.

[GUP 97] GUPTA V., HENZINGER TH. A., JAGADEESAN R., "Robust timed automata", in *Proc. International Workshop on Hybrid and Real-Time Systems (HART'97)*, vol. 1201 of *LNCS*, Springer, p. 331–345, 1997.

[HEN 97] HENZINGER TH. A., HO P.-H., WONG-TOI H., "HyTech: a model-checker for hybrid systems", *Journal on Software Tools for Technology Transfer*, vol. 1, num. 1–2, p. 110–122, 1997.

[HEN 03] HENZINGER TH. A., HOROWITZ B., KIRSCH C. M., "Giotto: A time-triggered language for embedded programming", in *Proc. of the IEEE*, vol. 91, num. 1, p. 84–99, 2003.

[HIG 52] HIGMAN G., "Ordering by divisibility in abstract algebras", in *Proc. London Mathematical Society*, vol. 2, p. 326–336, 1952.

[JAU 11] JAUBERT R., REYNIER P.-A., "Quantitative robustness analysis of flat timed automata", in *Proc. 14th International Conference on Foundations of Software Science and Computation Structures (FoSSaCS'11)*, LNCS, Springer, 2011, To appear.

[KAR 69] KARP R. M., MILLER R. E., "Parallel program schemata.", *Journal of Computer and System Sciences*, vol. 3, num. 2, p. 147-195, 1969.

[LAR 95] LAROUSSINIE F., LARSEN K. G., WEISE C., "From timed automata to logic – and back", in *Proc. 20th International Symposium on Mathematical Foundations of Computer Science (MFCS'95)*, vol. 969 of *LNCS*, Springer, p. 529–539, 1995.

[LAS 05] LASOTA S., WALUKIEWICZ I., "Alternating timed automata", in *Proc. 8th International Conference on Foundations of Software Science and Computation Structures (FoSSaCS'05)*, vol. 3441 of *LNCS*, Springer, p. 250–265, 2005.

[MAH 05] MAHATA P., Model checking parameterized timed systems, PhD thesis, Department of Information Technology, Uppsala University, Uppsala, Sweden, 2005.

[OUA 03] OUAKNINE J., WORRELL J. B., "Revisiting digitization, robustness and decidability for timed automata", in *Proc. 18th Annual Symposium on Logic in Computer Science (LICS'03)*, IEEE Computer Society Press, 2003.

[OUA 04] OUAKNINE J., WORRELL J. B., "On the language inclusion problem for timed automata: closing a decidability gap", in *Proc. 19th Annual Symposium on Logic in Computer Science (LICS'04)*, IEEE Computer Society Press, p. 54–63, 2004.

[OUA 05] OUAKNINE J., WORRELL J. B., "On the decidability of metric temporal logic", in *Proc. 19th Annual Symposium on Logic in Computer Science (LICS'05)*, IEEE Computer Society Press, p. 188–197, 2005.

[PNU 77] PNUELI A., "The temporal logic of programs", in *Proc. 18th Annual Symposium on Foundations of Computer Science (FOCS'77)*, IEEE Computer Society Press, p. 46–57, 1977.

[PUR 00] PURI A., "Dynamical properties of timed automata", *Discrete Event Dynamic Systems*, vol. 10, num. 1-2, p. 87–113, 2000.

Chapter 10

Distributed Control

10.1. Introduction

While verification techniques ensure that a given system is correct with respect to its specification, another challenging problem is to *control* a system in order to fulfill a specification. In this context, the system to control is *open* (it interacts with an environment), and the controller (or supervisor) restricts its behaviors in order to maintain a correct execution. Controller synthesis investigates the possibility of automatically synthesizing such controllers. Instead of verifying all the possible executions of a system, we are now interested in dynamically controlling the system in order to stay within the range of acceptable behaviors. Another question that derives from the verification problem is the synthesis problem: is it possible to automatically derive a correct system from its specification?

In other words, given a model $\mathcal{M}$ and a specification φ, the verification problem consists of checking that all the behaviors of the model satisfy the specification. In the control problem, we are given a controllable system G (called a plant), and a specification (φ) and we *look for* a controller C such that, whatever the actions of the environment E are, the executions of the system controlled by C (noted C/G) satisfy the specification. Finally, the synthesis problem is the following: given a specification φ, one *looks for* a program P such that, whatever the actions of the environment E are, all its executions satisfy the specification. In fact, the synthesis problem can be seen as a special case of the control problem: whereby the plant under supervision is trivial. The program that requires synthesis is actually the controller of such a system.

Chapter written by Claude Dutheillet, Isabelle Mounier and Nathalie Sznajder.

However, problems studied in the literature are not simply subcases of control problems. Often, the specifications considered for studying control problems are simpler when, for the synthesis problem, they are more general.

One of the frameworks of interest in this chapter has been introduced by Ramadge and Wonham [RAM 89] under the name of *supervisory control*. There, the system that requires control (the plant) is modeled by a discrete event system (DES). A DES is a dynamic system with a (not necessarily finite) state space, whose behavior is event-driven: modification of the state is triggered by discrete events occurring during the computation, real-time is abstracted [CAS 06]. Under this category fall numerous classical formalisms, among them finite automata, Petri nets, and process algebras. The events (or actions) of systems requiring control are usually partitioned into the set of *controllable* events and the set of *uncontrollable* events. Of course, the desired controller is only able to restrict the controllable events.

The following problem illustrates the control problem, it is presented in [RAM 89]. A cat and a mouse are placed in the maze of Figure 10.1. Each doorway in the maze is either for the exclusive use of the cat (they are denoted by c_i), or for the exclusive use of the mouse (they are denoted by m_i), and must be traversed in the direction indicated. Initially the cat is in room 2 and the mouse in room 4.

The objective is to find a controller that permits the cat and the mouse the greatest possible freedom of movement but which also guarantees that the controlled system satisfies the following specification φ:

1) the cat and the mouse never occupy the same room simultaneously;

2) it is always possible for the cat and the mouse to return to the initial state, i.e. the state in which the cat is in room 2, and the mouse is in room 4.

To fulfill the above requirements, controller C can open or close each door (controllable events), with the exception of door c_7 whose opening or closing depends on environment E (uncontrollable events).

The behaviors of the mouse and the cat are defined by the set of actions that they can execute, depending on the room in which they are. The system to control G is the shuffle product of the behaviors of the mouse and the cat.

Synthesis problem is also called Church's problem [CHU 63]. The problem of deciding whether such a program exists is called the *realizability* problem, and the problem of automatically producing such a program is called the *synthesis* problem. In the framework established by Church, the goal is to synthesize programs for *open* and *reactive* systems: systems that maintain an ongoing interaction with an uncontrollable environment.

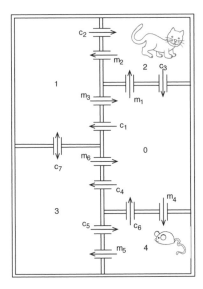

Figure 10.1. *A maze example*

It is well established ([BÜC 69]) that solving one of the above problems amounts to solving a *game*. Indeed, we can establish the following correspondence: the system modeled as a transition system is the arena of the game, the controller is the protagonist while the environment represents the antagonist. Then, the controllable events are possible moves for the protagonist and uncontrollable events are possible moves for the antagonist. Then, a behavior of the system is a play of the corresponding game, and the specification of the system is the winning condition of the game. Now, synthesizing a controller amounts to finding a winning strategy for the protagonist.

In the investigation of distributed systems, the problem of distributed control arises naturally. In such systems, it is desirable (with respect to design and implementation complexity for instance) to also obtain a distributed controller, i.e. a set of controllers, each of them controlling one component of the distributed system. The problems of control and synthesis can now be stated, respectively, by: given a specification φ and a plant G composed of subcomponents $G_1, G_2, \ldots, G_n$, do controllers exist $C_1, C_2, \ldots, C_n$, one for each component, such that whatever the actions of the environment E, the parallel executions of the controlled subcomponents (C_i/G_i) satisfy the specification, and for the synthesis problem, given n sites communicating through a fixed architecture and a specification φ, find programs $P_1, \ldots, P_n$ such that the behaviors of all the programs in parallel and interacting with the environment satisfy the specification?

An extension of the maze problem previously presented was proposed as a benchmark at WODES'08 [WOD 08]. It considers a tower composed by n identical levels. Each level is a maze as presented in Figure 10.1. A controllable bidirectional passageway connects room j of level $(5 * i + j)$ to room j of level $(5 * i + j + 1)$, for $i = 0, 1, 2 \ldots$, and $j = 0, 1, 2, 3, 4$. Therefore, levels 0 and 1 (5 and 6, 10 and 11, $\ldots$) are connected through room 0. Levels 1 and 2 (6 and 7, 11 and 12, $\ldots$) are connected through room 1. Levels 2 and 3 (7 and 8, 12 and 13, $\ldots$) are connected through room 2. Levels 3 and 4 (8 and 9, 13 and 14, $\ldots$) are connected through room 3 and levels 4 and 5 (9 and 10, 14 and 15, $\ldots$) are connected through room 4. Level 0 is only connected with level 1 and level $n - 1$ (the last level) is only connected with level $n - 2$. Initially all the cats are in room 0 of the maze of level 0 and all the mice (as many as cats) are in room 4 of the maze of level $n - 1$.

The objective is the same as for the initial one. This last version of the maze can easily be decentralized by looking for a set of controllers, one per level: each controller C_i controls the doors at its level, except for c_7, and the inter-level passageways connected to level i. An inter-level passageway is thus controlled by more than one controller.

To study the distributed control and synthesis problems, the following questions should be answered regarding the precise model of distributed systems:

Synchronous vs. asynchronous systems. The first decision to undertake concerns the semantics of the distributed system: is it synchronous or asynchronous? If the system is supposed to be synchronous, then a global clock governs the evolution of all the components: at each tick of this global clock, each of them takes an action. If we are interested in distributed protocols, the synchronous assumption cannot hold and we consider asynchronous systems: there all the components evolve at their own speed. In such asynchronous systems, the communication mechanism should also be considered carefully: is communication itself synchronous or asynchronous?

Models of communication. The different components of the system are expected to cooperate to achieve the specification and, to attain that goal, communication is a key element. The precise model of communication that will be used (shared variables, handshaking, first in first out (FIFO) channels, $\ldots$) is an important parameter to consider.

Type/expressiveness of the specifications. There is a balance to be obtained between the expressiveness of the specification and the feasibility of the result. According to the type of specifications considered, the results obtained may change drastically. In the centralized case, the synthesis and control problems are decidable for any specification given by a (ω)-regular language. This is no longer true in the distributed case, as we will see.

The choice of decentralizing the controllers implies that each of them only has a *partial view* of the state of the system. A first step towards a distributed control is then to obtain a controller under partial observation ([LIN 90, ARN 03, KUP 00]). Then several approaches have been adopted for distributed control. For the control community, decentralized control consists of synthesizing several controllers, each of them controlling a different subset of the system. The specifications can then be either local or global. In some cases, a same event can be controlled by several controllers; different policies may then be considered: if there is no unanimity among the controllers, should the transition be enabled or disabled? Another direction for distributed control has been taken by Pnueli and Rosner [PNU 90], following the line of Church (and followed then by quite a few other authors), in which the system is represented explicitly by a set of processes and communication channels, and each site is associated with exactly one controller. Section 10.2 is devoted to the presentation of the former problem and section 10.3 to the latter. The game framework is still relevant in the distributed case, except that multiplayer games are considered. These specific types of games are linked to logics that allow the properties induced by strategies of the different players to be expressed, such as ATL. This is presented in section 10.4.

10.2. Decentralized Control

The left part of Figure 10.2 illustrates the problem when the observation is global, meaning that the controller observes every action of the plant. One controller C observes all the actions of plant G and decides which controllable actions of G are enabled. The right part of Figure 10.2 illustrates the problem when the centralized controller has only a partial view of the plant. The actions of G observable by C are defined by P. In this case, C has to decide with a partial knowledge of the behavior of G.

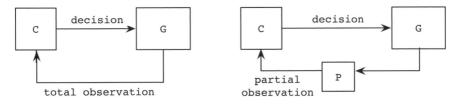

Figure 10.2. *Centralized control with total or partial observation*

The decentralized control problem is illustrated by Figure 10.3. It exhibits a new parameter of the problem, the arbiter. Each controller C_i can enable/disable a subset

En_i of the controllable actions of the plant. The arbiter is the procedure that determines whether an action controlled by more than one controller should be enabled or not in case there is no consensus among the controllers.

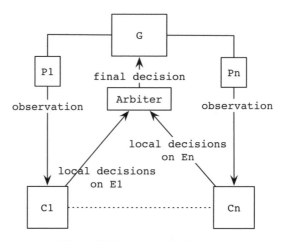

Figure 10.3. *Decentralized control*

The general decentralized control problem can therefore be expressed as follows: given a plant G, a specification φ, action sets P_1, ..., P_n (observable actions) and En_1, ..., En_n (controllable actions), do finite-state controllers C_1, ..., C_n and an arbiter exist such that the controlled behavior of the plant satisfies φ?

A controller that can act on any controllable action of the plant is said to be global while a controller that can control only a subset of the controllable actions of the plant is a local controller. The same distinction is made for the specifications: a specification that concerns the whole plant is a global one, while a specification that concerns only a part of the plant is local.

In the following, as in the literature, we present the problems for two supervisors but all the results can be generalized to any fixed number of supervisors. The results we present consider several cases: is the expected specification expressed globally or locally to each controller? Do the controllers communicate with each other?

The control problem may be considered with or without tolerance. In the first case, the controlled system may have a behavior that is slightly different from the expected behavior while in the second, the behavior must be exactly as expected .

The most common representation of the control problem models the plant to be controlled by a transition system

$$G = (Q, \Sigma, f, q_0, Q_m)$$

where Q is the set of states, Σ is the input alphabet of actions or events, $f \subset \Sigma \times Q \times Q$ is the transition relation, $q_0 \in Q$ is the initial state, and $Q_m \subseteq Q$ is the set of terminal or *marker* states. The set Σ must be finite, whereas Q and Q_m may be infinite. We denote by $\Sigma_{uc} \subseteq \Sigma$ the set of uncontrollable actions of the plant G and by $\Sigma_o \subseteq \Sigma$ the set of observable actions of plant G.

The transition systems of Figure 10.4, G^{cat} and G^{mouse}, model the movements of the cat and the mouse in the maze of Figure 10.1. $G^{cat} = (Q^{cat}, \Sigma^{cat}, f^{cat}, q_0^{cat}, Q_m^{cat})$ where $Q^{cat} = \{0_c, 1_c, 2_c, 3_c, 4_c\}$, $\Sigma^{cat} = \{c_1, c_2, c_3, c_4, c_5, c_6, c_7\}$, $q_0^{cat} = 2_c$, $Q_m^{cat} = \{2_c\}$ and $G^{mouse} = (Q^{mouse}, \Sigma^{mouse}, f^{mouse}, q_0^{mouse}, Q_m^{mouse})$ where $Q^{mouse} = \{0_m, 1_m, 2_m, 3_m, 4_m\}$, $\Sigma^{mouse} = \{m_1, m_2, m_3, m_4, m_5, m_6\}$, $q_0^{mouse} = 4_m$ and $Q_m^{mouse} = \{4_m\}$. The transition relations f^{cat} and f^{mouse} are defined by the automata of Figure 10.4.

The transition system G of the whole system is the shuffle product of G^{cat} and G^{mouse}, i.e., $G = (Q^{cat} \times Q^{mouse}, \Sigma^{cat} \cup \Sigma^{mouse}, f, (2_c, 4_m), \{(2_c, 4_m)\})$ with $(s, (x^{cat}, x^{mouse}), (y^{cat}, y^{mouse})) \in f$ iff $(s \in \Sigma^{cat}$ and $(s, x^{cat}, y^{cat}) \in f^{cat}$ and $x^{mouse} = y^{mouse})$ or $(s \in \Sigma^{mouse}$ and $x^{cat} = y^{cat}$ and $(s, x^{mouse}, y^{mouse}) \in f^{mouse})$.

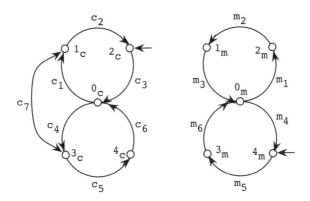

Figure 10.4. *Transitions systems: G_{cat} and G_{mouse}*

G is characterized by two subsets of Σ^*, where Σ^* is the set of all finite strings over Σ, including the null string ϵ: the set $L(G)$ of all possible action sequences that the plant may generate, called the *closed behavior* of G, and a subset $L_m(G)$ of $L(G)$, called the *marked behavior* of G, which contains sequences whose end-state belongs to Q_m. This subset is intended to represent completed tasks.

Formally, a controller C is a pair (S, ψ) where S is an automaton that recognizes a language over the same event set Σ as the plant G and ψ is a mapping that determines for every state x of S and every action s in Σ whether s is enabled in x. ψ must be such that $\forall x \in X, \forall s \in \Sigma_{uc}, \psi(x, s) = $ enable, where X is the set of states of S. S changes state according to the events generated by G and at each state x of S, $\psi(x, s)$ is used to determine whether s is enabled or not in the corresponding state of G. Usually, the automaton S is labelled only with actions observable by the controller, therefore, it represents the evolution of the controller in response to the outputs of the plant. The mapping ψ represents the control exerted by the controller on the plant.

Consider $L(C/G)$ the language that describes the behavior of plant G under the supervision of controller C. $L(C/G)$ is the set of sequences of events that are generated by both G and C and such that each event of the sequence is enabled by ψ. $L_m(C/G)$ is the subset of $L(C/G)$ containing sequences whose end-state is marked by both G and C. Considering the maze problem, a controller that ensures the second part of the specification (the system can always return to the initial state) is a proper controller when the initial state of the system is a marked state.

A controller C is said to be a *proper* controller if

$$\overline{L_m(C/G)} = L(C/G)$$

where the overbar notation denotes the prefix-closure, i.e. all strings in $L_m(C/G)$ and all their prefixes, including the empty string. A proper controller guarantees that the system is *non-blocking*, i.e. that every string in the closed-loop system can be completed to a marked string in the system.

A controller $C = (S, \psi)$ is said to be *complete* for G if for every string σ in Σ^* and every event s in Σ, the conditions $\sigma \in L(C/G)$, $\sigma s \in L(G)$ and $\psi(x, s) = $ enable together imply that $\sigma s \in L(C/G)$, where x is the state reached by C after the execution of σ. This ensures that suitable transitions are defined in S for every possible closed loop action. It is always possible to obtain a complete controller from an incomplete one.

The most common representation of the specification that the controlled system must satisfy is a language K such that $K \subseteq L(G)$. For the control problem to be solvable, it is necessary that K satisfies the *controllability* property [RAM 82]. A language is controllable if whenever a legal sequence (sequence that belongs to K) can be extended by an uncontrolled action, the resulting sequence is still legal. Then, controllability can be paraphrased by: *"If you cannot prevent it, then it should be legal"* [LAF 02].

DEFINITION 10.1 (controllability) *Let K be a language such that $K \subseteq L(G)$. K is a controllable sublanguage of $L(G)$ (controllable with respect to G) if*

$$\overline{K}\Sigma_{uc} \cap L(G) \subseteq \overline{K}$$

where $\overline{K}\Sigma_{uc} = \{\sigma s \mid \sigma \in \overline{K} \wedge s \in \Sigma_{uc}\}$.

When considering centralized control, if K is not controllable, there exists a unique supremal controllable sublanguage of K (possibly the empty language) [WON 87]. The author proposes an algorithm to compute this language when K and $L(G)$ are regular languages. The starting point is the automaton that recognizes K. This automaton is reduced by deleting the states (and the associated arcs) from which an uncontrolled event may be executed with respect to $L(G)$ but is not authorized by K (the execution of the uncontrolled event leads to a sequence that does not respect the specification). The reduction is iterated until a fix-point is reached. The obtained automaton is such that each accepted sequence, prolonged by an uncontrolled event with respect to $L(G)$, is an accepted sequence too. The obtained automaton recognizes the supremal controllable sublanguage of K and models the controller of the plant. In this algorithm the automata are always trim, i.e. they are reduced to automata such that all the states are reachable from the initial state and can reach a marked state.

Considering the maze problem, we first compute the system G that is the shuffle product of G_{cat} and G_{mouse}. To respect the specification, the states where the cat and the mouse are in the same room are suppressed as well as the states that do not allow the initial state to be reached (this state is the only marked state). The obtained automaton is the starting point of the algorithm. The computation of the fix-point leads to the controller of Figure 10.5.

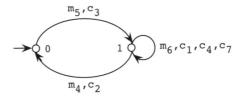

Figure 10.5. *Controller of the maze*

We now focus on particular distributed control problems for which solutions have been proposed.

10.2.1. *Local and modular specifications*

Local and modular approaches both tackle the complexity of the control problem by decomposing it into subproblems. The modular approach is adapted when the specification is a task that can be decomposed into subtasks. A set of controllers is defined, each of them have the aim of achieving one of the subtasks. To do so, every controller can act on any controllable action of the system. On the contrary, locality decomposes the plant into subsystems. Each subsystem corresponds to a subset of actions of the system, and a local specification is defined at the subsystem level. The goal is to combine the local controllers in order to achieve a specification at the system level. Local and modular approaches have both shown to be appropriate for some manufacturing system problems [WON 88, LIN 90].

Regarding the maze problem, a local approach may consist of having a controller for each level and one for each inter-level passageway. Each controller ensures that in the controlled level (or passageway) a cat and a mouse can never be in the same room (or in the inter-level passageway). Each level controller also ensures that the mice and cats present in the level can always go back to rooms 4 and 2, respectively. A modular approach may be to have two controllers for the whole system, each realizing a subpart of the global specification. A first controller should ensure that a mouse and a cat are never in the same room of a same level and that each cat can return to room 2 and a mouse to room 4. A second controller should ensure that a cat and a mouse never pass each other in an inter-level passageway.

Formally, in the local approach, each subsystem i is characterized by a non-empty subset $\Sigma_i \subseteq \Sigma$ of actions. We restrict the presentation to two subsystems, i.e. $i = 1, 2$, but the approach is general. Let P_i be the projection of Σ on Σ_i and G_i the system such that $L(G_i) = P_i(L(G))$. A minimal acceptable behavior $A_i \subseteq L(G_i)$ and a maximal legal behavior $E_i \subseteq L(G_i)$ are defined for the subsystem. The local control approach aims to find a set of controllers C_i such that $A_i \subseteq L(C_i/G_i) \subseteq E_i$ and such that the combination of the local controllers satisfies a global specification. Let $\tilde{C}_i$ be the controller that extends C_i to G by enabling all controllable actions that do not belong to $\Sigma_{i,c}$. Then $L(\tilde{C}_i/G) = L(G) \cap P_i^{-1}(L(C_i/G_i))$ is such that $L(G) \cap P_i^{-1}(A_i) \subseteq L(\tilde{C}_i/G) \subseteq L(G) \cap P_i^{-1}(E_i)$. By combining local controllers, it is then possible to find a global controller such that:

$$L(G) \cap \bigcap_{i=1}^{2} P_i^{-1}(A_i) \subseteq L(\tilde{C}_1 \wedge \tilde{C}_2/G) \subseteq L(G) \cap \bigcap_{i=1}^{2} P_i^{-1}(E_i)$$

This control problem is known as *local specification for local control with tolerance* [RUD 92]. In [LIN 90], the authors give sufficient conditions under which a solution to this problem exists.

Modular control [WON 88] considers the case where the specification can be defined as a set of properties. For each property $prop_i$, a set $L_i \subseteq L(G)$ of strings that satisfy the property is defined. The problem is then to find controllers C_1 and C_2 such that $L(C_i/G) \subseteq L_i$ and $L(C_1 \wedge C_2/G) \subseteq L_1 \cap L_2$. When equality cannot be achieved, the goal is to find the largest controllable behavior that satisfies the constraint. Four instances of this problem are presented in [WON 88], depending on whether non-blocking is required for the resulting controller or not, whether languages L_i are included in $L_m(G)$ or not, and whether they are closed or not. For each problem, sufficient solvability conditions are given and modular supervisors that satisfy the specification are proposed. The construction of solutions mainly relies on the so-called "non-conflicting" property of languages $(\overline{L_1 \cap L_2} = \overline{L_1} \cap \overline{L_2})$.

Local and modular approaches have been combined for systems that are represented as the composition of a set of susbsystems [QUE 00]. An efficient test has been proposed in [PEN 09] for detecting conflicts that can result in the blocking of such systems when the local controllers are combined.

10.2.2. Global specifications

The need for a formulation of the control problem that admits global specifications arose from the investigation of communication protocol synthesis [RUD 90]. In [RUD 92] the following definition of the control problem of *global specification for local control* is given. The control problem of *global specification for global control* is not presented since it is similar to the centralized control problem.

DEFINITION 10.2 (global specification for local control without tolerance) *Given a plant G over an alphabet* Σ, *a legal language E such that* $\emptyset \neq E \subseteq L_m(G)$ *and sets* $\Sigma_{1,c}, \Sigma_{1,o}, \Sigma_{2,c}, \Sigma_{2,o} \subseteq \Sigma$, *construct local (complete) controllers* C_1 *and* C_2 *such that* $\tilde{C}_1 \wedge \tilde{C}_2$ *is a proper controller for G and such that*

$$L_m(\tilde{C}_1 \wedge \tilde{C}_2/G) = E$$

DEFINITION 10.3 (global specification for local control with tolerance) *Given a plant G over an alphabet* Σ, *a legal language* $E \subseteq L_m(G)$, *a minimally adequate language* $A \subseteq E$, *and sets* $\Sigma_{1,c}, \Sigma_{1,o}, \Sigma_{2,c}, \Sigma_{2,o} \subseteq \Sigma$, *construct local (complete) controllers* C_1 *and* C_2 *such that* $\tilde{C}_1 \wedge \tilde{C}_2$ *is a proper controller for G and such that*

$$A \subseteq L(\tilde{C}_1 \wedge \tilde{C}_2/G) \subseteq E$$

In both definitions, $C_i, i = 1, 2$ is a controller that can observe only actions in $\Sigma_{i,o}$ and can control only actions in $\Sigma_{i,c}$ and $\tilde{C}_i$ is the global extension of C_i ($\tilde{C}_i$ acts on Σ while C_i acts on $\Sigma_{i,c}$). The set of uncontrollable actions Σ_{uc} is understood to be $\Sigma \backslash (\Sigma_{1,c} \cup \Sigma_{2,c})$.

A controller that implements *control with tolerance* is called *safe* [LAF 02].

In the case that some actions of the system are controlled by more than one controller such as, for instance, the inter-level passageways of the maze example, the definition of an arbiter is necessary. Different arbitration policies have been proposed for defining the enabling conditions of a multi-controlled action. The conjunctive arbiter requires a consensus among the controllers, the disjunctive arbiter accepts only one enabling controller, while the general arbiter may apply conjunctive or disjunctive policy depending on the action under consideration. The choice of a specific controller is closely related to the specification. The following co-observability properties give conditions under which the decisions made by local controllers are compatible with the realization of the specification.

Co-observability

The conjunctive arbiter enables an action if, and only if, it is enabled by every local controller. As a consequence, the default action of a controller under insufficient information is to enable an event ("pass the buck" or permissive policy), so that it does not interfere with the global decision. In other words, a controller disables an action only if it is sure that, by doing so, it will not prevent a legal sequence from occurring. The definition of conjunctive and permissive (C&P) co-observability is given here for two controllers. Point 1) of the definition considers the case of a multi-controlled event s and states that, if the execution of s after a sequence σ is possible but illegal (i.e. $\sigma s \in L \wedge \sigma s \notin \overline{K}$), then at least one of the controllers that controls s can distinguish σ from any sequence after which s is legal (in case it is C_1, $\forall \sigma'$, $P_1(\sigma) \neq P_1(\sigma') \vee \sigma' s \notin \overline{K}$). Hence, by disabling s after σ this controller will not remove any legal behavior. Points 2) and 3) state similar conditions for mono-controlled actions.

DEFINITION 10.4 (C&P co-observability) *[YOO 02] A language $K \subseteq L = \overline{L}$ is said to be C&P co-observable with respect to a language $L, \Sigma_{o,1}, \Sigma_{c,1}, \Sigma_{o,2}, \Sigma_{c,2}$ if*

$$\forall \sigma, \sigma', \sigma'' \in \overline{K}, \ (P_1(\sigma) = P_1(\sigma') \ \wedge \ P_2(\sigma) = P_2(\sigma'')) \Rightarrow$$

1) $(s \in \Sigma_{c,1} \cap \Sigma_{c,2}) \wedge (\sigma s \in L) \wedge (\sigma' s \in \overline{K}) \wedge (\sigma'' s \in \overline{K}) \ \Rightarrow \sigma s \in \overline{K}$;
2) $(s \in \Sigma_{c,1} \backslash \Sigma_{c,2}) \wedge (\sigma s \in L) \wedge (\sigma' s \in \overline{K}) \ \Rightarrow \sigma s \in \overline{K}$;
3) $(s \in \Sigma_{c,2} \backslash \Sigma_{c,1}) \wedge (\sigma s \in L) \wedge (\sigma'' s \in \overline{K}) \ \Rightarrow \sigma s \in \overline{K}$.

This definition can been completed with an additional condition on the marked language [RUD 92], which states that any marked sequence that cannot be distinguished from sequences in K and that is a prefix of a sequence in K must belong to K. The resulting property is simply called co-observability.

DEFINITION 10.5 *A language $K \subseteq L_m(G)$ is co-observable with respect to G if*

1) K is C&P co-observable with respect to $L(G), \Sigma_{o,1}, \Sigma_{c,1}, \Sigma_{o,2}, \Sigma_{c,2}$

2) $\forall \sigma \in L(G), \forall \sigma', \sigma'' \in K$ s.t. $P_1(\sigma) = P_1(\sigma') \wedge P_2(\sigma) = P_2(\sigma'')$;

$\sigma \in L_m(G) \cap \overline{K} \Rightarrow \sigma \in K.$

The disjunctive arbiter enables an action as soon as it is enabled by one of the local controllers. As a consequence, the default action of a controller under insufficient information is to disable an event ("antipermissive" policy), so that its decision does not interfere with the global decision. In other words, a controller enables an action only if it is sure that its execution will not cause any violation of the specification. The definition of disjunctive and antipermissive (D&A) co-observability is given here for two controllers. Point 1) of the definition considers the case of a multi-controlled event s and states that, if the execution of s after a sequence σ is possible and legal (i.e., $\sigma s \in L \wedge \sigma s \in \overline{K}$), then at least one of the controllers that controls s can distinguish σ from any sequence after which s is illegal (in case it is $C_1, \forall \sigma', P_1(\sigma) \neq P_1(\sigma') \vee \sigma's \notin \overline{K}$). Hence, by enabling s after σ this controller will not enable an illegal behavior. Points 2) and 3) state similar conditions for mono-controlled actions.

DEFINITION 10.6 (D&A co-observability) *[YOO 02] A language $K \subseteq L = \overline{L}$ is said to be D&A co-observable with respect to a language $L, \Sigma_{o,1}, \Sigma_{c,1}, \Sigma_{o,2}, \Sigma_{c,2}$ if:*

$\forall \sigma, \sigma', \sigma'' \in \overline{K}, \ (P_1(\sigma) = P_1(\sigma') \wedge P_2(\sigma) = P_2(\sigma'')) \Rightarrow$

1) $(s \in \Sigma_{c,1} \cap \Sigma_{c,2}) \wedge (\sigma s \in L) \wedge (\sigma's \in L\backslash\overline{K}) \wedge (\sigma''s \in L\backslash\overline{K}) \Rightarrow \sigma s \in L\backslash\overline{K}$;

2) $(s \in \Sigma_{c,1}\backslash\Sigma_{c,2}) \wedge (\sigma s \in L) \wedge (\sigma's \in L\backslash\overline{K}) \Rightarrow \sigma s \in L\backslash\overline{K}$;

3) $(s \in \Sigma_{c,2}\backslash\Sigma_{c,1}) \wedge (\sigma s \in L) \wedge (\sigma''s \in L\backslash\overline{K}) \Rightarrow \sigma s \in L\backslash\overline{K}$.

We recall the main results for the different arbitration policies.

Main results

The general arbiter applies to an architecture where the set of controllable actions is partitioned *a priori* into actions for which the disjunctive policy is applied ($\Sigma_{c,d}$) and actions for which the conjunctive policy is applied ($\Sigma_{c,e}$). It can be particularized into a conjunctive arbiter ($\Sigma_{c,d} = \emptyset$, and point (3) of the theorem becomes meaningless) or a disjunctive arbiter ($\Sigma_{c,e} = \emptyset$, and point (2) of the theorem becomes meaningless). The following theorem gives the conditions under which the global problem with zero tolerance can be solved:

THEOREM 10.7 *[YOO 02] Let $K \in L_m(G)$, $K \neq \emptyset$ and let $\Sigma_{c,d} \cup \Sigma_{c,e}$ be a partition of Σ_c. There exists a non-blocking controller C such that $L_m(C/G) = K$ and $L(C/G) = \overline{K}$ iff the following conditions hold:*

1) K is controllable with respect to $L(G)$ and Σ_{uc};

2) K is C&P co-observable with respect to $L(G), \Sigma_{o,1}, \Sigma_{c,e,1}, \ldots \Sigma_{o,n}, \Sigma_{c,e,n}$;

3) K is D&A co-observable with respect to $L(G), \Sigma_{o,1}, \Sigma_{c,d,1}, \ldots \Sigma_{o,n}, \Sigma_{c,d,n}$;

4) K is $L_m(G)$-closed, i.e. $K = L_m(G) \cap \overline{K}$.

The set of languages that can be generated using a general arbiter is a strict superset of the union of the sets of languages obtained by means of a disjunctive arbiter and by means of a conjunctive arbiter. It is also a strict subset of the set of languages generated by means of a centralized controller.

Besides the construction of the local controllers, the problem here is to find the partition $\Sigma_{c,d} \cup \Sigma_{c,e}$. [YOO 02] proposes a polynomial time algorithm to decide whether the partition exists and, if so, to build it. For the construction of the local controllers, the algorithm is as follows. A state x_i of C_i is a set $P_i^{-1}(P_i(\sigma))$, where $\sigma \in \overline{K}$. Each state is actually an equivalence class of sequences, where equivalence is defined by identical projections. The intial state $x_{0,i}$ is the equivalence class of ϵ. There is an arc from x_i to x_i' labeled by $s \in \Sigma_{o,i}$ if $\exists \sigma \in x_i, \exists \sigma' \in x_i', \sigma.s = \sigma'$. Functions ψ_i are given by:

$$\psi_i(x_i, s) = \text{enable} \quad \Leftrightarrow \quad (s \in \Sigma_{c,d,i} \wedge \psi_i^{DA}(x_i, s) = \text{enable})$$
$$\vee \quad (s \in \Sigma_{c,e,i} \wedge \psi_i^{CP}(x_i, s) = \text{enable})$$
$$\vee \quad s \in \Sigma_{uc} \vee s \in \Sigma_{c,e} \backslash \Sigma_{c,e,i}$$

where ψ_i^{DA} is the local mapping that would apply to events controllable by C_i in a (purely) disjunctive controller:

$$\psi_i^{DA}(x_i, s) = \text{enable} \quad \Leftrightarrow \quad \forall \sigma \in x_i \cap \overline{K}, \forall s \text{ s.t. } \sigma.s \in L(G), \sigma.s \in \overline{K}$$

and ψ_i^{CP} is the local mapping that would apply to events controllable by C_i in a (purely) conjunctive controller:

$$\psi_i^{CP}(x_i, s) = \text{enable} \quad \Leftrightarrow \quad \exists \sigma \in x_i, \sigma.s \in \overline{K}$$

A representation of the general controller C can then obtained by a shuffle product of the local controllers where the global decision for control actions that belong to $\Sigma_{c,e}$ is obtained by intersection, whereas the decision for control actions that belong to $\Sigma_{c,d}$ is obtained by union.

The control problem with tolerance has been studied in [RUD 92] for the case of a conjunctive controller. From theorem 10.7, it appears that this problem can be solved if, and only, if there exists a controllable and co-observable language K such that $A \subseteq K \subseteq E$.

THEOREM 10.8 *[RUD 92] If $A \neq \emptyset$ then the global problem with tolerance is solvable if and only if the smallest prefix-closed, controllable, and co-observable language containing A is contained in E.*

When the system under consideration can be specified by regular languages, [RUD 92] proposes an algorithm for computing the smallest prefix-closed, controllable and co-observable language containing A.

Another definition of observability in the decentralized context has been introduced, namely joint observability [TRI 04b], which is not comparable with the definitions of C&P or D&A co-observability. Assuming that K represents the correct behaviors, joint observability states that if σ is a correct behavior and σ' an incorrect behavior, then at least one observer i has a different view of σ and σ'. Unfortunately, the problem of checking whether K is jointly observable with respect to L is decidable only in the case of a single observer Σ_1, i.e. in a context of centralized control with partial observation. As soon as two observers $\Sigma_1, \Sigma_2 \subseteq \Sigma$ are considered, the problem becomes undecidable. From this result, it follows that the decentralized control problem where the behavior of the controlled system must be non-blocking and included in some regular language E, i.e. $L_m(C_1 \wedge C_2/G) \subseteq E$, is undecidable [TRI 04b, THI 05].

10.2.3. *Cooperative control*

The aim of this approach is to allow local controllers to exchange information when their local view is not sufficient to make a decision. In [WON 96] the problem is presented as follows: *for a given control task and set of observed actions a question is whether there is sufficient information obtained through the observed actions set for a controller to synthesize the given control task. In the situation where the observed actions set does not provide sufficient information but there is another controller observing the same system with another observed actions set, the problem might be overcome by communication from the other controller.* This is the case when a controller cannot distinguish between two sequences of actions (when it is necessary to take the "good" control decision) while another controller has enough information to distinguish between the two sequences. The controllers must be able to communicate as shown by Figure 10.6.

Considering the maze problem with one controller for each level and inter-level passageway, it seems obvious that each level controller needs information from its connected passageways to ensure that connected rooms never contain a cat and a mouse. Therefore, to solve this problem is will be necessary to "adapt" the set of observable actions of each controller.

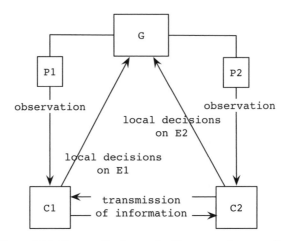

Figure 10.6. *Decentralized control with cooperative controllers*

The problem is formally introduced in [WON 96]. Let G be a plant over the alphabet Σ and K be a non-empty, prefix-closed, and controllable sublanguage of $L(G)$. K is decomposed into two sub-specifications K_1 and K_2 that must be respectively ensured by the controllers C_1 and C_2 that respectively observe actions of $\Sigma_{1,o}$ and $\Sigma_{2,o} \subseteq \Sigma$ ($\Sigma_{1,o} \cap \Sigma_{2,o} = \emptyset$) and respectively control actions of $\Sigma_{1,c}$ and $\Sigma_{2,c} \subseteq \Sigma$ ($\Sigma_{1,c} \cap \Sigma_{2,c} = \emptyset$). Consider the case where $\Sigma_{1,o}$ is not sufficient, i.e. C_1 has not enough information to "correctly" control actions of $\Sigma_{1,c}$. Then find a set $\Sigma_o \subseteq \Sigma_{2,o}$, if possible, such that there is a new controller $C_{1_{new}}$ that observes $\Sigma_{1,o} \times \Sigma_o$ with $L(C_{1_{new}}/G) = K_1$. This problem is solvable if, and only if, K is *co-observable* with respect to L, $\Sigma_{1,o}$, $\Sigma_{2,o}$, $\Sigma_{1,c}$ and $\Sigma_{2,c}$. Furthermore, if the problem is solvable, there exists at least one minimal set Σ_o that solves the problem (i.e., $\nexists \Sigma'_o \subseteq \Sigma_{2,o}$ with $|\Sigma'_o| < |\Sigma_o|$ that solves the problem). This solution is not dynamic since the information shared between controllers is statically computed, so the controller has access to it even when it is not necessary.

This formalization considers that each controller observes a projection of $L(G)$. The results presented in [WON 96] are more general since they consider a map instead of a projection, i.e. several actions can be mapped to a single action which is not possible with a projection.

10.2.4. *Alternative approaches*

In [RIC 97], the authors present the problem in terms of knowledge. Their central hypothesis is that *it is easier to reason about what controllers know or do not know instead of what sequences of events must or must not be recognized by the controllers.* To model knowledge they use a modal epistemic logic based on the possible-worlds model presented in [HAL 90]. At each step, from the actions it observes, each controller builds the set of possible global states of the plant, i.e. possible worlds. At one step, a controller decides to disable an action it controls if, and only if, it will take the same decision whatever the possible worlds. If several controllers can act on a same action, it is disabled when at least one controller makes this decision. In some cases, at some steps, one controller may have insufficient knowledge to make a control decision (i.e. it cannot decide to disable an action even if it is the right decision to make). When it cannot decide, a controller may be able to reduce the set of possible worlds by using the knowledge of some other controllers. This sharing of knowledge is called *pooling knowledge*.

In [RIC 99], the authors argue that if the controllers communicate only when one of them cannot make a decision, it is sometimes impossible to solve the control problem even if a solution exists. If the controller had previously received information it may be able to take the right decision. The authors overcome this limitation by identifying locations where pooling knowledge is helpful.

Since communications are costly, in [RUD 99] they develop a strategy and propose an algorithm to minimize communication between controllers. The aim is to obtain a consistent set of communications that provides enough information for controllers to solve the control problem and such that no subset of it satisfies the two previous conditions. The consistency ensures that, if in a global state gs a controller communicates with another one, it must communicate the same way in all global states it cannot differentiate from gs. These results are used in [RIC 99].

[GRA 10] studied the control problem with specifications that are priority policies (when two actions may be executed simultaneously the one with the highest priority has to be executed). It extends a work presented in [BAS 09] to share information when necessary. The controllers do not communicate directly, but when necessary, controlled processes may synchronize to pool their knowledge. A controller can therefore exploit this pooling to take the right control decision. With model-checking techniques, communication points where processes may be synchronized are pre-calculated. Before and after these points, they can act independently.

10.3. Controller synthesis for distributed systems

Independently from the aforementioned work, and from a more theoretical point of view, Pnueli and Rosner have extended the line of research initiated by Church by considering the synthesis problem for distributed systems [PNU 90]. This framework has then been used to study different variants of the problem, including the more general case of the control problem. This approach is, in some sense, more general and control is more difficult to achieve: the problem is, in general, undecidable, and for the decidable sub-cases, the theoretical complexity is very high. The main difference with the model described in the previous section is that here the controllers explicitly communicate in a way that is determined by the description of the system: its *architecture*, that defines a set of processes and their possible communications, with the restriction that the variables of the system form a *partition* of the set of processes. A variable *belongs* to the partition corresponding to a process if it can be modified by this process. This implies that at most one process can have writing access to a given variable.

This notion of architecture is very general, and a lot of modeling choices are still to be made. The most prominent have already been listed in the introduction, and we take another look at these parameters in the light of this specific model.

10.3.1. *The different variants of the model: an overview*

Synchronous vs. asynchronous systems

The model presented in the previous section in some sense hid the question of the synchronous or asynchronous nature of the systems considered, by representing them by a single automaton controlled by different controllers. Here, to describe the executions of a given architecture, it is necessary to explicitly provide the chosen semantics.

Models of communications. For synchronous systems, it is usually assumed that controllers communicate through *shared* variables. These variables are shared for reading only, and they can only be written by a single process: at each step of the computation, the different processes write simultaneously on the variables they own. Thus a variable written by one process and read by another serves to transmit information from the writer to the reader. In asynchronous systems, such a communication mechanism is very weak when it comes to distributed systems; Pnueli and Rosner [PNU 89], and then Anuchitankul and Manna [ANU 94] and Vardi [VAR 95] considered shared variables for communications between the environment and the system in the case of centralized synthesis. A more powerful mechanism consists of communicating through rendez-vous, i.e. synchronized execution of common actions or by signal (a sort of asymmetric rendez-vous initiated by only one of the processes).

Type/expressiveness of specifications. Since we are interested here in reactive systems, the specifications are usually assumed to be given in some temporal logic or similar formalism. Besides the classical alternative between linear time and branching time setting, and the expressiveness of the chosen specification language, the specifications may also differ in *the set of communications* they can constrain: can the specification concern all the communications of the system, even internal communications (we will call them *total specifications*)? Or can only the input-output behavior of the system be specified, seen as a black box (we will call them *external specifications*)?

10.3.2. *Synchronous systems*

The synthesis problem for synchronous distributed systems is the framework chosen by Pnueli and Rosner in their seminal paper [PNU 90]. In their paper, an architecture is formed by several processes that communicate with each other and with the environment through *shared variables*. In this subsection, we start with the results obtained for the synthesis problem, before showing an extension of this framework to the control problem.

The synthesis problem

An *architecture* describes a set of sites (called the processes) and a set of variables for the processes. Formally, we define an architecture by a tuple $\mathfrak{A} = (\text{Proc}, V, E, (S^v)_{v \in V}, s_0, (d_p)_{p \in \text{Proc}})$, where:

– Proc is the set of processes;

– V is the set of variables;

– $E \subseteq (\text{Proc} \times V) \cup (V \times \text{Proc})$ indicates which variables are read or modified by which process;

– S^v is the domain of the variable $v \in V$;

– $s_0 = (s_0^v)_{v \in V} \in \Pi_{v \in V} S^v$ is the initial state;

– and d_p is the delay associated with the process $p \in \text{Proc}$.

For $x \in \text{Proc} \cup V$, we write $E(x) = \{y \in V \cup \text{Proc} \mid (x, y) \in E\}$, and $E^{-1}(x) = \{y \in V \cup \text{Proc} \mid (y, x) \in E\}$, that represent, respectively, the set of the successors and predecessors of x in the graph of the architecture. Since it is bipartite, for $p \in \text{Proc}$, $E(p) \subseteq V$ and $E^{-1}(p) \subseteq V$ and for $v \in V$, $E(v) \subseteq \text{Proc}$, and $E^{-1}(v) \subseteq \text{Proc}$. Moreover, $|E^{-1}(v)| \leq 1$ (since we assume that a variable can be modified by at most one process). Intuitively, an edge $(p, v) \in E$ means that process p can write on variable v, and an edge (v, p) means that the variable v can be read by process p. The special process environment is not represented in the architecture, thus some variables may have no predecessor (they are written by the environment) or no successor (they are read by the environment) in the graph $(V \cup \text{Proc}, E)$. We will distinguish them as *input* and *output* variables formally defined respectively by $V_I = \{v \in V \mid E^{-1}(v) = \emptyset\}$ and $V_O = \{v \in V \mid E(v) = \emptyset\}$.

For $U \subseteq V$, we denote by S^U the set $\Pi_{v \in U} S^v$. A configuration of the architecture is given by a tuple $s = (s^v)_{v \in V} \in S^V$ giving the value of all variables. For all $s \in S^V$, for all $U \subseteq V$, we will write $s^U = (s^v)_{v \in U}$ the projection of s onto the variables of U. A *run* of an architecture $\mathfrak{A}$ in the synchronous framework is a word

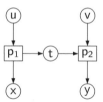

Figure 10.7. *Example of an architecture*

$\sigma = s_0 s_1 \cdots \in (S^V)^{\omega}$, where s_0 is the initial state of $\mathfrak{A}$. The projection of σ onto U is $\sigma^U = s_0^U s_1^U \cdots$. Finally, for a sequence $\sigma = s_0 s_1 \cdots \in (S^U)^{\omega} \cup (S^U)^*$, for all $0 \le i \le j$, we write $\sigma[i..j]$ for $s_i \cdots s_j$.

It is sometimes assumed that a *delay* occurs in the transmission of information between processes, corresponding to the time interval between the moment a process reads the variable and the moment the value it will consequently write on its output variables will be available to others. This is formalized by the value of d_p for each process p given in the architecture. In most of the models the processes have the same delay, but the results can be extended to the general case, where each process has a distinct delay of transmission [GAS 09].

Example 10.1

Figure 10.7 shows an example of an architecture, in which the variables are represented by circles, and the processes by squares. The input variables are then $V_I = \{u, v\}$, and the output variables $V_O = \{x, y\}$. A run of such an architecture is a sequence

$$s_0 s_1 s_2 \cdots = \begin{pmatrix} u_0 \\ v_0 \\ t_0 \\ x_0 \\ y_0 \end{pmatrix} \begin{pmatrix} u_1 \\ v_1 \\ t_1 \\ x_1 \\ y_1 \end{pmatrix} \begin{pmatrix} u_2 \\ v_2 \\ t_2 \\ x_2 \\ y_2 \end{pmatrix} \cdots$$

If there is no delay, then at each time step i, the value y_i depends on the sequence $\begin{pmatrix} t_0 & \cdots & t_i \\ v_0 & \cdots & v_i \end{pmatrix}$, *including* the values computed at the same time step i. But if the process p_2 has a delay of 1 for instance, then the value y_i depends only on the sequence $\begin{pmatrix} t_0 & \cdots & t_{i-1} \\ v_0 & \cdots & v_{i-1} \end{pmatrix}$, the value computed at the same time step being unavailable to the process. Observe that the value of the variable y does not depend on the value of the variables u and x. This is formalized in the definition of a program.

According to the information locally accessible to a process, a *program* (or *strategy*) for this process is a map that gives, the next value to be written in the variables it can modify. Formally, a *distributed program* (or *distributed strategy*) for $\mathfrak{A}$ is a tuple $F = (f^p)_{p \in \text{Proc}}$ such that, for any $p \in \text{Proc}$, $f^p : (S^{E^{-1}(p)})^+ \to S^{E(p)}$ — each program provides the next value to give to the variables modified by the process, according to the history of values taken by the variables read by the process. Such a strategy is called with *local memory*. Indeed, as already outlined, $S^{E^{-1}(p)}$ is the domain of the set of variables that process p can read, and $S^{E(p)}$ is the domain of the set of variables it can modify. Moreover, in its computation, a program must take into account the delay associated with the process. Formally, for all sequences of inputs $\sigma, \sigma' \in (S^{E^{-1}(p)})^i$ such that $\sigma[0..i - d_p] = \sigma'[0..i - d_p]$ we have $f^p(\sigma) = f^p(\sigma')$.

With these definitions, we say that a *run* $\sigma = s_0 s_1 \cdots \in (S^V)^\omega$ is compatible with a distributed strategy $F = (f^p)_{p \in \text{Proc}}$ if, for each $i > 0$, for each $p \in \text{Proc}$, $s_i^{E(p)} = f^p(\sigma^{E^{-1}(p)}[0..i])$ (recall that the sets $E(p)$ are pairwise disjoints). Moreover, if there is some process $p \in \text{Proc}$ with delay 0, we require the architecture to be acyclic (to see a definition of cyclic architectures with 0-delay processes, see [BER 06]).

Example 10.2 Consider again the architecture illustrated in Figure 10.7, and suppose that all the variables range over $\{0, 1\}$. If the processes are both 0-delay, define the (memoryless) strategies $f^{p_1}(\sigma \cdot s) = (s \oplus 1, s)$ for any $\sigma \in (S^u)^*$, where the first component is the value of the variable x and the second component is the value of the variable t, and for any $s \in S^u$, and $f^{p_2}(\sigma \cdot (s_t, s_v)) = s_t \oplus s_v$, for any $\sigma \in (S^{t,v})^*$, and for any $(s_t, s_v) \in (S^{t,v})$. The symbol $\oplus$ indicates the addition modulo 2. Then, at each instant, variable x is different from u, variable t transmits to the process p_2 the value of u. Then, variable y is equal to the exclusive or (xor) of the two input variables t and v, hence to the xor of u and v. The following is a prefix of a run compatible with this strategy:

$$
\begin{array}{cccc}
u: & \begin{pmatrix} 0 \\ 0 \\ 1 \\ 0 \\ 0 \end{pmatrix} & \begin{pmatrix} 1 \\ 0 \\ 0 \\ 1 \\ 1 \end{pmatrix} & \begin{pmatrix} 1 \\ 1 \\ 0 \\ 1 \\ 0 \end{pmatrix} & \cdots \\
v: & & & & \cdots \\
x: & & & & \cdots \\
t: & & & & \cdots \\
y: & & & & \cdots
\end{array}
$$

Recall that the value of u and v are controlled by the environment, not by the system. Hence, there are as many runs compatible with a given strategy as possible choices for the environment for the sequence of input values.

Specifications are given by either a Büchi automaton over $(S^V)^\omega$, or a temporal logic formula (linear-time or branching-time) with atomic propositions of the form

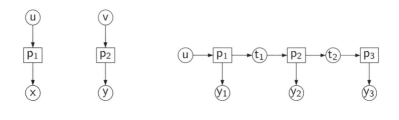

(a) Totally oblivious architecture   (b) Pipeline

Figure 10.8. *The two extremes of the decidability results*

$(v = a)$, for any $v \in V$ and $a \in S^v$ (see Chapter 7 for a definition of temporal logic and a description of the link between **LTL** and Büchi automata). The *synthesis problem for distributed systems* is then:
Input: an architecture $\mathfrak{A} = (\text{Proc}, V, E, (S^v)_{v \in V}, s_0, (d_p)_{p \in \text{Proc}})$, and a specification φ;
Output: a distributed program $F = (f^p)_{p \in \text{Proc}}$ such that every run compatible with F satisfies φ. [1]

This problem is actually twofold: a decision problem called the *realizability problem* that takes an architecture and a specification as input and decides the existence of a distributed program, and, if such a distributed program exists, the *synthesis problem* asks for a specific program to be produced. With slight abuse, we will say that the synthesis problem is decidable (respectively undecidable) if the corresponding realizability problem is decidable (respectively undecidable).

THEOREM 10.9 ([PNU 90]) *The synthesis problem for distributed systems is undecidable, for **LTL** or **CTL** specifications.*

The proof of this theorem is based on results on multi-player games by Peterson and Reif [PET 79], and gives undecidability even for the simple architecture of Figure 10.8(a).

It is nevertheless possible to decide the realizability problem and synthesize distributed programs in some identified subcases. For instance, a *pipeline* (represented

---

1. In case of branching-time specifications, one needs to define *run-trees* that gather all possible computations into one model. This can be done in a fairly straightforward way.

on Figure 10.8(b)) is an architecture in which information flows linearly from input to output variables. Then, we obtain the following theorem:

THEOREM 10.10 ([PNU 90, KUP 01]) *The synthesis problem for distributed systems is decidable for total* CTL^* *specifications, when restricted to pipeline architectures.*

For total specifications, a decidability criterion has been exhibited in [FIN 05]: for the problem to be decidable, the architecture considered must be *totally preordered* with respect to information. This means that all the processes of the architecture can be ordered in the following sense: process p is greater than process p' if p' has a better knowledge of the global state of the system: if all the variables that can be used to transmit information from the environment to process p can be *read* by p', then p' is able to know as much as p. Otherwise the architecture has an *information fork* and the problem is undecidable (see Figure 10.9(b)).

Total specifications are more powerful than external ones, so as far as positive results are concerned, it is more interesting to obtain the result for total specifications. However, it might be too strong a requirement, as shown with the architecture of Figure 10.7. The problem is undecidable for this architecture with total specifications ([FIN 05]), but becomes decidable if we relax the specifications to external ones [PNU 90]).

A specification is *external* if it only constrains the value of the input and output variables of the system. The problem of finding a decidability criterion for the synthesis problem for distributed systems, when restricted to external specifications is a challenging one, and is still an open question. We know what can cause undecidability though: the problem with external specifications is undecidable if the architecture is with *uncomparable information*, i.e., we can find two *output* processes with a set of *co-accessible* input variables that are not comparable (in the sense of set inclusion).

Figure 10.9 shows examples to illustrate the differences between the different notions. The architecture of Figure 10.9(a) is with uncomparable information: the set of coaccessible input variables of p_2 is $\{x_0, x_1, x_2\}$, which is not comparable with the set of co-accessible input variables of p_3 : $\{x_1, x_2, x_3\}$. It is then undecidable for both external and total specifications. Architectures of Figure 10.9(b) have an *information fork*: for instance, in the architecture on the right, process p_4 has access to x_2, but x_2 is not read by p_3, and reciprocally, process p_3 is linked to input variable x_1 that cannot be read by process p_4. However, the set of co-accessible input variables is the same for the two processes: $\{x_1, x_2\}$. In fact, when we are restricted to external specifications, the problem can be decidable for this architecture [GAS 09]. The architecture illustrated in the last part of the figure is totally preordered and thus the problem is decidable for this architecture for both external and total specifications.

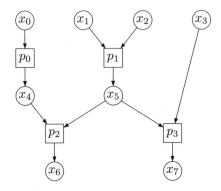

(a) Architecture with uncomparable information

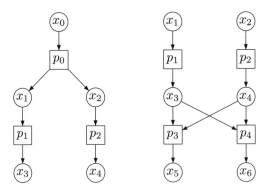

(b) Architectures with information fork but without uncomparable information

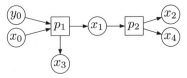

(c) A totally preordered architecture

Figure 10.9. *Examples of architectures with uncomparable information or linearly preordered*

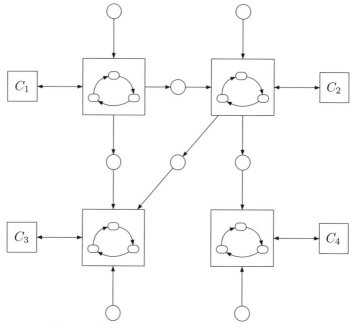

Figure 10.10. *A plant with its controllers*

A control problem with local specifications

To consider a *control problem* in this setting, we should incorporate the notion of a *plant* in the model. To that matter, to each site we add a (finite-state) program of the process to be controlled. This program is represented by a transition system, whose set of states can be seen as an additional private variable, local to the process, that memorizes its control state. Its transition function maps a local state and a tuple of values on the variable readable by the process to the next possible local states, and the next acceptable values for the shared variables modified by the process. Here it is assumed that the architectures are zero-delay (and hence acyclic). Formally, a *plant* is a couple $(\mathfrak{A}, \hat{P})$, where $\mathfrak{A} = (\mathrm{Proc}, V, E, (S^v)_{v \in V}, s_0)$ is an architecture, and $\hat{P}$ is a tuple of programs for the processes: $\hat{P} = (P^p)_{p \in \mathrm{Proc}}$, and each $P^p = (Q^p, q_0^p, \delta^p)$ is a transition system with Q^p is the set of states, $q_0^p \in Q^p$ is the initial state and $\delta^p : Q^p \times S^{E^{-1}(p)} \to 2^{Q^p \times S^{E(p)}}$ is the transition function.

The problem is then to automatically synthesize *local controllers* for the processes. Formally, a controller for process p is a function $f^p : Q^p \times (S^{E^{-1}(p)})^+ \times Q^p \times S^{E(p)}$ such that, for all $q \in Q^p$, for all $\sigma \cdot s \in (S^{E^{-1}(p)})^+$, $f^p(q, \sigma \cdot s) \in \delta^p(q, s)$. Hence, a local controller is an *advice function* that gives, according to the current state of the process, and the history of input values, the next move the program should take. A *distributed controller* is then a tuple $F = (f^p)_{p \in \mathrm{Proc}}$ of local controllers.

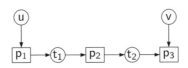

Figure 10.11. *Clean pipeline*

Given a distributed controller $F = (f^p)_{p \in \text{Proc}}$, a F-*controlled run* is a sequence $\sigma = (q_0, s_0)(q_1, s_1) \cdots \in (Q^{\text{Proc}} \times S^V)^\omega$ such that:

(C_1) $q_0 = (q_0^p)_{p \in \text{Proc}}$ is the tuple of initial states for the processes;

(C_2) for all $p \in \text{Proc}$, for all $i \geq 0$, if $f^p(q_i^p, (s_0 \cdots s_i)^{E^{-1}(p)}) = (q, s)$, then $q_{i+1}^p = q$, and for all $v \in E(p)$, $s_i^v = s^v$. Since the set of variables modified by the system forms a partition of the processes, this is well defined.

The condition (C_1) ensures that all the programs start in their initial state, while the condition (C_2) enforces the evolution of the system to respect the controllers advice. Observe that since the controller is a deterministic function, there is only one controlled run that matches a given sequence of values for the input variables of the system.

The *control problem* is then:
Input: a plant $(\mathfrak{A}, \hat{P})$, and a specification φ;
Output: a distributed controller $F = (f^p)_{p \in \text{Proc}}$ such that every F-controlled run satisfies φ.

It turns out that decidability results obtained in theorem 10.10 extend to the control framework. Madhusudan and Thiagarajan have studied the control problem in this framework, and advocating that global specifications as those presented in the previous subsection are unreasonably powerful, have investigated the problem with *local* specifications. In this context, a specification is said to be *local* if it is defined on the sequence of local states for each process.

A *clean pipeline* is an architecture in which the processes communicate in a chain, and the input variables are read by the first and the last process of this chain (see Figure 10.11). Observe that the output variables are not represented anymore: they are incorporated in the local states of the processes.

THEOREM 10.11 ([MAD 01]) *The control problem with local LTL specifications is decidable for clean pipelines.*

Since pipelines of Figure 10.8(b) are special cases of clean pipelines, this result extends the class of decidable architectures when we consider local specifications.

Unfortunately, local specifications also to lead to undecidability quite quickly too.

THEOREM 10.12 ([MAD 01]) *The control problem with local* **LTL** *specifications is undecidable for any architecture that is not a subarchitecture of a clean pipeline.*

10.3.3. *Asynchronous systems*

The *synthesis problem* for asynchronous systems was first studied in the centralized framework, with asynchronous communications (through shared variables) ([PNU 89, ANU 94, VAR 95]), but it is a very weak means of communication for the processes in the distributed case. This specific problem was addressed in [FIN 06]. Other works ([MAD 02, GAS 04a, MAD 05, CHA 09]) have assumed synchronous communications, mostly by rendez-vous.

The model

In asynchronous distributed systems, two events may occur independently on two different sites. We may chose to represent executions of such systems by *words* representing possible interleavings of independent events. This formalism translates the notion of *concurrency* between two events into a *non-deterministic* choice. To precisely describe and analyze executions of such systems, Mazurkiewcz traces have been introduced [MAZ 77, MAZ 86] (see also [ROZ 95]). In this setting, the concurrency between two events is preserved, since a specific order between two events is assumed only if the events are linked by a causality relation, encoded in the model by the notion of *dependency*. Since executions of asynchronous architectures will be represented by Mazurkiewicz traces, we first define these objects.

DEFINITION 10.13 (dependence alphabet) *A dependence alphabet is a pair* (Σ, D) *where* Σ *is a finite set of events and* $D \subseteq \Sigma \times \Sigma$ *is a reflexive and symmetric relation called* dependence relation. *The complementary relation* $I = \Sigma \times \Sigma \setminus D$ *is called* independence relation.

DEFINITION 10.14 (Mazurkiewicz trace) *A* Mazurkiewicz trace *over the dependence alphabet* (Σ, D) *is (up to isomorphism) a* Σ-*labeled partial order* $t = (V, \leq, \lambda)$ *(with* $\lambda : V \to \Sigma$ *a labeling function) such that:*

1) *for all* $x \in V$, *the set* $\{y \in V \mid y \leq x\}$ *is finite;*
2) *for all* $x, y \in V$, $x \lessdot y \implies \lambda(x) \ D \ \lambda(y)$;

3) for all $x, y \in V$, $\lambda(x)$ D $\lambda(y)$ $\implies$ $x \leq y$ or $y \leq y$.

There is a mapping between the infinite words over Σ and the infinite Mazurkiewicz traces over (Σ, D). In fact, every word is the linearization of a *unique* Mazurkiewicz trace over (Σ, D), and a Mazurkiewicz trace admits at least one linearization over Σ^ω.

Given a set of processes Proc, we consider a *distributed alphabet* (Σ, loc), where Σ is a finite set of actions, and $\mathsf{loc} : \Sigma \to 2^{\mathrm{Proc}} \setminus \emptyset$ is a total function mapping each function to the set of processes that take part into its execution. An action $a \in \Sigma$ is said to be *local* if $|\mathsf{loc}(a)| = 1$. Moreover, Σ is partitioned into the sets of controllable and uncontrollable actions denoted Σ_c and Σ_{uc}, respectively, and all the uncontrollable actions are assumed to be local. Now, the system to be controlled is an *asynchronous automaton* [ZIE 87].

In other words, in this framework, an *architecture* is given by a tuple

$$\mathfrak{A} = (\mathrm{Proc}, \Sigma, \mathsf{loc}, (S^p)_{p \in \mathrm{Proc}}, s_0, (\delta_a)_{a \in \Sigma})$$

where Proc is a set of processes, (Σ, loc) form a distributed alphabet over Proc, and moreover, $\Sigma = \Sigma_c \uplus \Sigma_{uc}$ is partitioned into the set of controllable and uncontrollable actions, S^p is the finite set of states of process p, $s_0 = (s_0^p)_{p \in \mathrm{Proc}}$ is the global initial state, formed by the initial local states of each process, and for all $a \in \Sigma$, $\delta_a \subseteq S^{\mathsf{loc}(a)} \times S^{\mathsf{loc}(a)}$ is the transition function associated to the action a, giving the evolution of the states of all the processes involved in the execution of a. In the following, we will write Σ^p for the set of actions in which p is involved, i.e. actions a such that $p \in \mathsf{loc}(a)$.

Runs of such architectures are Mazurkiewicz traces over the alphabet (Σ, D) where, for all $a, b \in \Sigma$, a D b if and only if $\mathsf{loc}(a) \cap \mathsf{loc}(b) \neq \emptyset$. Indeed, two events are dependent if one process participates in the execution of both. Otherwise, they can occur independently. Alternatively, we can see them as words over Σ^ω (i.e. as the possible interleavings). Then, the global system can be seen as a transition system $TS_\mathfrak{A} = ((S^p)_{p \in \mathrm{Proc}}, \Sigma, \to, s_0)$, where the transition relation $\to \subseteq (S^p)_{p \in \mathrm{Proc}} \times \Sigma \times (S^p)_{p \in \mathrm{Proc}}$ is given by $(s, a, s') \in \to$ if, and only if, $(s^p)_{p \in \mathsf{loc}a}, (s'^p)_{p \in \mathsf{loc}a} \in \delta_a$, and for all $p \notin \mathsf{loc}(a)$, $s^p = s'^p$. The runs of the system are then sequences of elements in $\{s_0\} \cdot ((S^p)_{p \in \mathrm{Proc}} \cdot \Sigma)^\omega$ respecting the transition relations $\to$. Observe that, in that case, the set of runs is *trace-closed*: if a word is a run of the system, then all the other linearizations of the unique corresponding Mazurkiewicz trace are also runs of the system.

Consider the architecture illustrated in Figure 10.12, adapted from [MAD 02]. It is part of an architecture modeling the dining philosopher's problem. Here we only have pictured one philosopher and one fork. In this problem, n philosophers are around

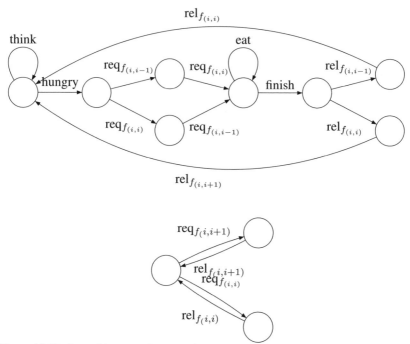

Figure 10.12. *An architecture of an asynchronous system: one philosopher and one fork*

a table, and n forks are available: one fork between two philosophers. The upper process in Figure 10.12 models the philosopher i. He thinks for a while, and then becomes hungry. He picks one the left or the right fork, then the other one, and eats for a while. When he is finished, he puts his forks back on the table. The uncontrollable actions are think, hungry, eat, and finish and are local actions (do not involve any other processes). The actions $\text{req}_{f_{(i,j)}}$ and $\text{rel}_{f_{(i,j)}}$ stand for "philosopher i requests the fork j" and "philosopher i releases the fork j" respectively. Observe that the request action involves both the fork and the process, then $\text{loc}(\text{req}_{f_{(i,j)}}) = \{philo_i, fork_j\}$. If the fork is already used by another philosopher, philosopher i cannot take the transition $\text{req}_{f_{(i,j)}}$, it will only be possible when the other philosopher releases its fork.

Representation of executions by Mazurkiewicz traces provides two natural ways of defining history available to local controllers for the processes. The first has already been presented in the chapter and is called *local memory*. A controller for a process $p \in \text{Proc}$ is with local memory if its decisions are based on the history of events $a \in \Sigma$ such that $p \in \text{loc}(a)$, i.e. it depends only on the actions that are locally visible. This is in some sense the minimal amount of information can be provide to the controllers. Now, a controller is with *causal memory* if it depends on all the events in the *past* of the last local event, in the trace representing the run. An algorithm for the processes to compute this relation has been given by Mattern with the introduction of *vectorial clocks* [MAT 89]. This can be seen as the maximal amount of information that can be allowed while keeping the distribution of the controllers. This is less unrealistic than it may seem at first glance, and the amount of information to transmit is actually bounded.

When controlling such asynchronous automata, a choice can also be made between controlling the processes (process-based controllers) or controlling the actions (action-based controllers). In the process-based version, each process decides which action to undertake. An action is then undertaken if all the processes involved agree to do so. In the action-based version, each action is declared executable or not, regarding the state of all the processes involved.

Controllers with local memory

We present here the model defined by Madhusudan and Thiagarajan in [MAD 02]. The goal is to synthesize a set of controllers, one for each process, whose actions are determined only by the history of actions locally visible to the process. Formally, a strategy (or controller) for process p is a function $f^p : (\Sigma^p)^* \cdot S^p \to 2^{\Sigma^p}$ that maps a current local state of the process and a sequence of actions in which p is involved to a set of allowed actions. Of course, the strategy always allows all the possible uncontrollable actions. Moreover, if we write, for $s \in S^p$, $en(s) = \{a \in \Sigma^p \mid \exists s', s'' \in (S^p)_{p \in \text{loca}}, s'^p = s \text{ and } (s', s'') \in \delta_a\}$ the set of locally enabled actions for process p, we require that $f^p(\sigma, s) \subseteq en(s)$, for any $\sigma \in (\Sigma^p)^*$, $s \in S^p$. This enforces the fact that the controller can only restrict the allowed behavior.

The specification is given by an ω-regular language over Σ, the alphabet of actions. Recall that we have stated that the runs of the system are trace-closed. Without this requirement, it could lead to specifications that do not respect the asynchronous aspect of the system, by discriminating between two linearizations of the same partial order. Moreover, we state the following theorem:

THEOREM 10.15 *[MAD 02] If the specification language is not trace-closed, the control problem for asynchronous systems is undecidable.*

Madhusudan and Thiagarajan [MAD 02] show that if the specification language is trace-closed, in the very restricted case where the strategies are *clocked* and *com-rigid*, the problem becomes decidable. A strategy is *clocked* if it only depends on the current local state, and on the *number* of actions already taken, the exact history remaining unknown. It is *com-rigid* if, at each instant, the actions it allows are actions that involve the same set of processes.

Controllers with causal memory

The previous restrictions can be released if we consider causal memory. Informally, a controller with causal memory is a controller that depends on all the actions that are in the causal past (i.e. in the past in the partial order of the Mazurkiewicz trace) of the last action locally visible to the controller. To understand this, it is useful to see the executions of the system as Mazurkiewicz traces, i.e. partial orders of actions. All the actions of a given process are totally ordered, but actions on other processes may be concurrent. Consider the architecture illustrated in Figure 10.13(a). The dependence relation for the different actions can be computed and built from the linear execution *abcadcadb* the partial order of Figure 10.13(b), where fortuitous orders between events have been erased. At this point, the local view of process p_1 is simply aaa, whereas its causal view is illustrated in Figure 10.13(c): all the events in the past of the maximal event occurred on p_1 (here a) are included. The causal view of the *action* a now takes the maximal events that have occurred on all the processes involved in a, and can view all the events in the causal past of these elements. In our example, it means that the local view of a also includes the last b (as illustrated in Figure 10.13(d)). Hence, action-based controllers are more powerful than process-based controllers, since, they can simultaneously observe the state of several processes (those that are involved in the action). We will return to that observation later.

It has been shown in [MAD 05] that for *connectedly communicating processes* (CCP) and trace-closed specifications, the control problem is decidable. An architecture is a CCP if there exists some bound on the number of steps a process p can execute without communicating with q (directly or indirectly) and communicate with him again later. In other words, the bound k is such that, if p executes k steps without communicating with q, they will never communicate again.

Controllers with causal memory have also been studied by Gastin, Lerman, and Zeitoun (see [GAS 04a]) in the case of controllers distributed among *actions* (in fact, controllers with causal memory have been introduced in [GAS 04b]). To describe their decidability result, we need the following definition: a dependence alphabet is a *co-graph* if it can be obtained from singletons using serial and parallel compositions (given (A, D_A) and (B, D_B) two dependence alphabets, the parallel composition is of the form $(A \cup B, D_A \cup D_B)$ and the serial product is $(A \cup B, D_A \cup D_B \cup A \times B \cup B \times A))$. Behaviors on co-graphs are called series-parallel. In [GAS 04a], the authors show that the control problem is decidable for architectures with a dependence alphabet that is a co-graph and trace-closed ω-regular specifications.

As we have already pointed out, action-based controllers are more powerful than process-based controllers. In fact, there exist an architecture and a specification such that there exists a distributed winning strategy for action-based controllers, but none for process-based controllers ([MUS 09]).

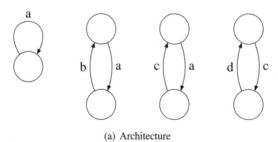

(a) Architecture

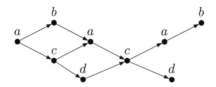

(b) The execution viewed as a Mazurkiewicz trace

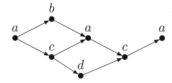

(c) Causal view of process p_1

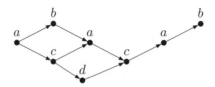

(d) Causal view of action a

Figure 10.13. *Different views for the controllers*

10.4. Multi-player games

As pointed out in the introduction to the chapter, there is a natural relation between the (distributed) control problem and (multi-player) games: the controllers are a team of players that cooperate against an opponent - the environment. In this section we present some of theoretic approaches used in games to the distributed control problem.

10.4.1. *ATL*

The logic ATL (alternating-time Ttemporal logic) [ALU 97] has been introduced as a specification language particularly adapted to *open systems*, in which several agents can influence the behavior of the system. While LTL mainly allows the description what *will* arrive and CTL what *can* arrive, ATL can express the fact that some agent (or coalition of agents) can *control* the system in order to enforce a given property. In that sense, it can be seen as an extension of CTL, since it offers *selective quantification* over paths that are possible outcomes of a game.

If a Kripke structure is the model on which linear-time and branching-time logics are interpreted, alternating-time temporal logics are interpreted on *multi-agents systems*, such as concurrent game structures. In a concurrent game structure, all the players of the game are given the ability to undertake actions simultaneously. These structures are then well adapted to describe concurrent and synchronous games. However, we will see that it is flexible enough to also describe turn-based games by offering only one action to all the players but one in a given state, and asynchronous games by adding an additional player acting as a scheduler.

DEFINITION 10.16 (**Concurrent Game Structure**) *A concurrent game structure (CGS) is a tuple $S = (k, Q, \Pi, \pi, d, \delta)$ such that:*

– k is a natural number representing the number of players, identified by numbers ranging from 1 to k;

– Q is a finite set of states;

– Π is a finite set of propositions;

– π is a labeling function, such that for each state $q \in Q$, $\pi(q) \subseteq \Pi$ indicates the set of propositions true at q;

– for each player $a \in \{1, \ldots, k\}$, and each state $q \in Q$, the natural number $d_a(q) \geq 1$ gives the number of moves available to player a at state q. These moves are identified with the numbers $1, \ldots, d_a(q)$. At each state $q \in Q$, a move vector is a tuple $(j_1, \ldots, j_k)$ such that for each player a, $1 \leq j_a \leq d_a(q)$. We define also a move function D that gives for each $q \in Q$, the set of possible move vectors: $D(q) = \{1, \ldots d_1(q)\} \times \cdots \times \{1, \ldots, d_k(q)\}$;

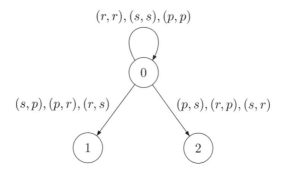

Figure 10.14. *A concurrent game structure*

    – δ *is a transition function defined for each* $q \in Q$ *and each move vector* $(j_1, \ldots, j_k) \in D(q)$ *by a state* $\delta(q, j_1, \ldots, j_k) \in Q$ *that results from state* q *when every player* a *plays the move* $d_a(q)$.

    In a concurrent game structure, at each state, each player chooses a move among the set of available moves. The choice is made concurrently: a player does not know the moves chosen by the others. By applying the transition function to the resulting tuple and the current state, the next state of the run is obtained. The concurrent game structure illustrated in Figure 10.14 represents a "rock/paper/scissors" game (example taken from [LAR 10]). In this two-player game, the players choose simultaneously between the rock, the scissors, and the paper. The rock breaks the scissors but is wrapped in the piece of paper, that is itself cut by the scissors. In the CGS, a pair (c_1, c_2) represents the move c_1 of player A_1 and c_2 of player A_2, where r stands for rock, p for paper and s for scissors. In state 1, A_1 wins the game, in state 2, A_2 wins. This example shows the concurrency of the model.

    Open systems are also commonly represented by *turn-based* synchronous games, in which the players play one at a time. It is, in fact, a special case of a concurrent game structure, in which at each state q, only one player has a choice of moves, for any other player a, $d_a(q) = 1$. Consider for instance the classical example of the gate controller ([ALU 97]): a train arrives at a crossing and needs to drive through a gate. Whether or not the train is allowed to enter the gate is decided by a controller. Figure 10.15 illustrates the associated concurrent game structure. The labeling function gives:

    – $\pi(q_0) = \{out\_of\_gate\}$: the train is outside the gate;

    – $\pi(q_1) = \{out\_of\_gate, request\}$: the train is outside the gate and has requested to enter;

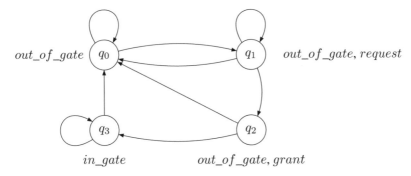

Figure 10.15. *The gate controller*

 – $\pi(q_2) = \{out\_of\_gate, grant\}$: the train is outside the gate and has been given permission to enter;

 – $\pi(q_3) = \{in\_gate\}$: the train is in the gate.

Here, the states q_0 and q_2 belong to the train, and the states q_1 and q_3 belong to the controller. In state q_0, the train can request to enter the gate or can chose to stay out of the gate. In state q_1, the controller can either grant the train permission to enter, or deny it, or delay the handling of the request (by staying in q_1). In state q_2, the train can either enter the gate or cancel its request and go back to q_0. In state q_3, the controller can chose to keep the gate closed (by staying in q_3), or decide to open it to new requests.

Alternatively, it is possible to encode turned-based asynchronous game structures in concurrent game structures, which is useful to model transmission protocols for instance. To that matter, an additional player playing the role of a *scheduler* is required. In every state, the scheduler selects one of the players, that will be the one to choose its move at the next state.

Syntax and semantics of ATL

Given a set Π of propositions, and a finite set $\Sigma = \{1, \ldots, k\}$ of players, an ATL formula φ is described by the following grammar:

$$\varphi ::= p \mid \neg\varphi \mid \varphi \vee \varphi \mid \langle\!\langle A \rangle\!\rangle X\varphi \mid \langle\!\langle A \rangle\!\rangle G\varphi \mid \langle\!\langle A \rangle\!\rangle \varphi U \varphi$$

where $p \in \Pi$ is a proposition, and $A \subseteq \Sigma$ is a coalition of players. As in CTL, the modalities X, G, and U are temporal operators, intuitively meaning respectively "next", "always" and "until", and the operator $\langle\!\langle \rangle\!\rangle$ is a *path quantifier*, selecting those paths enforced by some strategies for the players of A.

An **ATL** formula is interpreted over states of a concurrent game structure having the same sets of propositions and players. Formally, consider the concurrent game structure $S = (k, Q, \Pi, \pi, d, \delta)$. A strategy for a player $a \in \Sigma$ is a function that determines the next move for player a, after a finite sequence of states. Formally, we define $f_a : Q^+ \to \mathbb{N}$ such that, if $\lambda \in Q^+$ ends with the state q, $f_a(\lambda) \leq d_a(q)$. Hence, the strategy always offers a possible move. Given a coalition A, and a set F_A of strategies for the players in A, given a state $q \in Q$, we define the possible outcomes of F_A from q (denoted $\text{outcome}(q, F_A)$) to be the set of computations $q_0 q_1 \ldots$ such that $q = q_0$, and for all $i \geq 0$, there is a move vector $(j_1, \ldots, j_k)$ such that (1) $f_a(q_0 \ldots q_i) = j_a$, for all $a \in A$, and (2)$\delta(q_i, j_1, \ldots, j_k) = q_{i+1}$.

Consider a state $q \in Q$. The semantics is given inductively by:

$S, q \models p$	if p labels the state q;
$S, q \models \neg\varphi$	if $S, q \not\models \varphi$;
$S, q \models \varphi_1 \vee \varphi_2$	if S, q satisfies either φ_1 or φ_2;
$S, q \models \langle\!\langle A \rangle\!\rangle \mathsf{X}\varphi$	if there is a set F_A of strategies for the players in A such that, for all computations $q_0 q_1 \cdots \in \text{outcome}(q, f_A)$, $S, q_1 \models \varphi$;
$S, q \models \langle\!\langle A \rangle\!\rangle \mathsf{G}\varphi$	if there is a set F_A of strategies for the players in A such that, for all computations $q_0 q_1 \cdots \in \text{outcome}(q, f_A)$, for all $i \geq 0$, $S, q_i \models \varphi$;
$S, q \models \langle\!\langle A \rangle\!\rangle \varphi_1 \mathsf{U}\varphi_2$	if there is a set F_A of strategies for the players in A such that, for all computations $q_0 q_1 \cdots \in \text{outcome}(q, f_A)$, there is some $i \geq 0$, such that $S, q_i \models \varphi_2$ and for all $0 \leq k < i$, $S, q_k \models \varphi_1$.

It is also useful to consider the dual notion of $\langle\!\langle \rangle\!\rangle$, that will be denoted $[\![ ]\!]$. Intuitively, if the formula $\langle\!\langle A \rangle\!\rangle \varphi$ means that the coalition of players A can enforce φ, $[\![A]\!] \varphi$ cannot "avoid" φ (they cannot cooperate in order to make it false). Then, for a coalition A, we can write $[\![A]\!] \mathsf{X}\varphi$ for $\neg\langle\!\langle A \rangle\!\rangle\mathsf{X}\neg\varphi$ $[\![A]\!] \mathsf{G}\varphi$ for $\neg\langle\!\langle A \rangle\!\rangle\mathsf{F}\neg\varphi$, and $[\![A]\!] \mathsf{F}\varphi$ for $\neg\langle\!\langle A \rangle\!\rangle\mathsf{G}\neg\varphi$.

If we consider the example of the gate controller illustrated in Figure 10.15, we can express in **ATL** the following properties (taken from [ALU 97]) that are all satisfied in the initial state of our CGS. In the following properties ctr represents the controller:

– whenever the train is out of the gate and has not been granted the permission to enter the gate, the controller can prevent it from entering the gate:

$$\langle\!\langle \rangle\!\rangle \mathsf{G}((out\_of\_gate \wedge \neg grant) \to \langle\!\langle ctr \rangle\!\rangle \mathsf{G}\ out\_of\_gate.)$$

Observe that this formula could not been expressed in **CTL** nor **CTL***. In this CGS, whenever the train is out of the gate and does not have the permission to enter the gate, there exists a computation in which the train finally enters the gate, so the **CTL** formula $\mathsf{AG}((out\_of\_gate \wedge \neg grant) \to \mathsf{EG}out\_of\_gate)$ is not satisfied. What we express in the **ATL** formula, is that, *however* the train behaves, the controller *can enforce* it to stay out of the gate;

– whenever the train is out of the gate, the controller cannot force it to enter the gate:

$$\langle\langle\rangle\rangle \mathsf{G} \; (out\_of\_gate \rightarrow [\![ctr]\!] \; \mathsf{G} \; out\_of\_gate);$$

– whenever the train is out of the gate, the train and the controller can cooperate so that the train will enter the gate

$$\langle\langle\rangle\rangle \mathsf{G} \; (out\_of\_gate \rightarrow \langle\langle ctr, train\rangle\rangle \mathsf{F} \; in\_gate).$$

Note that in that case, since there are only two players, it is indeed the same than the CTL formula AG $(out\_of\_gate \rightarrow$ EF $in\_gate)$: the fact that they can both cooperate in order to obtain some result amounts then to the existence of a path obtaining the result;

– whenever the train is out of the gate, it can eventually request a grant for entering the gate, in which case the controller decides whether the grant is given or not:

$$\langle\langle\rangle\rangle \mathsf{G} \; (out\_of\_gate \rightarrow \langle\langle train\rangle\rangle \mathsf{F} \; (request \wedge (\langle\langle ctr\rangle\rangle \mathsf{F} \; grant) \wedge (\langle\langle ctr\rangle\rangle \mathsf{G}\neg grant)));$$

– whenever the train is in the gate, the controller can force it out in the next step:

$$\langle\langle\rangle\rangle \mathsf{G} \; (in\_gate \rightarrow \langle\langle ctr\rangle\rangle \mathsf{X} \; out\_of\_gate).$$

Model-checking

If we want to verify whether controller exists that can enforce a given specification for instance, we need to *model-check* the corresponding ATL formula stating that the controller has a strategy to enforce the specification. The model-checking problem for ATL asks, given a CGS $S = (k, Q, \Pi, \pi, d, \delta)$ and an ATL formula φ, for the set of states in Q that satisfy φ. Model-checking algorithms are similar to those used for CTL, except that instead of a pre-image operator, we need here a *controllable predecessor* operator, computing the set of predecessor states in which the players can cooperate and enforce the next state to be the one asked for. We will not detail this algorithm here, interested readers can refer to [ALU 97]. ATL model-checking is PTIME-complete, and is implemented in MOCHA [ALU 98].

As for every logic, several extensions of ATL exist. We present some of them here.

An extension of ATL: ATL*

Like CTL is a fragment of CTL*, ATL is a fragment of a logic called ATL*. Formulae of ATL* are formed by two types of formulaes: *state* formulae, and *path* formulae. Formally, a ATL* state formula φ is of the form:

$$\varphi ::= p \; | \; \neg\varphi \; | \; \varphi \vee \varphi \; | \; \langle\langle A\rangle\rangle \psi$$

for $p \in \Pi$ is an atomic proposition, $A \subseteq \Sigma$ is a set of players, and ψ is a ATL* path formula defined by:

$$\psi ::= \varphi \mid \neg\psi \mid \psi \vee \psi \mid X\psi \mid \psi U\psi.$$

An ATL* formula is a state formula. The semantics of a ATL* is, given a CGS S, a state q and a path λ, defined as follows:

$$
\begin{aligned}
&S, q \models p && \text{if } p \text{ labels the state } q; \\
&S, q \models \neg\varphi && \text{if } S, q \not\models \varphi; \\
&S, q \models \varphi_1 \vee \varphi_2 && \text{if } S, q \text{ satisfies either } \varphi_1 \text{ or } \varphi_2; \\
&S, q \models \langle\!\langle A \rangle\!\rangle \psi && \text{if there is a set } F_A \text{ of strategies for the players in } A \text{ such that,} \\
& && \text{for all computations } \lambda \in \text{outcome}(q, f_A), \text{ then } S, \lambda \models \psi; \\
&S, \lambda \models \varphi && \text{for } \varphi \text{ a state formula, if } \lambda = q_0 q_1 \cdots \text{ and } S, q_0 \models \varphi; \\
&S, \lambda \models \neg\psi && \text{if } S, \lambda \not\models \psi, \\
&S, \lambda \models \psi_1 \vee \psi_2 && \text{if } S, \lambda \text{ satisfies } \psi_1 \text{ or } \psi_2, \\
&S, \lambda \models X\psi && \text{if } \lambda = q_0 q_1 \ldots \text{ and } S, q_1 \models \psi; \\
&S, \lambda \models \psi_1 U \psi_2 && \text{if } \lambda = q_0 q_1 \ldots \text{ and there is some } i \geq 0, \text{ such that} \\
& && S, q_i q_2 \cdots \models \varphi_2 \text{ and for all } 0 \leq k < i, S, q_k q_{k+1} \cdots \models \varphi_1.
\end{aligned}
$$

The formula $\langle\!\langle A \rangle\!\rangle FG\neg req \vee GF grant$ expressing that a coalition of players can enforce that an infinite number of requests implies an infinite number of grants is neither expressible in ATL nor in CTL*.

The model-checking of ATL* is 2EXPTIME-complete (the lower bound is obtained by a reduction to the LTL realizability problem [PNU 89]), and PTIME-complete when restricted to ATL* formulae of bounded size.

ATL with incomplete information

The definition of ATL assumes that each player of the game has complete information about the state of the CGS: strategies for the player depends on the history of the global states visited so far. However, in the distributed control framework, it is generally admitted that controllers have a *local view* of the system. The definitions of CGS and ATL can be adapted to model such games with incomplete information.

In a turn-based synchronous CGS with incomplete information, each player can observe only a subset of the set of propositions. In particular, we use special atomic propositions, p_a for each player a. If p_a holds in one state, it means that it is player a's turn. We note $\sigma(q)$ the player that can play in q. This proposition p_a is always observable by the player a (each player can observe when it is its turn to play), but not necessarily by the other players (the other players might not be able to determine which player plays). Moreover, we require that the CGS respects the following property: in some state q where p_a holds, if there is a move from q to q', then the set of propositions that are *unobservable* to a is the same in q and q', except from $p_{\sigma(q')}$ that can appear in q': this information might be unobservable to a, and still appear in q'. Besides, from two states q_1 and q_2 where p_a holds and the set of atomic propositions observable to a is the same, if there is a move from q_1 to q'_1, then there is a move from q_2 to q'_2 for every state q'_2 verifying: 1) the set of propositions observable to a in q'_2 is the same than in q'_1 and 2) the set of propositions unobservable to a is the same in q'_2 and q'_1, except from $p_{\sigma(q'_2)}$ that might be different from $p_{\sigma(q'_1)}$.

To specify properties on such CGS with incomplete information, we need to restrict ourselves to a syntactic fragment of ATL. As a matter of fact, if some property p is not observable by a player a, the formula $\langle\langle a \rangle\rangle \mathsf{true} \mathsf{U} p$ makes no sense: if the player a cannot observe the property to reach, we cannot require him to have a strategy to attain such a state. Hence we require that each player in a coalition is able to observe all the properties involved in the task the coalition is required to attain. For formal definitions of CGS with incomplete information and of the corresponding fragment of ATL, the interested reader can again refer to [ALU 97].

Unfortunately, the model-checking problem for CGS with incomplete information is undecidable. The proof of this result relies on results of Yannanakis [YAN 97]. However, if we are restricted to *single-player* ATL, i.e., formulae in which coalitions are restricted to singletons of players, the model-checking problem for CGS with incomplete information becomes decidable, though EXPTIME-complete [ALU 97].

Other logics

Other logics have been proposed in the last years to increase the expressiveness of ATL and ATL*. For instance, strategy logic [CHA 07] extends LTL with first-order quantifications over strategies. It subsumes both ATL and ATL* and allows us to express properties for non-zero sum games, but is restricted to two-player games.

Definition of ATL semantics implies that, when quantification on strategies are nested, the outmost strategies are not taken into account by the innermost ones. In [DAC 10], an alternative definition of ATL is given, named ATL with strategy contexts, in which players *commit* to their strategies, which apply to evaluate the whole subformula. This logic is very expressive and can be model-checked.

A special framework of distributed games with incomplete information has been defined in [MOH 03]. In this case, an arena is composed of a synchronous product of several arenas, one for each player. Each local arena is bipartite: the moves of the player and the environment alternate. In the global arena, a state is controlled by the environment if all the local arenas are in an environment-controlled state. A move from such a state consists of a move in at least one local arena, leading to a player-controlled state. From a player-controlled state, all the players activated (i.e. those that are in a player-controlled state on the local arena) move on their local arena. The players that were not activated are even unaware of the existence of a move by other players. This model, though slightly abstract, is very flexible and allows numerous synthesis and control problems to be encoded, both in synchronous and asynchronous settings. They provide simplification theorems on the distributed games obtained, which often leads to games where a distributed strategy can be computed. Using this technical tool, they offer a uniform (and often simpler) way of solving classical problems of distributed control and synthesis.

10.5. Conclusion

Automatically controlling a distributed system in a distributed way respecting the structure of the plant is a challenging problem. We have presented two different approaches for this problem, respectively from the control and formal method communities. While the latter approach considers controllers whose actions should ensure that the infinite behavior of the plant belongs to the language of the specification, the former often looks for *maximal* controllers, i.e. controllers ensuring that the set of (often finite) behaviors is the language of the specification.

We have presented the main results regarding the control problem. Our presentation is obviously not exhaustive. For each presented problem we have not mentioned all the works concerned and we have not presented all the possible problems. Regarded the presented works, the controller must be a finite state controller. In [PUR 01, THI 09] the authors investigated infinite state controllers. Another supposition made in the results presented is that communications between the controllers and the plant are synchronous. In [TRI 04a] the authors investigated asynchronous communications.

To overcome the state explosion problem due to the study of a complete system, the hierarchical control of discrete event systems has been studied. It was first introduced in [ZHO 90]. A summary of the problem is presented in [GRI 05].

Some tools are proposed to solve the control problem. Some of them have been used to solve the Wodes benchmarks such as libFAUDES [MOO 08], STSlib [MA 08], and SUPREMICA [MIR 08]. The first two are library and the third is a complete tool. The tool DESUMA [RIC 06] is a tool integrating the UMDES [UMD 06] library dedicated to the study of discrete event systems modeled by finite-state automata.

10.6. Bibliography

[ALU 97] ALUR R., HENZINGER T. A., KUPFERMAN O., "Alternating-time temporal logic", in *Proceedings of the 38th Annual IEEE Symposium on Foundations of Computer Science (FOCS'97)*, Los Alamitos, CA, USA, IEEE Computer Society, p. 100-109, 1997.

[ALU 98] ALUR R., HENZINGER T. A., F.Y.C. M., QADEER S., RAJAMANI S. K., S. T., "Mocha: modularity in model checking", in *Proceedings of the 10th International Conference on Computer Aided Verification (CAV'98)*, Lecture Notes in Computer Science, Springer, p. 521-525, 1998.

[ANU 94] ANUCHITANKUL A., MANNA Z., "Realizability and synthesis of reactive modules", DILL D. L., Ed., in *Proceedings of the 6th International Conference on Computer Aided Verification (CAV'94)*, vol. 818 of *Lecture Notes in Computer Science*, Stanford, California, USA, Springer, p. 156–168, 1994.

[ARN 03] ARNOLD A., VINCENT A., WALUKIEWICZ I., "Games for synthesis of controllers with partial observation", *Theoretical Computer Science*, vol. 1, num. 303, p. 7–34, 2003.

[BAS 09] BASU A., BENSALEM S., PELED D., SIFAKIS J., "Priority scheduling of distributed systems based on model checking", BOUAJJANI A., MALER O., Eds., in *Computer Aided Verification*, vol. 5643 of *Lecture Notes in Computer Science*, p. 79–93, Springer Berlin / Heidelberg, 2009.

[BER 06] BERNET J., JANIN D., "On distributed program specification and synthesis in architectures with cycles", NAJM E., PRADAT-PEYRE J.-F., DONZEAU-GOUGE V., Eds., in *Proceedings of the 26th IFIP WG6.1 International Conference on Formal Techniques for Networked and Distributed Systems (FORTE'06)*, vol. 4229 of *Lecture Notes in Computer Science*, Springer, p. 175–190, 2006.

[BÜC 69] BÜCHI J. R., LANDWEBER L. H., "Solving sequential conditions by finite-state strategies", *Transactions of the American Mathematical Society*, vol. 138, p. 295–311, American Mathematical Society, 1969.

[CAS 06] CASSANDRAS C. G., LAFORTUNE S., *Introduction to Discrete Event Systems*, Springer, Secaucus, NJ, USA, 2006.

[CHA 07] CHATTERJEE K., HENZINGER T. A., PITERMAN N., "Strategy logic", in *Proceedings of the 18th International Conference on Concurrency Theory (CONCUR'07)*, vol. 4703 of *Lecture Notes in Computer Science*, Springer, p. 59-73, 2007.

[CHA 09] CHATAIN T., GASTIN P., SZNAJDER N., "Natural specifications yield decidability for distributed synthesis of asynchronous systems", in *Proceedings of the 35th International Conference on Current Trends in Theory and Practice of Computer Science (SOFSEM'09)*, Lecture Notes in Computer Science, Springer, 2009.

[CHU 63] CHURCH A., "Logic, arithmetics, and automata", in *Proceedings of the International Congress of Mathematicians*, p. 23–35, 1963.

[DAC 10] DA COSTA A., LAROUSSINIE F., MARKEY N., "Expressiveness and decidability of ATL with strategy contexts", LODAYA K., MAHAJAN M., Eds., in *Proceedings of the Conference on Foundations of Software Technology and Theoretical Computer Science (FSTTCS'10)*, Leibniz International Proceedings in Informatics, Leibniz-Zentrum für Informatik, 2010.

[FIN 05] FINKBEINER B., SCHEWE S., "Uniform distributed synthesis", in *Proceedings of the 20th IEEE Annual Symposium on Logic in Computer Science (LICS'05)*, IEEE Computer Society Press, p. 321–330, 2005.

348 Models and Analysis in Distributed Systems

[FIN 06] FINKBEINER B., SCHEWE S., "Synthesis of asynchronous systems", PUEBLA G., Ed., in *Proceedings of the International Symposium on Logic-based Program Synthesis and Transformation (LOPSTR'06)*, vol. 4407 of *Lecture Notes in Computer Science*, Springer, p. 127–142, 2006.

[GAS 04a] GASTIN P., LERMAN B., ZEITOUN M., "Causal memory distributed games are decidable for series-parallel systems", LODAYA K., MAHAJAN M., Eds., in *Proceedings of the 24th Conference on Foundations of Software Technology and Theoretical Computer Science (FSTTCS'04)*, vol. 3328 of *Lecture Notes in Computer Science*, Springer, p. 275 – 286, 2004.

[GAS 04b] GASTIN P., LERMAN B., ZEITOUN M., "Distributed games and distributed control for asynchronous systems", FARACH-COLTON M., Ed., in *Proceedings of the 6th Latin American Theoretical Informatics Symposium (LATIN'04)*, vol. 2976 of *Lecture Notes in Computer Science*, Springer, p. 455–465, 2004.

[GAS 09] GASTIN P., SZNAJDER N., ZEITOUN M., "Distributed synthesis for well-connected architectures", *Formal Methods in System Design*, vol. 34, num. 3, p. 215-237, 2009.

[GRA 10] GRAF S., PELED D., QUINTON S., "Achieving distributed control through model checking", TOUILI T., COOK B., JACKSON P., Eds., in *Computer Aided Verification*, vol. 6174 of *Lecture Notes in Computer Science*, p. 396-409, Springer Berlin / Heidelberg, 2010.

[GRI 05] GRIGOROV L., Hierarchical control of discrete-event systems, Survey paper, School of Computing, Queen's University, Canada, 2005, Available at http://www.banica.org/research/.

[HAL 90] HALPERN J. Y., MOSES Y., "Knowledge and common knowledge in a distributed environment", *J. ACM*, vol. 37, p. 549–587, ACM, 1990.

[KUP 00] KUPFERMAN O., VARDI M. Y., "μ-calculus synthesis", NIELSEN M., ROVAN B., Eds., in *Proceedings of the 25th International Symposium on Mathematical Foundations of Computer Science (MFCS'00)*, vol. 1893 of *Lecture Notes in Computer Science*, Springer, p. 497–507, 2000.

[KUP 01] KUPFERMAN O., VARDI M. Y., "Synthesizing distributed systems", HALPERN J. Y., Ed., in *Proceedings of the 16th IEEE Annual Symposium on Logic in Computer Science (LICS'01)*, IEEE Computer Society Press, 2001.

[LAF 02] LAFORTUNE S., YOO T.-S., ROHLOFF K., "Recent advances on the control of partially-observed discrete-event systems", CAILLAUD B., XIE X., DARONDEAU P., LAVAGIN L., Eds., *Synthesis and Control of Discrete Event Systems*, Kluwer Academic Press, 2002.

[LAR 10] LAROUSSINIE F., "Temporal logics for games", *EATCS Bulletin*, vol. 100, 2010.

[LIN 90] LIN F., WONHAM W., "Decentralized control and coordination of discrete-event systems with partial observation", *Automatic Control, IEEE Transactions on*, vol. 35, num. 12, p. 1330 -1337, 1990.

[MA 08] MA C., WONHAM W., "STSLib and its application to two benchmarks", in *Proceedings of the 9th International Workshop on Event Systems (WODES'2008)*, p. 119 -124, May 2008.

[MAD 01] MADHUSUDAN P., THIAGARAJAN P. S., "Distributed control and synthesis for local specifications", OREJAS F., SPIRAKIS P. G., VAN LEEUWEN J., Eds., in *Proceedings of the 28th International Colloquium on Automata, Languages and Programming (ICALP'01)*, vol. 2076 of *Lecture Notes in Computer Science*, Springer, p. 396–407, 2001.

[MAD 02] MADHUSUDAN P., THIAGARAJAN P. S., "A decidable class of asynchronous distributed controllers", BRIM L., JANCAR P., KRETÍNSKÝ M., KUCERA A., Eds., in *Proceedings of the 13th International Conference on Concurrency Theory (CONCUR'02)*, vol. 2421 of *Lecture Notes in Computer Science*, Springer, p. 145–160, 2002.

[MAD 05] MADHUSUDAN P., THIAGARAJAN P. S., YANG S., "The MSO theory of connectedly communicating processes", RAMANUJAM R., SEN S., Eds., in *Proceedings of the 25th Conference on Foundations of Software Technology and Theoretical Computer Science (FSTTCS'05)*, vol. 3821 of *Lecture Notes in Computer Science*, Springer, p. 201–212, 2005.

[MAT 89] MATTERN F., "Virtual time and global states of distributed systems", *Parallel and Distributed Algorithms*, North-Holland, p. 215–226, 1989.

[MAZ 77] MAZURKIEWICZ A., Concurrent program schemes and their interpretations, DAIMI report PB 78, Aarhus University, 1977.

[MAZ 86] MAZURKIEWICZ A. W., "Trace theory", BRAUER W., REISIG W., ROZENBERG G., Eds., *Petri Nets: Central Models and Their Properties, Advances in Petri Nets 1986, Part II, Proceedings of an Advanced Course, Bad Honnef, 8.-19. September 1986*, vol. 255 of *Lecture Notes in Computer Science*, Springer, p. 279–324, 1986.

[MIR 08] MIREMADI S., AKESSON K., FABIAN M., VAHIDI A., LENNARTSON B., "Solving two supervisory control benchmark problems using Supremica", in *Proceedings of the 9th International Workshop on Discrete Event Systems (WODES'2008)*, p. 131 -136, May 2008.

[MOH 03] MOHALIK S., WALUKIEWICZ I., "Distributed games", PANDYA P. K., RADHAKRISHNAN J., Eds., in *Proceedings of the 23rd Conference on Foundations of Software Technology and Theoretical Computer Science (FSTTCS'03)*, vol. 2914 of *Lecture Notes in Computer Science*, Springer, p. 338–351, 2003.

[MOO 08] MOOR T., SCHMIDT K., PERK S., "libFAUDES - An open source C++ library for discrete event systems", in *Proceedings of the 9th International Workshop on Discrete Event Systems (WODES'2008)*, p. 125 -130, 2008.

[MUS 09] MUSCHOLL A., WALUKIEWICZ I., ZEITOUN M., "A look at the control of asynchronous automata", LODAYA K., MUKUND M., R. R., Eds., *Perspectives in Concurrency Theory*, p. 356–371, Universities Press, 2009.

[PEN 09] PENA P., CURY J., LAFORTUNE S., "Verification of nonconflict of supervisors using abstractions", *IEEE Transactions on Automatic Control*, vol. 54, num. 12, p. 2803 -2815, 2009.

[PET 79] PETERSON G. L., REIF J. H., "Multiple-person alternation", in *Proceedings of the 20th Annual IEEE Symposium on Foundations of Computer Science (FOCS'79)*, p. 348–363, IEEE Computer Society Press, 1979.

[PNU 89] PNUELI A., ROSNER R., "On the synthesis of an asynchronous reactive module", AUSIELLO G., DEZANI-CIANCAGLINI M., ROCCA S. R. D., Eds., in *Proceedings of the 16th International Colloquium on Automata, Languages and Programming (ICALP'89)*, vol. 372 of *Lecture Notes in Computer Science*, Springer, p. 652–671, 1989.

[PNU 90] PNUELI A., ROSNER R., "Distributed reactive systems are hard to synthesize", in *Proceedings of the 31st Annual IEEE Symposium on Foundations of Computer Science (FOCS'90)*, vol. II, IEEE Computer Society Press, p. 746–757, 1990.

[PUR 01] PURI A., TRIPAKIS S., VARAIYA P., "Problems and examples of decentralized observation and control for discrete event systems", in *Proceedings of the IEEE; special issue on Dynamics of Discrete Event Systems*, Kluwer Academic Publisher, p. 0–7923, 2001.

[QUE 00] QUEIROZ M. H. D., CURY J. E. R., "Modular supervisory control of large scale discrete event systems", in *Discrete Event Systems: Analysis and Control. Proc. WODES'00*, Kluwer Academic, p. 103–110, 2000.

[RAM 82] RAMADGE P. J. G., WONHAM W. M., "Supervision of discrete-event processes", in *Proceedings of the the 21th IEEE Conference on Decision and Control*, vol. 3, p. 1228–1229, 1982.

[RAM 89] RAMADGE P. J. G., WONHAM W. M., "The control of discrete event systems", in *Proceedings of the IEEE*, vol. 77, IEEE Press, p. 81–98, 1989.

[RIC 97] RICKER S. L., RUDIE K., "Know means no: incorporating knowledge into decentralized discrete-event control", in *Proceedings of the 1997 American Control Conference*, p. 2348–2353, 1997.

[RIC 99] RICKER S., RUDIE K., "Incorporating communication and knowledge into decentralized discrete-event systems", in *Proceedings of the 38th IEEE Conference on Decision and Control*, vol. 2, p. 1326 -1332 vol.2, 1999.

[RIC 06] RICKER L., LAFORTUNE S., GENC S., "DESUMA: A Tool Integrating GIDDES and UMDES", Presented at *the 8th International Workshop on Discrete Event Systems (WODES'2006)*, p. 131 -136, 2006.

[ROZ 95] ROZENBERG G., DIEKERT V., Eds., *Book of Traces*, World Scientific, Singapore, 1995.

[RUD 90] RUDIE K., WONHAM W. M., "Supervisory control of communicating processes", in *Proceedings of the IFIP WG6.1 Tenth International Symposium on Protocol Specification, Testing and Verification X*, Amsterdam, The Netherlands, North-Holland Publishing Co., p. 243–257, 1990.

[RUD 92] RUDIE K., WONHAM W. M., "Think globally, act locally: decentralized supervisory control", *IEEE Transactions on Automatic Control*, vol. 37, num. 11, p. 1692–1708, 1992.

[RUD 99] RUDIE K., LAFORTUNE S., LIN F., "Minimal communication in a distributed discrete-event control system", in *Proceedings of the American Control Conference*, vol. 3, p. 1965-1970, 1999.

[THI 05] THISTLE J., "Undecidability in decentralized supervision", *Systems and Control Letters*, vol. 54, num. 5, p. 503 - 509, 2005.

[THI 09] THISTLE J. G., LAMOUCHI H. M., "Effective control synthesis for partially observed discrete-event systems", *SIAM Journal on Control and Optimization*, vol. 48, num. 3, p. 1858-1887, SIAM, 2009.

[TRI 04a] TRIPAKIS S., "Decentralized control of discrete-event Systems with bounded or unbounded delay communication", *IEEE Transactions on Automatic Control*, vol. 49, num. 9, p. 1489 - 1501, 2004.

[TRI 04b] TRIPAKIS S., "Undecidable problems of decentralized observation and control on regular languages", *Information Processing Letters*, vol. 90, num. 1, p. 21 - 28, 2004.

[UMD 06] UMDES, 2006, http://www.eecs.umich.edu/umdes/toolboxes.html.

[VAR 95] VARDI M. Y., "An automata-theoretic approach to fair realizability and synthesis", WOLPER P., Ed., in *Proceedings of the 7th International Conference on Computer Aided Verification (CAV'95)*, vol. 939 of *Lecture Notes in Computer Science*, Springer, p. 267–278, 1995.

[WOD 08] WODES, 2008, Benchmark presented at the 9th International Workshop on Event Systems (WODES'2008).

[WON 87] WONHAM W. M., RAMADGE P. J., "On the supremal controllable sublanguage of a given language", *SIAM Journal on Control and Optimization*, vol. 25, num. 3, p. 637-659, SIAM, 1987.

[WON 88] WONHAM W. M., RAMADGE P. J., "Modular supervisory control of discrete-event systems", *Mathematics of Control, Signals and Systems*, vol. 1, p. 13–30, 1988.

[WON 96] WONG K., VAN SCHUPPEN J., "Decentralized supervisory control of discrete-event systems with communication", in *WODES 96, IEEE*, p. 284–289, 1996.

[YAN 97] YANNANAKIS M., "Synchronous multi-player games with incomplete information are undecidable", 1997, Personal Communication.

[YOO 02] YOO T.-S., LAFORTUNE S., "A general architecture for decentralized supervisory control of discrete-event systems", *Journal of Discrete Event Dynamical Sytems: Theory and Application*, vol. 13, num. 3, p. 335–377, 2002.

[ZHO 90] ZHONG H., WONHAM W. M., "On the consistency of hierarchical supervision in discrete-event systems", *IEEE Transactions on Automatic Control*, vol. 35, num. 10, p. 1125–1134, 1990.

[ZIE 87] ZIELONKA W., "Notes on finite asynchronous automata", *ITA*, vol. 21, num. 2, p. 99–135, 1987.

List of Authors

Béatrice BÉRARD
LIP6
Pierre & Marie Curie University
France

Christine CHOPPY
LIPN
University of Paris 13
France

Stéphane DEMRI
LSV
CNRS
France

Claude DUTHEILLET
LIP6
Pierre & Marie Curie University
France

Serge HADDAD
LSV
Ecole Normale Supérieure de Cachan
France

Fabrice KORDON
LIP6
Pierre & Marie Curie University
France

Isabelle MOUNIER
LIP6
Pierre & Marie Curie University
France

Laurent PAUTET
LTCI
Telecom ParisTech
France

Laure PETRUCCI
LIPN
University of Paris 13
France

Denis POITRENAUD
LIP6
University of Paris Descartes
France

Pascal POIZAT
LRI
Evry Val d'Essonne University
France

Jean-François PRADAT-PEYRE
LIP6
University of Paris West Nanterre
France

Pierre-Alain REYNIER
LIF
University of Provence
France

Nathalie SZNAJDER
LIP6
Pierre & Marie Curie University
France

Yann THIERRY-MIEG
LIP6
Pierre & Marie Curie University
France

Thomas VERGNAUD
SC2
Thales
France

Index